REPARATIONS: INTERDISCIPLINARY INQUIRIES

Reparations: Interdisciplinary Inquiries

Edited by

JON MILLER AND RAHUL KUMAR

OXFORD
UNIVERSITY PRESS

OXFORD
UNIVERSITY PRESS

Great Clarendon Street, Oxford OX2 6DP

Oxford University Press is a department of the University of Oxford.
It furthers the University's objective of excellence in research, scholarship,
and education by publishing worldwide in

Oxford New York

Auckland Cape Town Dar es Salaam Hong Kong Karachi
Kuala Lumpur Madrid Melbourne Mexico City Nairobi
New Delhi Shanghai Taipei Toronto

With offices in

Argentina Austria Brazil Chile Czech Republic France Greece
Guatemala Hungary Italy Japan Poland Portugal Singapore
South Korea Switzerland Thailand Turkey Ukraine Vietnam

Oxford is a registered trade mark of Oxford University Press
in the UK and in certain other countries

Published in the United States
by Oxford University Press Inc., New York

First published 2007

British Library Cataloguing in Publication Data
Data available

Library of Congress Cataloging in Publication Data
Data available

Typeset by SPI Publisher Services, Pondicherry, India
Printed in Great Britain
on acid-free paper by
Biddles Ltd., King's Lynn

978-0-19-929991-1

1 3 5 7 9 10 8 6 4 2

Preface

Reparations is an idea whose time has come. From civilian victims of war in Iraq and South America to descendents of slaves in the United States to citizens of colonized nations in Africa and South Asia to indigenous peoples around the world—these groups and their advocates are increasingly arguing that the solution to present-day inequalities must include reparations programs targeted at redressing historical injustices.

As important and potent a tool for social justice as reparations may be, demands for reparations and reparations programs are also of interest because of the conceptually complex issues that require exploration in any serious inquiry into the normative foundations of reparations claims and policies. These issues can be roughly characterized as falling into four general clusters. First, there are questions about the *identity* of those to whom reparations are owed and to whom the duty to make reparations falls. What, for example, is the significance of the fact that in certain cases what is sought are reparations for injustices originally perpetrated against the long-dead ancestors of those pressing the demand for reparations, by particular individuals whose ancestors are also long gone? In cases where reparations are targeted at a particular group, say, members of an Aboriginal tribe in Australia, or African Americans, how ought the conditions for membership in that group to be specified? Second, there are important issues concerning what form reparations should take—money, land, apologies, public memorials and museums, changes in the law, changes in political institutions, enhanced educational opportunities, the introduction of policies designed to educate the general public about the character of past injustices, some combination of these, or something else altogether? Is there a single best form that reparations should take in all cases or ought the form to vary from case to case? Third, there is the question of

Most of the chapters in this volume were originally presented at the conference, 'Reparations: An Interdisciplinary Examination of Some Philosophical Issues', held at Queen's University in February 2004. We are pleased to acknowledge the major financial support for the conference provided by the Social Sciences and Humanities Research Council of Canada. Significant additional funds were also provided by the Forum for Philosophy and Public Policy, the Department of Philosophy, the Office of Research Services, the Faculty of Arts and Sciences, and the School of Law, all at Queen's. We are grateful to these bodies for their support. Thanks are also owed to Mary Taslimi for her excellent work proofreading the final manuscript. And last but not least, we wish to say thanks to the commentators and participants at the conference, including Bruce Berman, Jacqueline Davies, André Gombay, Matt James, Michael Kocsis, Will Kymlicka, Alistair Macleod, Colin Macleod, Margaret Moore, Natalie Oman, Daniel Osabu-Kle, Paula Schwebel, James Sterba, Margaret Walker, Mark Walters, Daniel Weinstock.

the relationship between reparations programs and policies and other goals of social justice. Should reparations programs aim only to provide redress for past injustice, narrowly conceived, or should they also aim to move society and the general global order to a more just state?

The fourth, and arguably most fundamental cluster of issues, which has implications for all the others, has to do with the general *aim* of reparations programs. With some exceptions, philosophical theorizing about the normative foundations of reparations claims and policies have assumed that they fall under the paradigm of matters having to do with compensatory, or corrective, justice. So conceived, the aim of reparations programs has been taken to be that of altering the current state of affairs so that it at least approximates the character of the state of affairs before the wrongdoing or injustice for which reparations are being sought took place. Questions of culpability, the conceptual coherence of understanding those who claim reparations for past wrongdoing to actually have been harmed by past wrongdoing or injustice, and the (to whatever extent possible) quantification of the harm done by the relevant wrongdoing, have loomed large in discussions of reparations that treat them as demands for some form of compensation.

Though these issues are certainly of philosophical interest, they have their natural home in a way of thinking about what drives reparations claims and what reparations programs hope to achieve that many partisans in debates over reparations do not share. In the real-world debates, the issue is often less about how to restore the *status quo ante* and more about how to repair broken relationships between people. Antagonists argue about things like how to repair the 'sacred bond' established by treaties between indigenous leaders and European or American governments, how to acknowledge the sense of betrayal felt by members of historically oppressed groups, how to reconcile formerly warring groups and restore trust, and what obligations current generations might have to participate in redressing the sins of past ones, regardless of issues of strict culpability.

Understanding reparations claims and programs in this way, as reparations advocates conceive of them, still requires the kind of conceptual clarification that is the particular expertise of philosophers. But it crucially also requires drawing on the expertise of other disciplines. The input of historians is needed, for example, to shed light on what is often a murky and contested historical record. Legal specialists and political scientists with an expertise in different institutional arrangements are needed for the exploration of the legal mechanisms available for institutionalizing reparations, and what changes—legal, institutional, and constitutional—must be made to accommodate and successfully implement reparations programs. Psychologists need to speak to issues concerning the mental costs of injustice, and how broad-based reparations programs can be sensitive to what individuals need in order to facilitate the healing of psychic scars. Insights of the representatives of NGOs are also essential; in light of their concrete experiences dealing with victims and implementing programs designed to help them, they are in a good position to speak authoritatively on how demands for reparations for programs are best presented and what kinds of reparations measures are most likely to be effective.

This volume is a contribution to the advancement of, and in an important sense, is an argument for, an understanding of reparations claims and programs as an inherently interdisciplinary inquiry. With that in mind, it collects mainly newly commissioned essays from a number of well-known and emerging scholars from a variety of disciplines: law, economics, political science, history, psychology, and philosophy. Though the contributors come from different disciplines, their contributions are all philosophically minded in their care to take account of important conceptual issues that are important for understanding the basis of different reparations claims and policies.

The volume is structured around four modules or types of reparations cases: those involving indigenous peoples, slavery and Jim Crow in the United States, conflict, and colonialism, respectively. Each module consists of both papers that are attentive to the particular features and history associated with certain reparations claims and those which prescind from the details of particular cases in order to discuss issues that arise concerning the particular relevant type of reparations claim. Our division of the volume into four modules is motivated by two general considerations. First, different types of cases raise different types of questions; by grouping them in discrete sections, it is possible to display and understand what is unique about each type as well as what all the types share in common. Second, arranging the chapters together by type allowed greater dialog among the authors writing on that type. Authors were encouraged to respond to each other, especially to those who were writing on the same case; by placing them together, we hoped their different approaches to and perspectives on the same broad type of case may be more easily grasped.

Jon Miller
Rahul Kumar

Contents

Notes on Contributors xi

Introduction: Reparation: A Moral and Political Dilemma 1
Elazar Barkan

PART I. REPARATIONS FOR INDIGENOUS PEOPLES

1. Why is Indigeneity Important? 23
Jeremy Waldron

2. Acknowledging the Past to Heal the Future: The Role of Reparations for Native Nations 43
Rebecca Tsosie

3. Coming to Terms with the Past in Australia 69
Janna Thompson

PART II. REPARATIONS FOR SLAVERY AND JIM CROW

4. Transgenerational Justice—Compensatory Versus Interpretative Approaches 87
Glenn C. Loury

5. Reconsidering the Case for Black Reparations 114
Andrew Valls

6. Further Trouble for Unsettled Waters: Attention to Gender in the Debate on Black Reparations 130
Carolyn Benson

PART III. REPARATIONS FOR CONFLICT

7. Justice and Reparations 153
Pablo de Greiff

8. Countering the Wrongs of the Past: The Role of Compensation 176
Debra Satz

9. Justice and Reparations in World Politics 193
Catherine Lu

PART IV. REPARATIONS FOR COLONIALISM

10. How Should We Respond to the Cultural Injustices of Colonialism? 215
Rajeev Bhargava

11. Reparations as Symbol: Narratives of Resistance, Reticence, and Possibility in South Africa 252
Brandon Hamber

12. Colonialism, Reparations, and Global Justice 280
Kok-Chor Tan

Conclusion: Essential Elements of Healing after Massive Trauma: Some Theory, Victims' Voices, and International Developments 307
Yael Danieli

Bibliography 323
Index 338

Notes on Contributors

Elazar Barkan is a Professor of International and Public Affairs at Columbia University.

Carolyn Benson is doctoral candidate in philosophy at the University of St. Andrews.

Rajeev Bhargava is Senior Fellow and Director of the Programme of Social and Political Theory, Centre for the Study of Developing Societies, Delhi.

Yael Danieli is a clinical psychologist in private practice, a victimologist, traumatologist, cofounder and Director of the Group Project for Holocaust Survivors and their Children in the New York City area.

Pablo de Greiff is Director of Research at the International Center for Transitional Justice in New York City.

Brandon Hamber, Ph.D. is currently an Honorary Fellow of INCORE, a United Nations Research Centre for the Study of Conflict at the University of Ulster.

Glenn C. Loury is the Merton P. Stolz Professor of the Social Sciences and Professor of Economics at Brown University.

Catherine Lu is Associate Professor of Political Science at McGill University.

Debra Satz is Associate Professor of Philosophy and, by courtesy, of Political Science at Stanford University.

Kok-Chor Tan is Associate Professor of Philosophy at The University of Pennsylvania.

Janna Thompson is Associate Professor and Deputy Director of the Centre for Applied Philosophy and Public Ethics and the Head of the Melbourne University Division of the Centre.

Rebecca Tsosie is Professor of Law and William H. Pedrick Distinguished Research Scholar at Arizona State University.

Andrew Valls is Assistant Professor of Political Science at Oregon State University.

Jeremy Waldron is a Professor of Law and Philosophy at the New York University School of Law.

Introduction: Reparation: A Moral and Political Dilemma

Elazar Barkan

On December 11, 2005, the *The Observer* in London published a story under the headline 'JP Morgan faces boycott over slave trade reparations'. In it, the paper reported on a campaign calling on American students to boycott the bank's student loans business, a business reportedly worth US$9 billion a year. If the story escaped your attention, you may excuse yourself. A search on both Nexis and Google suggests that no major US media outlet reported on the proposed boycott. So while boycott may overstate the situation, nonetheless the story is interesting. Foremost because JP Morgan, which had bought two Louisiana banks who had owned slaves, did set up earlier in the year a scholarship fund for black students in Louisiana 'to acknowledge the past and improve the future'. The bank did not admit liability, and so far law suits that attempted to impose reparations on American companies in connection with past history and association with slavery have been dismissed. Wachovia bank acted similarly to JP Morgan, as did Aetna. Activists denounced the scholarship plans as 'insulting', though the initial apology from Aetna a couple of years earlier had been welcomed.

A more tangible demand for redress caught the headlines earlier in 2005. The Getty museum in Los Angeles had its shady acquisitions of antiquities exposed. Based on internal documents, it was claimed that the museum was involved in acquiring looted art, suggesting that perhaps as many as half of its antiquities masterpieces may be tainted. Italy demanded the return of tens of objects (forty-two items).[1] The Getty is not unique, merely a younger institute with a larger acquisition budget than most. But the issue bedevils most large and not-so-large museums. The repatriation of cultural property from human remains to antiquities and works of art has become central to the rethinking of identity, culture, and human rights. It has reframed the way museums think of their collections and acquisitions, the ethics and the practice of it. But not only prospective policies are at stake, the actual collections and the rationale for holding or repatriating them, are intertwined with the very notion of the identity of the museum. The British Museum and the dispute over the Elgin Marbles is the most famous of these controversies. Elginism is becoming a synonym for the pretense to endow looted art with respectability.

The increased attention to redress in politics and by academics and its integration into the human rights discourse coincided with the post-cold war years, a period in which human rights became prominent in international law and transitional politics captured a central segment of the discourse of politics and morals. Since 9/11 however, the place of morality has been transformed: embraced by neoconservatives as legitimizing aggressive policies of expansion (the exporting of democracy), and hesitantly embraced by liberals who are often overpowered by the fear of national security rhetoric. How did these changes impact the place of redress in politics? I would like to suggest that redress for historical injustices embodies in a particular way the democratization of international law and its impact on domestic politics. Redress remains central, and may have even grown in importance in explaining the triangulation in international politics of justice, morality, and human rights, and the reciprocal tension. The following comments are directed at placing reparation and redress in the context of human rights and engage several of the issues raised by other essays in the book.

The core of liberal rights enveloped by social and cultural values stemming from local traditions and preferences informs the debate over human rights. Although from certain perspectives universal considerations dominate the discussion, the critical discourse involves a vague set of values which is cognizant of the tension between the group and the individual, and is committed to address both while refusing to privilege either. I have referred to this previously as a neoenlightenment synthesis.[2] It privileges voluntary local resolutions and rejects the notion of a general global moral system as an abstract theoretical solution. Rawls, for example, maintained that principled rights outweigh any other consideration, including the general welfare and the will of the majority. He emphasized an a priori framework of rights rather than a framework based on a specific content. In contrast, human rights and redress are more likely to be understood by supporters as a matter of social justice emboldened by rights language. Contemporary theories of justice cannot be said to have successfully resolved this tension, and the appeal to abstract rights detached from any historical context has long been under criticism. The multiple international conventions and instruments that enact and celebrate the rights language have strengthened this reciprocal connection. Privileging of the Enlightenment notions of equality and toleration has successfully eliminated from large segments of Western society the justification of prejudiced policies on the basis of a natural or historical superiority of one group over another. Yet the legacy of these discriminations has not been attended to, and provides a strong rationale for bridging the rights language with redress. The debate over liberalism focuses on the nature and substance of equality and opportunity, and on the extent of toleration, but no longer seriously questions the desirability of these principles.

Today, liberal societies are more likely than most to recognize past public injustices. But other governments, NGOs, commercial companies, and even individuals may take the burden of the past on themselves. As political realism grows societies are often forced to recognize that certain historical, nonliberal, and unjust policies played a central role in their past, even if at times these may be viewed as having been unavoidable. But being part of liberal society also means that public opinion expects justice and feels guilty when implicated by injustice, even historical injustice. To search for the source of this guilt, we would do well by going back to Adam Smith who viewed justice as a result of our sympathy with individuals who suffer and explicitly denies any utilitarian benefits as a motive. Thus, it is only when people believe that their society is fundamentally just and that their fellow beings are fair, can market economy and a relative lack of regulations succeed. In the post-civil rights and postcolonial society many more individuals and groups make political claims on such social sympathy. More recently it has been translated into the question of historical justice and its present-day effects. Tan picks up a similar argument when arguing for reparation as morally significant 'even if egalitarian arguments are available to support the same kinds of demands' and these might be particularly persuasive if we focus on groups—'corporate agency and responsibility'. Expanding the view of society from individualism to a neo-enlightenment perspective enables the inclusion of redress within the liberal view.

Redress in this sense is negotiated among various groups with specific political identities and agendas. Thus, any settlement is both a political and a social treaty. In amending gross historical immoralities, redress replaces a universal comprehensive standard of justice with a negotiated justice among the opposing parties in specific cases. Social guilt is a powerful political tool because of its vagueness and because of the voluntary nature of accepting responsibility. The perpetrator's growing willingness to recognize the legitimacy of the victim's claims, even a gaze, becomes the victim's political power. This attempt to bridge vague global morality and local conditions is done through international shaming—a revered human rights tactic—and is proving effective in pressuring politicians to apologize and repent.

I.1. THE LIMITS OF REDRESS: HOW TO READ THE WCAR IN DURBAN

Some of the best-known agreements and demands for reparation and compensation stem from the crimes of World War II. Others are a response to various racist policies and colonialism. Perhaps the most prominent item on the international agenda regarding redress is the demand over reparation for slavery. The demand received most attention in the buildup and during the Durban conference in September 2001. These were the days of the end of the long 1990s—the period between 1989—the end of the cold war—and 9/11; when the Age of Optimism dominated and the daily sustenance of 'irrational exuberance' was just beginning to recede.

In the first days of September 2001, the attention of the world was focused on the World Congress against racism (WCAR) in Durban. Let me quote from some newspaper reports to help us regain the flavor of the time. In an article under the headline 'Africans toughen reparation demands', *The Guardian* wrote on September 5, 'African countries have made tougher demands in connection with the slave trade and colonialism . . . They include explicit apologies to all victims from individual countries . . . and reparation in the form of debt cancellation, markets open to African exports, health care funding, the return of plundered art objects, and the acceleration of aid.' That same day, *The Independent* added that 'Africa and Europe [remain] deadlocked over demand for reparations . . . [T]he moderate stance adopted by South Africa and Senegal—for an expression of "regret" and reparations in the form of debt relief and directed aid—had lost out to a militant lobby.'

Over the next couple of days the standoff deteriorated and the result was 'The Durban debacle' as the conference 'degenerated into . . . name-calling and hateful rhetoric' (*St. Petersburg Times*, Florida). *The Oregonian* talked about 'the mirage of reparations' and the *Irish Times* described it more sympathetically: 'Delegates fail to rise to occasion. Political bickering and horse-trading over painful injustices of the past and present transformed the UN racism conference from a "forward-looking and progressive" event into an acrimonious and tense gathering.'

Arab states tried to equate Israel and Zionism with racism. Many viewed anti-Semitism as rampant at the conference, terror was still primarily part of the intifada in Palestine and not yet a global war. In protest, the United States and Israel walked away from the conference. (The pro-reparation activists viewed the Unites States walkout over anti-Semitism as a pretense to avoid the conflict over reparation.[3] Given the US track record in support of Israel in international fora, it is hardly a pretense for another policy, though no doubt it rejected the call for reparation.)

The debate among those who stayed at Durban revolved around the question of whether the Europeans would admit that slavery was a crime against humanity and apologize for the slave trade. The resolution was inconclusive. In the final hours of the conference an agreement was reached. European nations 'crossed a huge historical and psychological barrier', said the *Irish Times*, 'when they agreed to "apologise" for the slave trade', if Africa 'drops a call for financial reparations and for an admission that slavery was a crime against humanity.' An alternative interpretation was, as *The Observer* noted, 'Africans back down at the UN race talks': 'the final agreement reveals a fudged text that carefully skirts all direct reference to European culpability.'

'The best the Africans get is a call for support for the continent's Marshall Plan—the New African Initiative—and in a host of areas such as debt relief, funds to combat AIDS, the recovery of stolen government funds transferred to the West by former dictators and their cohorts, and an end to the trafficking in people. But nowhere does the word "reparations" appear.' Whether the principled commitment, not a specific plan, for foreign aid and assistance was a victory for claims of redress—as activists tried to present—is highly doubtful. In the process, the Europeans who were divided, regrouped around the British position. The United Kingdom was less accommodating to the African demands; while the African nations had initially followed the extreme position, led by Zimbabwe, but eventually retreated from it. At the end everybody lost. Certainly the legitimacy of redress or any move in the direction of reparation for slavery lost.

International administrators however have a way of seeing reality in their own way. UNESCO attempted to validate the result of the conference in Durban ('In defence of Durban: racism is back on the agenda') and concluded that 'For the first time, the international community recognized that slavery and the slave trade formed a "crime against humanity,"'and that the highlight of the conference was the 'declaration of principle over the "moral obligation" to pay financial compensation for wrongs committed' which was viewed by some as 'stronger than a "legal obligation."'[4] Factually these were wishes and proposals not a decision, or an obligation.

For some the defeat did not last long. *The Independent* announced the next frontier on the following day: 'west dodges blame at racism conference; slavery as one route to compensation is closed, Namibians seek another by claiming US$2 billion from Germans for colonial massacre.'

The conference was particularly interesting for many reasons. Let me make the following observations: The framing of the conference was the formulation of demands for social justice as reparation, and to the question of redress as rights. Demands that have been part of the international conversation were reformulated to be part of the seemingly winning rhetoric of the day.

The question of whether reparation is a social justice movement or a moral justice claim is never clear, and the movement often trips over its own lack of clarity. It is intriguing to speculate on the reasons for the failure. There is always the possibility that the Europeans were never going to engage seriously in the process, and this was merely an exercise in diplomacy. That the conference was a sham to begin with. But if we imagine for a moment that this was not the case and that there was a chance of success, it would be fair to suggest that politics, not the principle of reparation, failed.

The political failure in Durban resulted among others because the demands for redress were cast primarily as moral demands, and to a very limited degree the Europeans with few exceptions would have gone along with the moral component. But there was an attempt to impose a code of behavior that did not square with those who demanded it. Utter disregard to human rights by some of the loudest advocates, such as Zimbabwe, and their lack of admission of any violations of human rights on their own behalf, diminished the moral force of the claim. The demands were presented and gained legitimacy from the groups of activists, where the concerns of the other side (the governments) were not presented adequately. This was preaching to the choir, not negotiated agreement. For the spectator it seemed that a clear declaration by activists had higher priority than a muddy agreement. The Europeans had to be lobbied, seduced, to accept and acknowledge a responsibility which would push the conventional wisdom and practice of a government's obligation to past injustices. Instead, the Europeans were presented with an uncompromised position, and demands, not a process.

In the short space allotted for these comments, I would like to briefly address questions related to reparation as a proxy for social justice, especially for colonialism and slavery. Who is entitled to reparation, and under what rationale? What is an adequate compensation and how to get the perpetrators to pay? And what are the limits of reparation? Not surprisingly, although these issues are not resolved in this book, each is made more complex, rejecting any simple binary division.

I.2. REPARATION AS A PROXY FOR SOCIAL JUSTICE

What would adequate reparation look like? The rhetoric of reparation often implies rather than explicates a rationale. One possible implicit image of fair reparation is the redress of the damage done and a return to the *status quo ante*. Indeed the intuitive political call to amend and attend for 'the full range of wrongs for which reparations are due' can easily garner sympathy. How else is one to think of a just solution? Alas, such an ideal situation can never be approximated. Given the immense disparity between aspirations and available reparation, it is not surprising that the victims and the claimants are frustrated, and will continue to be.

This vague goal underscores the conflicting demands of reparation, including its tension with public policy. Is reparation a proxy for attending to other human rights or policy obligations? Human rights generally claim to overlook the identity of the individual and her community. Redress in contrast is directed precisely at the intersection of the individual and the specific community. The challenge for reparation theory is to delineate the relation of reparation in respect to both the individual and the group, and in particular the relation and tension between these sets of claims. How far to recognize the group as an entity and how to quantify the obligations? It is the nature of human interaction that we find it is easier to quantify tangible material loss, and hence most cases of reparation are limited to compensation for material loss. Lost education opportunities, political oppression, community breakup, and family disintegration are just some of the glaring examples that are not computed into the reparation equation, but clearly inform the demands for redress and the frustration at the outcome.

Looking at the reparation debate from the standard welfare economist's view of compensation, which frequently provides the philosophical and legal context, it becomes clear that victims of gross violations of human rights seek compensation as one part of a campaign to gain political and economic power. Given the multiple goals, some might settle for financial reparations as welfare. The route of filling policy goals through reparation is not without its problems. It might be attractive for a host of reasons, including that it is potentially a smaller obligation. But why should public obligations be framed as reparations and redress? Is the society better off for it? Is that the best way to achieve social justice? Are the victims better off? They most likely do not receive any material benefits they could not receive otherwise under a different social policy. Or perhaps it is only the perpetrators, who remain the powerful class and the elite in the society, who get off cheaply?

If reparation is made available especially in cases where economic and social needs are otherwise not provided, does that mean that the reparation is the wrong method and that the government should not be allowed 'to get away with it'? This dilemma is raised most often in the context of a general scarcity of resources, where the government is not fulfilling its social and economic obligations to aid the poor. By not responding to those needs through either employment of economic and social rights or social welfare, but choosing to partially fulfill these duties while employing reparation rhetoric, the victims seem to be ill-served. The dilemma revolves around the anticipation of what would be the economic policies of the government if reparation rhetoric were not available. Those who believe that other reforms would be forthcoming would most likely be against reparation, but the reality is often otherwise; societies in transition are not involved with redistribution of wealth. So it is left to reparation to ameliorate economic deprivation in societies that emerge from intense political violence. Is that a good or bad development? Put differently, we may ask, should reparation be burdened with the task of amending systematic, or exceptional, situations? If the class of injured is so large that any reparation would amount to economic policy, does it make sense to talk about reparation? Is reparation a useful policy toward achieving economic and social justice?

Two global historical injustices are receiving most attention these days in redress discourse: colonialism and slavery. The centrality of reparation to redress colonialism is often asserted in general postcolonial rhetoric. Slavery as the central experience in the history of discrimination is the core of reparation demands by descendants of slaves. The centrality of redress demands by African Americans and African diaspora is contested within the group/community, as is the discussion regarding reparation to African states which straddles both issues: slavery and colonialism.

The illegitimacy of colonialism may imply that the demands for redress would be straightforward. Bhargava's multilayer analysis on 'the cultural injustices of colonialism' illuminates in contrast a more complex power dynamics which must be considered, although it makes life and interpretation of reparation much more multifaceted. Bhargava shows colonialism to be diverse in its motivation and impact, and underscores the internal diversity in the colonial world, where some have suffered extremely while others benefited. A world, where elites predated the colonial imposition and where modernity was to advance regardless of colonialism. Not only did cultural injustices predate colonialism, but Bhargava reminds us, colonialists—by some measures—suffered too, at least to the degree that their oppressive sides came to dominate their own culture not only the colonized. Similar point is made about postapartheid South Africa, where much has changed (even if not enough for many people). As the new black elite prosper, and the inter-black inequality increases—it is estimated to be greater than between blacks and whites—the binary division in a post-transition society between victims and perpetrators becomes more obscured. Indeed this raises a central identity issue for the discussion: who represents the group? Are the poor and victimized descendants of a victimized group more 'authentic' than the prosperous and economically or professionally successful members of that group? Are the former more authentic African Americans or postcolonials?

How is one to navigate within this complexity? Is the discussion over reparation to be all-encompassing? We may want to begin by limiting the conversation and exclude cases related to events and relationships which have long ceased to impact contemporary society and are not of concern to living people and cultures. This comment is directed primarily at critics of reparation, who mock claims as outdated, such as slavery. The retort: 'why not have the Normans or the Crusaders pay reparation?' is not serious. (To explicate: it is not serious because there are no bona fide groups who consider themselves to be 'victims' of those actions; whether these were right or wrong. It is not the distance in time, but the lack of claimants.) But it is also a reminder for supporters of redress that there is a need to prioritize. It is clearly sensible to focus on past and continuing injustices. Injustices which cannot be attended to neither by retribution nor by restoration—both of which are either impossible or morally unsustainable—demand an alternative redress and shift the attention to a form of compensation. This is a crucial point: reparative responses have to attend to real people. The strength of the argument is informed by real suffering, not abstract theorizing.

It is one thing to recognize the political demands to limit the claims of reparation in order to make the conversation feasible, it is quite another to propose ways of doing it, without seeming to be harsh or uncaring toward certain victim groups. An intriguing and challenging observation of such a limitation is proposed by Thompson who calls attention the case of the Aborigines of Tasmania. Assumed to be a separate culture that vanished by the end of the nineteenth century, Tasmanian Aborigines, Thomson argues, have by now to be regarded as belonging to mainstream society. Although there remain a small number of people of Aboriginal ancestry, there is not, culturally speaking, an Aboriginal community. The lack of cultural link becomes a determining factor, and excludes them from claims of restitution: 'They cannot claim a right to a heritage from which their families have for so long been separated.' Their claims instead ought to be limited to historical memory and recognition of the injustices. This attempt at establishing an objective criterion is controversial, but corresponds to Waldron's and Bhargava's view. One is reminded of the Mashpee in Massachusetts which having lost control of their traditional area, filed a lawsuit to recover land but were rebuked by the jury which found them not to be a tribe (1978).[5]

Bhargava points out that the most important reparable class of injustices is that of cultural injustices. But given the impact of modernity and the dynamic cultural interaction and ambivalence, which changes amount to injustices? Clearly not any change is a violation. Rather, only those changes that are inflicted on the group, and its members, by denying it autonomy. Bhargava is happy to recognize the extensive autonomy, especially in the private sphere, which the colonized had maintained. Colonialism, he reminds us, was not an unambiguous, unmitigated disaster for the colonized, it was also a civilizing force. Indeed, change was a source of internal protest, not merely an external imposition. Rebellion against tradition was not limited to the West. These multiple perspectives are important not because at the end of the day colonialism served the interests of the colonized, but because it frames the extent of the colonial injustice as an issue of 'cultural autonomy, not merely as gains and losses'. While the demands for reparation are built on the argument that the cultural injustices continue, Bhargava underscored the continuity of the 'unequal relations of colonial rule' as these are 'reinscribed in current practices of post-colonial societies'. His aim is both at the current elites as well as the former colonial powers: 'It is no longer possible then, as it once might have been, to identify all perpetrators of injustice as western and all victims as non-western'. Similar to the colonizers who have an obligation to the colonized, so do, the colonized elites have obligation toward the colonized victims. The colonized victims are victims both because of the impact of colonialism, as well as for lack of impact, for having been left behind in the race to modernity. In this sense, reparatory cultural work is not limited to retrieving intellectual traditions, to reviving old text, but rather 'connecting with those people who escaped the deep impact of colonial modernity and who, therefore, are still steeped in traditions'. (Bhargava)

Glen Loury represents the legacy of slavery in analogous terms. It 'was the relegation of the black slaves and their progeny to a status of social pariahs, which constituted the severest harm'. Indeed Loury demonstrates that it is '*racial stigma*, not *racial discrimination*' that 'constitutes the deepest and most enduring historical harm done to blacks in the U.S.' and is very much a deep cultural infliction. Indeed both Bhargava and Loury reject the notion of a *status quo ante* as an adequate measure of repair.

The real damage is constructing a value natural inferiority which *led 'to "objective" racial inequality which is de-coupled from the discriminatory acts of individuals, carries over across generations*'. The racial divide is not the 'limited opportunities for development' which were suffered by others, but the construction of the belief of 'limited innate capacities to develop' which produces a 'vicious circle which, though it originates in the distant past, has now taken on a life of its own'. '*Stigma-influenced dynamics in the spheres of social interaction and self-image, shapes political and social-cognitive sensibilities in the citizenry, makes racial disparity appear "natural" and non-dissonant, stymies reform, and locks-in inequality*.' This is the demand from the American society, that it 'should fully acknowledge its wrongful past'. Loury rightly expands this to a critique of 'color-blind liberalism' that displays 'sociological naiveté' and lacks recognition of 'historical developments... when liberal political theory is brought to bear on the problem of race'.

Yet, although Loury underscores the guilt and responsibility of American society in causing the racial stigma and suffering of contemporary African Americans, he rejects reparations for 'political as well as epistemological reasons'. He divorces his call for 'the public, the political elite, the opinion-shaping media', to take responsibility for 'the contemporary plight of the urban black poor, and to understand them in a general way as a consequence of an ethically indefensible past' from reparation because he thinks it is counterproductive—it is bad for the country, and bad for black people—because it 'squanders blacks' dwindling political capital and misses our chance to show genuine moral leadership in this nation, as the early civil rights era heroes had done.' The solution for Loury ought to be part of the larger social justice agenda. Perhaps. But it might be possible to think of reparation as a general demand, and of the remedies as specific. The discussion of social justice may provide a first approximation of the difficulties, but would counter the negation of reparation as a rhetorical tool.

Carolyn Benson challenges the redress movement from an internal perspective, namely the lack of attention to gender. At one level there is little distinction between the various critics: all focus on the psychological effects of slavery as the fundamental damage to blacks. The focus on 'historical storytelling' is a powerful device to bring about empathy with reparatory demands, with 'the construction of a collective cultural narrative that is able both to reveal the truth about America's history of "freedom", "fairness" and "equality" and to diffuse the dangerous myths about race and responsibility that continue to infect American consciousness.' Benson emphasizes on the need to think of race and gender as realities that are not 'wholly separate' but rather intertwined are well taken, and at least in certain discourses would be taken for granted. The redress movement may have in time to embrace it too.

The distinction emerges in the approach to the material reparation. Here Benson differs from Loury, and her concerns are not so much the legitimacy of material reparation, but who the beneficiaries would be. The interests of the black community cannot be identified—she emphasizes—with those of the black man; gender is a crucial component. Benson's attention to gender is right as far as the cultural and psychological aspects are discussed. The discussion over who the beneficiaries of reparation ought to be seems to take for granted the potential success of the redress movement. Benson adds to the fundamental issues of reparation also the concern of what would a just 'catching up' with the white society be. As she rightly points out, with either white or black society widely internally diverse, how are we to know what catching up means? Benson is concerned with gender, but as Bhargava points out there are multiple differentiations within each society, community, and gender.

This is clearly the case in South Africa, whereas Hamber reminds us 'it is now estimated that inter-black inequality is greater than between blacks and whites.' Hamber similar to Loury emphasizes the psychological component of reparation as an acknowledgment, but contrary to Loury he sees in the monetary reparation a component of the acknowledgment. The relationship of acknowledgment and material reparation is particularly complex in South Africa, because the great achievement of the Truth and Reconciliation Commission (TRC) was supposedly the formal acknowledgment of the crimes of apartheid. What would be a greater recognition psychologically than the riveting hearings of the commissions and the public acknowledgment? One way to think about it is as a recognition of scarcity, but it was the former chairman of the TRC Desmond Tutu who has come over the years to regret that the TRC did not award reparation, arguing that the commission should have had a mirror track of reparation to the victims as it granted amnesty to perpetrators. The material reparation in real time would have given the needed added value. Perhaps the lesson of South Africa ought to be that 'reparations—whether individual, community, or broader' will be characterized by its frustration rather than satisfaction. Dealing with such horrific crimes against humanity, the legitimization of the desire for reparation—including 'the process of granting reparations' and the frustration that goes along with it—may provide the only viable psychological redress.

This shifts the focus on the need to rebuild relations of trust and mutual respect in the context of a torn past. This means relationship, which requires both sides to come together, not merely to rebuild the confidence of the victims through assertion of rights. Such a relationship necessitates revisiting the question of who is entitled to reparation, and under what rationale? How to distinguish between victims? There is no threshold of suffering or type of injury that is viewed as unwarranted of reparation, yet it is clear to everyone that not all violations can or ought to be redressed. So how are victims to be ranked? Differentiated? Validated? The mere choice of language may inflict the violation, before the conversation ever begins.

Most often this limbo is exploited by critics to negate reparation. Jeremy Waldron has been for more than a decade engaging the question of historical injustices.[6] Here Waldron presents a simple but challenging observation. Simple because it is seemingly self-evident, challenging because it strikes at the core of the claims of victimology: namely that some victims, in this case indigenous peoples, as members of a group, as a class, have suffered more egregious injustices, and therefore are worthy of reparation more than immigrant groups, religious minorities, or slaves and their descendants. Waldron is interested in challenging the rationale of the justification for such a primacy (Principle of First Occupancy) but from a wider perspective. He raises the issue of ranking injustices, and secondarily the corresponding remedial measures. When redistribution is adequate and when only restoration of rights of sovereignty and property are adequate? The lack of clarity over who is indigenous and why (first occupants or penultimate occupants—the last ones before colonialism) goes to the heart of the rationale for reparation: is it a subjective or a global, universal definition that ascribes these rights? The question to be asked is why do certain claims seem to be politically legitimate, at least to a degree, even if—as Waldron shows—these hardly stand the test of coherence? Another way to look at it is why do the claims of some indigenous peoples carry different weight than others? One possible answer is the identity of the perpetrators, the ability to claim from people who are still powerful and willing to listen. This is not a coherent, but a political answer.

The multiple facets of reparation are inherently often in conflict with each other. Satz suggests some of the ways in which this is problematic, including the dilemma of preferring imperfect justice to no justice. Any attempt to try to homogenize wrongs or redress would likely come up short. Satz suggests certain principles (target the wrong, respect varied harms, and understood relationally between the parties) which might be beneficial in examining whether the effort can be considered adequate and why the economic view of compensation is unlikely to be satisfying. This is true particularly in cases where the object carries extra economic meaning such as land, ancestral remains, and works of art, for example. Even in cases where compensation can play a central role, the goal of intergenerational compensation is in the final analysis to 're-establish relations of trust and mutual respect'.

Quantifying reparation is another way of ranking suffering. What is an adequate compensation? In part the answer relates to the construction of reparation as a symbolic act or as a real legal and economic measure that has to be adequate? 'Adequate' as defined by courts, or precedents. What if the magnitude of adequate reparation is 'too large' for the society to absorb, either subjectively (unwillingness) or objectively (too large relative to the GNP)? Does reparation have a symbolic role? This leads to a related set of issues of recognition: What constitutes recognition through reparation? Oftentimes the claim is that it is not about the money, but the recognition, the acknowledgment. Indeed that the symbolic is primary, the money is a secondary consideration. Yet the critique of reparation is often about inadequate sums. What does 'adequate' mean?

One school views the return of victims to a prior level of existence or at least satisfaction and often would eschew money as a means of compensation. This for example is most evident in the case of the Black Hills and the Lakota Indians, where hundreds of millions of dollars are accruing (very low) interest by the US government, but the descendants of the victims refuse to accept the court judgment and instead demand a return of the land. Tsosie sees in this refusal an embodiment of the dilemma of native people between looking to reparation as a form of 'reconciliation', and the resistance of reparation in order to avoid the politics of assimilation or in a more nuanced way, the efforts of 'reidentification'. The dilemma is that 'Native peoples, who seek continuing recognition of their separate political and cultural identities, as well as social and economic justice within contemporary society' would undermine their own experience by participating in reconciliation. It is clear that native peoples are split over the question. Those who believe that being treated with respect and equality, and a measure of reparation, can to the degree possible constitute a redress. Others, particularly activists and proponents of native national independence, emphasize a state which results from the cultural destruction of a 'psychological dependency' which is not really repairable. Tsosie herself points more to the reconciliation tradition among native people, especially referring to the Hawaiian tradition of 'Kala'.

This dilemma of reconciliation through reparation, or privileging separate identity, can be formulated as a tension between the group and the individual. If the Native people as individuals are better off, but that leads to assimilation, should native people seek reparation? This almost became an issue for the Sioux when in 1987 Senator Bill Bradley advanced a plan to compensate the Sioux with $18 billion. Bradley's bill aimed at restoring sovereignty to the Sioux through a 1.3 million acre increase in their reservation and the creation of a Sioux National Council as a forum of Sioux national revival. Even the bill's supporters found the sum too large to contemplate, especially because it would hinder Congress in future settlements by establishing a standard that would be too expensive for the government.[7] This and other reasons caused the plan's failure. But would that sum have been declined? Why would hundreds of millions of dollars for the Sioux not constitute recognition, but billions would? Would the restituted property (including water and mineral rights) be alienable (could be sold to outsiders)? Increasing resources in native tribes, especially from gambling, suggest that there are numerous middle ways, and the question of assimilation is not a burning one. Yet the nature of tradition is that it changes over time, and native culture is not always best interpreted to accommodate it. So are reparation and reconciliation a matter of principle, or merely inadequate at a certain level but not another? Would comparable sums be adequate in South Africa? Is there a class of victims which is more deserving than others or are these all proxies for a political debate?

Indeed, cash compensation to individual members of a tribe might only aggravate the infliction (e.g. when members of a Native American tribe who suffer from high rates of alcoholism, due largely to the original injustices suffered by the tribe, might serve only to exacerbate the effects of those injustices)

(Satz). But even a positive response by a Native American on the individual level, such as for example using the reparation money to build a new life and assimilate outside the tribe, would accelerate the disintegration of the tribe. The Bradley plan stipulated limiting the individual benefits to advance tribal existence, in part by not allowing beneficiaries to sell land rights. Group compensation and group existence constitute in this view a higher good than the potential individual improvement. The Native Americans would have to subscribe, abide, by a higher good. The complexity of the plan ensured that were it to be approved, the existence of the Sioux as a nation, a group, took precedence over the welfare of the individual Sioux as subjectively understood.

The TRC in South Africa raised the expectations of victims to receive reparation. It had a subcommittee (Reparations and Rehabilitations Committee) and its report advanced several reparatory measures. The TRC opted to view reparation as a right on the basis of victimization, not according to a means test. Those strategies that did not involve money, were more straightforward, including commemorative and legal amnesty for crimes committed in the anti-apartheid struggle. When it came to money reparations, however, the sums promised were small and decreasing with new programs, aimed primarily at those who testified for the TRC. It is intriguing to compare the sums of money in other cases (discussed elsewhere in the book): the sums rejected by the Sioux (no individual figures, but hundreds of millions at present value), demands for 'adequate' reparation in Peru (in line with the inter-American Court guidelines for individual compensation of about US$150,000+, that would entail a total payment of US$6 billion), and that advanced in South Africa (of US$4,900 per individual; US$80 million or compared with US$460 million recommended by the TRC.) The South African system could not accommodate the demands for reparation, and the struggle spilled from South Africa into the US courts.

I.3. HOW TO GET THE PERPETRATORS TO PAY?

Despite the great diversity of situations, former victims who claim reparation do share certain circumstances. Foremost, they remain relatively or absolutely poor, are weak, and dependent in some measure on the perpetrators for welfare and reparation. The essential recognition here is that the victims have no free agency in determining their reparation; they are dependent on the willingness of the perpetrators to collaborate. If that were not the case, the victims could appropriate the disputed resources. This may (or may not) bring a greater measure of justice, but would not be viewed as reparation, more as a revenge. For example, the Tutsi in Rwanda won the war, the Kosovars returned under NATO's cover. In both cases the victims reclaimed property, and even expelled (ethnically cleansed 'part of') former perpetrators. In neither case reparation is an important explanatory component for the justice on behalf of the victims.

The old tradition of imposing war reparation by the victors, Lu reminds us, was not used last in the aftermath of World War I, but also following the First Gulf War. Lu aims to explore the way material reparations may serve as retributive justice in addition to restorative efforts. But as she shows the moral efficacy depends on numerous political factors, and the failure to exact reparation in both Germany and Iraq does not make a strong case for the success of reparation as punishment in a situation where sovereign agents are involved. The moral obligation can be met by an agreement, which even under pressure is different than punishment. This is clearly not the case when the guilty party can be compelled to pay. This is most evident in the domestic court system, where perpetrators are forced to pay reparations.

Despite many attempts, there have been too few examples of successful Court-mandated reparations for cases of historical crimes and injustices. One possibility is to prosecute perpetrators and even sue in civil courts, including in the US, where many perpetrators and even more collaborators and bystanders conduct business. Indeed during the Nineties much news coverage was devoted to it, and activists continue to pursue this route. Under the American Alien Tort Claims Act, activists sought to circumvent the political mechanism, and to sue for reparation. So far it has failed. This is not to suggest it is impossible, yet the Alien Tort Claims Act has proven in practice so far a very limited tool. Although the risk of losing in the US courts can be deterring for governments, and some like the Swiss banks, or insurance companies, may even pay, to avert a potential of a much higher judgment and the accompanying negative publicity of the trial. But it is also evident that the courts are reluctant to intervene. Women victims of Japanese crimes during World War II lost in the courts, while the Holocaust claims were settled out of court and in neither did the victims receive satisfaction by the courts. The failure of activists to win in court elicited calls on businesses to take the moral high ground and acknowledge their responsibility or guilt. That would call for building a community, for collaboration between the victims and the perpetrators. Court action stifles such collaboration. This clearly remains a possibility, but the nature of the judicial system is that it attends to the exceptional, while structural changes have to come through the political system. In these, redress has great affinity to economic social and cultural rights. To translate these demands into policies, to enact these, the change has to come through the political system. Excluding force or court ruling, reparation is the result of an agreement between the perpetrators and the victims. At times under pressure, but always involving the recognition by both parties that their interests are best served by the agreement, and they can do no better under the circumstances. Pablo de Grief reminds us that the prosecutorial and the reparative are both complementary elements of justice: criminal justice is directed primarily against perpetrators while reparation is an effort on behalf of victims. No retributive justice can be widely applied and only the guiltiest (even in an ideal scenario) are brought to justice. In contrast, reparation and restitution as ideal aspire to attend to all victims. Since this desire is never fulfilled, alternative goals have to be designated. It may not be surprising that those are recognition, civic trust, and social solidarity. This demarcation underscores the shift from the legal discourse to the political arena.

I.4. WHAT ARE THE LIMITS OF REPARATION?

Reparation as a political agreement has to include both sides, especially if the perpetrators maintain power, political or economic. The interest of the victims though under the new regime is subject to intense dispute. This entails building a relationship, even when one side is odious and even if the relationship has to be viewed only as a necessity not a welcomed outcome. To achieve this, building relationship with the perpetrators is an effort on behalf of the victims. The outcome is not a zero-sum game, and reciprocity is essential for the benefit of both sides. This perspective is enhanced when we are reminded that we cannot assume that there is such a thing as the 'victims' ' perspective. South Africa postapartheid regime is a good example among many. 'The victims' in South Africa, although in power for over a decade, handle with great care, not to say reluctance and even resistance, any demands for reparation or redress that entails economic ramifications. 'The victims' in this case refers to those in power, not the many more that remain poor. While the government could have easily appropriated extensive parts of the whites' property as reparation, or inflict reparation payments on domestic and even international companies, it chose not to do so. The concern of the government is that it would either debilitate the companies or scare them off, and either result might have a negative impact on the very people it tries to assist. This government view is subject to intense criticism. Two observations are in order. First, the critics are correct in anticipating that not every reparatory arrangement would have the catastrophic outcome on the economy as the government stipulates. The government has been so reluctant, that one has to conclude that although it represents the victims, it also represents the victims who have done exceptionally well under the new regime, and therefore may not feel as passionate as others about economic redress. The victim's perspective depends on one's position in society. Second, the empirical analysis is subject to legitimate disagreement. Notwithstanding these empirical differences of opinion, the principle that building relationship is in the interest of the victims, not only the perpetrators, is crucial in formulating reparation agreements.

I.5. CONCLUSION

The scope of historical and immediate past injustices is breathtaking. There is little doubt in reading the various essays here that the classes of people deserving reparation, restitution, compensation, or other forms of redress is too large to contemplate, as is the scope of their rights and demands. Yet, as the various writers in the book suggest, there are numerous difficulties of how to adjudicate the various claims, and even harder to theorize and demarcate the various classes of claims. Moral intuition goes a long way to explain who benefits from redress, and who does not, even when the benefits are almost uniformly more symbolic than redistributive. Such theoretical dilemmas are not unique to redress, and it is rather difficult to think of confining such global phenomena into a theoretical frame. Yet there is little doubt that as redress becomes central to our understanding of a theory of justice which moves from the abstract to the specific, grounded as it is in local situations and violations, privileging specific wrongs to a universal theory.

The success of restitution as a moral political theory will be measured by its ability over time to imagine a cultural diversity that eschews a universal notion of the good but subscribes to vague shared values that provide models for conflict resolutions otherwise unavailable. By recognizing the merit in both individual and group rights as they exist in an unjust world, the starting point for restitution aims at providing a mechanism for negotiating rivalries and recognizing identities rather than ignoring them. Restitution as a theory of international relations proposes a process, not a specific solution or standard. It underscores a milieu in which many nations and minorities see greater benefits to themselves in conducting a dialog and reconstructing a shared past as the basis for both a recognition of their identity and a reconciliation. The process of restitution negotiation leads to a reconfiguration of both sides. While the perpetrators hope to purge their own history of guilt and legitimize their current position, the victims hope both to benefit from a new recognition of their suffering and for certain material gains.

One end of the reparation can be inadequate in the absence of other manifestations of truth and acknowledgment. By itself, apology can easily be considered as an empty gesture, as cheap and inconsequential talk. The critique of restitution—reparations and apologies—as too little too late—overlooks the continuous presence and effect of historical injustices in the life of the victims and the perpetrators, particularly in relation to identity, and hence the need to even partially amend these violations.[8] The novelty of restitution leaves us with a dilemma. Are we to celebrate the proliferation of restitution as a modest beginning of a new international morality, or is it merely the latest twist in contemporary escapism from moral responsibility and social justice?

NOTES

1. Felch and Frammolino (2005). The latest in the repatriation saga (which in the Getty involves institutional and personal issues) was the anticipated agreement with Greece ('Getty Director to Seek Return of Antiquities to Greece', *New York Times*, May 17, 2006).
2. Barkan (2000).
3. Winbush (2003).
4. Sané (October 2001). Sané is assistant director general for social and human sciences of UNESCO and former secretary-general of Amnesty International.
5. Clifford (1988: 277–347).
6. Waldron (1992).
7. Barkan (2000: 185–7).
8. Barkan and Karn (2006).

Part I

Reparations for Indigenous Peoples

1

Why Is Indigeneity Important?

Jeremy Waldron

1.1. AN ABSTRACT QUESTION

The term 'indigeneity' is something of a mouthful.[1] You would not find it in the *Oxford English Dictionary*, which insists on 'indigenousness' or the ugly 'indigenity' (which it describes as rare). Like its near-synonym, 'aboriginality', the word 'indigeneity' forms an abstract noun from an adjective we use to apply to certain peoples. The *Oxford English Dictionary* defines 'aboriginality' as '[t]he quality of being aboriginal; existence in or possession of a land at the earliest stage of its history'. In a similar way, 'indigeneity' is derived from 'indigenous' which means '[b]orn or produced naturally in a land or region; native or belonging naturally to (the soil, region, etc.)', from *indu*, an old Latin root meaning 'within' (like the Greek *endon*) and *gignere* meaning 'to beget'.[2]

Though it is not in the dictionary—not yet—'indigeneity' is already a term of art in the politics and philosophy of cultural rights and the rights of First Peoples. The etymology is fascinating, but I am mainly interested in the abstract idea of indigeneity. My discussion therefore lacks the richness and concrete focus of the chapters in this volume by Rebecca Tsosie and Janna Thompson. But I make no apology for talking about abstractions, because the question I want to ask in this chapter is about the bearing of the abstract idea of indigeneity on situations of the sort that Tsosie and Thompson describe. My discussion is in some ways critical of theirs, but it is intended at least at the outset to be complementary. They offer the riches of thick description; I add to that the analytics of conceptual analysis. For I want to ask: what does it add to our understanding of the predicaments and choices that Tsosie and Thompson set out for us, to describe Aboriginal peoples of Australia (the Wik people of the Cape York peninsula, e.g.) or Native Peoples in North America (the Great Sioux Nation, e.g.) as the *indigenous* people of those countries? And of course, despite my philosophical austerity, I have my own concrete points of reference: what does it add to our understanding of the predicaments and choices facing the people and government of New Zealand, to describe Maori (the Ngai Tahu people of New Zealand's South Island, e.g.) as the *indigenous* people of that country?

Like Tsosie and Thompson—indeed like all the authors in this collection—I want to pursue this particularly with regard to the issue of the remediation of injustice, and so my question can be focused as follows. In the process of trying to come to terms with the historic injustice perpetrated by white settlers and by colonial and postcolonial authorities in Australia, New Zealand, Canada, the United States, and other countries over the past 300 years, how important is it to bear in mind that some of these injustices were perpetrated *against the indigenous inhabitants of those countries*? No doubt people and governments acted oppressively to many groups; no doubt they still do. But it is widely believed that injustices perpetrated against Maori, or Aborigines or Native Americans are more egregious—or at least different in kind—than injustices against immigrant groups, or religious minorities, or slaves and their descendants. It is thought that injustice against Australian Aborigines, or Native Americans or Maori is specially salient, not only on account of its extent and its human consequences, but just because it was perpetrated against the original people of the land.

So: what is important about indigeneity? And I want to ask also: what principles does indigeneity invoke, which account for its importance? Rebecca Tsosie is quick to point out, at the beginning of her chapter, that we must not assume that it is appropriate to respond to all claims made by indigenous peoples in the same way: '[T]he starting and ending points might differ considerably from group to group'.[3] But if the concept of indigeneity has any meaning it presumably makes a difference to each of the (different) contexts in which it is deployed, and it can make a consistent difference—the same difference—to those contexts and its users can be acquitted of any charge of equivocation, without our having to hold that all injustice to indigenous peoples must be responded to in the same way.

One particular idea, which I should like to pursue quite closely, is this. Long before people became interested in indigeneity as such, or in the postcolonial situation of indigenous peoples or in the public morality and constitutional law of settler societies—long before people took an interest in any of that, legal and political thought in our tradition came up with what is known as *the Principle of First Occupancy*. This principle holds that the first person, or the first people, to take possession of a piece of land acquire special rights over it, so far as property and sovereignty are concerned. Many who *now* talk about indigeneity seem to believe that this venerable principle is key to understanding the importance that attaches to the description of a people as indigenous. It is key, they say, to distinguishing the claims of groups like

Maori or Native Americans from the claims of other groups—like immigrant groups or the descendants of slaves—in these modern societies. That is what I want to discuss. My fear is that theorists of indigeneity have taken up this Principle of First Occupancy without sufficient examination: they have taken it up in a relatively uncritical way.[4] I think it needs more careful examination.

I have a particular interest in theories of justice—I grew up philosophically under the indirect influence of John Rawls—and I have always been intrigued by the way in which the concept of indigeneity cuts through and transforms what would otherwise be a forward-looking discussion of social justice. Let me explain this, because it will be important in what follows. We might think in a good-hearted and pragmatic way that a decent society ought to struggle to make things more just, here and now and into the future for all the people and communities who are trying to make a life around here. If the resources of our society are wrongly distributed—if land, wealth, income, and power are wrongly distributed—then distributive justice demands a readjustment. Such redistribution has happened on a large scale and small scale in the past. Maybe it should happen again. But that is not enough—say some writers and politicians—if the issue is indigeneity. Indigeneity calls for a more radical approach: not just remedial measures to address maldistribution, but a *restoration* to the descendants of indigenous peoples of some or all of the rights—rights of sovereignty, rights of property—that were once held by their ancestors. Thus Duncan Ivison and his coeditors in the 'Introduction' to their collection of essays on *Political Theory and the Rights of Indigenous Peoples* are adamant that 'the distinctiveness of indigenous claims ... is lost or rendered opaque in discussions of distributive justice. ... Indigenous claims are not just for rights to any fair share of Australian or Canadian resources, but to a particularized share ...'.[5] The idea of indigeneity is supposed to transform the discussion from a general debate about justice to a debate phrased in more Nozickian, even Lockean terms, about the priority of certain entitlements and the particular connection of owners or sovereigns to particular pieces of land or territory.[6] Ivison, Patton, and Sanders are quite explicit about the privilege and priority that is claimed for these entitlements over and above, say, the grievances and claims of other disadvantaged groups. Immigrants may complain of prejudice and discrimination, African Americans may seek reparations for slavery, but these demands for justice are different in kind from indigenous claims. The theory of indigeneity, they say, is preoccupied with 'the problem of distinguishing indigenous claims from the claims of other kinds of cultural or "societal" groups'.[7] And throughout their book, they treat it as a point against any putative definition of indigeneity that it may tend to minimize this distinction.

1.2. TWO KINDS OF DEFINITION

Let us begin by reviewing some of the ways in which indigeneity may be defined. Indigeneity is a relative term: a people is described as indigenous in relation to a certain land or territory. Sometimes the term is treated as doubly relative, so that a people is called indigenous, first in relation to a certain territory, and second, in relation to some other people, who arrived in the land at a time subsequent to them. So we say the Maori are the indigenous inhabitants of New Zealand because they were its first human inhabitants. And we say they are its indigenous inhabitants relative to the Europeans, who settled several hundreds of years after the Maori as part of the colonial enterprise.

So immediately, we have two styles of definition, which I will call style (a) and style (b). The original definition put forward at the 1975 World Council of Indigenous Peoples was a style (a) definition: it referred to the 'descendants of the earliest populations living in the area'. But the same organization offered a style (b) definition in its draft covenant of 1984, referring to the descendants of peoples 'who lived in the territory before the entrance of a colonizing population'.[8]

The two concepts may be coextensive, as in New Zealand and Australia, where the populations that confronted European colonists in the late eighteenth century are plausibly regarded as the descendants of the first inhabitants of these lands. But still it is necessary to be aware of these alternative styles of definition, because indigeneity in sense (b) may ground different sorts of claims than indigeneity in sense (a), and it may make a difference which ones we rely on. It makes a difference, too, because in some circumstances the ideas *will* come apart. In India, for example, if indigeneity is defined in terms of literal *first* occupancy, we have to go way back before the Mughal empire of the sixteenth century, before the Vedic period on which present Hindu nationalist mythology is presently based, before the Indo-Aryan invasions in the latter half of the second millennium BC, even before the early Harrapan period that laid the foundation for the Indus Civilization; we have to go all the way back to the Paleolithic peoples who settled the Indian subcontinent as early as the eighth millennium BC. If on the other hand, we are talking about prior occupancy relative (say) to the wave of European incursions into India that began in the sixteenth century or the establishment of the British Raj in the eighteenth century, then we are saying that what commands respect is a complex mosaic of layered titles, claims, and civilizations (many established by conquest or incursion in the more distant past) that just happened to exist there at a particular point in time.[9] Plainly indigeneity in sense (b) is a variable term, depending on which empire or conquering power one is contrasting it with.

Even if you just concentrate on definition (a), there is still considerable indeterminacy. There is a distinction, which is no doubt difficult to pin down but interesting nonetheless, between being descended from the first inhabitants of a given territory and being descended from people who inhabited a given territory since the dawn of human history. It would be silly to describe the first European whalers who reached the subantarctic islands in latitudes below New Zealand—Auckland Island, Campbell Island, for example—as indigenous to those islands, even though they are, strictly speaking, the First Peoples of those islands, in the sense of not having been preceded there by any other human group. But apparently it is not silly to describe the first human inhabitants of New Zealand/*Aotearoa* as indigenous, even though they came there less than a thousand years ago, with ancestral memories of migration from a quite different homeland. Nor, presumably, should there be any difficulty in applying the same term indigenous to the Maori as to the Australian Aborigines, even though the ancestors of the latter migrated to Australia tens of thousand years before the ancestors of the former sailed to New Zealand.

The fact is that humans have been migratory animals since our emergence in Africa more than a hundred thousand years ago, and it is plain that the application of the term indigenous to human populations is always going to be somewhat different from its application to plants, for example. Humans are not indigenous in the way that plants are. We have not sprung from the earth or evolved within the territories with respect to which we claim to be indigenous. Usually what is emphasized is that indigenous peoples have strong ancestral links to the land because they have made a life there for many generations.[10]

For type (b) definitions of indigeneity, there are also intriguing riddles on the other side of the equation. If indigeneity means priority over the colonizing population, does it imply that the occupation by the colonists has gone on for a relatively short period? F.M. Brookfield mentions the case of certain Nordic countries, which have recognized the indigeneity of the Sami peoples despite the fact that the peoples relative to whom the Sami are said to be indigenous have also occupied the lands in question for millennia.[11] Type (b) definitions often suggest not just temporal priority—the indigenous peoples were here before the settlers—but also a great disparity between the few generations that have passed since colonization compared to the millennia in which their indigenous predecessors occupied the territory.

These definitional conundrums are well known. Benedict Kingsbury observed in 1998 that '[t]he development of "indigenous peoples" as a significant concept in international practice has not been accompanied by any general agreement as to its meaning'.[12] The issue has become particularly fraught in Asian countries where there is resistance to any definition of indigeneity that does not reference colonization. Kingsbury notes that 'several governments of Asian states argue that the concept of "indigenous peoples" is so integrally a product of the common experience of European colonial settlement as to be fundamentally inapplicable to those parts of Asia [like China] that did not experience substantial European settlement'.[13]

It is not my intention to make anything of this definitional uncertainty as such. Kingsbury may well be right when he suggests that traditional analytic or positivist modes of definition are inappropriate.[14] The Draft UN Declaration of the Rights of Indigenous Peoples at present contains no definition at all, and maybe that is the most sensible course.[15] We have already taken notice of Rebecca Tsosie's warning that the experiences and predicaments of First Peoples in various parts of the world are quite different.[16] If this is true, one possible implication is that the term indigenous tells us very little. Ken Coates suggests that the point is to let indigenous peoples define themselves, and not worry too much about any common meaning conveyed by the term.[17] But I suspect this still assumes that nonindigenous peoples will not try to muscle in on the act, and that assumption itself must based on some implicit conviction about what distinguishes indigenous from nonindigenous claims.

1.3. THE SIGNIFICANCE OF INDIGENEITY

We have seen that indigeneity is always defined relative to a given territory and the special relationship to *the land* that is key to most indigeneity claims means that claims bound to affect property, the distribution of resources, and resource use policies as well as issues relating to territorial sovereignty.[18] Those who believe that indigeneity is important believe that its importance consists in the challenge it poses to current patterns of sovereignty and property rights. The logic is quite simple. Indigenous peoples were not just waiting to be colonized in the eighteenth and nineteenth centuries. They were living and thriving with their own systems of polity, law, and economy. Those systems were *there first*; and they have a continuing moral status that is grounded in that priority. Colonization disrupted that, often brutally. Such disruption establishes the current regime of property and sovereignty as presumptively illegitimate. Now, in some cases where a present regime is judged illegitimate, the appropriate response is to look forward to arrangements that might be more just or appropriate. But with this sort of illegitimacy—the illegitimate disruption of an indigenous regime—the remedy involves looking back to *pre*-existing arrangements, and finding a structure now that is more respectful of those arrangements than the colonial and settler regimes have been to date.

Nothing like this, it is said, can be claimed by other minorities (immigrants, e.g. or the descendants of slaves). Their claims are no doubt very impressive from a moral point of view, but they are utopian: they look for justice where it has not yet existed. The claims of indigenous peoples are more grounded than in preexisting reality.

In its strongest version, the indigenous claim is, as Julie Cassidy has argued, a claim of *reversion*—she means the international law doctrine of reversion—based on the continuity of *de jure* sovereignty even under adverse conditions like colonization:

> The right of an ousted sovereign to have sovereignty restored under the laws governing belligerent occupation is derived from ultimate *de jure* title or territorial sovereignty. Sovereign rights do not inure in a belligerent occupant, much less an occupant whose entry was unlawful.... The sovereignty of the dispossessed peoples continues, awaiting reversion, despite the loss of territory and even total illegal annexation.... [W]here people have been forcibly subjugated, their sovereign title continues in abeyance and can later be restored.[19]

Of course, one seldom hears an argument for complete reversion to the status quo that confronted the European colonizers. What people say is that '[o]bsolete versions of absolute sovereignty are being discarded for indigenous equivalents that emphasize an autonomy both relative and relational', or something of the sort.[20] Still the claim to preexisting entitlements is there in the background, underwriting the widespread belief that governments presently in power in countries where there are indigenous minorities should be pressured to make considerable changes in current arrangements for governance and in current arrangements for land ownership and resource use. The power of the idea of indigenous entitlement means that it is not thought inappropriate to disrupt current patterns of property and sovereignty—to shake them up and reorganize them in various ways—to reflect the priority of the self-determination claims and the economic and proprietorial claims of indigenous peoples.

1.4. TWO ARGUMENTS

I have talked about two approaches to the definition of indigeneity. What I called the type (a) definition identifies those whose ancestors were the first humans to occupy the territory in question. The type (b) definition, by contrast, talks about *prior* occupancy, not First Occupancy. For this definition it is enough that indigenous peoples occupied and governed the territory at the time of colonization. For definition (b), it matters not whether they were the first to inhabit a land: what matters is that they were the last to inhabit it before the catastrophic incursions of European settlement.

The types of definition we have been considering correspond to two different arguments based on indigeneity. One is based, as I said earlier, on the venerable Principle of First Occupancy; the other is based on a more pragmatic conservative principle of respecting existing arrangements (even if those arrangements were set up only a few generations prior to the colonizing events complained of). So we have a Principle of First Occupancy, corresponding to type (a) definitions of indigeneity and what I shall call a Principle of Established Order corresponding to the type (b) definition, that is, corresponding to the idea that the would-be colonists ought to have respected the order already in existence among the indigenous peoples they sought to subjugate.

Let me say a little about each of these principles. First Occupancy first. The principle holds that the first person or community to take possession of a resource or a piece of land gets to be its owner. Or: the first people or community to take possession of a territory get to be (or choose) its sovereign. According to this argument, aboriginal peoples gained an entitlement to their ancestral lands by being the very first human communities to claim them. Of course, the first occupant may sell his property or cede its sovereignty to another, on whatever terms they please, and then those to whom the title has been transferred in this way may transfer it again, if they choose, to another person or group and so on. A theory of this kind has a nice recursive logic to it, which Robert Nozick elucidated in his book *Anarchy, State and Utopia*.[21] Justice-in-transfer is predicated on the idea that no one can be dispossessed except by his own consent, and the Principle of First Occupancy respects that too: the reason why the first occupant acquires good title is not because of anything special about *occupancy*[22] but because of simple priority. The first occupant did not have to disturb anyone else's rights in order to gain his title; but subsequent occupants would have had to disturb someone else's rights; and that is why, for second and subsequent occupants, the principle of consent is required.

First Occupancy has a venerable history in the theory of property and sovereignty. There is a version of it in John Locke's writings on property[23]—though for Locke the elements of labor and cultivation are crucial, whereas in the pure Principle of First Occupancy, 'occupancy' is a neutral term, referring to more or less any way in which a person or community might use or take possession of resources. Occupancy can include hunting, gathering, gardening, agriculture, recreation, or just residence—virtually any form of land use qualifies. There is a version of the principle in Blackstone, though it is a very hesitant version indeed.[24] You will find it in traditional textbooks of natural and international law.[25] It continues to be used in modern arguments about property and economics, in Richard Epstein's and Robert Nozick's work, for example.[26] It is a powerful and appealing principle, keying in as it does to intuitions we have all known since childhood: 'First come, first served', and all of that.

Many texts on indigeneity say that indigenous people's claims are based on something called 'original occupancy', and that can certainly be read as appealing to the logic of the First Occupancy principle which I have just outlined.[27] But sometimes the term that is invoked is 'prior occupancy', and that is something rather different. So we move on to the second of my two principles, corresponding to the type (b) definition.

In the crudest sense, the difference between the Principle of First Occupancy and a principle respecting prior occupancy, which I think of as the Principle of Established Order, is the difference between first and last, or (to speak more precisely) the difference between first and penultimate. The Principle of First Occupancy looks to the dawn of time, to the moment at which the land in question was first taken peacefully into human use and possession. The Principle of Established Order looks to what was happening at a moment just before the present, just before the first European ships came over the horizon.

It is not just a matter of time and relativity. The Principle of Established Order is opposed to First Occupancy in a deeper sense. Established Order is a conservative principle, not a reactionary one. Its aim is to vindicate and preserve an established existent status quo, not delve into tangled historical questions about any *status quo ante*. It recognizes the opacity of the past and the dangers of holding existing systems hostage to legitimist inquiry. Irrespective of how an existing distribution came about—whether it is a distribution of property or a distribution of sovereign authority—the Principle of Established Order gives it a prima facie right to be left undisturbed and allowed to develop according to its own dynamic. 'To disturb any one in the actual and long possession of territory', said Hugo Grotius, 'has in all ages been considered as repugnant to the general interests and feelings of mankind'.[28] Established Order refers to the human interest in stability, security, certainty, and peace, and for the sake of those values it prohibits overturning existing arrangements irrespective of how they were arrived at. Of course it cannot be an absolute principle: there may be compelling reasons for overthrowing and reforming an existing regime. (A regime of slavery, e.g. in New Zealand's Chatham Islands, cries out for redress, however long it has been established.)[29]

Now Established Order is undoubtedly an appropriate basis for condemning the injustice that took place at the time of colonization. For in the lands that were colonized there *was* a flourishing political and customary-legal system; there were established rules of property and recognized titles of sovereignty and governance; there was an order which had a claim to be respected, not on account of its antiquity but on account of its existence. European settlers might try to raise questions about the origins of the order they confronted: they might wonder whether the native chieftains had acquired their authority by violence and conquest. They might query whether the existing inhabitants of the land had appropriated their property in strict accordance with Lockean principles. And they might try to take advantage of these doubts to vindicate their expropriations on the grounds of the problematic origins of native title. But the Principle of Established Order simply prohibits that approach. Never mind its origins, the principle says. The native order existed as a stable and flourishing system when you arrived on the scene; and it was entitled to recognition and respect as such. If indigeneity is supposed to key into these values, then it can make a powerful case for reproaching the damage that colonial settlement inflicted.

1.5. PRIOR OCCUPANCY: INJUSTICE AND DISRUPTION

There is, on the other hand, an obvious difficulty with using the Principle of Established Order as a basis for remedial or reversionary claims to property and sovereignty by indigenous peoples in the twenty-first century. The principle certainly supports the claim that injustices were perpetrated when the precolonial order was disturbed and displaced. But precisely because it is a conservative principle, Established Order has the characteristic that while it condemns injustice at one particular point in time, it can equally work to vindicate established patterns of settlement that are founded on that injustice.

I said a moment ago that Established Order is a conservative principle. Based on the human interest in stability and security, it prohibits overturning existing arrangements. It deliberately refrains from legitimist inquiry into the past, for it holds that irrespective of how an existing distribution of property or sovereign authority came about, it has a prima facie right to be respected and left undisturbed. Of course, it is just a prima facie principle: there may be things about the modern situation that require redress or even revolution, in which case the Principle of Established Order must give way. But that cannot be for historical reasons alone;[30] and that is an important conclusion, because it indicates that a type (b) notion of indigeneity rooted in Established Order is incapable of adding anything distinctive to independent justice-based lines of argument for reform and change in the present.

Elsewhere I have argued that some claims based on historical injustice may be overtaken by events which make the distributional situation, which was established by the injustice, now just and appropriate to modern circumstances.[31] The argument I am making today illustrates a similar point, but in a slightly different way.[32] If the basis of M's complaint of injustice is that M held resources in a stable pattern of established occupancy and P disturbed that pattern, then whether reversion is an appropriate remedy will depend in part on whether P has now established a stable pattern of occupancy, which is entitled to respect on exactly the same principle as M's was. If the date of the injustice and the date of the claimed reversion are sufficiently close, that may not hold. But where, as in New Zealand, they are separated by a century or two, the application of Principle of Established Order to disturb current patterns of resource use or current patterns of sovereignty is problematic to say the least. The Principle of Established Order prohibits disrupting current patterns of land use and governance just as it (unsuccessfully) prohibited their disruption in the middle of the nineteenth century.

1.6. WHAT DOES FIRST OCCUPANCY ADD?

If Established Order—and the type (b) definition of indigeneity that appeals to it—will not support radical disruption of present arrangements, what about the purer and the apparently more principled idea of First Occupancy? Surely the descendants of the original inhabitants of a land have compelling claims against the present in virtue of being indigenous in sense (a).

I have two sets of things to say about First Occupancy theory, some relating to the principle itself, and some relating to its application.

(1) So far as application is concerned, obviously any notion of indigeneity based on First Occupancy is tremendously demanding on the resources of historical inquiry. It requires us to go back to the beginnings of human habitation in a particular territory, and determine who were the early occupants of that territory and whether there is any group which took possession of it peacefully, without dispossessing anyone else. In some contexts that is challenging beyond belief—I mentioned India earlier in the chapter, where a literal application of First Occupancy requires us to go back millennia before the events reported in Hindu mythology and even before the emergence of the Indus Civilization.

You may say—'Well, that is just the price of literalism'. But if we are not working with *literal* First Occupancy, then we are using some other principle like Established Order, and that runs into the difficulties I have already described. First Occupancy is an unforgiving theory, and there is no point using it unless you are prepared to embark on literal historical inquiry. (This is what I meant when I said that the choice of principles associated with indigeneity is sometimes careless or opportunistic.)

Let me focus on the New Zealand case for a moment, because I know it best. (Janna Thompson may want to say something exactly similar about the Australian Aborigine case.)[33] A defender of Maori rights may say: 'Well, whatever the case in India, at least in New Zealand things are clear. It is well known that the Maori *were* the first human occupants of New Zealand. So the literal application of the term "indigenous" to them in sense (a), and the literal application of First Occupancy arguments, is straightforward'. Is it? I wonder. We know that Polynesian seafarers did not settle New Zealand *as Maori*, but in distinct groups, which developed into *iwi* in possession of various territories, with quite distinct habitats, and often at war—including territorially acquisitive war, wars of conquest—with one another. We speak easily of 'the Maori people', but for the thousand-odd years before the arrival of Europeans, New Zealand was inhabited by diverse descent groups who shared a language perhaps, and to a certain extent a common culture, but did not conceive themselves as one people. These issues—particularly inter-*iwi* conflict, conquest, and expropriation—may be glossed over for various purposes, and probably they should be glossed over. But they cannot be glossed over if we persist in relying on a definition of indigeneity that is supposed to hook up with a Principle of First Occupancy. For of course First Occupancy is *intensely* interested in the history of territorial warfare; it is *intensely* interested in whether the titles for which vindication is currently sought, were established peacefully or by violence. If they were established by war and violence, then First Occupancy has no application. That is the whole point of the principle. That is because of the special moral force with which it is supposed to invest some claims and grievances, with which the Principle of Established Order (the more conservative, pragmatic principle) cannot invest them. Professor Brookfield puts the point very clearly when he says this:

> [T]he concept of indigenous people, if we confine it to a territory's original occupants, is morally relevant to the extent that their taking possession of an empty land gives legality to their presence (in the sense that their customary legal order becomes operative in the territory) but simultaneously gives full legitimacy as well. After all, there were no rights of prior occupancy requiring to be legally and morally extinguished. *Yet if an indigenous people... recognizes principles of conquest and seizure of power... in their inter-tribal relations, the moral relevance of their status as strictly indigenous people in relation to intruders from another culture cannot be great.*[34]

Maybe as a matter of comity between (say) English Common Law and Maori customary law, principles of acquisition by conquest should be recognized. Maybe we should recognize the custom of acquisition by conquest as a legal principle in what Professor Brookfield calls in a recent article the 'miniature international society' that operated among *iwi*.[35] Brookfield makes that case in his book, when he says that:

> Where the conquest was by one tribal polity over another ethnically the same as the conqueror, it may be (as in Maoridom) that inter-tribal custom was also a legitimating force: the defeat is experienced less as an 'intrusion' than conquest from outside the quasi-international society of the tribes of the same ethnicity.[36]

But even if the custom of acquisition by conquest is credited, that does not help at all with the application of the Principle of First Occupancy. The gist of First Occupancy is that special rights may attach to the *peaceful* occupation of unoccupied lands. Recognition of the custom does not license us to pretend that war was peace or that fighting was nonviolent.

Of course it is distasteful to bring up these issues of ancient (or not-so-ancient) history in the context of a good-hearted attempt undertaken at present to make a country like New Zealand more just.[37] But the perspective from which it seems distasteful, the moral perspective from which this sort of historical inquiry seems like a distraction, is not and cannot be a First Occupancy perspective. It is either an entirely presentist perspective, a forward-looking perspective aiming at distributive justice, which most aficionados of indigeneity reject. Or, if it has anything to do with indigeneity, it has to do with indigeneity in sense (b), in which case the same Principle of Established Order—respect for existing settlements, however they were established—which condemns this historical inquiry will also (as we saw) condemn any attempt to replace existing present-day arrangements with structures of property and governance more akin to those that existed in 1839.

Thus, my argument here has the form of a dilemma. Either we accept that a First Occupancy inquiry will have to sort through various indigenous claims, putting aside those that rest ultimately on war or conquest. Or we close that line of inquiry down, but only at the cost of also precluding an equivalent inquiry into more recent war, invasion, conquest, and seizure, figuring that if the conservative Principle of Established Order functions to protect violently established arrangements in 1839, it also functions to protect violently established arrangements in 2005.

(2) In any case, First Occupancy has always been a problematic principle, and the traditional writers on property and sovereignty, like Blackstone, are right to have been hesitant about it. The principle accords moral privilege to an occupant, in virtue of that occupant's not having dispossessed anyone else. The title of such an occupant is supposed to have absolute priority over anyone whose occupancy was affected by war or violence. But in relation to territory and resources, violently dispossessing another person or another people is not the be-all and end-all of injustice, and it is not the only basis on which we might raise a moral question mark over an entitlement. Refusing to share resources with others is also a form of injustice; refusing to modify a holding based on First Occupancy in response to demographic or other

changes in circumstances is an injustice. Taking more than you need, or occupying so much that subsequent arrivals have nothing to occupy, is an injustice.

All this has been understood and argued through by theorists of First Occupancy since John Locke's time. We know that Locke felt it necessary to qualify his version of the Principle of First Occupancy with the condition that there be 'enough and as good left for others' after the occupation.[38] And the formulation and reformulation of this 'Lockean proviso' have seemed essential in the modern discussion of theories of this sort. No one now that I know of in the theory of property is willing to argue for a First Occupancy principle that is not qualified in this way,[39] and very few are willing to deny that this proviso may also call one's holding into question at a later time, when circumstances change.[40] In brief, it is well understood in the literature on property that First Occupancy cannot stand on its own to legitimate disproportionate possession of land by one people to the exclusion of others who have no place else to go, simply because the former people came on the scene first. And I guess that is my point. This has all been thought through, in a complex and important literature, but it is the bare Principle of First Occupancy that gets seized on opportunistically by defenders of indigenous rights in a way that is completely impervious to these details and qualifications.

What I am saying is that people need to be a little more careful about the type of property theory they implicitly buy into when they privilege indigeneity. Simple slogans like 'First come, first served' and 'We were here first' have never been particularly attractive sentiments in the history of property theory, and they become no more attractive by being associated with revulsion from historic injustice.[41] They have often been associated with righteous indifference to others' interests, indifference even to others' needs, as people seek to retain possession of resources purely on the basis of historic priority. Since 1974, we have had the benefit—if that is the right word—of having a fully worked theory in front of us, based on exactly these intuitions, in the forms of Robert Nozick's theory of historical entitlement,[42] and for more than ten years after the publication of Nozick's book, the advantages and disadvantages of theories of his kind were comprehensively discussed by social and political philosophers. True the theory presented in *Anarchy, State and Utopia* was radically individualist in flavor, organized around the idea of absolute *individual* rights, whereas in the present context we are talking about the rights of communities or whole peoples. But as Nozick recognized, the logic is basically the same, and so are the difficulties.[43] In both cases, people who may have an interest in resources, for example people who may need to make use of them, are being excluded simply because they were not in the right place at the right time. I guess in the end any theory of property is going to have this sort of consequence: property is almost always exclusive in some regard, and the right to exclude is generated along with other property rights by contingent events. But just for that reason, great care needs to be taken in specifying what the contingent events are that give rise to these exclusive rights, and in specifying how they may be conditioned by circumstances. The most plausible theories of historical entitlement do this with some sort of Lockean proviso; but as we have seen that is exactly the sort of device that is likely to cast most doubt on simplistic claims of entitlement based on pure indigeneity.

Once we recognize that First Occupancy does raise serious problems of exclusion and that it does have this potential for a curious imperviousness to latter-day circumstances, then we can begin to appreciate the dangers of any simple-minded application of it or of a concept of indigeneity founded on it. Quite apart from the inherent *creepiness* of its underlying legitimism, there are considerable dangers in exposing modern distributions of power and property to the arcane details of recondite historical and prehistorical inquiry. For example:

> recognition of special rights and entitlements for having been the earliest or original occupants might spur and legitimate chauvinist claims all over India.... Claims to historical priority already feature in some 'communal' conflicts and incipient chauvinist movements abound, as with the pro-Marathis, Hindu-nationalist Shiv Sena party in Maharashtra. In effect, if some people are 'indigenous' to a place, others are vulnerable to being targeted as nonindigenous, and groups deemed to be migrants or otherwise subject to social stigma may bear the brunt of a nativist 'indigenist' policy.[44]

These dangers are not aberrations. They are part and parcel of what First Occupancy inquiries, for that principle itself purports to license some people, on grounds of historical priority, to repudiate and marginalize the claims of others. First Occupancy looks all very well when one considers only that the very first occupants did not have to dispossess anyone else. But if having established their occupancy, they hold the resources exclusively against everyone else in a way that is impervious of the needs of newcomers, then there is a very grave moral danger.

1.7. IS THAT ALL THERE IS?

Some will say that the account I have given is excessively analytic—picking apart the notion of indigeneity, and confronting it with this crude dilemma: either an Established Order claim, which precludes any radical reversionary remedy, or a First Occupancy claim, which is both inherently objectionable and anyway historically precarious. What could be better proof, my critics will say, of the proposition that the analytic techniques of Western political philosophy are out of place in this area and that 'liberal arguments are ... unable to comprehend what is distinctive about indigenous claims to land and self-government'.[45]

Maybe they are right. Or maybe I should turn the point around and say that, if the discourse of indigeneity really *is* incompatible with the conceptual structure of Western political philosophy, then what are the aficionados of indigeneity doing appropriating principles like First Occupancy and Established Order from John Locke and Hugo Grotius? We cannot have it both ways. If we want to make *indigeneity* respectable with these venerable principles of natural law, then we have to also be prepared to buy into all their difficulties, and face up to them responsibly.

If, on the other hand, indigeneity is a *sui generis* notion, as the Canadian theorist James Tully has argued, generating a set of claims that, in Tully's words:

> do not derive from any universal principles, such as the freedom or equality of peoples, the sovereignty of long-standing, self-governing nations, or [even] the jurisdiction of a people over land they have occupied to the exclusion and recognition of others peoples since time immemorial[46]

then it is difficult to know what to say. It cannot be that discussion is over as soon as someone mentions the word indigenous and associates a set of claims with it. Such claims are not self-justifying. They are supposed to be heard and understood, and subject to reason and criticism and examination, on both sides of the divide.

I am aware that my discussion here is far from exhausting the debatable content of indigeneity; I said that at the beginning. I am aware, too, that the concept does have an ineffable, almost mystical element, which is difficult to fathom. Is it fair to say, as Bill Oliver says, that '[t]he notion of indigenousness often leads ... to the ascription of a timeless and sacred quality to what was simply prior occupation', a merely 'rhetorical heightening of the unexceptionable fact of having been here first'?[47] It may be an unexceptional fact; but what I have been doing in this chapter is trying to explore some of the principles in our tradition that might make it significant. And the conclusion I rest with is not the mundaneness of the question 'Who was here first?' but some sense of its difficulty and danger. There are places in the world—India is one, perhaps Bosnia is another, Israel/Palestine is a third,[48] various places in Africa provide a further and distressing set of examples—places where making *that* the crucial question is a deadly and vicious ingredient in social and political pathology. These frightful situations are too distant for those to worry about who talk most confidently of the rights of indigenous peoples. For me, however, there are places closer to home—Fiji, for example—where insistence on the question Who was here first? has already done great harm. The difficulties, the harm and the dangers may be less apparent in Australia, New Zealand, Canada, and the United States; but if we are seeking to buy into the *general* discourse of indigeneity then we had better be aware of the volatile substance we are playing with.

NOTES

1. This chapter is an adaptation of my (2003). Versions of it were presented at a conference on 'Reparations' at Queen's University, Ontario in 2004 and most recently at the 2005 Annual Meetings of the American Political Science Association, in Washington, DC.
2. *Oxford English Dictionary*, online edition, last accessed 10/02/05.
3. Tsosie (p. 44).
4. So I come at this issue in part from my work on First Occupancy in the theory of property: see my (1988) and in part from my work on the rectification of historic injustice—e.g. my (1992).
5. Ivison, Patton, and Sanders (2000: 10).
6. cf. Nozick (1974: ch. 7) and John Locke, *Two Treatises of Government* [1689], II, Ch. V.
7. Ivison, Patton, and Sanders (2000: 3).
8. Cited by Kingsbury (1998: 422).
9. The *OED* gives this as a second special meaning of 'aboriginal':

    2. spec. Dwelling in any country before the arrival of later (European) colonists. 1788 BURKE Sp. agt. W. Hastings Wks. XIII. 64 This aboriginal people of India.

10. However, this too is sometimes made relative to other peoples—in a definition (b) sort of way—as in the rather informal definition we find at the beginning of Anaya's (2004: 3). Anaya talks of peoples' being 'indigenous because their ancestral roots are embedded in the lands in which they live... much more deeply than the roots of more powerful sectors of society living on the same lands or in close proximity'.
11. Brookfield (1999: 78).
12. Kingsbury (1998: 414).
13. Ibid. 418.
14. Ibid. 457.
15. See Anaya (2004: 185 ff). However, in international law circles, consensus seems to have moved toward type (b) definitions of indigeneity—like the one in ILO Convention 169 of 1989, which talks about people being 'regarded as indigenous on account of their descent from populations which inhabited the country... at the time of conquest or colonization or the establishment of

present state boundaries'. [Article 1 (1)(a) of ILO Convention (# 169) concerning Indigenous and Tribal Peoples. Adopted at Geneva, June 27, 1989.]

16. See Tsosie (p. 44).
17. See Coates (1998: 76).
18. However, as Tsosie emphasizes, (p. 44), these are not the only issues. Indigeneity is also said to be important for cultural rights and language issues—though there too the precedence that it asserts over other cultural claims or other language-rights claims depends in part on the special significance indigeneity is supposed to have in respect of land and territorial sovereignty.
19. Cassidy (1998: 117). In discussing reversionary claims, Kingsbury (2002: 118), offers the following examples:

    When Estonia, Latvia, and Lithuania broke away from the Soviet Union in 1991, they claimed simply to be restoring a pre-existing sovereignty that had been illegally interfered with by unlawful forcible incorporation into the USSR in 1940–1941.... In New Zealand, the argument is made that Maori were sovereign prior to 1840, that this collective sovereignty... was never lawfully surrendered, and... should now be revived and made operational.

20. Maaka and Fleras (2000: 93).
21. Nozick (1974: ch. 7).
22. This is a contrast with John Locke's Labour Theory, which is based on something special about *labor*: John Locke, *Two Treatises*, II, Ch. 5.
23. Ibid.
24. Blackstone (2001: Vol. II: ch. 1, p. 4).
25. Such as Twiss (1884: 194–5): 'a person may take possession of a thing which has no owner, so as to acquire Rightful Possession of it; and Property is in such a case acquired simultaneously with Possession.... Such being the Law of Nature in regard to primitive acquisition on the part of individuals, the Law of Nations is in perfect accord with it'.
26. Epstein (1985) and Nozick (1974: ch. 7).
27. Cf. Maaka and Fleras (2000: 94): 'Indigenous peoples have the right of sovereignty by virtue of original occupancy'.
28. Hugo Grotius, *The Rights of War and Peace*, Bk. II, Ch. 4. 2 (Campbell trans.) (In the same passage, Grotius also quotes Cicero, from the second book of his *De Officiis*, asking 'what justice there can be in depriving an owner of the land, which he has for many ages quietly possessed?')
29. See Brookfield (1999: 160). See also Tribunal (2001: 63 ff). The Chatham Islands lie several hundred miles to the east of New Zealand. In 1835, they were invaded by people of Ngati Mutunga *iwi* from the mainland, and their indigenous occupants—called Moriori, a Maori people who had lived there for centuries in isolation from the mainland—were killed and eaten or enslaved, and their lands occupied. Since the invasion took place before 1840, the descendants of Ngati Mutunga have insisted that the New Zealand government recognize their title under its general recognition of native entitlement in the Treaty of Waitangi, which was signed in 1840.

30. The Principle of Established Order directly condemns—it does not just compete with—recourse to reasons relating to historic injustice per se. So it cannot sensibly be balanced against such reasons.
31. See Waldron (1992). The argument may be illustrated as follows: Imagine two societies living on a large plain, each with its own source of water. One of those societies—from the north—descends in predatory fashion on the other in the south, and insists on using the southerly water supply as well. That's an injustice. But if, subsequently to that, the northerly water source dries up, then the situation that the northerners established by violence now becomes the situation that justice requires. The two societies must now share the same watering hole. So in this case, you cannot move automatically from a finding of historic injustice to anything like reversion as a remedy.
32. I emphasize that not all claims based on historical injustice can be finessed in this way. Janna Thompson insists in her chapter in this volume (p. 6) that '[i]t is difficult to deny that Aborigines are owed something for the injustices that they have suffered in the past'. I am sure she is right. The supersession argument that I have put forward elsewhere—Waldron (1992)—does not relate direct claims for compensation for injustice (though those have other well-known difficulties). It affects only claims of a reversionary character, and claims of compensation oriented to the failure subsequently to give back what was taken. And even there, the argument is that supersession may take place, not that it inevitably does. See also my (2004: 237).
33. See her chapter in this volume.
34. Brookfield (1999: 80–1) (my emphasis).
35. Brookfield (2002: 128–9). There are limits on this, of course, which become clear in relation to the events of 1835 in the Chatham Islands, whose Maori inhabitants were plainly 'not part of that miniature international society'. See above note 29.
36. Brookfield (1999: 79).
37. Similarly it would be distasteful to inquire into the history and prehistory of the holdings of war, conquest, and territorial holdings as among various First nations in the American context. Rebecca Tsosie, in her chapter in this volume, wisely does not delve into this issue.
38. John Locke, *Second Treatise*, Ch. V, paragraph 33.
39. See especially Nozick (1974: 174–82). I have discussed these issues in my (1988: Chs. 6, 7).
40. See Nozick (1974: 179 f). See also my (2005: 81).
41. Cf. Waldron (1992: 28).
42. See Nozick (1974: 149–82).
43. Nozick (1974: 178) 'We should note that it is not only persons favoring private property who need a theory of how property rights legitimately originate. Those believing in collective property, for example those believing that a group of persons living in an area jointly own the territory, or its mineral resources, also must provide a theory of how such property rights arise; they must show why the persons living there have rights to determine what is done with the land

and resources there that persons living elsewhere don't have (with regard to the same land and resources)'.

44. Kingsbury (1998: 435).
45. Ivison, Patton, and Sanders (2000: 9). And Dianne Otto has said—in her (1995: 97), —that all this just reflects the tendency of liberalism 'to conflate broad human experience into rigid dichotomous stereotypes'. She goes on: 'To recognize multiplicities would free indigenous peoples from the current imperative to present themselves as a unified category. It would enable a construction of indigeneity that was diverse, multi-layered and shifting'.
46. Tully (2000: 47).
47. Oliver (1998: 223).
48. See Waldron (2004).

2

Acknowledging the Past to Heal the Future: The Role of Reparations for Native Nations

Rebecca Tsosie

2.1. INTRODUCTION

For Native peoples, the discussion about reparations is not an intellectual exercise. It is a discussion of how the past, present, and future are cojoined and interdependent, just as the contemporary descendants of those who lived through the 'Indian wars' of the past couple of centuries are inseparably linked to their ancestors. The 'past' encompasses our family, our people, our nations. It is the story of how we came to be who we are today. As John Borrows, a Canadian First Nations scholar suggests, tribal narratives and stories are also important repositories for understanding the principles and laws that guide Native peoples in their interactions with one another and with the European societies that 'settled' these lands.[1] Any discussion of contemporary Native/non-Native relations is thus incomplete without a reference to Native normative frameworks.

In keeping with that premise, this essay discusses the concept of 'reparations' as one that is simultaneously emotional and spiritual, political and social. The framework for understanding the role of 'reparations' for Native nations necessarily must be intercultural. It must account for the different historical experiences of Native nations with the Europeans that colonized these lands, and it must address Native epistemologies. There is no 'uniform' theory of reparations that fits all cultures, all nations, and all peoples. This essay explores the potential contours of a theory of reparations for Native peoples, while simultaneously acknowledging that the theory may and likely will differ, depending on the particular historical context and cultural framework that applies.

The project of this essay is thus quite different from that of the other contributors to this volume. Janna Thompson's chapter offers a theory of reparative justice as it might apply to contemporary discussions about achieving justice for the Native peoples of Australia. Her chapter acknowledges the importance of historical context, but is highly dependent on prevailing moral theories of justice and desert among citizens in pluralistic societies. Jeremy Waldron's chapter is even more abstract, defining the concept of 'indigenous' as a method to assess whether rights claims are appropriate or justified at all. Both Waldron and Thompson appear to conceive of reparations under a 'tort model of reparations', as essentially being compensation for 'past wrongdoing', while still factoring in the equitable interests of contemporary citizens, both Native and non-Native. In comparison, this essay addresses what an intercultural framework for reparative justice might look like, and suggests that the starting and ending points might differ from group to group. In particular, Native peoples are asserting claims for recognition of cultural and political rights, as separate governments, which distinguishes their claims for reparations from those of any other group. This essay suggests that the concept of reparations should respond to the need to heal wounds that relate to past wrongdoing, as well as contemporary forms of injustice against Native peoples.

2.2. IDENTIFYING THE 'STARTING POINT'

To avoid abstraction and motivate this discussion, I start by examining one case study of a particular Native nation and its experience with the US government. The story of the Great Sioux Nation, which comprised several autonomous political bands of Lakota, Dakota, and Nakota peoples, and its battle against the United States is the subject of a great deal of popular American fiction. The most popular modern account exists in the 1990 box office hit, '*Dances with Wolves*'. This movie relates the romantic story of an American cavalryman who joins the Sioux Indians in their last fight for freedom before they succumb to 'conquest' by the United States. The Sioux Indians are noble, spiritual, and brave. The cavalrymen are corrupt, dirty, and mean. It is a sad story, because the tragic demise of the Sioux is inevitable, and no matter how hard the hero tries, there is nothing to be done. *Dances with Wolves* was a huge hit with the American public. It also did wonders for the South Dakota tourist economy. Suddenly, everyone wanted to visit the Black Hills (now under state, private and federal ownership) and see the glorious past of the Sioux Indians. Well, what about the present? The governor of South Dakota at the time, George Mickelson, got into the spirit of things and announced a 'Year of Reconciliation' between the state of South Dakota and the Sioux Indians. This, however, turned out to be largely a photo opportunity.[2] Some

Sioux Indians asked whether the government would give back any of their lands, particularly the sacred sites that they still use for religious purposes in the Black Hills. Some Sioux people wondered whether the government would issue an apology, say it was sorry for stealing their treaty-guaranteed lands, for murdering their patriot chiefs—men like Sitting Bull and Crazy Horse, or for turning their backs on the many solemn promises made in the treaty commissions. No apology ensued. No attempt was made to give land back. In fact, today, the Lakota people on the Pine Ridge Reservation live in the poorest county in the United States. They not only have the highest poverty rate in the United States, but among the highest rates of unemployment, alcoholism, domestic violence, suicide, and incarceration.

So, do the contemporary Sioux people 'deserve' reparations? We can argue about why, in the words of Janna Thompson, 'existing citizens of a political society owe reparation for injustices that they had no role in perpetrating'.[3] Or we can discuss why contemporary Lakota individuals should have the right to make any 'claims in respect to wrongs done to their parents and ancestors'.[4] At first glance, these seem to be perfectly useful intellectual inquiries that ought to concern diverse citizens of a pluralistic society. In fact, the US Supreme Court ventured part of the way down that path in its 1980 opinion in *United States* v. *Sioux Nation* which held that the 1877 statute that appropriated the Black Hills from the Lakota people was an unconstitutional taking of the treaty-guaranteed lands of the Sioux Nation, and that the United States was legally obligated under the Fifth Amendment to pay 'just compensation' to the contemporary descendants of the bands that were parties to the treaty.[5] The United States subsequently discharged its 'debt' by paying the requisite amount of money into a trust account set aside for the Indian people. Was this an attempt at reparations for a past wrong? That all depends on what the starting point is for the discussion of reparations.

Interestingly, many years later and despite severe economic challenges, the Sioux Indians continue to refuse to accept the award, which now stands at over US$500 million with accrued interest. How could this be? Does this mean that the Sioux Indians are not in favor of reparations? Does this mean that Governor Mickelson's suggested 'reconciliation' between Native and non-Native 'citizens' in South Dakota is in fact impossible? Could it be that the Sioux people understand reparations and reconciliation much differently than the non-Indian politicians and citizens of South Dakota? Clearly, the starting and ending points are much different for the Sioux people than for the non-Indians in South Dakota. The non-Indians claim to want a reconciliation, by which they mean a final effort to 'put the past where it belongs'. The Supreme Court decision says this is only possible if the United States makes amends for its illegal appropriation of the Black Hills. In the American legal system, money is an adequate means to compensate for loss of property. The loss of property is in the past. The compensation operates in the 'present' to redress past wrongs. However, for the Sioux people, the wrongdoing continues because the United States still maintains control over the lands that are seen as fundamental to Sioux political and cultural identity and because the United States continues to deny the several bands of the Sioux Nation their sovereign right to protect their land, and the natural and cultural resources comprised within those lands. The United States not only appropriated Sioux 'property', but actually tried to eliminate the Sioux people themselves. The Sioux people perceive the appropriation of the Black Hills as inseparably linked to the US government's genocidal military campaign against them, which culminated in the 1890 massacre at Wounded Knee. Moreover, they see the physical genocide of the nineteenth century as related to more contemporary efforts to extinguish Sioux political identity. In the words of Sioux attorney, Mario Gonzalez, 'the killings at Wounded Knee and the theft of the Black Hills are not separate, unrelated stories [but rather] our repeated efforts to liberate our homeland [constitute] a political matter directly related to this country's effort to destroy Lakota identity'.[6]

If we understand reconciliation as a process of 'healing' between groups who have experienced bitter and painful relations, and if we use the concept of reparations as a means to identify specific steps in that process, then we cannot be afraid to engage the full story of the Sioux Nation's encounters with the US government, including the Wounded Knee Massacre. The basic facts of the event are not disputed. In December of 1890, a Lakota leader, Big Foot, brought his band of sick and starving people to a military post and surrendered to the United States after an official government order authorized the US military to kill all Sioux Indians who were attempting to hunt and survive on their traditional lands and had not submitted themselves to the Indian agency. The US cavalry separated the men from the women and children and disarmed the men. After an unidentified shot was fired, the US cavalry began firing on the Indian men, who fled from the soldiers. The soldiers had surrounded the camp, however, and they began firing their Hotchkiss guns not only on the men, but on the women and children who were waiting in the camp. Individual soldiers pursued the Indians, butchering them as they ran. In the end, over 300 Sioux Indians were killed, two-thirds of them women and children.

Although the basic facts are not contested, the perspectives given in historical accounts vary widely. American history books generally refer to Wounded Knee as the 'last of the Indian wars'. The pervasive account is that the US cavalrymen overreacted to the 'unidentified shot' due to their fear of the Sioux people and their belief that the messianic Ghost Dance religion practiced by Big Foot and his followers was a violent movement. The history books relate that the soldiers began firing indiscriminately on men, women, and children due to their overwhelming fear of the Sioux Indians. The Sioux people, in comparison, are adamant that this was a 'massacre' and not a 'battle'. Moreover, the survivor accounts hint at a much darker story. Alice Ghost Horse, a survivor of the massacre, told of what happened that day, as her father helped her mother, brothers, and sisters hide from the soldiers in a ravine. She tells how he was wounded, but left them to look for survivors and never came back. She says that she and the other survivors hid until nightfall, and that they heard shots ring out for hours until dusk fell. Then, they heard a wagon searching for the dead.[7] Her story concludes: 'I have never touched a white man during my lifetime. I just could not trust any white men and never will because they killed my father and brother for no reason at all'.

Of course, Mario Gonzalez and other Lakota Nationalists would assert that the United States did in fact have a 'reason' to commit murder, and that reason was to conquer the Lakota people and appropriate their lands and resources. And yet, if the Sioux Nation's claim is distilled into an inquiry about compensation for 'property rights', how can we address the larger claim for reparative justice? Waldron's essay focuses on the rights that accrue from indigenous status, which primarily relate to land and title, and he suggests that the very assessment of 'injustice' is dependent on a careful look at the equities between Native and non-Native peoples in contemporary society. Thus, the entire question of whether 'historical titles' to land can persist may be relative to the needs and expectation interests of the non-Native peoples who by now have occupied and asserted title to the lands for a couple of centuries. This perspective, in fact, informs the US Supreme Court's holding in a recent case, *City of Sherrill* v. *Oneida Indian Nation*, that the 'Tribe cannot unilaterally revive its ancient sovereignty, in whole or in part' over parcels of land that the tribe purchased in fee within the boundaries of its original treaty reservation, which had never been disestablished by the US government.[8] Thompson's essay goes further, suggesting that ownership is not the only basis for Native claims, but that there are many other claims that might arise from 'past injustices', some of which may have persisted into the contemporary era. She suggests that many of these claims might be redressed by providing tangible opportunities (e.g. to employment or education) that could in fact 'equalize' the disparate experiences of Native and non-Native citizens. Finally, with respect to the category of claims that relate to cultural harm (e.g. forcible acculturation in government-sponsored boarding schools), Thompson suggests that, although some claimants might be justified in making reparative claims as 'heirs to a culture or the benefits of a community', this entitlement would necessarily end when the 'cultural link with the past has been severed', and living members of the culture no longer are able or willing to value their aboriginal culture.[9]

Compare the accounts offered by contemporary Sioux scholars and claimants with the accounts given by Waldron and Thompson. For the Sioux people, the fight for land is coextensive with their fight to maintain a separate political and cultural identity. They perceive themselves as rights holders by virtue of their inherent existence as a separate people and it is not up to any foreign government, legal system, or moral system to define their 'rights' or entitlements to land and culture. For Waldron and Thompson, Native claims can be parceled out into claims for 'ownership', for 'equal opportunity' as citizens, or for 'cultural rights'. Within the moral universe of Western liberal thought, these claims are weighed and adjudicated for their 'contemporary' validity. The two frameworks are radically different and lead to very different accounts of what 'reparative justice' might look like in a contemporary era. With that in mind, this essay now turns to offer an intercultural framework to evaluate the multiple dimensions of Native claims for reparative justice.

2.3. NATIVE AMERICAN REPARATIONS: A HISTORICAL SURVEY

In a legal sense, reparations are only appropriate where one group has suffered some legally cognizable 'harm' at the hands of another. As the preceding section demonstrates, the Sioux Nation and the various bands of Lakota, Dakota, and Nakota people have experienced a variety of harms. These are representative of the harms suffered collectively by Native people in the United States, and are simultaneously legal and moral in nature.

First, there are what I will describe as 'political' harms that ensued in the conflicts between Native people and the United States. Some of these harms relate to the forced appropriation of treaty-guaranteed lands and resources. For example, the 1868 Fort Laramie Treaty between the United States and the Sioux Nation promised the Sioux people that they would live in peace, in perpetuity, on the 'Great Sioux Reservation', an area that encompassed most of what are now the states of Montana, North Dakota, South Dakota, Nebraska, and Wyoming. In direct violation of the treaty provisions and by force and fraud, the United States seized most of this land. Today, the Sioux people are divided into minute reservations, on lands that comprise a mere fraction of what they once held. In turn, much of the land on these small reservations was taken in the early 1900s and given to white settlers, to the states, and to the US government for use in reclamation projects, national parks, and national monuments. The Sioux Nation has thus lost valuable rights to lands and associated resources (e.g. timber, minerals, and water) and has also suffered the moral and dignitary harms of treaty breach and subsequent treatment as a 'conquered nation'.

Some of these harms occurred as the US government, its officials, and its citizens confiscated the bodies of the Indians who died during this process of dispossession and refused to give them back. For example, in the late 1800s, the US Surgeon General issued an official order which required US cavalrymen to dismember Indian bodies recovered on the battlefield and send them to Washington, DC for 'scientific' analysis. This gruesome policy had many analogs at the local level, as frontier vigilantes and US soldiers murdered Indian people and plundered their bodies and campsites for regalia, weapons, and sacred objects which were kept as trophies in some cases, and turned over to museums and agency collections in other cases. Indian people suffered further harm from the public display of their ancestors' remains and sacred objects in museums and the open sale and trade of these remains and sacred objects at 'Wild West' conventions and trade shows. Native legal claims to repatriate their dead or their cultural objects were routinely denied until 1990, when Congress issued corrective legislation on the subject in the form of the Native American Graves Protection and Repatriation Act (NAGPRA).[10] As of 1990, conservative estimates speculated that there were approximately 250,000 sets of Native American human remains in federal repositories and museums. We now know that this number was much higher, and today, only a fraction of those remains and sacred objects have been returned to Native communities.

Second, the Sioux, like all Native people, have suffered a variety of cultural harms. They were subjected to a forced campaign of civilization, which outlawed their religious ceremonies and cultural practices. Individuals were imprisoned and fined for engaging in their religious practices without any form of court hearing or trial. Native children were forcibly seized and removed to distant boarding schools, where they were forbidden to speak their language and were taught that Indian culture was 'primitive, heathen, and bad'. Their traditional governments were shut down, and the Indian Bureau set up alternative government structures (tribal councils) for them. They were displaced from their sacred lands and barred from engaging in their traditional economies and life ways. Instead, they were coerced into a forced dependency, which made their very survival contingent on appropriations of 'rations' from the US government, most of which were illegally pilfered by the Indian agents and sold at a profit to non-Indian settlers.

It is hard to describe the impact of these harms and their profound legacy for contemporary Native people. The intergenerational harm of these policies continues to haunt Native people. In the words of Assistant Secretary for Indian Affairs, Kevin Gover:

> The trauma of shame, fear, and anger has passed from one generation to the next, and manifests itself in the rampant alcoholism, drug abuse, and domestic violence that plague Indian country. Many of our people live lives of unrelenting tragedy as Indian families suffer the ruin of lives by alcoholism, suicides made of shame and despair, and violent death at the hands of one another.

What possible framework is available for redress of these harms? I will first discuss the general framework within legal theory for reparations, and then discuss the experience of Native peoples in the United States.

2.3.1. A Framework for Understanding Native American Reparations

The concept of reparation carries with it a multitude of meanings. Webster's dictionary defines reparation in alternative ways: first, as 'the act of making amends, offering expiation (atonement), or giving satisfaction for a wrong or injury;' and second, as 'compensation in money or materials payable by a defeated nation for damages to or expenditures sustained by another nation as a result of hostilities with the defeated nation'. These alternative definitions indicate that, broadly construed, the concept of reparation is applicable to relationships between individuals, groups, and nations. It is designed to restore what has wrongfully been taken and to atone for injury, whether material or moral in character. The concept of reparation is accepted by the United States and the international community. It is a concept that has value across cultures and time periods because all peoples recognize that certain acts are 'wrong' and that harms must be remedied.

In many ways, the concept of reparation is consistent with legal principles designed to redress harms for breach of contract or tort injuries. Unlike criminal actions, which are designed to punish individuals for wrongdoing, civil actions generally seek to restore the appropriate relationships between injured parties. Thus, for contractual injuries, we seek to place the injured party back into the position that he would have been in without the breach. The doctrine of restitution in contract cases, for example, calls for the breaching party to restore or give equivalent value for any loss, damage, or injury. Similarly, in tort cases, we offer victims compensatory relief for economic loss through actions for damages. Where the harmful conduct has caused an unjust enrichment, the law can impose a 'constructive trust' on the profits in favor of the victim.

According to Martha Minow, reparations embodies an ideal of 'restorative justice'.[11] Restorative justice aims to 'repair the injustice', to make up for it and institute future changes to correct the injustice. Drawing on Minow's work, there are several different forms of reparative justice for historical wrongs. Reparations offers money or resources in symbolic redress of violations. 'Restitution' returns wrongfully appropriated property, artifacts, and human remains. 'Apology' offers verbal acknowledgment of responsibility for wrongdoing and affords victims the chance to forgive or refuse to forgive. Notably, reparative justice can entail both economic and symbolic acts: monetary payment, health and social services, restitution of property, public apologies, and memorials. There is a material component to this process and also an intangible, psychological component. At a minimum, it is important to emphasize the humanity of victim and offender, to repair social connections and instill a sense of peace rather than ongoing conflict. There is an emphasis on healing. For example, victims need to move beyond a sense of powerlessness, and may need to tell their own stories and have the public acknowledge this.

There are many problems in adopting a theory of reparation that does not acknowledge these dual components. For example, it would be wrong to suggest that once compensation is made, the events need not be discussed again. Nor is it appropriate to suggest that a monetary remedy can cure a nonmonetary harm. Furthermore, we need to evaluate cases within an intercultural context. If we apply the concept of reparation to intergroup relations, the normative frameworks that we use will be informed by different cultural values and by different perceptions that stem from our respective historical experiences. Although American people 'share' a history in some sense, our perception of that history differs depending on whether we are descended from Native people, African people brought here involuntarily as slaves, British colonists, or the many ethnic groups that voluntarily immigrated to the United States, but then found themselves categorized and stereotyped in particular ways because of their original ethnicity. Similarly, our contemporary experience in the social, political, and economic realms of American society can vary drastically depending on these same considerations. Thus, not surprisingly, many American citizens view the concept of reparation with a great deal of suspicion. 'What do THEY want now?', 'How much will this cost US?'. The response exemplifies the problem.

It is important to separate the question of *entitlement* to reparations from the question of what *measures* are necessary to achieve reparations. For example, within international law, reparations between nations entail both monetary compensation and satisfaction.[12] Damages are available for moral and material injury. 'Material injury' involves 'damage to persons or property'. Monetary compensation is the most common reparation form. A moral injury to a state is an 'injury to the dignity or sovereignty of a state', for example a violation or breach of a treaty. The remedy for this might be an award of monetary damages, punitive sanctions issued against the wrongdoer, an apology to the victim, an acknowledgment of wrongdoing by the guilty party, or any other measures necessary to prevent the recurrence of the illegal act. In any case, the point of reparation is to 'wipe out all the consequences of the illegal act and reestablish the situation which would, in all probability, have existed if that act had not been committed'.[13] With respect to Native Americans, the doctrine of reparation as it applies to nations forms an appropriate model because of their continuing status as separate sovereigns with distinctive cultures and continuing ties to their aboriginal territories. I want to acknowledge, however, that in some cases, individual Native Americans will have a claim for reparations based, for example, on discrete instances of abuse, such as occurred at many government-run boarding schools.

Native peoples in the United States continue to suffer from a profound legacy of historical injustice that has political, legal, social, economic, moral, and spiritual dimensions. These are integrated in such a way that the concept of reparations, for Native people, must simultaneously address the dispossession of their lands, natural resources, ancestral remains, and cultural property, as well as the suppression of their political autonomy and their cultures. To reduce these components into a claim for monetary compensation is ludicrous. The measures used to redress these harms will require a significant restructuring of America's basic institutions, including its political and legal institutions. The concept of reparations has been used within Critical Race Theory (CRT) to advocate arguments for structural changes in society, on the theory that our existing institutions (political, educational, etc.) are fundamentally unequal because they were created to maintain the dominance of the racial elite who founded this country. I accept the truth of that statement in the context of discussions about the nature of injustice, and so part of my argument for Native peoples proceeds along similar lines to the arguments of CRT scholars: that we need to make structural changes to our basic institutions in order to ensure justice. What those changes should be, of course, will depend on the nature of the injustice. I am arguing for a theory that evaluates the experience of each group (e.g. African Americans, Native Americans) independently.[14] Thus, for Native Americans, reparations may well be (in the words of Mari Matsuda), a 'legal concept that has transformative power'.[15]

2.3.1.1. *The Experience of American Indian Nations With Reparations*

American Indian claims for reparations, to date, have been largely within the context of land claims litigation and claims for repatriation of ancestral human remains and sacred objects.

Land Claims

In the case of land claims, reparation for the loss of American Indian lands and resources has depended on a *compensable breach* of a treaty right or right conferred by statute, as well as the willingness of federal courts to substantiate the breach with a damages award. So, for example, in *County of Oneida* v. *Oneida Indian Nation*, the Court found that the 1790 and 1793 Trade and Intercourse Acts, which forbade the purchase of lands from Indian tribes without the consent of the United States, invalidated the state of New York's 1795 purchase of Oneida land.[16] This decision clouded the title to thousands of acres of land in New York, currently occupied by non-Indians. Although the Oneidas prevailed in their legal claim, the case is still being litigated to determine the remedy for this wrongful act.

The main vehicle to redress violations of American Indian land rights was the Indian Claims Commission Act (ICCA) of 1946.[17] Until the ICCA was passed, individual tribes had to petition Congress to enact a special statute in order to adjudicate their claims against the government. Not surprisingly, very few tribal claims had actually been eligible for adjudication prior to 1946. The ICCA outlined five categories of claims that would be justiciable before the Commission, including claims in law or equity arising under 'the Constitution, laws, or treaties of the United States', tort claims, equitable causes of action (such as fraudulent conduct by government officials), takings of tribal lands without compensation, and 'claims based on fair and honorable dealings that are not recognized by any existing rule of law or equity'. The Act, as it was interpreted and litigated, offered monetary compensation to Indian nations for the wrongful appropriation of their lands, and for other violations of tribal rights guaranteed by treaty or statute.

The Lakota brought an action for the breach of the 1868 Treaty and the taking of their sacred Black Hills in the 1920s under a special Congressional statute. After nearly twenty years, the Claims Court held that this was merely a 'moral' claim that had no legally cognizable basis for redress. After the ICCA was passed, the Lakota again got Congressional permission to reopen the case under that statute's standard for legal redress. This time they prevailed, but were merely awarded monetary damages for the taking of the land and associated resources.[18] Because the Lakota sought repatriation of the lands, rather than monetary compensation, they were not satisfied with the reparations process under the ICCA.

The ICCA also failed to redress other moral and dignitary wrongs. Tribes that pursued claims that arguably fell into the 'fair and honorable dealings' category were sadly disappointed with the Claims Commission's narrow interpretation of that provision. For example, the Ft. Sill Apache Tribe's claim for redress of injuries suffered during their twenty-seven year imprisonment was held not to be compensable under the fair and honorable dealings clause of the ICCA.

Thus, the ICCA is an example of the government's tendency to view Native American reparations as a monetary settlement of property claims rather than a means to account for moral or dignitary harms. The harms to Native American sovereignty and culture have been addressed through legislation dealing with repatriation, language rights, self-government (e.g. the Indian Reorganization Act, and the Indian Self-Determination Act), and the Indian Child Welfare Act. These pieces of legislation affirm the status of Indian nations as 'domestic dependent nations' under the federal trusteeship. Thus, the federal government may 'restore' and 'protect' aspects of Native sovereignty that were wrongfully impaired, such as the right to hold cultural property and the right to determine guardianship rights to Native children.

Repatriation Claims

Along with their land base, Native Americans suffered loss of significant cultural resources, including sacred objects and objects of cultural patrimony, which were removed by artifact collectors and anthropologists. In addition, Native American human remains were also collected by federal agencies and museums for scientific study. In addition to the plundering that took place under the Surgeon General's order and the activities of frontier vigilantes, Native American gravesites on state and federal lands were plundered by archaeologists and amateur 'artifact collectors' to recover human remains and funerary objects. In the 1900s, the US government passed legislation providing that Native American remains on federal land were 'federal property'. This constrained the activities of the amateur collectors to some extent, but provided federally licensed archaeologists with a legal right to dig up Native American remains and take them to museums for scientific study.

These practices continued largely unabated until the enactment of the NAGPRA in 1990.[19] Native American Graves Protection and Repatriation Act is one of the only federal statutes to ever provide enforceable protections for Native American cultures. Native American Graves Protection and Repatriation Act is an important piece of legislation, enacted pursuant to the federal government's trust responsibility to Indian people, which protects the unique cultural rights of these groups. Thus, NAGPRA's provisions must be interpreted consistently with the federal government's duty to protect Indian tribes from actions undertaken by the dominant society which seek to destroy Native cultures and peoples. This duty of protection was a solemn pledge that the federal government made to Indian people when it entered treaties with them. Many tribal leaders counseled against ceding any lands, in part because they feared that they would lose any ability to protect their ancestors' remains.

They were assured by federal negotiators that the white people sought only to settle the lands and not to harm the Indian people. Native American Graves Protection and Repatriation Act thus reflects a moral as well as legal duty to safeguard Native cultures.

Native American Graves Protection and Repatriation Act protects the rights of Native American people, including American Indian tribes, Native Alaskan groups, and Native Hawaiians, to four categories of cultural items: human remains, associated and unassociated funerary objects, objects of cultural patrimony, and sacred objects. While 'human remains' and 'funerary objects' have their usual meanings, 'objects of cultural patrimony' and 'sacred objects' have statutory definitions which largely rely on Native American tradition and law to define the nature of the object and the standards for rights of possession, disposition, and alienation of these objects. Native American Graves Protection and Repatriation Act is fairly unique among federal statutes because of its explicit reference to cultural knowledge and the role of tribal law in establishing concepts of ownership and 'cultural affiliation'.

The mandate of NAGPRA to repatriate Native American human remains and cultural objects back to Native people is considered a form of reparations. Arguably, the right to bury the remains of one's ancestors and protect the sanctity of ancestral burial sites are basic 'human rights' that most American citizens have always enjoyed. Thus, perhaps NAGPRA merely ensures that Native peoples are treated 'equally' to non-Native peoples. However, NAGPRA is intended to remedy the significant cultural harm caused by the historical appropriation of human remains, funerary objects, sacred objects, and objects of cultural patrimony from Native peoples. In that sense, the statute is a form of reparative justice. Indeed, with the exception of NAGPRA, there has been little effort to address the cultural harm caused by past and present government policies that have harmed Native cultures, including harms to religion, land, and resources.

2.4. NATIVE AMERICAN REPARATIONS: A PROSPECTIVE ANALYSIS

In an article on treaty rights that was published a few of years ago, I drew on work by Eric Yamamoto and Mari Matsuda to assert that intercultural justice will ultimately depend on the willingness of various cultural groups to recognize group injustices, both past and present, and attempt to define a strategy to heal, to reconcile, and to reaffirm the rights of distinctive groups within American society.[20]

My discussion with respect to intercultural justice depends on two foundational points. I start with the premise that the concept of reparation is critical to achieve 'intercultural justice' between contemporary groups in American society. However, because of the very different historical positions of the respective groups that comprise 'American society', the specific measures used will vary. Thus, my second premise is that the concept of reparation must be flexible and account for the different historical experiences of particular groups.

2.4.1. Defining Intercultural Justice

Professor Eric Yamamoto has written a comprehensive account of interracial justice that provides a good foundation for the idea of intercultural justice.[21] According to Yamamoto, 'interracial justice entails hard acknowledgment of the historical and contemporary ways in which racial groups harm one another, along with affirmative efforts to redress justice grievances and rearticulate and restructure present-day relations'.[22] Interracial justice is fundamental in healing broken relationships between different groups and in establishing 'right relationships' between those groups.[23] Yamamoto suggests that interracial justice involves four components of 'combined inquiry and action': (*a*) recognition of group harms and grievances, (*b*) accepting group responsibility for healing the wounds, (*c*) reconstructing intergroup relations through particular acts (e.g. forgiveness, apology), and (*d*) reparations, which involves making material changes (social, economic, and political) to rebuild the structure of the relationship in a tangible way (not 'just talk').[24]

Yamamoto's model is centered on race relations rather than cultural relations. Race and culture share an important intersection, however, which Yamamoto acknowledges, and which makes the model of interracial justice constructive to defining intercultural justice.[25] As Albert Memmi observed, aspects of cultural difference, both real and imagined, are used by dominant racial groups to single out racial minorities as 'the other' and justify unequal, exclusionary, and even violent treatment of those groups.[26] Moreover, cultural imperialism by the dominant group depends on suppression and/or assimilation of minority cultures. The resultant cultural loss has devastating consequences for members of the minority cultures, who 'experience a loss of identity' that often results in psychological trauma and social dysfunction (e.g. substance abuse, incarceration, and domestic violence).[27]

2.4.2. Acknowledging the Past

William Chapman writes: 'the past is at its best when it takes us to places that counsel and instruct, that show us who we are by showing us where we have been, that remind us of our connections to *what happened here*'.[28] Indian people and Euro-American people share a history of their encounter, and, for better or worse, they share the legacy of that encounter. Indian nations suffered huge losses, whether measured in lives, lands, or other resources. However, they also maintained lands and cultural identities that support their claims to sovereignty and self-determination today.

The history that has characterized the relations between American Indians and the United States has been one of tremendous violence, treachery—and yes, pure 'evil'. The genocide that took place on this continent is of staggering dimension. According to James Sterba, as of 1890, when the Indian wars concluded with the massacre at Wounded Knee, 98 percent of the Native population that existed during pre-Columbian times had been killed.[29] Up to ninety-four million Indians lost their lives during the conquest of the Americas (as compared to sixty million Africans during slavery, and six million Jews during the Holocaust).[30]

Of course, it is not the sheer magnitude of the genocide that characterizes the evil of conquest for American Indian nations; it is their subsequent treatment by the dominant society. Building on Laurence Mordekhai Thomas's work in *Vessels of Evil: American Slavery and the Holocaust*, Sterba examines the continuing evil wrought by the dominant society's justification of the conquest and dispossession of Native peoples through stereotyping. Thomas differentiated the evils of American slavery from the Holocaust through the concept of 'natal alienation' which Sterba asserts is also a feature of Indian–White relations. Natal alienation is the forcible destruction of the minority group's cultural context by the dominant society: 'There is natal alienation in the lives of an ethnic group when the social practices of the society into which they were born forcibly prevents most of them from fully participating in, and thus having a secure knowledge of their historical-cultural traditions'.[31] Sterba claims that the lack of equal respect and opportunity is what has barred the flourishing of these groups.[32]

Sterba's argument suggests that if Blacks, Indians, and other racial minorities are given equal respect and opportunity as citizens, then the wrongs that have been done to them through cultural destruction can be overcome. To some extent, Janna Thompson's essay shares the same conclusion. Many Native people would disagree with this assessment, at least with respect to Native peoples. For example, Haunani-Kay Trask asserts that it is the fact of this cultural destruction which is responsible for the 'psychological dependency' that continues to traumatize Native peoples: 'generations become addicted to the worst cultural habits of the colonial society which increases both ignorance of and alienation from, the Native culture'.[33] The increasing alienation of Native people from their traditional cultures cripples them in the dominant society and in their aboriginal societies.

Indeed, the poverty rate among American Indians, the low life expectancy, high suicide rate, and high rates of alcohol-caused mortality indicate that 'American Indians suffer from extreme social and economic injustice'.[34] Trask notes a similar set of social ills among Native Hawaiian people, and attributes this to the 'continuing impact of Western imperialism'.[35] Whether couched in terms of injustice or 'imperialism' the end question is the same: how do the different groups that comprise 'American' society come to terms with the evils of the past and attempt to overcome the continuing consequences of that past in an effort to achieve intercultural justice?

2.5. HEALING THE FUTURE: NOTIONS OF RECONCILIATION AND JUSTICE

In any process of group reconciliation it is necessary to first acknowledge the complex and pervasive nature of the harm, both as a legal and as a moral matter. It is then necessary to construct a vision for the future that can encompass notions of intercultural 'justice' within a framework for healing and reconciliation. Building on Yamamoto's account of interracial justice, it appears that there are two essential requirements for effective reconciliation.[36] First, the groups must reconstruct their relationship through acts, such as apology, that indicate acknowledgment of wrongdoing and a commitment to 'make things right'. Second, true reconciliation entails a commitment to make tangible amends which will facilitate the material economic, social, and political changes necessary to achieve justice.

2.5.1. Reconstruction

The process of reconciliation is largely framed by the government's approach to acknowledging historical injustice. Building on the post-slavery reconstruction process, Robert Meister suggests that there are two different approaches to 'posttraumatic reconciliation'.[37] One approach asks all Americans to acknowledge the pain and suffering that the United States has inflicted on *others*. This approach represents a constitutional politics of *representation*, which implies that preexisting identities are fixed and require recognition.[38] Under a politics of representation, it is vital for the nation to recognize the separate identities of the victims and to meet their claims to redress past and present injustice. The perpetrators (or their descendants) are required to *acknowledge* wrongdoing as a way to start healing the wounds of the past. Under this model, 'truth' about the past is essential, and national politics and histories must be opened to include the voices of those who have been excluded.

In the context of American slavery, Meister contrasts the 'Lincolnian' approach, which is to ask all Americans 'to identify *themselves* as victims who survived the experience of slavery and the Civil War'.[39] This approach exemplifies a 'constitutional politics based on *reidentification*', which implies a national rebirth based on a new collective identity that bridges the gap between 'self' and 'other'.[40] The goal of a politics of reidentification is not necessarily to set things right for the victims, but to help the entire nation recover from its 'toxic guilt' which is ultimately destructive to the common goal of national citizenship. The 'Union' is the survivor in this model, and victims and perpetrators are asked to mutually identify with one another as 'survivors' of past events, and to acknowledge the equal moral footing that they now share. Under the Lincolnian view, 'Americans' are the survivors, and there is no need for any particular group to 'survive'. In fact, a politics of reidentification discourages an emphasis on group differences, which are seen as contrary to the spirit of reconciliation that should guide the present condition of all Americans. Not surprisingly, any notion of group apology is likely to be inconsistent with this notion of the 'common' identity of victims and perpetrators as survivors of a less than glorious past.

A politics of reidentification may be suitable for groups that are committed to equal citizenship and opportunity, and for whom reconciliation implies an end to past policies that disadvantaged them from equal citizenship. However, it is not suitable for groups such as Native peoples, who seek continuing recognition of their *separate* political and cultural identities, as well as social and economic justice within contemporary society. The treaties between the United States and Indian nations exemplify the commitment to tribalism and group-based separatism that Indian nations look to today in their efforts to gain recognition for their rights to self-determination. Thus, it is possible, as some Aboriginal people in Australia have asserted, that group-based claims for self-determination are in fact inconsistent with the national governments' efforts to achieve reconciliation, to the extent that such efforts are based on a 'politics of reidentification' which intend to unify the constituent members of a multicultural society around a unitary ideal of citizenship.[41] Importantly, however, Native rights to self-determination are not independent of their claims for redress for historical injustice. On the contrary, one of the great harms of colonialism has been the denial of the inherent right of self-determination for Native peoples. Thus, the concept of reparations for Native peoples MUST include recognition of their right to self-determination. This is not some vague agreement to allow tribes to govern themselves within the colonial bureaucracy, but an actual commitment to honor the types of bilateral treaty relationships that *nations* enjoy, as well as the right to maintain their distinctive tribal cultures (through, e.g. the protection of sacred sites and ancestral human remains under standards that are suited to Native claimants).

In any case, to be effective as a means to achieve intercultural justice, a 'politics of representation' must involve an *intercultural* dialog on the normative foundations necessary to achieve healing and justice between groups. The next section of this chapter examines the use of apology as a tool to start that process of intercultural dialog.

2.5.2. Apology as a Means of Intercultural Dialog

There are only two instances in which the United States or its representatives have attempted to apologize for past wrongs toward Native Americans. The first occurred in 1993, when the US Congress issued a resolution apologizing to the Native Hawaiian people for the 1893 overthrow of the Hawaiian Kingdom by a band of insurgents backed by the US military and asking for the process of reconciliation to commence. The second occurred in September 2000, when Kevin Gover, a Pawnee Indian and the Assistant Secretary for Indian Affairs, apologized to Native people for the past wrongs committed by the Bureau of Indian Affairs (BIA) and for the continuing harm suffered by contemporary Native communities as a result of these wrongs. Because the latter apology is most relevant to the harms I have described above for the Lakota people, I focus on this apology.

Assistant Secretary Gover made his remarks on the occasion of the 175th Anniversary of the BIA, which he characterized not as a 'celebration', but as a 'time for reflection and contemplation, a time for sorrowful truths to be spoken, a time for contrition'. He started the apology by reciting several historical harms that BIA policy and actions perpetrated on Native peoples. Most importantly, he acknowledged that the original mission of the Office of Indian Affairs, which started out in the Department of War and was then moved to the Interior Department after most of the Indian wars had been concluded, was to pave the way for the United States to appropriate lands from tribal ownership for the benefit of US citizens. This, in turn, was accomplished by 'ethnic cleansing' intentional physical harm 'on a scale so ghastly that it cannot be dismissed as merely the inevitable consequence of the clash of competing ways of life':

> the deliberate spread of disease, the decimation of the mighty bison herds, the use of poison alcohol to destroy mind and body, and the cowardly killing of women and children in massacres such as those at Sand Creek, the banks of the Washita River, and Wounded Knee.

Assistant Secretary Gover then listed the BIA's subsequent efforts to 'annihilate Indian cultures' and destroy Indian economies by inculcating a forced dependency on the United States and the BIA. Gover concluded that 'poverty, ignorance, and disease have been the product of this agency's work'.

Until this speech, it was unheard of for a US government official to talk about US Indian policy as ethnic cleansing. After all, the 'official version' of the United States dispossession of Native nations generally hinges on the justification that because of the 'savage' character of the tribes, they were unable to 'hold property rights' on the same level as civilized people, and thus were 'necessarily' conquered by a more civilized nation.

When Assistant Secretary Gover's apology acknowledged the truth of United States/Indian relations, as Indian people have experienced that history and as they continue to experience it, he started an intercultural dialog about acknowledging the past in order to heal the future. Assistant Secretary Gover stressed that by accepting the historical legacy of the BIA as one of 'racism and inhumanity' the Agency must also accept 'the moral responsibility of putting things right'. Admittedly, this apology came from a federal agency and not from the US government. Yet the apology is historically significant because it represents the first official attempt ever to acknowledge moral responsibility for past wrongs against American Indian people committed by the United States and its agents. The apology thus served several important purposes.

First, the apology issued a corrective history to evaluate past conduct. American history books and law books are replete with the justificatory approach to past bad acts toward Native Americans. For years, history books instructed American school children that the savagery of Indian people was responsible for their demise in the face of 'civilization'. This understanding, in turn, has been used by Supreme Court justices and policymakers to justify the denial of Native rights. In *Tee-Hit-Ton* v. *United States*, for example, the savage nature of the Tee-Hit-Ton Indians, as a group of itinerant 'hunter-gatherers' excuses the United States from any contemporary Constitutional obligation to pay just compensation for the taking of their traditional lands.[42] In a different context, Chief Justice Rehnquist's dissent in *United States* v. *Sioux Nation* relies on the same rationale to excuse the obligation to pay the Lakota for the taking of treaty-guaranteed lands. Relying on the *Oxford History of the American People*, Rehnquist alludes to the savage nature of the Lakota people, who 'lived only for the day, recognized no rights of property, robbed or killed anyone if they thought they could get away with it, inflicted cruelty without a qualm, and endured torture without flinching'.[43] Rehnquist's conclusion is telling:

> That there was tragedy, deception, barbarity, and virtually every vice known to man in the 300-year history of the expansion of the original 13 Colonies into a Nation which now encompasses more than three million square miles and 50 states cannot be denied. But in a court opinion, as a historical and not a legal matter, both settler and Indian are entitled to the benefit of the Biblical adjuration: 'Judge not, that ye be not judged'.[44]

The impact of this history and its popular understanding on Native peoples is profound. Not only does the United States fail to acknowledge the vast and complex nature of the harm that it has wrought on Native peoples, but it appears to place the blame for this harm squarely on Native people themselves. The message to Native people is simple: 'If only you had been more like us, things might have been different for you'.[45]

Second, and building on this historical foundation, Assistant Secretary Gover's apology locates responsibility where it belongs: on the original wrong-doers and those in privity with them. Gover acknowledges that 'the BIA employees of today did not commit these wrongs', but they must 'acknowledge that the institution we serve did'. All employees of the BIA 'accept this inheritance, this legacy of racism and inhumanity. And by accepting this legacy, we accept also the responsibility of putting things right'. In this sense, Assistant Secretary Gover's approach builds on what Peter French and others call 'collective responsibility'. Some scholars locate collective responsibility for past wrongs under a 'benefits theory'. Peter French, however, makes a compelling case for collective responsibility among contemporary governments, groups, and institutions for past wrongs based on the idea of collective ownership of 'public memory'.[46] 'Public memory casts the past into our present', French argues, 'and well it should because it is our past or what we are jointly committed as a group to being our past. We, as a collective, are the continuation of the projects of our collective's past'. Public memory is the repository of our collective identity, and to the extent that officials, governments, and institutions manage it publicly, it represents our commitment to a collective past for our contemporary group. Thus, Assistant Secretary Gover's remarks are particularly important because they recast the collective memory of the United States and American citizens as a way to acknowledge collective responsibility for past wrongs.[47]

In that respect, the third important function of Assistant Secretary Gover's apology is to differentiate the impacts of the harms and show the continuing nature of the historical wrongdoing. So, Gover's apology speaks not only to the historical physical harm (e.g. ethnic cleansing) perpetrated on Native peoples, but also the economic harm (destruction of traditional food sources and economies, forced dependency), and the cultural harm (prohibiting Native language and religion). All of these harms resulted from tangible and overt laws and policies of the United States.[48] However, the result of these harms is far more complex: a constellation of emotional and spiritual trauma that extends from generation to generation within Native communities. For example, Assistant Secretary Gover refers to the tragic legacy of the BIA boarding schools and asserts that 'the BIA committed these acts against the children entrusted to its boarding schools, brutalizing them emotionally, psychologically, physically, and spiritually'.

Assistant Secretary Gover affirmatively states that 'These wrongs must be acknowledged if the healing is to begin'. And in that sense, the single most important purpose of the apology was to set the process for healing in motion.

2.5.3. Reconciliation and Reparations

According to Matsuda, the idea of reparations builds on the Constitutional norm of liberty and 'recognizes the personhood of victims'.[49] Lack of legal redress for racist acts continues the injury perpetrated by the initial wrongdoing by signifying 'the political nonpersonhood of victims'.[50] The grant of reparations, on the other hand, declares: 'You exist. Your experience of deprivation is real. You are entitled to compensation for that deprivation. This nation and its laws acknowledge you'.[51]

Although many citizens view the concept of reparations as coextensive with *monetary* compensation, the idea of reparations is much more complex and has social, economic, and political dimensions. In fact, some groups would dispute that monetary damages could ever be a satisfactory replacement for the loss of certain tangible resources. For example, the Lakota seek the return of the Black Hills and refuse to take compensation in the form of damages. The idea of reparations clearly must involve recognition of Native peoples' rights to enjoy their distinctive cultural and political identity. Thus, many Native American claimants argue for recognition of their rights to practice their religion at certain sacred sites and for their political right to 'self-determination'. Finally, the concept of reparations may depend as much on process as on substance for its effectiveness at achieving true reconciliation. As Matsuda notes, the 'very process of determining the validity of claims will force collective examination of the historical record. The discovery and acknowledgment of past wrongs will educate us and help us to avoid repeating the same errors'.[52] In that respect, Assistant Secretary Gover's apology engaged the forward-thinking questions of what it might mean to 'heal' Native communities and what the BIA's moral responsibility might be in this process. The apology itself intended to commence this process in at least three different respects. First, it is intended to set a moral boundary against which to measure future behavior:

> Never again will this agency stand silent when hate and violence are committed against Indians. Never again will we allow policy to proceed from the assumption that Indians possess less human genius than other races. Never again will we be complicit in the theft of Indian property. Never again will we appoint false leaders who serve purposes other than those of the tribes. Never again will we allow unflattering and stereotypical images of Indian people to deface the halls of government or lead the American people to shallow and ignorant beliefs about Indians. Never again will we attack your religions, your languages, your rituals, or any of your tribal ways. Never again will we seize your children, nor teach them to be ashamed of who they are. Never again.

Second, the apology is intended to inspire a policy template to deal with legal and political redress for past wrongs, which are often reflected by the current needs of Native communities. It is clear from Gover's remarks that the harms are much too complex and serious for a 'quick fix'. Perhaps Native economies can be bolstered by gaming policies. Perhaps Native governments can be supported by the self-determination and self-governance statutes and policies. But the process of healing for Native communities will require a much more nuanced version of federal policy dedicated to a moral, as well as legal, commitment to the notion of self-determination. What does it mean to facilitate 'tribal self-determination' if the tribal government is still under the control of the federal government and its larger agenda to American citizens? How can a 'tribal community' be a vibrant repository for self-determination if a significant portion of Native adults are incarcerated and in poverty, and if a significant portion of Native families are torn apart by substance abuse and domestic violence? These are the paradoxes of contemporary Indian policy that Gover acknowledges, and with which the process of healing must engage.

Finally, Assistant Secretary Gover's apology is intended, on a spiritual level, to set in motion the process of redirecting blame, healing spiritual trauma, and promoting a larger sense of collective responsibility on the part of the US government and its citizens. Importantly, the apology *alone* cannot actually do any of those things. Rather, it is intended to start that process in motion and begin a dialog about what must be done to heal the past. As Gover says, 'we desperately wish that we could change this history, but of course we cannot'. The most that can be done is to 'accept the moral responsibility for putting things right'.

2.6. CONCLUSION

The intellectual puzzle about reparations and reconciliation is really quite simple: We cannot heal the future if we cannot honestly acknowledge the truth of the past. This requires the reformulation of public memory, from an exercise of justification to an admission of past wrongdoing and an acknowledgment of current inequities.

It is important to think about the process of healing from historical trauma as both a *cultural* and an *intercultural* process. For example, Senator Daniel Akaka from Hawaii linked the Congressional apology to Native Hawaiian people, which focused on reconciliation with the Hawaiian cultural concept of 'ho'oponopono', which means 'to make things right' and is a technique used to resolve interpersonal conflicts.[53] Senator Akaka observed that:

> The process of reconciliation is a process of healing, which should not be viewed as one particular issue or a narrowly defined process. It should be viewed as a multitude of positive steps between Native Hawaiians and the federal government to improve the understanding between each party, to improve the social and economic conditions of Native Hawaiians, and to resolve long standing matters of political status and land claims.

Within the tradition of 'ho'oponopono', the healing process is both emotional and spiritual and is premised on the idea that the perpetrator and the person wronged are bound together in a relationship of negative entanglement called 'hihia'. The healing process must 'untangle' these negative emotions to facilitate a mutual understanding of the 'emotional truth' of what happened, a sincere appreciation of the effects of the bad behavior, a confession of the wrongdoing and seeking of forgiveness by the perpetrator, the act of granting forgiveness and, ultimately, the 'release' of all negative emotions. The final phase of 'kala', which means to 'release, untie, free each other completely'—follows the phase of forgiveness. Thus, the idea of 'kala' is importantly distinct from that of 'forgiveness'. The actual phrase, 'Ke kala aku nei 'au ia 'oe a pela noho 'I 'au e kala ia mai ai' means 'I unbind you from the fault, and thus may I also be unbound by it'. As Manu Meyer observes, 'kala seeks to strip the incident of its pain-causing attributes'.[54]

In issuing the Joint Resolution, the US government took an important first step by acknowledging its complicity in the illegal overthrow of the Hawaiian monarchy and its regret for the resultant hardships that occurred for the Native people. However, although the Joint Resolution expresses regret for the deprivation of Native Hawaiian rights to self-determination, and specifically acknowledges their attachment to their 'ancestral territory' and 'their cultural identity', it does not express support for Native peoples' contemporary rights to self-determination or their legal rights to land or cultural resources. Thus, the pain cannot heal because the Native people still suffer from their dispossession from their lands and their distinctive cultural and political rights.[55] For Native Hawaiians, as for other Native people, the idea of intercultural reconciliation involves both the values essential to reconstruction (e.g. the notions of apology and forgiveness) and the need for tangible reparations as a way to make things right.

Native governments have demonstrated their tenacity and determination to exist in perpetuity. Through many treaties and laws that exemplify the 'trust doctrine', the US government has committed itself to protect Native governments, to respect their rights as separate peoples, and to work cooperatively to solve contemporary problems. Given this reality, engaging the process of intragroup and intergroup healing is not even an 'option' for the United States and the Indian nations. It is a requirement to achieve intercultural justice in the future.

NOTES

1. Borrows (2002).
2. See Gonzalez and Cook-Lynn (2001: 91)(quoting Lakota scholar Vine Deloria, Jr as stating that the Year of Reconciliation was simply 'twelve months of symbolic maneuvering for publicity and renewal of political images'.).
3. Thompson at p. 69.
4. Ibid.
5. *United States* v. *Sioux Nation*, 448 U.S. 371 (1980).
6. See Gonzalez and Cook-Lynn (2001: 82).
7. Ibid. at 15–21.
8. *City of Sherrill* v. *Oneida Indian Nation*, 125 S. Ct. 1478, 1483 (2005).
9. Thompson at p. 69.
10. 25 U.S.C. §§3001–3013.
11. Minow (1998: 91–117).
12. Chock (1995: 495).
13. Ibid. at 495 (citing Chorzow Factory case from Permanent Court of International Justice).
14. Tsosie (2005).
15. Matsuda (1987).
16. 470 U.S. 226 (1985).
17. 25 U.S.C. §70–70v.
18. *United States* v. *Sioux Nation*, 448 U.S. 371 (1980).
19. 25 U.S.C. §§3001–3013.
20. See Tsosie (2000).
21. Yamamoto (2000).

22. Ibid. at 9–10.
23. Ibid. at 10.
24. Ibid.
25. Ibid. at 90–7.
26. Ibid. at 95–6.
27. Ibid. at 94–5.
28. Keith Basso, Wisdom Sits in Places, 4 (citing William Chapman), Preserving the Past 46 (1979) (emphasis in original).
29. Sterba (1996).
30. Ibid.
31. Sterba (1996: 437).
32. Sterba (1996: 438–9).
33. Trask (1994: 260).
34. Sterba (1996: 439).
35. Trask (1994).
36. My argument builds on Yamamoto's discussion of 'reconstruction' and reparation, in his account of interracial justice. See Yamamoto (2000: 190–209).
37. Meister (1998).
38. Ibid.
39. Ibid.
40. Ibid.
41. Some indigenous Australians argue that the Australian government's program for reconciliation is essentially an effort to incorporate Native people into the larger polity and thus may actually impede a movement toward 'real self-determination', which should entail development of a sovereign Aboriginal nation and promote tangible political and economic rights for the Native people. See Cunnen and Libesman (1995).
42. *Tee-Hit-Ton* v. *United States*, 348 U.S. 272 (1955).
43. *United States* v. *Sioux Nation*, 448 U.S. 371 (1980). The majority of the Court held that the treaty-guaranteed nature of these lands did require the United States to pay just compensation to the Lakota for the taking of these lands.
44. Ibid.
45. *Johnson* v. *McIntosh*, 21 U.S. (8 Wheat.) 543 (1823).
46. French (2003).
47. French's account is importantly different from Thompson's argument that 'people acquire historical obligations by being members of an intergenerational society that committed wrongs against another such society'.
48. For example, the 19th cent. Code of Federal Regulations expressly criminalized the practice of Native religions and customs.
49. Matsuda, supra note 17 at 74.
50. Ibid.
51. Ibid.

52. Ibid.
53. See Meyer (1995).
54. Ibid. at 35.
55. See generally MacKenzie (1991). Mackenzie offers one of the most comprehensive treatments of the unique legal position of Native Hawaiian people. The persistent refusal of the courts to recognize the religious rights of the Native Hawaiian people is documented at pages 229–41.

3

Coming to Terms with the Past in Australia

Janna Thompson

Reparative justice, as it is traditionally understood, requires that the perpetrators of injustice return what they have taken from their victims and/or compensate them for harm done, with the objective of returning them, so far as possible, to the situation that existed before the injustice was done. Aristotle, for example, thought of reparation as a matter of righting the moral balance by ensuring that perpetrators would not profit from ill-gotten gains and that victims would recoup their losses.[1] My brief is to describe and discuss issues of reparative justice in respect to injustices done to Aborigines and their communities during the course of Australian history. But this job cannot be done without a critical examination of the traditional idea of reparation. Public debates in Australia about justice for Aborigines have made it clear that demands for reparation are difficult to justify or fulfill when there are disagreements about who (if anyone) now counts as a perpetrator or a victim or what justice requires when a return to an ante-injustice state of affairs is neither possible nor morally desirable.

I will discuss three issues which pose difficulties for an account of reparative justice in cases of historical injustices. First, the problem of explaining why existing citizens of a political society owe reparation for injustices that they had no role in perpetrating. Second, the problem of determining what counts as just reparation and how this should be determined; and third, the difficulty of explaining how individuals can make claims in respect to wrongs done to their parents or ancestors. In the course of my discussion of these issues, I will propose an alternative interpretation of reparative justice and its requirements.

3.1. A HISTORY OF INJUSTICES

Few people doubt that serious injustices were done to Aborigines and their communities during the course of European settlement of Australia. In some respects, the history of relations between Europeans and the indigenous people of Australia is similar to other histories of European settlement. In Australia, as in Canada, the United States, South America, etc., native people were pushed aside to make way for Europeans and their activities, and when they resisted they were punished. As in Canada and the United States, the culture of the native peoples was subverted and their communities were often forcibly relocated or destroyed. As in other countries, indigenous people were subjected to prejudice and discrimination and to authoritarian regimes of control.

What makes Australian colonial history different from other histories is the fact that British officials and Australian governments refused to acknowledge the status of indigenous people. Australia was declared '*terra nullius*', giving Europeans the right to settle and exploit the land as they pleased.[2] No treaties were made with indigenous communities; no recognition was given to their claims of ownership or to their communal traditions and laws. This meant that Aborigines had no official place in Australian society and, in fact, were not even recognized as citizens until the middle of the last century. Policy toward Aborigines up to recent times was dominated by the assumption that the presence of Aborigines in Australia was only temporary. It was believed that full-blooded Aborigines, as members of a weaker race, would die out, and half-caste individuals, of which there were an increasing number, could be integrated into the European population, so that in the course of time Aboriginal blood and Aboriginal culture would fade away.

However, Aborigines and their communities have not disappeared and in the last fifteen years, political and legal developments have forced non-Aboriginal Australians to face some of the injustices of the past. A judgment by the Australian High Court in 1992 declared that British sovereignty and European settlement had not necessarily extinguished indigenous rights to property. This decision was followed by a High Court judgment which ruled that Aboriginal communities could legitimately claim land now leased by farmers and graziers (which includes most of outback Australia).[3] *Terra nullius* was officially dead.

The Labour government then in power consolidated the rulings of the Court with a Native Title Act which provided a framework for making claims and offered compensation to those who were not able to claim. This legislation, along with the establishment of a Council for Aboriginal Reconciliation, was intended to bring about a historic change in the relations between Aboriginal and non-Aboriginal Australians. Awareness of past injustices and their present day consequences was also heightened by two National Inquiries. The first, into Aboriginal deaths in custody,[4] found that Aborigines were more likely than members of the non-Aboriginal population to end up in prison where they were often subjected to insensitive or even brutal treatment. The later Inquiry into the separation of Aboriginal and Torres Strait Islander children from their families[5] revealed the practice, only recently ended, of removing half-caste Aboriginal children from their families and communities and bringing them up in orphanages or white foster homes.

These developments of the late 1980s and early 1990s were a high water mark in the attempt of Australians to come to terms with the past. The Liberal government, which came to power in 1996, was attentive to the fears of leaseholders, and sponsored legislation to reduce the ability of Aborigines to claim land or to prevent mining and agricultural activities on the land that they possessed. This government has largely ignored or sidelined the reconciliation process. Prime Minister Howard refuses to offer an official apology for the injustices of the past. Presently existing Australians, he insists, should not be held responsible for deeds done by past generations, and he favors what he describes as 'practical reconciliation'—that is, policies aimed at improving services and conditions for Aborigines. Public attention in recent times has shifted to dysfunctions within Aboriginal communities and political groups, and some commentators play down the importance of historical injustices and suggest that Aborigines, or their culture, are largely responsible for their present day problems, or argue that Aborigines as beneficiaries of Australian society have no right to make reparative demands.[6]

The political backlash against Aborigines and their supporters is the result of many political and economic factors. But it has been aggravated by the above-mentioned conceptual difficulties in applying requirements of reparative justice to historical injustices. Why should present day Australians, many of whom recently arrived in the country, regard themselves as responsible for past injustices to Aborigines? And what can reparative justice demand in a situation where so many Australians depend on resources that were unjustly taken from Aborigines? The difficulties of applying reparative justice to this case of historical injustice motivate a further question. Why focus on the past at all? Why not concentrate on removing the disadvantages from which Aborigines now suffer (as the Prime Minister seems to prefer)? I will answer these questions in the following sections.

3.2. APOLOGY AND COLLECTIVE RESPONSIBILITY

It is wrong to punish people for the crimes of others, and it seems equally wrong to make them pay reparations for wrongs they did not do. If presently existing citizens are supposed to make reparations for injustices done by past officials or citizens of their nation, then this must be justified by some account of collective responsibility. But according to common theories of collective responsibility, there is no responsibility without participation, active or passive.[7] Citizens of a democracy might be regarded as responsible for the policies of their elected officials but it is more difficult to see how they can be responsible for policies pursued by their nation before they were born, came of age, or arrived in the country.

A communitarian conception of collective responsibility might seem more appropriate for cases of historical obligation. Alasdair MacIntyre thinks that responsibility follows from the fact that we are bearers of a particular social identity.

> I am someone's son or daughter, someone else's cousin or uncle... I belong to this clan, that tribe, this nation. Hence what is good for me has to be the good for one who inhabits these roles. As such I inherit from the past of my family, my city, my tribe, my nation, a variety of debts, inheritances, rightful expectations and obligations. These constitute the given of my life, my moral starting point.[8]

The trouble is that not all individuals reason from this moral starting point. MacIntyre himself thinks that 'individualist' selves are becoming more common, and even those who do regard themselves as attached in an essential way to others are likely to have different ideas about the relations which form their identity. Some people regard their family as central to their lives but have little interest in their nation. The immigrant may continue to derive his self-identity from the land of his ancestors. Nor does acceptance of responsibility necessarily follow from identification. A person can locate herself within a history or identify with a group without thinking that she is obliged to do anything about the commitments or injustices of past members. And there is no necessary connection between feeling shame or regret for the sins of predecessors and taking responsibility for reparative justice. A communitarian account of the self can explain why some people are prepared to take responsibility for past injustices of their community, but it cannot persuade those who do not share MacIntyre's starting point or explain why the stance taken by Prime Minister Howard is wrong.

The approach to collective responsibility that I defended in my book, *Taking Responsibility for the Past*,[9] is premised on the existence and moral desirability of intergenerational relationships and practices which enable members of certain kinds of collectives, like nation-states, to make commitments which future members are obliged to fulfill. A treaty is such a commitment, and the assumption that nations should keep their promises depends on the idea that their members can legitimately impose obligations on their successors as well as themselves. That members of nations, or of other kinds of organized collectivities, should be able to make transgenerational commitments, formal or informal (and indeed may be morally obliged to make them in certain circumstances) has to do with the value to members of establishing and maintaining intergenerational relations of respect among communities. Those who engage in the practice of making such commitments are obligated to keep the commitments of their predecessors (all things being equal) and, as a corollary of this practice, to make reparation for a failure of themselves or their predecessors to keep past commitments.

No treaties were made with Aboriginal communities in Australia, but nevertheless a similar argument explains why non-Aboriginal citizens of Australia have historical responsibilities. Justice in an intergenerational society requires that communities establish just relations with each other—relations which are assumed to be ongoing and which thus impose obligations on future as well as present generations. The reconciliation process between Aboriginal and non-Aboriginal Australians is assumed to be a watershed in the history of interactions between the two peoples: a commitment to maintaining just relations into the future. Reconciliation requires a commitment between members of communities with moral implications for present and future generations. Presently existing non-Aboriginal Australians are committing their successors to maintaining relations of respect toward Aboriginal communities. To justify making a commitment which morally binds future citizens, they are obliged to acknowledge and make recompense for those past actions and attitudes that were incompatible with relations of respect.

This account of why present citizens have a collective responsibility for making recompense for the wrongs of the past is not necessarily the only account of why this responsibility exists, but it does have some advantages. First of all, it does not rely on the feelings of citizens or their sense of self. And it does not depend on ancestry. People acquire historical obligations by being members of an intergenerational society that committed wrongs against another such society. On the other hand, it does not rest content with the insistence that citizens have these obligations simply because they are citizens. It says something about the moral mechanisms behind treaty keeping and related 'obligations of state' and thus provides an explanation of why responsible citizens should accept the sacrifices that these duties entail.

However, the account presents a number of challenges to the standard conception of reparative justice. First of all, it implies that injustice encompasses more than dispossession and related harms. Inherent in unjust acts committed against Aborigines was a lack of respect for them as individuals and as members of communities. The doctrine of *terra nullius* was in itself an injustice, quite apart from the acts of dispossession which it sanctioned. But this means that any plausible idea of the requirements of reparation must include acts that acknowledge such failures of respect and demonstrate the intention to be respectful in the future. This is why so many Aborigines regard an official apology as being essential to reconciliation. Second, this account of collective responsibility makes acts of reparation forward, as well as backward, looking, insofar as they are motivated by an intention to establish or repair respectful relations. This orientation, as I will suggest in the next section, plays a major role in determining the form that reparations should take for dispossession and other injuries.

3.3. LAND CLAIMS AND REQUIREMENTS OF REPARATION

According to the standard account, reparation requires return of what was wrongly taken or appropriate compensation in cases where a return is no longer feasible. The decisions of the Australian High Court seem to offer a legal means of achieving reparative justice for Aborigines—at least in some cases. But in practice, the courts have not served Aboriginal communities all that well. After a ten-year battle, the Yorta Yorta people who claim land around the Murray River in Victoria and New South Wales had their case rejected by the High Court.[10] It failed in part because they could not produce written evidence that they had retained a connection to the land from the time of dispossession to the present. Evidence that came from their oral tradition was not regarded as adequate. The problem is that legal claims to restitution have to be made in Australian courts in accordance with Australian laws and the conception of property and legal procedure embedded in this law. Aborigines with their different ideas about law and land are at a disadvantage.

Aboriginal communities that have been able to negotiate a settlement with pastoralists, miners, local councils, and national park officials have often fared better than those that have relied on legal procedures. Such negotiations not only attempt to reach an agreement concerning land use which is supposed to take into account the interests and points of view of all parties. They have also ranged over present issues of concern to Aborigines—for example, access to employment and education. However, from the perspective of traditional views of reparative justice, such settlements seem perverse. The Native Title Act forces Aborigines to make compromises, but from a moral point of view it seems natural to wonder why Aborigines should be expected to give up anything that is rightly theirs. Why should the interests of present land users matter when they are benefiting from stolen property? And is it not simply a confusion to bring issues of equity in education and employment into a discussion of reparations? I will argue that problems associated with reparative justice, especially in cases of historical injustice, not only make negotiated settlements politically advisable, but that such settlements are the only just way of dealing with historical injustice, given present circumstances and the moral importance of establishing and maintaining respectful relations.

Negotiations serve a number of important purposes in achieving reparative justice. One of them is to make each party aware of the perspective of the other. Reparative justice requires an understanding of what kind of injustice was done to the victims—what was taken from them. Aborigines and non-Aborigines have very different ideas about land, history, and relationships. For example, Western ideas about property stress its economic value, and this is reflected in assumptions about what counts as suitable compensation for dispossession. Aborigines' connection to the land is also spiritual and nothing can compensate them for loss of significant ceremonial sites. Before justice can be done such differences must be understood.

However, negotiations play a more central role in the determination of what is just. Supporters of Aboriginal land rights seem to face the dilemma discussed by Jeremy Waldron in his critique of 'indigeneity'.[11] Either they have to insist that Aborigines retain their entitlement to the land even in the face of the needs of the non-Aboriginal population and all the changes that have occurred since dispossession; or it seems that they have to allow that these changes make a crucial difference. The first alternative is unattractive, first of all, because it seems to depend on the problematic idea that Aboriginal communities possess an unchallengeable 'original title' to their land based on first or prior occupancy; and second, because it seems difficult to defend the idea that their entitlement, however established, is immune to reassessment in the light of the needs and situation of others.[12] 'We were here first', as Waldron says in another place, has always been an unpleasant way of denying present aspirations or resisting current claims of need.[13] But if we choose the second alternative and allow that present possessors also have a claim, we are faced with the problem of determining how their claims and Aboriginal claims should be adjudicated. Given the difficulty of defending the existence of historical titles or of determining to what extent they can persist through time and change, it might be thought that equity should be the only consideration: that land rights for Aborigines should depend on their current needs, relative to the needs of non-Aborigines.[14] However, this suggestion is also unattractive. It is difficult to deny that Aborigines are owed something for the injustices that they have suffered in the past—and not just because they are relatively disadvantaged members of the Australian population. Respect for a community seems to require not only an acknowledgment of past injustices but attention to claims that arise from these injustices.

Why these claims should be taken seriously can be better understood in the light of a particular example. The Wik people consist of a number of communities inhabiting the western part of Cape York Peninsula.[15] In the early days of colonization, Wik communities suffered the fate of many Aboriginal groups. Their lands were overrun by pastoralists and miners and their efforts to fight this encroachment were met by violence. Some were transported to other localities; others were press-ganged into the pastoral or pearl fishing industries; others found refuge on mission stations. Despite determined attempts of the Queensland state government to destroy their culture, many of these groups managed to maintain contact with their land and their cultural practices. When in the 1970s the government granted bauxite mining leases over a large area of Wik territory without consulting the Wik, the communities fought back through a national campaign and court actions. Throughout this period, the Queensland authorities did whatever they could to frustrate Wik efforts to gain some control over the land and to reestablish their cultural life. Mining leases continued to be granted without reference to Wik needs or desires; Wik attempts to settle on what they thought of as their land were vigorously resisted. At one point, land was declared a national park in order to keep the Wik from using it.

This history can be used to make a number of points. First of all, the Wik people did not suffer a single historical injustice. They were subjected to a history of injustices which began in the early days of colonization and persisted up to recent times. These injustices were closely related in that they resulted from the pursuit by the Queensland government of a policy of control and assimilation or from its determination to prevent the Wik from gaining any control over the land and its resources. It thus seems reasonable to insist that any attempt to come to terms with the past in a way that demonstrates respect for the Wik as a people would have to address this history—and not merely isolated acts of injustice like original dispossession.

Second, the Wik were not the passive victims of injustice, but resisted by finding ways of maintaining their culture and connection to the land and protesting against government actions. From their point of view, this struggle is the main theme of their recent history. It is this history, and the way it is understood by the victims, which makes it right to insist that appropriate reparation for the injustices—reparation which demonstrates respect for the Wik and their point of view—is to return to their control some of the land that they once possessed.[16] This way of understanding the requirements of reparative justice appeals to a history of injustices and the way in which a community, in reacting to them, has formed its identity and understands its relation to the past. It does not depend on an appeal to original rights of ownership. It does not imply that every historical case of dispossession requires restoration or that the victims must receive everything that was taken from them or enjoy all of the rights that they formerly possessed. And it allows present interests and needs to be taken into account.

This understanding of reparative justice also requires that the interests of non-Aboriginal land users be taken into account. The issue of how conflicting interests are to be adjudicated might be decided by an independent arbiter, like a court, but proper appreciation of points of view and respectful relations between relevant communities are more likely to be achieved if the decision can be the result of a negotiation in which the parties are motivated by the objective of coming to terms with injustices of past in a way that establishes the basis for respectful relations in the present and future. Reparative justice would be achieved when the harm done by injustice to relations of respect between individuals or communities is repaired or compensated for by the perpetrators (or their successors) in a way such that each party can, from its point of view, regard the settlement as a just basis for future coexistence and cooperation.[17] This ideal may never be fully realized in practice, but it can nevertheless serve as a guiding idea. Since the ideal of justice is forward as well as backward looking, it does not preclude taking into account interests that figure in demands for equity—like opportunities for employment or education. Aboriginal communities which incorporate these demands into their negotiations about native title can reasonably expect that they will be given a priority that they might not otherwise receive if they were merely a disadvantaged group of people. What Prime Minister Howard calls 'practical reconciliation' seems to mean only that Aborigines count as members of the Australian population whose needs should be considered when budgetary restrictions allow.[18]

3.4. REPARATION AND HARM TO INDIVIDUALS

The wrongs that I have so far discussed are injustices to communities as intergenerational groups which possess transgenerational entitlements and obligations. Because such communities and their entitlements persist through many generations, there is no conceptual difficulty in understanding how a community can be entitled to reparation for harms done to it in an earlier part of its history. But not all harms done to Aborigines were harms to communities and not all Aborigines who suffer disadvantage because of injustices of the past are members of Aboriginal communities. In fact, some of the policies that we now regard as wrong were designed to break up communities or separate individuals from them. Individuals who, as a result of these policies, have no contact, or only a tenuous relation, with the communities of their ancestors, or whose communities no longer exist, are not likely to benefit from reparative acts directed to communities. This seems unfair. These nonmembers are also victims of a history of injustice—in many cases, a history that is responsible for their inability to benefit. Are they also owed reparation?

Most people would agree that individuals who suffer hardship or loss of opportunity due to an injustice are owed compensation—even if the injustice was actually committed against their forebears.[19] But the case for compensation is weakened if doubts arise about whether a victim's situation can be blamed on the injustice. One of the difficulties faced by Aboriginal individuals who claim to be victims of past government policies is establishing that these policies harmed *them*. This problem is particularly acute in the case of the 'stolen children'.

The policy of taking half-caste children away from their families was pursued by most Australian state governments over many decades up into the 1960s. In early years legislation allowed children to be removed without consent of their parents. They were simply abducted from Aboriginal camps or homes and transported to a distant location, and attempts of family members to visit or communicate with them were systematically thwarted. Though removal of children depended in later years on the agreement of the parents, consent was often obtained by coercion, and parents were given misleading information about where their children were being taken and how long they would be away. Many of the removed children never saw their families again, some not for twenty or more years and had by this time lost the ability or inclination to participate in the life of their kin or community. The policy of removal was visited on Aboriginal families generation after generation, and many of those who were taken away as children had their own children removed. The purpose of the policy was mainly to assimilate to mainstream society those children who were deemed to be worthy of rescue, but in its later days it was also regarded as a welfare measure—the assumption being that the children would have better lives if they were separated from their families and Aboriginal communities.[20]

There are many reasons for regarding the policy as wrong. It was a terrible injustice to parents who were coerced or tricked into giving up their children; it demoralized families and communities; it created fear and distrust. But the family members who were directly affected are mostly dead, and the question before the courts and society is whether those who were removed can now claim compensation for the harms that they were caused. Many of those who gave evidence to the National Inquiry into the Separation of Aboriginal and Torres Strait Islander Children From Their Families were clearly victims of harm. They were put into institutions where they were abused, mistreated, undernourished, and denigrated. They were required to accept the values of whites in a society that refused to regard them as equals. They were often given only a minimal education and sent out to work for no pay.

Children sent to foster families were also frequently abused and treated like slaves.

However, not all the removed children did suffer these harms. Some outcomes fulfilled the hopes of the more humanitarian policymakers. Some children were taken away from their mothers at birth before they had a chance to form a bond with their Aboriginal family. Some were put into loving foster homes where they received opportunities that they would not have had if they had not been removed. Those who criticized the report of the Inquiry could point to individuals who regarded themselves as beneficiaries of the policy. But even in those cases where children did suffer some harm, it might be argued that they were made better off than they would have been if they had remained with families whose poverty made them unable to provide their children with a decent life. This suggests that a distinction could be made between the policy itself and the way it was carried out. Governments should have taken more care to ensure that the removed children were well cared for and properly educated; more effort should have been made to integrate them into mainstream society; and if these things had been done fewer would have been able to complain of maltreatment or exploitation. In fact, some Australians continue to insist that the policy, though badly implemented, had a humanitarian justification. How, then, can the policy be blamed for harming the children?

The harm is not explained by the fact that the children were separated from their biological kin. Some adopted children do suffer from not knowing their biological parents, but if this is a harm, then it seems to be one that can be outweighed by other considerations. The practice of adoption is not generally wrong. Nor can the wrong be accounted for by stressing the value to individuals of having a cultural reference point.[21] Many individuals who were removed as children complain about cultural alienation, but their problems could be blamed on the way that the policy was implemented. Presumably, if it had succeeded in the way that its humanitarian defenders intended, it would have provided the children with a secure identity in mainstream society. Nevertheless, it seems hard to deny that a wrong has been done that requires the children to be compensated even in those cases where they suffered no trauma, abuse or maltreatment and have been able to live satisfactory lives in mainstream society.

The assumption that needs to be questioned is that compensation is owed only to those who, as individuals, have suffered physical or psychological damage from the doing of a wrong. But individuals can also have entitlements that exist because of their relationship to others. Obvious examples are the right of bequest and the corollary right to receive an inheritance. A society that regards it as ethically important that individuals have the right to pass on things that they value to their descendants owes compensation for wrongfully interfering with this right, and if the people directly wronged no longer exist, then compensation is owed to their intended heirs. Since it is reasonable to assume that parents and other community members intended to pass on their Aboriginal heritage to their descendants, and that government policies violated their right to do so, and as a result, the right of the children to receive their inheritance, then it follows that the children are entitled to compensation for this wrong.

The rights of bequest and inheritance, and the requirement of compensation that goes with it, has sometimes been challenged by those who regard inheritance as contrary to requirements of distributive justice or to the idea that people should be rewarded according to desert. But the objections that can be rightly made to a state of affairs in which a few families, through laws of inheritance, have been able to monopolize the wealth of a society, should not prevent us from acknowledging the right of parents to pass on to their descendants some things that are of family significance or that people especially want their children to have. The relations between parents and children: the love and affection that often exists between them and the fact that parents are likely to regard themselves as having special responsibilities to their children, are good reasons for societies to allow and protect a right of gift or bequest, and thus the children's right to inherit at least some things that their parents want to give them. And if the parents were prevented by an injustice from passing on such an inheritance to their children, then the children as heirs are owed reparation.[22] Not to get what they are owed is not only a wrong to their parents, but is also a violation of their entitlement as heirs.

Among the things that parents generally want to pass on to their children are the opportunities to appreciate certain values, to engage in particular activities or to enjoy particular goods. For example, they may want their children to be exposed to particular religious values, to learn about cultural norms, to appreciate the ideals that they regard as important, and more generally, to be able to live in their cultural community and participate in its activities. They may even think that they have a duty to provide their children with these things—not just because they think that it is important that a child have a cultural identity (such an abstract reason may never cross their minds), but because they value the values and traditions of their culture and because they want to pass on the practices and traditions that make meaningful communication between generations possible. In general, it seems reasonable that parents should be able to provide such an inheritance to their children (given that they value it) and that children have a right to receive it. An inheritance does not have to be accepted. The children may decide to reject their heritage, turn their back on their religion, or leave their cultural community. But nevertheless, if an injustice prevents them from obtaining what we can presume that their parents wanted them to have, then they have a right to compensation.

It might be argued that making governments responsible for compensating people for a loss of a cultural inheritance overlooks the problem of contingency discussed by Waldron.[23] If the abductions had not occurred, some of the parents might have chosen to leave their culture; they might have decided that their children should be raised in mainstream society. In the face of such a possibility, how can we assume that a wrong was done to either them or their children by denying the children an Aboriginal inheritance? One way of answering this question is to argue that it is not likely that Aborigines would voluntarily give up their culture, and that we can reasonably assume that they would have wanted to provide their children with an Aboriginal heritage. But another way of answering is to argue that such contingencies are irrelevant. If we regard it as important that parents ought to be able to provide an inheritance for their children—particularly a cultural inheritance—and that the children have a right to receive it, then we ought to defend these rights by ensuring that compensation is given for violations even in cases where doubt about parental intentions is possible.

The difficulty remains of determining what form of compensation is owed to the Aboriginal children who were subjected to the injustice of removal. In some cases, the nature of the loss, and what should be done in compensation, is relatively clear. Because they were removed from their community and have no place in it, the children (now grown) cannot be regarded as members and thus cannot benefit from land claims or other forms of reparation which the community might receive. The children are being denied economic benefits that they would have received if they had not been taken away. The Report of the Inquiry rightly recommends that these individuals receive compensation for this loss. However, there is no obvious form of rectification for loss of a cultural heritage. Children who have grown up alienated from the culture of their parents are not likely to be able to return to it—even if they want to. Nevertheless, there are things that can be done that would count as recompense. One of them is to issue an official apology—an action that many of the victims regard as appropriate. The Report of the Inquiry also recommends that those who wish should get assistance in locating their kin and learning about the culture they have lost.[24] Those who have been injured or traumatized by their treatment as children or the discrimination that they have faced in mainstream society are, of course, entitled to other forms of compensation.

I have argued that Aboriginal individuals can be justified in making reparative claims as heirs to a culture or the benefits of a community. It is necessary to say something about the limits of this entitlement. There is no obvious reason why the children of children who were removed cannot also regard themselves as entitled to recompense. The loss of a familial or communal heritage might be regarded as similar in important respects to the loss of a family heirloom. But a family's right to a lost heirloom does not last indefinitely, and neither does the entitlement to be compensated for a lost heritage, as the following example indicates.

The Aborigines of Tasmania were, apparently, of a race and culture distinct from the Aborigines of mainland Australia. Disease, guerrilla warfare, starvation, and imprisonment resulted in the death of all full-blooded Aborigines by the end of the nineteenth century and the destruction of their culture.[25] There remain in Tasmania a number of people of Aboriginal ancestry, but they are not members of a traditional Aboriginal community. The cultural link with the past has been severed, and no one knows very much about the values and traditions of Tasmanian culture. I do not think that it is possible for existing Aborigines in Tasmania to regard themselves as being unjustly deprived of their rights as heirs to a cultural heritage. One of the reasons is the passage of time and the changes it brings. After so many generations it seems that Tasmanian Aborigines have to be regarded as belonging to mainstream society. They cannot claim a right to a heritage from which their families have for so long been separated. But the second, and probably more decisive reason, is that it is not possible to claim rights in respect to a culture that no longer exists or which has radically changed, or a culture that no one living is able or willing to value. To say that people of Aboriginal ancestry in Tasmania are not the heirs to an Aboriginal culture is not to deny that they are entitled to think of themselves as Aborigines or to regard themselves as having a link to their Aboriginal ancestors. They are entitled to demand that these ancestors be properly regarded and represented in histories of Australia and that it be remembered that injustices were committed against them. This duty is not only owed to them. It is owed by any society that has a proper respect for history and the dead.

NOTES

1. Aristotle (1955: 148).
2. For an influential account of the dispossession of Aborigines, see Reynolds (2003).
3. The 1992 Judgment was the result of a case brought by Eddie Mabo, a Torres Strait Islander, who laid claim to the land of his forebears. The second judgment resulted from a case brought by the Wik people of Cape York Peninsula. For more about the Wik, see below. In the view of Aboriginal activists who favor

a treaty between the Australian Commonwealth and Aboriginal communities, these judgments do not adequately recognize Aboriginal sovereignty.

4. *Royal Commission into Aboriginal Deaths in Custody* (1991).
5. Human Rights and Equal Opportunities Commission (1997).
6. e.g. Windschuttle (2003) argues that there were no significant injustices done to Aborigines. This and other attempts to downplay the significance of historical injustices are discussed in Macintyre and Clark (2003).
7. e.g. Feinberg (1968: 687) lists 'opportunity for control' as one of the necessary conditions for liability for an action or practice of a group.
8. MacIntyre (1981: 220). For an attempt to argue that national identity is the basis for taking responsibility for historical injustices, see Poole (1999: ch. 4).
9. Thompson (2002: chs. 1, 2) argue in more detail for the view outlined in this paragraph.
10. For details, see Strelein (2003).
11. See Waldron's paper in this volume.
12. Locke (1978: V) believed that individuals or groups gained such a title by mixing their labor with something that no one else had claimed. The historical view of how ownership is acquired and justified has some modern supporters, notably Nozick (1974), though Nozick does not accept Locke's account of labor mixing.
13. Waldron (1992: 28).
14. See Lyons (1977: 374).
15. The information in this paragraph is taken from Martin (1997: 8–10).
16. The same point can be made about the Lakota, whose struggle for their land and for their cultural resources is described in Tsosie's chapter in this volume.
17. Tsosie also emphasizes that reparative justice is forward as well as backward looking, that it involves a process of healing and repairing relationships.
18. Many people, including Aboriginal leaders, have doubts about the intention and performance of the Liberal government in respect to meeting the needs of Aborigines. See, e.g. O'Donoghue (2003).
19. Problems arise when the individuals in question would not have existed if the injustice had not been done. For a discussion, see Sher (1981). The position that I advocate below is not affected by this difficulty.
20. The policy of removing children from their families for the purposes of assimilation was not unique to Australian governments. Other nations have used similar strategies for assimilating minority cultures or dealing with social problems. Tsosie describes the policy pursued by the US government of seizing Native American children and removing them to distant boarding schools where they were supposed to unlearn their cultural ways and adopt the values of mainstream society. The Canadians adopted a similar policy of assimilation, and the Swiss attempted to deal with their Romany population by the same method. (Canadian and Swiss governments have apologized for these policies.)

21. Kymlicka (1989: 165ff.) argues that having a secure cultural framework counts as a basic good. However, it does not matter, according to his argument, how someone gets that good.
22. I defend these views about inheritance at greater length in Thompson (2001).
23. Waldron (1992: 8–9).
24. HREOC, 284ff.
25. The last full-blooded Tasmanian Aborigine, Truganini, died in 1876.

Part II

Reparations for Slavery and Jim Crow

*

4

Transgenerational Justice—Compensatory Versus Interpretative Approaches*

Glenn C. Loury

4.1. INTRODUCTION

Should African Americans, in keeping with an idea of transgenerational justice, receive 'reparations' for the historical crimes of slavery and Jim Crow segregation? That question is being asked with growing intensity across America. *If one understands by reparations the receipt of financial transfers as compensation for historical crimes, my answer to this question is a resounding, 'No'. On the other hand, if one intends by such advocacy to urge on the American people a sober reflection on and reinterpretation of those aspects of our history which gave rise to the current extent of unequal social and economic standing between racially defined subgroups of American society, my answer is a tentative, hopeful, 'Yes'.*

This essay draws on economics, sociology, politics, and philosophy, in an attempt to support this position. Despite my skepticism about the wisdom and moral necessity of race-based compensatory financial transfers, I leave room for the possibility that some claims arising from the many racial injustices perpetrated against them and their ancestors over the course of US history can be sustained on behalf of African Americans. But, before getting to my argument proper, I wish to put forward some common sense reasons to think that we black Americans have little to gain and much to lose from making 'Reparations Now' the next civil rights rallying cry:

[*Conceptualizing Harm*] Consider the complex character of the harm. To repair the consequences of historical crimes we need to begin with an understanding of what has been lost. Depriving the ancestors of current-day African Americans of the fruits of their labours was not, I argue, the gravest injury done them. Rather, it was the

* I wish to thank the participants at the conference where this paper was originally presented for their helpful comments.

relegation of the black slaves and their progeny to a status of social pariahs, which constituted the severest harm. This harm, I claim, will not be reversed, and may indeed be reinforced, by the successful advocacy for slavery reparations.

[*Political Challenges*] Consider the demographics. When it comes to race in America, 'them times, they are a-changin'. We are no longer, and will never again be, a nation of blacks and whites. Some 30 million immigrants, mostly of non-European origins, have arrived on our shores since the height of the civil rights movement. These new Americans and their children have a claim to the national narrative no less surely than do blacks. It is their country, too. Of course, new citizens of this republic are obligated like the rest of us to shoulder their share of national responsibilities, including the discharge of any debt the country has incurred as a result of historical wrongs. But, a racial reform movement built around the theme of paying reparations to blacks is unlikely to engage these newcomers, making the construction of political coalitions in support of progressive public policies that are essential for black flourishing less likely to occur.

[*Epistemological Problems*] Consider that there is no intellectually defensible way to put a price tag on slavery. Any sum mentioned is arbitrary. This is because the tort-law model underlying reparations advocacy—he who harms another must make the injured party whole—is hopelessly muddled when applied here. How would one even begin to demonstrate in quantitative terms the nature and extent of injury? Given the wide economic disparities to be observed among white Americans of various ethnic groups, who can know how blacks would have fared but for the wrongs of the past? Who can say what the out-of-wedlock birth rate for blacks would be, absent chattel slavery? How does one calculate the cost of inner-city ghettos, of poor education, of the stigma of perceived racial inferiority? The damage done by slavery and its aftermath is at once too subtle and too profound to be evaluated in monetary terms.

[*Issues of Interpretation*] Consider the symbolic tone of reparations advocacy. At the deepest level, it seems not even to be the money that animates most advocates. [See Robinson (2000) for an example of this rhetorical posture.] The deeper demand seems to be that America, by making amends, should fully acknowledge its wrongful past. While, as will become clear, I agree with this sentiment, I also think that it is rather late in the day for African Americans to be satisfied with a politics of symbolism. Substantive political gains for today's descendants of slaves require forging coalitions with those non-blacks who can see the need to extend greater opportunities to every American now being left behind. This means appealing to people on the basis of universal ideals, and proposing programs the benefits from which are available in principle to all who need them. I can see no way to fight black poverty, black imprisonment, inadequate black health care or deficient black education without, at one and the same time, fighting the poverty, imprisonment, poor health care and failed education that afflicts non-black Americans as well. Nor can I see any real justification for doing so.

[*Civic Construction Goals*] Reparations advocacy invites the majority of Americans to see the problem as one where 'we' do something for 'them'. What is needed, however, is to construct a we—meaning all Americans—capable of righting whatever social injustices plague our society—for 'our own sake' in this country, so that our moral pronouncements on the world stage will not be made into a hollow mockery. No doubt, the construction of this will be more readily achieved to the extent that citizens are made aware of the nature and extent of historical misdeeds undertaken by their government, or with its acquiescence. So, the concern expressed here about civic construction goals ought not be understood as precluding a vigorous, sometimes unsettling discourse about the past. Nevertheless, slavery's consequences will be minimized only when we have established a regime of social provision that affords every American the chance to live a full and satisfying life. For blacks to gain reparations without attaining this goal would be to win a false victory. For then, when the horrible consequences of our troubled racial past persist in the blighted lives of millions of poor black people, sceptical onlookers will be able to say, 'We'd love to help, but you Negroes have already been paid'.

This essay is organized as follows: Drawing on my book *The Anatomy of Racial Inequality* (Loury 2002), I offer in the next section a conceptual model of the propagation through history of racial injury. This model guides my thought about the problem of reparations and supports the conclusions here advanced. The core idea is that *racial stigma*, not *racial discrimination*, constitutes the deepest and most enduring historical harm done to blacks in the United States. Following this, I will consider the limitations of one frequently encountered argument against slavery reparations, which I will refer to as *color-blind liberalism*. I then take up some of the *epistemic difficulty* for inferring causal connections over long stretches of history, and the resulting implications of this difficulty for formulating a coherent conception of historical claims. Finally, I offer a statement of my proposed alternative approach, advocating an interpretative, as distinct from a compensatory, approach to meeting the imperative of historical justice in the case of black Americans.

4.2. UNDERSTANDING THE HARM: RACIAL STIGMA, NOT RACIAL DISCRIMINATION

I now briefly sketch the conceptual framework that guides my thinking about the problem of racial inequality in the United States. I have two broad aims: to outline a theory of 'race' applicable to the social and historical circumstances of the United States; and, to sketch a speculative account of why racial inequality in the United States is so persistent. Fundamental to my approach is the distinction between *racial discrimination* and *racial stigma*. Racial discrimination has to do with how blacks are treated, while racial stigma is concerned with how black people are perceived. My fundamental premise is that *reward bias* is now a less significant barrier than is *development bias* to the full participation of African Americans in US society. *Reward bias* refers to the unfair treatment of persons based on race in formal economic and bureaucratic transactions, limiting the rewards they can receive for the skills and talents they present to the market. *Development bias* refers to blocked access for persons in a subordinate racial group to resources that are essential for the development of human skills and the refinement of talents, due to the fact that resources of this kind often become available to persons as a by-product of informal, nonmarket-mediated but race-influenced social relations.

I do not claim these two kinds of bias to be mutually exclusive: the acquisition of skills can be blocked by market discrimination; and, the maintenance of a discriminatory order against the pressures of market competition may rely on various instruments of informal social control. Still, I think this distinction is useful for whereas the reward bias emerging from market discrimination presents a straightforward moral problem and calls forth the obvious and nearly universally embraced remedy of antidiscrimination law, development bias is a subtler, more insidious moral problem—one, I will argue, that may be difficult to remedy in any manner likely to garner a majority's support. This difficulty has both a cognitive and an ethical dimension. From a cognitive point of view, many observers, when seeking an explanation for a group's poor social performance, may not distinguish between limited opportunities for development and limited innate capacities to develop. From an ethical point of view, citizens who find the overt discrimination by race associated with reward bias to be noxious may be less offended by the covert social discrimination that underlies development bias.

All of this is relevant to a discussion of reparations because—given the facts of human developmental dynamics, the irreversibility of harms associated with blocked developmental opportunities, and the inability of financial transfers to offset those harms—the compensatory goal for reparations may lie beyond our grasp if I am right to think that development bias is the main culprit underlying contemporary racial inequality.

Fundamental to this argument is my conviction that the subordinate position of African Americans in today's social economy derives from the stigmatized status of blacks in the society, and not the other way around. Racial stigma (about which more momentarily) inhibits African Americans from gaining access to those networks of social affiliation where developmental resources are most readily appropriated.

The main difficulty today is not a race-influenced marketplace refusing to reward black talent, but race-influenced patterns of social intercourse refusing many black people a chance to reach their full human potential, and a race-influenced psychology of valuation that denies to African Americans the tacit presumption of equal human worth. My key point is that blacks' stigmatized status in the social imagination is reinforced, reproduced and justified by their subordinate position in the economic order, creating a vicious circle which, though it originates in the distant past, has now taken on a life of its own. Blacks' 'underperformance' is rooted in their social isolation and tacit devaluation, while this isolation and devaluation is legitimated and normalized by widely held perceptions about black underperformance. Unfortunately, reparations-centered advocacy (and, for that matter, other race-conditioned interventions such as affirmative action policies) will probably be insufficient to counteract this self-reinforcing dynamic.

My view on the ontological status of race undergirds and reinforces this way of thinking. As one who takes race to be a social construction, I place great weight on the subjective and intersubjective aspects of racial awareness. I take mainly a cognitive rather than a normative stance toward race-conscious behavior, looking to how human agents process social experience and how they organize their perceptions, examining the categories into which they sort those others whom they encounter in society. What we see in the phenomenon of race is that a field of human subjects characterized by morphological variability (differences in skin tone, hair texture, facial bone structure, and the like) comes through concrete historical experience to be partitioned into subgroups defined by some cluster of these physical markers. Information-hungry agents then hang expectations around these markers, beliefs that can, by processes I have discussed elsewhere in some detail (see Loury 2002: ch. 2), become self-confirming. Meaning-hungry agents invest these markers with social, psychological, and even spiritual significance. Markers become the basis of social and personal identities. Narrative accounts of descent are constructed around them. Collectivities of mutually susceptible agents—sharing feelings of pride, honor, shame, loyalty, and hope—come into existence based to some extent on their holding these race-markers in common. This vesting of reasonable expectation and ineffable meaning in objectively arbitrary markings of the human body comes, through social and political struggles mediated by economic and institutional structures, to be reproduced over the generations. It takes on a social life of its own, seems natural not merely conventional, and ends up having profound consequences for social relations obtaining among individuals within the 'raced' society.

Now, taking race to be a conventional, not a natural category, suggests that the *symbolic* connotations of racial categorization in American life may be helpful to understand the extent and durability of the subordinate position of black people. The conceptual frame I envision for this essay builds on the observation that, due to the history and culture of this society, powerful negative connotations have come to be associated with particular bodily marks carried by some citizens. I claim that this is decidedly the case with respect to the marks that connote 'blackness' in US society. [This claim is defended at length in Loury (2002: ch. 3.] To understand racial inequality in this society, I propose that scholars should place great emphasis on how observers perceive and interpret social data bearing on the status of disadvantaged racial groups—an approach that is to be distinguished from the traditional focus on some racial dislike or antipathy that members of the dominant group are said to harbor against members of the subordinate racial group.

I begin with the broad observation that we humans have the innate tendency to impute an ineffable significance to the artifacts that furnish our lives. That is, we look for and derive *meaning* from the material substratum in which we are embedded. Accordingly, human behavior is determined not only by material structures 'out there' in the world, but also by what those structures are understood to signify 'in here', inside our minds. The bodily markings associated with racial categories are among those material structures in the American social environment to which meanings about the identity, capability, and worthiness of their bearers have been imputed.

Once established, these meanings can come to be taken for granted, enduring unchallenged for generations. In a hierarchical society, a correspondence may develop between a person's social position and the physical marks taken in that society to signify race. Bodily signs that trigger in an observer's mind the sense that their bearer is ordained to be 'a hewer of wood and drawer of water', or is a member of a 'master race destined to rule the world', or is a 'social pariah best avoided at all costs' illustrate the possibilities. When the meanings connoted by race-symbols undermine an observing agent's ability to see their bearer as a person possessing a common humanity with the observer—as 'someone not unlike the rest of us'—then I say this person is 'racially stigmatized', and the group to which he belongs suffers a 'spoiled collective identity'.

Historical context is everything here, and for the matter at hand the key contextual factor is the historical institution of chattel slavery. In his 1982 *Slavery and Social Death*, historical sociologist Orlando Patterson shows that to understand slavery one must grasp the importance of *honor*. Slavery, he argues, is a great deal more than an institution allowing property-in-people. And further, 'the permanent, violent domination of natally alienated and generally dishonored persons'. By surveying this institution across five continents over two millennia, he shows that the hierarchy of social standing—masters over slaves, reinforced by ritual and culture—is what distinguishes slavery from any other system of forced labor. In the American context, obviously, the rituals and customs supporting this hierarchical order—the system of taken-for-granted meanings that made possible an adherence to high Enlightenment ideals in the midst of widespread human bondage—came to be closely intertwined in both the popular and the elite culture with ideas about race. As such, dishonor, shown so brilliantly by Patterson to be a general and defining feature of slavery, became, in the (American) case at hand, inseparable from the social meaning of race.

So my syllogism is this: in general, slaves are profoundly dishonored persons. In the American context, slavery was a thoroughly racial institution. *Ergo*, the social meaning of race emergent in American political culture at mid-nineteenth century was closely connected with the slaves' dishonorable status. Of course, that was a long time ago and it is true that many non-black Americans have ancestors who were profoundly dishonored in one way or another. Nevertheless, honest assessment of the contemporary American political landscape—debates over welfare, crime, schools, jobs, taxes, housing, test scores, diversity, urban policy, and much more—reveals the lingering effects of this historically engendered racial dishonor. By 'racial dishonor' I mean something specific: an entrenched if inchoate presumption of inferiority, of moral inadequacy, of unfitness for intimacy, of intellectual incapacity, harbored by observing agents when they regard the race-marked subjects. I assert that this specter of 'social otherness', of racial dishonor that emerged with slavery and that has been shaped over the post-emancipation decades by political, economic, and cultural forces specific to American society, remains yet to be fully eradicated. So my use of the term racial stigma alludes to this lingering residue in postslavery American political culture of the dishonor engendered by racial slavery.

It is crucial to understand that this is not mainly an issue of the personal attitudes of individual Americans. To reject my argument here with the claim that 'stigma cannot be so important because attitude surveys show a continued decline in expressed racism among Americans over the decades' is to thoroughly misunderstand me. I am discussing social meanings, not attitudes—specifically the meanings conveyed by race-related public actions and events. I am talking about the 'etiquette of public discourse' and the 'boundaries of legitimacy' that constrain politicians when they formulate and justify the policies they advocate. I have in mind the unexamined beliefs that influence how citizens understand and interpret the images they glean from the larger social world. I claim that the meaning of a policy—job preferences, say—can be quite sensitive to the race of those affected: Veterans are acceptable beneficiaries but blacks violate meritocratic principles. I assert that public responses to a social malady—drug involvement, say—depend on the race of those suffering the problem: The youthful city-dwelling drug sellers elicit a punitive response, while the youthful suburban-dwelling drug buyers call forth a therapeutic one.

Nothing in these examples, I claim, turns on the racial attitudes of the typical American. Everything depends, I am arguing, on racially biased social cognitions that cause some situations to appear anomalous, disquieting, contrary to expectation, worthy of further investigation, inconsistent with the natural order of things—while other situations appear normal, about right, in keeping with what one might expect, consistent with the social world as we know it. These cognitive distinctions tend to be drawn to the detriment of millions of racially stigmatized citizens, I assert, because of the taint of dishonor that is part and parcel of the social meaning of race in the United States. Now, I may be right or I may be wrong about this, but no attitude survey can decide the issue.

To illustrate, consider the debate over race and intelligence that has raged in recent years thanks in large part to the best-selling 1994 book, *The Bell Curve* by Richard Herrnstein and Charles Murray. What, I ask, does the typical well-educated American know about IQ differences among people from Tennessee, Texas, and Massachusetts? I venture that most Americans know next to nothing about such disparities, if any exist. Moreover, and this the key point, it would be illegitimate to make a factual claim about such differences in a public argument over policy—to object to the redistribution of resources between geographic regions within the country, for example, on the grounds that people in the less advantaged areas are already receiving their IQ-adjusted deserts.[1] Or I can put the point somewhat differently. The American population is aging. It is known that intelligence declines as a person ages, after some point in the life cycle. And, laws against age discrimination have invalidated mandatory retirement policies. These things taken together imply that the American workforce could become 'dumber' if we baby boomers insist on staying in the workforce beyond our prime years. Where can one read about the dire consequences of this development for our future economic productivity? Nowhere. Why not? The reason, I suggest, is that those older, soon-to-be-less-intelligent workers are our mothers and fathers (or, in some cases, ourselves!). We are not about to set those people to one side so as to conduct an elaborate discourse about their fitness. And if they are 'dumb', then they are our dumb moms and dads. Like those living in different regions, we who belong to different generations will not permit ourselves to be sundered by any civic boundary. We will sink or swim together.

The point here, once again, is that some social disparities are salient and others not. The salience of social facts is not determined in an entirely rational, deductively confirmed manner. It involves a mode of cognition that depends on some prior patterning or orientation that is not, itself, the product of conscious reflection. I want to deepen the received theory of racial discrimination for this reflection on reparations because, in the case at hand (namely, racial inequality in the United States) the disadvantaged racial group is often objectively less productive (i.e. has fewer useful skills on average than the dominant population according to conventional measures, commits more crimes, or whatever.) And yet, this 'objective' productivity gap is, I maintain, the outgrowth of a social process that is racially biased. This kind of thinking led me, in my doctoral thesis of twenty-five years ago (oh, my!), to coin the phrase 'social capital'. (And what a stroke of good luck that was for me! My writing down those two words led the late sociologist, James Coleman, in his treatise *The Foundations of Social Theory* to credit me with being one of the progenitors of the idea of social capital. And, given the way that the idea has taken off, that has proven to be a real windfall!) I was moved to use the phrase in my dissertation because it seemed to me then that the 'human capital' account of individual variation in labor market earnings gave insufficient attention to the socially conditioned processes through which people come to 'invest' in human capital, ignoring what is often the most interesting and morally problematic aspects of the inequality-generating processes. I argued that we should look not only to the rational calculation of the anticipated return on investment, but also to the factors which promote or impede an individual's access to resources critical to human development. This access, this social capital, depends on a person's inherited social position—who their parents are, who their neighbors are, what kind of community they grew up in, whom they were connected to, where they got their life-altering inspiration—things of this kind. So, if we want to understand inequality in this society, especially racial inequality, we must understand how such differences of social situation are produced and have been sustained over time. But the orthodox approach in economics did not invite us to think about that.

With this framework in mind, I wish to suggest that durable racial inequality can best be understood as the outgrowth of a series of what Myrdal (1944) referred to as 'vicious circles of cumulative causation'. I am particularly interested in how race can bias processes of social cognition. That is, I am trying to move from the fact that people take note of racial classification in the course of their social interactions, to some understanding of how this affects their *perceptions* of the phenomena they observe in the social world around them, and how it shapes their *explanations* of those phenomena. I am asking, when does the race of those subject to some problematic social circumstance affect whether powerful observers perceive there to be a problem, and if so, what follows from this. I am suggesting that the tacit social meanings associated with blackness in the public's imagination biases the social cognitions of observing agents, inducing them to make detrimental causal misattributions. Confronted by the facts of objective racial disparity of performance, observers must adopt some 'model' of what has generated their data. Their processes of social cognition and discernment, their awareness of anomaly, and their capacity for empathy will be influenced by widely held beliefs in this regard.

Because observers will have difficulty identifying with the plight of a group of people whom they (mistakenly) assume simply to be 'reaping what they have sown', there will be little public support for egalitarian policies benefiting a stigmatized racial group. This, in turn, encourages the reproduction through time of racial inequality because, absent some policies of this sort, the low social conditions of many blacks (say) persist, the negative social meanings ascribed to blackness are thereby reinforced, and so the racially biased social-cognitive processes are reproduced, completing the circle.

It may help to make this point with a nonracial example. So, consider gender inequality, disparity in the social outcomes for boys and girls, in two different venues—the schools and the jails. Suppose that, when compared to the girls, the boys are overrepresented among those doing well in math and science in the schools, and also among those doing poorly in society at large by ending up in jail. There is some evidence to support both suppositions, but only the first is widely perceived to be a problem for public policy. Why? My answer is that it offends our basic intuition about the propriety of underlying social processes that boys and girls do differentially well in the technical curriculum. Although we may not be able to put our fingers on exactly why this outcome occurs, we instinctively know that it is not right. In the face of the disparity we are inclined to interrogate our institutions—to search the record of our social practice and examine myriad possibilities in order to see where things might have gone wrong. Our base-line expectation is that equality should prevail here. Our moral sensibility is offended when it does not. And so, an impetus to reform is spurred thereby. We cannot easily envision a wholly legitimate sequence of events that would produce the disparity, so we set ourselves the task of solving a problem.

On the other hand, gender disparity in rates of imprisonment occasions no such disquiet. This is because, tacitly if not explicitly, we are 'gender essentialists.' That is, we think boys and girls are different in some ways relevant to explaining the disparity—different either in their biological natures, or in their deeply ingrained socializations. [Note well, the *essentialism* with which I am concerned need not be based solely or even mainly in biology. It can be grounded in (possibly false) beliefs about profound cultural difference as well.] As gender essentialists, our intuitions are not offended by the fact of vastly higher rates of imprisonment among males than females. We seldom ask any deeper questions about why this disparity has come about. And so, we see no problem.

We may be right or wrong to act as we do in these gender disparity matters, but my point with the example is to show that the bare facts of gender disparity do not, in themselves, suggest any course of action. To act, we must marry the facts to some model of social causation. This model need not be explicit in our minds. It can and usually will lurk beneath the surface of our conscious reflections. Still, it is the facts *plus* the model that lead us to perceive a given circumstance as indicative of some as yet undiagnosed failing in our social interactions, or not. This kind of reflection on the deeper structure of our social-cognitive processes, as they bear on the issues of racial disparity, is what I had hoped to encourage with my discussion of 'biased social cognition'. And, the role of race in such processes is what I am alluding to when I talk about racial stigma.[2]

This argument has important political implications. Imagine that an observer (correctly) takes note of the fact that, on the average and all else equal, commercial loans to blacks pose a greater risk of default, or that black residential neighborhoods are more likely to decline. This may lead that observer to withhold credit from blacks, or to move away from any neighborhood when more than a few blacks move into it. But, what if race conveys this information only because, when a great number of observers expect it to do so and act on that expectation, the result (through some possibly complex chain of social causation) is to bring about the confirmation of their beliefs? Perhaps blacks default more often precisely because they have trouble getting further extensions of credit in the face of a crisis. Or, perhaps nonblack residents panic at the arrival of a few blacks, selling their homes too quickly and below the market value to lower-income (black) buyers, and it is this process that ends up promoting neighborhood decline. If under such circumstances observers were to attribute racially disparate behaviors to deeply ingrained (biological or cultural) limitations of the African Americans—thinking, say, that blacks do not repay their loans or take care of their property because, for whatever reasons, they are just less responsible people on average—then these observers might well be mistaken. Yet, since their surmise about blacks is supported by hard evidence, they might well persist in the error. Such an error, persisted in, would be of great *political* moment, because if one attributes an endogenous difference (a difference produced within a system of interactions) to an exogenous cause (a cause located outside that system), then one is unlikely to see any need for systemic reform. This distinction between *endogenous* and *exogenous* sources of social causation, I am arguing, is the key to understanding the difference in our reformist intuitions about gender inequalities in the schools and in the jails: Because we think the disparity of school outcomes stems from endogenous sources, while the disparity of jail outcomes is tacitly attributed in most of our 'causal models' to exogenous sources, we are differentially moved to do something about the disparities.

So, the effect I am after when I talk about racial stigma and the reason I employ an apparently loaded phrase like biased social cognition is this: It is a politically consequential cognitive distortion to understand the observably disadvantageous position of a racially defined population subgroup as having emerged from qualities taken to be intrinsic to the group when, as a matter of actual social causation, that disadvantage is the product of a system of social interactions. I reiterate that it hardly matters whether those internal qualities *mistakenly* seen as the source of a group's observed laggardly status are biological or deeply cultural. What matters, I argue, is that something has gone wrong if observers fail to see *systemic, endogenous* interactions that lead to bad social outcomes for blacks, and instead attribute those results to *exogenous* factors taken as internal to the group in question. My contention is that in American society, when the group in question is blacks, the risk of this kind of causal misattribution is especially great. Given the facts of racially disparate achievement, the racially disproportionate transgression of legal strictures, and racially unequal development of productive potential, observers will have difficulty identifying with the plight of a group of people whom they (mistakenly) think are simply reaping what they have sown. So, there will be little public support for egalitarian policies benefiting a stigmatized racial group. This, in turn, encourages the reproduction through time of racial inequality because, absent some policies of this sort, the low social conditions of many blacks persist, the negative social meanings ascribed to blackness are thereby reinforced, and so the racially biased social-cognitive processes are reproduced, completing the circle.

This argument also has implications for how we social scientists interpret our data bearing on racial inequality. As I have been suggesting, individuals are embedded in complex networks of affiliations: They are members of nuclear and extended families; they belong to religious and linguistic groupings; they have ethnic and racial identities; they are attached to particular localities. Each individual is socially situated, and one's location within the network of social affiliations substantially affects one's access to various resources. Opportunity travels along the synapses of these social networks. Thus a newborn is severely handicapped if its parents are relatively uninterested in (or incapable of) fostering the youngster's intellectual development in the first years of life. A talented adolescent whose social peer group disdains the activities that must be undertaken for that talent to flourish is at risk of not achieving his or her full potential. An unemployed person without friends or relatives already at work in a certain industry may never hear about the job opportunities available there. An individual's inherited social situation plays a major role in determining his or her ultimate economic success. Some important part of racial inequality, on this view, arises from the way geographic and social segregation along racial lines, fostered by the stigmatized status of blacks—their social otherness—inhibits the development of their full human potential. Because access to developmental resources is mediated though race-segregated social networks, an individual's opportunities to acquire skills depend on present and past skill attainments by others in the same racial group.

4.3. PROBLEMS WITH COLOR-BLIND LIBERALISM

Seven generations after the end of slavery, and a half-century past the dawn of the civil rights movement, social life in the United States is still characterized by a significant degree of racial stratification and inequality. Numerous indices of well-being—wages, unemployment rates, income and wealth levels, ability test scores, incarceration and criminal victimization rates, health and mortality statistics—all reveal substantial disparity among different racial groups. Indeed, over the past quarter century the black–white gap along some of these dimensions has remained unchanged, or has even widened. Although there has been noteworthy progress in reversing historical patterns of racial subordination, there is today no scientific basis on which to rest the prediction that a rough parity of socioeconomic status between blacks and whites in the United States will obtain in the foreseeable future.[3]

'So what?' one might reasonably ask. As long as the individual members of a disadvantaged racial minority group are not being discriminated against, why should citizens in the United States, or in any liberal democracy for that matter, care about racial inequality per se? This is an important question for anyone reflecting on matters of social justice in a pluralistic society. It is especially crucial for adherents of a certain version of political liberalism, who hold that a properly structured analysis of the justness of social arrangements should derive from a consideration of the welfare of individuals, and not from the economic or social position of population subgroups.

While I am arguing against the payment of reparations to black Americans for the harms of the past, I wish to stress that I reject the view that only individuals and never groups can be the subjects of a discourse on social justice. As such, I undertake here to criticize the manner in which this 'color-blind' version of liberal political theory deals with the ethical problems raised by the pronounced and durable social-economic disadvantage of African Americans. My topic, then, is 'racial justice'.

To fix ideas, consider the formidable intellectual edifice that is modern social choice theory. This literature at the junction of economics and philosophy pursues the formal, logical derivation of implications for public decision-making that issue from various postulates chosen to capture our ethical intuitions about social justice.[4] A near universally imposed constraint on collective decision-making in this literature is the so-called *Anonymity Axiom*. This postulate denies the ethical legitimacy of distinguishing for purposes of social choice between two states of affairs, A and B, that differ only in the identities of the people located in various positions of the social order. Thus, imagine that states of affairs A and B entail the same number of persons living in poverty, suffering from inadequate health care, held in prison, and the like, but that a different group of people suffer these conditions in state A than in state B. The Anonymity Axiom then requires that a just public decision-making process be indifferent between these two states. It follows as an immediate corollary of this requirement that the diminution of racial inequality for its own sake would not be a legitimate social goal.

The crux of my argument in this essay, and the outlines of my alternative proposal for how to deal with the racial harms of America's past, can be seen by considering the case I wish to make against this implication of the Anonymity Axiom. I question the adequacy of color-blind liberalism as a normative theory, in view of the historical facts of racial subordination, and the continuing reality of racial inequality. There seem to be questions of social justice arising under these conditions, in societies, such as the United States, that are sharply stratified along racial lines, to which this theory can give no good answers.[5]

The phenomenon of racial stigma poses intractable problems for this brand of individualism. For there is a sphere of intimate social intercourse, governed to some degree by raced perceptions in individuals' minds, that, out of respect for liberty and the dignity of human beings, should not become the object of political or bureaucratic manipulation. Yet I hold that such race-preferential associative behavior perpetuates a regime of development bias against blacks, largely due to a protracted, ignoble history during which reward bias against blacks was the norm. Thinking in terms of racial stigma, I believe, provides insight into race-constrained social interactions and into race-impacted processes of social cognition, helping us to see the forces at work in a raced society like the United States that create causal feedback loops perpetuating racial inequality, and that impede their identification. Moreover, as expanded on below, this way of looking at things has an important implication for political philosophy. In particular, it leads us to reject color blindness (or the related notions of race-neutrality, or racial impartiality) as *the* moral standard in regard to issues of social justice and racial inequality in the United States.

Indeed, I argue that color blindness—a quintessential icon of liberal neutrality—is a superficial moral standard, one that reveals how starkly under-socialized is the entire intellectual project within which it is embedded. It will be important now to stress that I do not think of this weakness as irremediable. The root of my argument is not to announce a bedrock philosophical inadequacy; it is to decry a sociological *naiveté*. I do not attack liberalism in a wholesale manner. But I long to see liberalism enriched by taking seriously the relational structures that mediate the contacts between autonomous, dignity-bearing subjects, who are the concern of liberal political theory. I want the socially situated context of these subjects to be integrated into the philosophical project itself. Thus, I do not defend simpleminded racial utilitarianism—the idea that we aggregate the incomes or utilities of people defined by superficial racial characteristics, and use this sum as an indicator of the goodness of society. But I insist that reflection about the rights of individuals and the vitality of the institutions that influence individual interactions, should take seriously the raced historical and social structures within which those individuals function.[6]

So, my core objection to color-blind liberalism has to do with this sociological *naiveté* and the limited place for historical developments to enter when liberal political theory is brought to bear on the problem of race. Sure, the so-called 'underclass' in the ghettos of America is behaving badly, in self-destructive and threatening ways. But those patterns of behavior, embodied in those individuals, reflect structures of human development mediated by social relations that are biased against those persons because of a history of racial deprivation and oppression. The result then is to produce, in our time, wide disparities in some indicia of behavior across racial groups. What does the abstract individualism of liberal theory (LT) suggest that we do now? Throw up our hands? There are no questions of justice raised? Scratch our heads? We do not quite know what to do. Too bad. We lament, but . . . There is, I believe, a gaping hole in liberalism as a normative framework if no better answer is to be had.

My fundamental point is that the selves that are the enshrined subjects of LT are not given a priori. Rather, they are products of social relations, and of economic and political institutions. They are creatures, to some not inconsiderable degree, of the very system of laws, social intercourse, and economic relations that normative political theory is supposed to assess. Neither their ideas about the good life, nor (crucial for my purposes here) their self-understandings as raced subjects, come into being outside of the flow of history and the web of culture.[7] The diminished selves, the self-doubting, alienated, nihilistic selves—these are social products, and I want to attend to this fact within the project of political theory. This leads to a rejection of color blindness as a normative standard because I cannot abide the imposition of abstract strictures of neutrality on a game in which, systematically, nonneutral practices have left so many raced and stigmatized outsiders with so few good cards to play. My core concern is about racial stigma and development bias. Succinctly stated, my argument with liberalism is that it fails to comprehend the following. *Stigma-influenced dynamics in the spheres of social interaction and self-image production lead to objective racial inequality which is decoupled from the discriminatory acts of individuals, carries over across generations, shapes political and social-cognitive sensibilities in the citizenry, makes racial disparity appear 'natural' and nondissonant, stymies reform, and locks-in inequality.*

4.4. EPISTEMIC DIFFICULTIES

One aspect of this perspective should be commented on. History has been invoked here as a factor conditioning the ethical assessment of contemporary social arrangements. And yet, the explicit channels of historical influence, on which social scientific work can shed some light, must of necessity remain opaque, and vaguely specified. What might be called an 'epistemological fog' obscures the causal dynamics at work across the generations and limits our ability to know in detail how past events have shaped current arrangements. Thus, it may be reasonable to assert in a general way that past racial discrimination in contract, together with present discrimination in contact, disadvantages blacks by impeding their acquisition of skills. But it is nearly impossible to say with any quantitative precision just *how much* of current racial inequality is due to this source of disadvantage.[8]

Now one could take the view, as some conservatives have done, that this knowledge limitation should short-circuit claims for racial egalitarianism that rely on the past unjust treatment of some racial group.[9] While acknowledging the plausibility of this view, I nevertheless reject it. Rather, I hold that a compensatory model, familiar from tort and liability law, is the wrong way to think about this question. My position, contrary to what I believe are simplistic applications of liberal neutrality that issue in mandates of color blindness, is that past racial injustice is relevant in establishing a general presumption against indifference to present racial inequality (thereby militating against the implications of the Anonymity Axiom mentioned earlier). But the degree to which social policy should be oriented toward reducing present racial inequality and the weight to be placed on this objective in the social decision calculus is not here conceived in terms of 'correcting' or 'balancing' for historical violation. Thus I argue that, even though quantitative attribution of causal weight to distant historical events is not possible, one can still support qualitative claims.

This distinction between quantitative and qualitative historically based claims is important, I think, because it casts doubt on the adequacy of purely procedural theories of justice when analyzing matters of race. Color blindness as understood by critics of affirmative action is one such theory. In general, procedural theories of social justice turn on the answers to two kinds of questions: What are people entitled to? And, what actions affecting the distribution of claims are legitimate? Then, any state of affairs that respects individuals' entitlements and comes about from procedurally legitimate actions is held to be just. Notice, however, that procedural theories are essentially incomplete because they cannot cope with the consequences of their own violations.

Suppose we are given a set of rules about how people are to treat one another. Suppose further that people happen not always to follow these rules. As just noted, history can be messy stuff. Teasing out causal implications across the centuries of historic procedural violations is impossibly difficult. So, if procedurally just requirements are not adhered to at some point—people entitled to the fruits of their labor are not rewarded accordingly, say—then, at some later point, perhaps a century on, there will be consequences rife in the interstices of society. But, as argued above, it will be impossible in principle to identify and to quantify these effects. What then would a procedural account have to say about this? Simple notions about providing compensation for identifiable historic wrongs may work when individual interactions are being considered, but they cannot possibly work for broad social violations—chattel slavery, for instance. A procedural theory leaves us with no account of justice under such circumstances. This is a fundamental incompleteness in the theory, one that is especially pertinent to a consideration of racial justice in the United States.[10]

To pursue this point somewhat more formally, let us call a system of rules about social justice *procedural* if it satisfies the following: (*a*) A list of rules or procedures is specified about how people are supposed to deal with one another. And, (*b*) a state of affairs is held to be just if it evolves from a just original state, where every step in the evolution is brought about by the freely chosen actions of mutually consenting agents, all of which are consistent with the rules specified in (*a*). Furthermore, call such a system *closed to moral deviation* if it meets the following test. Whenever some state of affairs is brought about through actions by some agents that breach the rules specified in (*a*), it is in principle possible to 'recover' from the effects of this breach through a series of counteractions that are themselves consistent with the rules set out in (*a*).

In other words, a *procedural* account of social justice is *closed to moral deviation* if one can correct the consequences of rule violation through actions that are themselves consistent with the rules. In the absence of this 'closure' property, a procedural theory would need to be supplemented by some non-procedural account of how to manage the states of affairs arrived at in the aftermath of the commission of procedurally unjust acts. Elsewhere I have demonstrated (in the context of a theoretical example) that notwithstanding the effective prohibition of discrimination in contract, historically engendered economic differences between racial groups can persist indefinitely when discrimination in contact continues to be practiced (see Loury 1977, 1995).

That is, nondiscrimination, once having been established in the sphere of contract but not in the sphere of contact, can admit of an indefinite perpetuation of the racial inequality originally engendered by historic contractual discrimination. Stated in terms of the language just introduced, my demonstration implies that the color blindness derived from the Anonymity Axiom—treat all subjects interchangeably and take note of no person's racial identity in the execution of social choice—when viewed as a procedural account of racial justice, is not closed to moral deviation. This, then, is the basis of my larger argument that, as a matter of social ethics, policies should be undertaken to mitigate the economic marginality of members of historically oppressed racial groups. This is not a reparations argument. *When the developmental prospects of an individual depend on the circumstances of those with whom he is socially affiliated, even a minimal commitment to equality of opportunity for individuals requires such policies.*

4.5. THE INTERPRETATIVE APPROACH

In June 2005, the US Senate passed Senate Resolution 39 by a unanimous vote. The Resolution offers a formal apology 'to the victims of lynching and the descendants of those victims' for the fact that the Senate consistently failed to pass anti-lynching legislation over the many decades during which this crime was widely practiced across the south. Indeed, each time the House of Representatives passed an anti-lynching statute (which occurred in 1922, 1937, 1940) Southern senators used a 'state's rights' argument, the filibuster or other devices to prevent a vote on the measure. This Resolution was the culmination of a concerted campaign of lobbying and public agitation which eventually succeeded in gaining the attention and the support of the US Senate. It is a model of what I mean by 'the interpretative approach' to the problem of dealing with our morally problematic history.[11]

Indeed, a sharp contrast can be drawn between two different ways of dealing with the problem of an ethically troubled past. One seeks reparations, conceiving the problem in compensatory terms. The other conceives the problem, let us say, in interpretative terms—seeking public recognition of the severity, and (crucially) the contemporary relevance, of what transpired. In the latter view, the goal is to establish a common baseline of historical memory—a common narrative, if you like—through which the past injury and its continuing significance can enter into current policy discourse.[12] What seems conceptually important, though, is to clarify that, while some reckoning with the racist history of the United States remains to be done, this reckoning may, for political as well as epistemological reasons, be inappropriately specified when cast in terms of reparations. What is required, instead, is a commitment on the part of the public, the political elite, the opinion-shaping media, and so on to take responsibility for such situations as the contemporary plight of the urban black poor, and to understand them in a general way as a consequence of an ethically indefensible past. Such a commitment would, on this view, be open-ended and not contingent on demonstrating any specific lines of causality. This, I wish to suggest, is the most powerful, enduring and appropriate reparation that could be proffered to black Americans in repair of the injuries of the past.

The national narrative—the agreed-on interpretation of a nation's history and its relevance to contemporary political issues—matters a great deal. Thus, in the United States we are often said to be a nation of immigrants. Thirty million newcomers have arrived on our shores since the liberalization of immigration laws in the 1960s. They have advanced up the escalator of opportunity, by and large. Now, what will the story be? Here is one possibility:

> We are a great nation, an open society, the land of opportunity. True, there are millions of laggard blacks, and that is too bad. It is regrettable that we need to lock up one million of them on any given day. And it is too bad that some two out of five of these black children depend on a public welfare system that has just been reformed in such a manner that, absent a boom economy, they may suffer a great deal. True, we have of late engaged in a discourse about the intellectual inadequacies of these blacks—a discourse that leaves it an open question whether or not, or the extent to which, those inadequacies are rooted in the inherent incapacities of their genetic endowments. But, as best we can determine, no individual's rights are being violated when he or she applies for an employment or educational opportunity, and we intend to make sure this remains the case. True, some blacks are falling behind, but most of the recent immigrants are not of European origins either, and they are doing pretty well by and large. So as far as racial justice is concerned, America is okay.

Now, is that simply racism? Yes and no, I would say. Yes, it is racism, but by no means is it *simply* racism. How, the question becomes, will it be contested? What will the argument be? 'Do not compare blacks to immigrants?' Frankly, my view is that analysts ought to be wary of such comparisons, but I do not see how they can be avoided. 'Do not publish those test score data?' I seriously doubt that anyone is going to put the genie back in the bottle on that one either. But how about this: Adopt as an axiom from the outset a belief in the equal humanity of these sons and daughters of slaves. Make this an a priori commitment that is not contingent on any empirical determination. The view would be that they are equal humanly with us, and that we swim or sink together. This view would be taught to the new Americans at their first step off the boat. We would not allow them to cluster in Miami, thinking that they have made a wondrous new world on the shores of industrial capitalism and liberal democracy, while the laggards over in Liberty City riot every now and then, and otherwise suck on the welfare tit. Before they get the citizenship paper, we would make sure they know the story of the country—that is, the decent story, the narrative that has some chance of being sustained under appropriate moral scrutiny. A central aspect of that story is that one-quarter or so of the black American population languishes in the Liberty Cities of the nation because we have a public culture in which the presumption of their equal humanity has not yet been fully extended.

This 'conservative line' on race in America today is simplistic. An alternative narrative would stress that the self-limiting patterns of behavior among poor blacks are not a product of some alien cultural imposition on a pristine Euro-American canvas. Rather, such 'pathological' behavior by these most marginal of Americans is deeply rooted in American history. This interpretation of our history would emphasize that black cultural marginality evolved in tandem with American political and economic institutions, and with cultural practices that supported and legitimated those institutions—practices that were often deeply biased against blacks. So, the line might go, while we should not ignore the behavioral problems of this so-called underclass, we should discuss and react to them as if we were talking about our own children, neighbors, and friends. This is an American tragedy. It is a national, not merely a communal disgrace. And we should respond to it as we might to an epidemic of teen suicide or a run of high school shooting sprees—by embracing, not demonizing, the perpetrators, who, often enough, are also among the victims.

And yet the conservative line on race downplays the fact that contemporary American society has inherited a racial hierarchy—the remnant of a system of racial domination that had been supported by an array of symbols and meanings deleterious to the reputation and self-image of blacks. A more appropriate interpretation of our history would recognize that the web of interconnections among persons that facilitate access to opportunity and shape the outlooks of individuals are raced—which is to say, processes of human development have been and are systematically conditioned by race.

Thus, racially disparate outcomes at the end of the twentieth century can be no surprise, either. The 'comparative narrative'—'structural reform is not needed; blacks may be lagging but nonwhite immigrants are progressing nicely, so America must be okay'—is sophomoric social ethics and naive social science. It is also unjust. Correcting this injustice is, I am arguing, what reparations for the crimes of slavery and of Jim Crow segregation should be all about. Saying this in no way commits me to the view that success is independent of effort, or that victims of racism should be exempted from mandates of personal responsibility. The problem with stigmatizing talk about 'black culture', 'black crime', and 'black illegitimacy'—when used as explanatory categories by the morally obtuse—is that such a narrative is adopted as an exculpatory device, a way of avoiding a discussion of mutual obligation. A distressing fact about contemporary American politics is that simply to make this point is to risk being dismissed as an apologist for the inexcusably immoral behavior of the poor. In truth, the moral failing here lies with those who would wash their hands of the poor, declaring 'we've done all we can'.

4.6. CONCLUSIONS

I wish in conclusion to return to my complaints against 'color-blind liberalism', and to describe what I take to be an appropriate context in which the intuitions of color blindness might yet prevail. Let us distinguish among three domains or venues of public action in a racially stratified society where the 'blindness' intuitions of liberal neutrality might be applied. First is the domain of policy implementation—where we decide on the instruments of public action. Here we are admitting students to college or hiring public employees or distributing social benefits. Some mechanism is being used to do this, and that mechanism may, or may not, take cognizance of a subject's race. Blindness here means structuring public conduct so that people from different racial groups who are otherwise similar can expect similar treatment. This is what most people have in mind when they insist that the government should be color-blind.

Second is the domain of policy evaluation—where we assess the consequences of public action. Here we are deciding whether to build a prison or a school, and if it is a school, whether it should serve the general population or only the most accomplished students. We are fighting a war on drugs and deciding whether to concentrate on the buying or the selling side of illicit transactions. As a general matter, prior to choosing a course of public action we need to assess the relative costs and benefits of the alternatives before us. The impact of an alternative on particular racial groups may, or may not, be explicitly reckoned in this assessment. Blindness here means not seeing a policy as more or less desirable on account of the race of those affected. This is what the Anonymity Axiom of social choice theory requires.

Third is what I will call the domain of civic construction—where we develop our nation's sense of shared purpose and common fate. Here we are building monuments, constructing public narratives, enacting rituals, and, most generally, pursuing policies that have an inescapably expressive as well as a directly instrumental effect. Blindness to race in this domain means deploying the instruments of civic pedagogy so as to promote a sense of national community that transcends racial divisions. This is what my Axiom 2 (on antiessentialism) requires, when it is embraced without reference to empirical assessments.

Veterans of the racial preferences wars are most familiar with the questions—having mainly to do with the unfairness of racial discrimination—that arise in the domain of implementation. To get a glimpse of the subtle dilemmas that arise in the domain of evaluation, imagine that the central bank is trying to decide whether or not to induce a recession, so as to lower the risk of inflation. Would it be legitimate to tolerate a somewhat greater chance of inflation while maintaining a strong demand for labor because doing so also manages to hold the unemployment rate of black youth at humane levels for the first time in a half-century? Can we reckon that this is a good policy because it contributes to overcoming racial stigma, draws blacks more fully into the mainstream of society, and permits them to earn the respect of their fellow citizens? (Here I mean to suggest that, but for this racial benefit, a different decision might be taken.) In other words, can we explicitly count as a benefit to society what we calculate to be the racially progressive consequences (reducing black economic marginality) of what is a race-blind action (electing to take a greater risk of inflation)?

The issues arising in the domain of civic construction are also subtle. Consider the practice of capital punishment, which may or may not deter murder, but which is most definitely the state-sanctioned killing of a human being. Would it be legitimate when deciding whether or not to undertake the powerfully pedagogic public ritual of executing lawbreakers to take note of what may be a large racial disparity in its application? (Here I am supposing for the sake of argument that the processes of policing, judging, and sentencing that lead to persons being executed are not racially biased, and I am asking whether we might nevertheless reject the use of capital punishment because of its racially disproportionate effects.) In other words, must we be blind to the possibility that such a racial imbalance could distort our civic self-understanding in the United States?

Or, to take a very different case, consider the conscious act of integrating the elite who exercise power and who bear honor in the society—the people to whom we delegate discretion over our lives. Suppose we undertake to ensure that there are, visibly, African Americans among those elite. Suppose this goal is pursued not to bestow benefits on black people, as such, but with the specific intent of integrating the national community by rubbing out in the consciousness of the populace a perception of racial difference in inherent capacities or deserved social standing. Would that be a valid enterprise? Such a project, after all, pays tribute to the idea of race-blindness, too: It seeks to diminish the sense within the polity that we consist of racial groups that are differently endowed or unequally worthy of respect, with some more deserving than others of inclusion in the prized venues of public life.

We have, then, these three domains—implementation, evaluation, and civic construction—giving rise to three classes of public questions: How should we treat individuals? How should we choose the goals to be pursued through our policies? And how much awareness ought we to have of the ways in which the conduct of public business can perpetuate into yet another generation the inherited stigma of race?

Color-blind liberalism seems to militate strongly in favor of 'blindness' in both the first and the second domains. I think this is wrong on both counts, because it is a-historical and sociologically naive. Color-blind liberalism fails, I will argue tomorrow, because (among other reasons) it is not closed to moral deviation. And a principled stand of race-indifference is unacceptable as well, because it rules out policies that are almost universally credited as being necessary and proper, given the history of race relations in this country. Few thoughtful people are prepared to import their love of the race-blind principle into the domain of evaluation. They may object to race-based selection rules, but they do not object to the pursuit of explicitly race-egalitarian outcomes through public policies that take no notice of race at the point of implementation. That is, using our linguistic convention introduced earlier, though they may embrace race-blindness they reject race-indifference.

Thus there is much (I think plausible) disquiet at the thought of constructing race-based electorates for the purpose of giving blacks greater political voice, but hardly any opposition to moving from at-large to nonracially drawn single-member voting districts when the intent is to produce a similar outcome. And, as mentioned, policies like the 10 percent plan in Texas, implemented through race-blind decision rules but adopted with the intent of benefiting blacks and Hispanics, are not controversial—politically or constitutionally—among most opponents of affirmative action.

I want to suggest that only in the domain of civic construction should some notion of race-blindness be elevated to the level of fundamental principle. The operative moral idea would be what Orlando Patterson has called the principle of infrangibility (i.e. the absence of boundary)—saying that we are One Nation, Indivisible, and taking that idea seriously enough to try to act (whether in a race-blind or a race-sighted fashion) so as to bring that circumstance about. Those people languishing at the margins, even if they are strange and threatening, are going to be seen as being, in the way that most fundamentally counts for our politics and civic life, essentially like us. We are going to prudentially and constitutionally, but determinedly and expeditiously, move so as to tear down, or certainly build no higher, the boundaries of race that divide the body politic.

There should be no race-mediated civic boundary, and where a boundary exists, it becomes our work to rub it out. That is a kind of race-blindness, too. Embracing this position would constitute reparations in its highest form. I hold that there is nothing in political liberalism, rightly understood, that should lead us to reject that practice. There is nothing wrong with a liberal, concerned about social justice, undertaking to fight racial stigma. There is nothing wrong with constructing a racially integrated elite in America. There is nothing wrong with fretting over 1.2 million African American young bodies under the physical control of the state. Indeed, I am led to wonder how any thoughtful person aware of the history and the contemporary structure of US society could conclude otherwise.

'Black Reparations' advocacy, on this account, is problematic not because (as many critics would have it) the people pushing it are quarrelsome jerks. It is problematic, and bad for this country, and bad for black people ourselves, because it squanders blacks' dwindling political capital and misses our chance to show genuine moral leadership in this nation, as the early civil rights era heroes had done. We are still a multiracial nation, and will be for as far into the future as anyone can see. The moral and political issues most salient in the context of blackness remain to be addressed (overcrowded prisons, ghettos from which opportunity for social betterment has fled, and so on), and 'compassionate conservatism' does not even begin to address them. But, then, neither will the payment of financial reparations for historical harm. The issue confronting those black leaders and intellectuals brave enough to think outside the box today is how to convert our historical inheritance of moral authority and our claim on the public's attention—an inheritance derived from the sufferings and heroic triumphs of our ancestors—into a moral *and political* currency that is relevant to our time. Mournful recitations of the old civil rights mantras are obviously inadequate to the task. The fact is that there are no problems facing the 'black community' that are not also problems for a vast number of brown, yellow, red, and white Americans. And there are no solutions for these problems that can, or should, be enacted solely (or even mainly) to assuage the legitimate concerns of blacks. But there is a criticism of the regnant interpretation of America's racial history in contemporary political discourses that can and should be made, in the name of historical and racial justice. I have tried in this essay to indicate what the broad outlines of such a criticism might be.

NOTES

1. In this sense, we operate under a tacit constraint on public discourse that might be called 'geographic anti-essentialism'. Under this tacit constraint, no public argument about regional policy is legitimate if it posits fundamental

differences in capacities (moral or intellectual, say) between inhabitants of distinct geographic regions (urban/rural, north/south, etc.) My view elaborated in Loury (2002: ch. 3) is that some comparable restraint is warranted on public discourse invoking inherent racial differences. I hold that such restraint is a necessary precondition to establishing a genuinely democratic order in the United States, in light of our history of racial subordination. This position of mine is to be distinguished from efforts to stifle scientific research on innate racial differences, which I do not support.

2. I see in the racially disparate impact of the enforcement of antidrug laws, and in the American public's general lack of interest in this racial disparity, a telling illustration of the value in this way of thinking. There could be no drug market without sellers and buyers. (Just so, there would be no street prostitution without hookers and johns.) Typically, those on the selling side of such markets are more deeply involved in crime and disproportionately drawn from the bottom rungs of society. Yet they are only one side of a two-sided transaction. They would not exist, but for the demand for their services. There is no sensible way in which they alone can be held to have 'caused' this problem. When we entertain various responses to the social malady reflected in drug use (or in street prostitution) we, in effect, weight the costs likely to be imposed on the people involved on either side of the illicit transactions. Our tacit models of social causation play a role in this process of evaluation. Have bad lawbreakers who sell drugs on our city streets imposed this problem on us? (Or, in the parallel situation, have bad women who sell their bodies on our streets brought this malady of prostitution into being?) Or, has a bored, spoiled middle class with too much time on its hands engendered the problem in its hedonistic pursuit of a good time? The answer for such a question is unlikely to be determined in a rational, data-driven manner, I maintain. How serious a given crime is seen to be by those who through their votes indirectly determine our policies, and how deserving of punishment for a given infraction various individuals are seen to be, will depend on the racial identities of those involved, I maintain, because the tacit causal accounts adopted by influential observers are likely to depend on the social meanings embedded in physical traits that serve as racial identifier.
3. See, e.g. the United States, Office of the President (1998: ch. 4), Farley (1996: ch. 6), Loury (2000, 2002: appendix), for documentation of these claims.
4. Further elaboration can be found in Arrow (1963), Sen (1970), and Elster and Hylland (1986).
5. I am using the term color-blind liberalism here and throughout in order to distinguish the object of my criticism from the broad theory of political liberalism as set out, e.g. in the work of Rawls. I am mindful of the fact that the embrace of this latter theory does not necessarily entail an endorsement of color blindness as a fundamental moral principle. However, so far as I know, the implications of Rawls's political liberalism (RPL) for the questions of racial egalitarianism with which I am here concerned have yet to be worked out in any comprehensive way. Doing so, in my opinion, remains an urgent philosophical project.

6. Just what might this mean in practice? I will argue (implicitly) below that a proper theory of social justice suitable for a raced society like the United States would be one satisfying the following desiderata:
   1. The social position of racial groups would count in the moral assessment;
   2. Social-political mobilization along lines of racial identity would be recognized as a necessary instrument of resistance for groups subject to historical racial subordination;
   3. Racial *stigma*, no less than racial *discrimination*, would be seen as a legitimate, and indeed an urgent, object of social approbation; and
   4. In the face of dramatic racial disparities in social performance, the imputation of responsibility to individuals for their 'choices' would be qualified by acknowledgment of the racially conditioned environments within which these individuals have to operate.
7. My critique of liberalism is thus similar in spirit to the communitarian arguments found in the work of Sandel (1982) and Taylor (1992), among others. As mentioned in note 5 above, the philosophical problem of deducing with some specificity what RPL implies about the problem of racial justice in the contemporary United States and like societies around the world remains an open one. Early critical discussion of this question in the literature—e.g. Charles Mills's critique of LT in *The Racial Contract* ('LT pretends to a universalism that it never obtains; the actual 'contract' is deeply and subtly a racial one') or Michael Sandel's more profound critique in *Liberalism and the Limits of Justice* (LT suffers from sociological naïveté and an inadequate philosophical anthropology [this regarding the nature of the self]: 'If the right is prior to the good then the self must be prior to its ends; but what manner of self might this be?')—do not seem to me to be sufficient. Although RPL does not imply the color blindness of today's antiaffirmative action racial libertarians, it remains unclear (despite much useful recent work on related questions by Amartya Sen, Anthony Appiah, Elizabeth Anderson, and Will Kymlicka, among others) as to just what, in a more positive vein, RPL does require for the just arrangement of social institutions (for the design of economic, political, educational, social welfare and criminal justice institutions, more specifically), given the fact of persistent social inequality between historically significant and culturally salient racial groups.
8. Consider the recent argument of Patterson (1998) on behalf of the proposition that the high rates of paternal abandonment of children among contemporary Afro-Americans is due to the devastating consequences for gender relations among blacks of American slavery, and of the racist system of Jim Crow segregation that followed. In my view, Patterson's argument is persuasive. But, even so, he can provide no answer to this crucial counterfactual query: What would family patterns look like among today's blacks in the absence of these historical depredations? This question is important because, without some sense of the

extent of damage caused by past violation, it is difficult to gauge the appropriate scope of remedy.

9. Thomas Sowell is perhaps the leading exponent of this view. A representative work is Sowell (1983).
10. Nozick (1974) provides a prototype of the procedural approach, in the sense being criticized here. I hasten to note that Nozick is himself aware of these difficulties, and proposes various amendments to his procedural theory in an effort to deal with them.
11. See Poverty & Race Research Action Council (2005) for details on the campaign for Resolution 39, and an informative interview with the one of its major proponents.
12. A crude analogy might be drawn here, suggested by the debate over the Truth and Reconciliation Commission in postapartheid South Africa: The compensatory approach is rather like putting as many past offenders as possible on trial, punishing them for their wrongdoing, and getting justice for survivors of the victims. The interpretative approach is a bit like waiving the pursuit of individual criminal liability in the interest of bringing to public light the true nature of what took place under apartheid.

5

Reconsidering the Case for Black Reparations

Andrew Valls

The issue of black reparations has received a great deal of attention in recent years. On the face of it, this development would seem odd. After all, we are more than one generation removed from the close of the civil rights era which ended *de jure* segregation and outlawed most forms of racial discrimination. Yet it is precisely the failure of policies adopted during the civil rights era to bring about racial equality that lies behind the attention that the issue of black reparations is currently receiving. The idea of black reparations provides a framework for advancing the stalled progress toward racial justice.

In the academic literature, discussion of black reparations is part of a broader development that gives attention to past injustices and ways of addressing their present-day legacies (e.g. Brooks 1999; Barkan 2000; Thompson 2002; and Torpey 2003). Here too it may be that the failure of previous theorizing to adequately account for and address the harms of the past lies behind the current scholarly interest in the legacies of colonialism, genocide, slavery, and related topics. It is important to see the current interest in black reparations as a part of this trend, which may reflect a general turn, among philosophers, at least, from ideal to nonideal moral and political theory.

In any case, the debate over black reparations—whether African Americans should receive compensation for the wrongs of the past—seems particularly fraught with strong passions on both sides. Moreover, while in many ways not dissimilar to issues pertaining to other groups and other injustices, the issue of black reparations seems particularly prone to caricature and misunderstanding. Whether purposeful or not, these misunderstandings both undermine a clear picture of what is at stake in the debate and may undermine the case for black reparations. With this in mind, this chapter attempts to clarify the issue of black reparations in the hope of thereby both advancing understanding of the issue and also strengthening the case in favor of black reparations. The chapter builds on arguments that I have made elsewhere (see Valls 1999, 2003*a*, 2003*b*), and some of the discussions below presuppose those arguments. Here the focus is on correcting pervasive misunderstandings in the debate over black reparations.

The chapter focuses on four sources of misunderstanding. The first is thinking of black reparations as reparations for slavery, as opposed to reparations for the whole history of racial injustice, including the Jim Crow era. I argue that this is inaccurate and has a way of undermining some of the strongest bases for black reparations. The second is the notion that reparations in general and black reparations in particular necessarily involve direct payments to individuals. This, I argue, is a mistaken understanding of the nature of reparations and ignores the wide range of policies that a reparations program could include. Third, I address the concern that focusing on black reparations is a strategic or political error because it draws attention to two things that many Americans seem not to want to discuss: the past and race. It is better, on this view, to pursue a class-based coalition that will also address racial inequality, if indirectly. I argue to the contrary that failure to draw attention to the past and to racial inequality itself weakens the argument for policies necessary to address racial inequality and is therefore a strategic mistake. I also argue that such strategic considerations do not touch the substantive moral issue of whether reparations are justified. Fourth, I consider philosophical arguments against focusing on the past and on race, particularly the argument that forward-looking egalitarian moral and political theories are superior to backward-looking arguments for black reparations. I argue to the contrary that race-blind egalitarian theories of justice fail to address—both materially and symbolically—the distinctive racial dimension of inequality in American society. In the conclusion I point to some hopeful—and some worrying—developments in the pursuit of black reparations and racial reconciliation.

5.1. REPARATIONS FOR SLAVERY?

The issue of black reparations is often couched in terms of whether there should be 'reparations for slavery' (see, e.g. Barkan 2000; Horowitz 2002). This way of understanding the issue is both mistaken and pernicious. It is mistaken because it ignores the full range of wrongs for which reparations are due, and it is pernicious because it thereby frames the issue of black reparations in a way that makes them appear less justified than they are.

Let us consider the distortion of American history first: focusing on reparations for slavery has the effect of eliding the whole history of segregation, discrimination, and oppression that followed the end of slavery. It ignores the fact that, after 1877, the federal government gave up on its commitment to ensure equal citizenship rights for African Americans, and left them to their fate at the hands of white southerners. It ignores the role of southern states in disenfranchising African Americans, and the federal government's complicity in this—culminating in the Supreme Court decision in *Plessy* v. *Ferguson* (1896), which held that 'separate but equal' was permissible under the US Constitution. That is, it ruled that racial segregation—in effect, racial subordination of black Americans—is compatible with the Constitution's guarantee of equal protection of the laws.

The Plessy decision, along with others, meant that state governments and private organizations were free to discriminate against African Americans. States did this by providing separate and inferior schools for African Americans, and by enforcing segregation in many other public services. Private enterprises discriminated by, for example, denying entry into many private schools, and by discriminating in hiring, contracting, and lending. Jim Crow was a system of discrimination that involved the cooperation and complicity of the federal government, state and local governments, as well as private enterprises.

The focus on slavery also slides over the active role of private groups and private citizens in keeping African Americans 'in their place' under the Jim Crow system in the south from the end of reconstruction until the 1950s and even into the 1960s. Groups like the Ku Klux Klan (KKK) were crucial in maintaining the Jim Crow system by terrorizing African Americans and thereby preventing them from mounting an effective opposition to Jim Crow. But the KKK was just a part of the Jim Crow system. Perhaps even more important was the support that it received from ordinary white folks in the south. This is reflected in the massive turnouts to watch lynchings that took place on a fairly routine basis. These events were the occasion for public gathering and entertainment. The recent exhibit of lynching photographs and the accompanying book, *Without Sanctuary* (Allen et al. 2000), bear this out. They are filled with pictures of black men hanging by their necks, surrounded by smiling white faces. These photographs were often made into postcards and sold as mementos of the event.

The focus on slavery, then, ignores both the state and the non-state actions that perpetrated a system of brutal racial oppression for the many decades between the end of reconstruction and the beginning of the civil rights movement. Nor was this only the case in the American South. For example, lynchings took place routinely outside of the South, and other forms of segregation and discrimination were common in the North and Midwest as well. This is not to say that African Americans were not generally better off outside the South—no doubt they were. Still, it is important to emphasize that Jim Crow was not merely a southern phenomenon. Both because of the complicity of the federal government in Jim Crow, and because of the discrimination that took place throughout the country, the crimes of this period are truly national crimes.

Yet to speak of reparations for slavery ignores all of this. It implies that no reparations are due for the systematic oppression under which African Americans labored for several generations after slavery ended. And it makes the wrongs for which reparations are due appear more ancient than they are, unfairly biasing the issue against reparations. It does so by implying that, after slavery, no grave wrongs were committed for which reparations might be due—after all, the topic of discussion is not reparations to African Americans for all of the wrongs suffered, but only reparations for slavery, which ended almost a hundred and fifty years ago. For those who are ignorant of the relevant aspects of American history, the focus on reparations for slavery may convey the false impression that, after slavery, African Americans were given a more or less fair chance at succeeding, and, instead of taking advantage of this, they choose to merely complain about past wrongs. But none of this is the case. Many of the wrongs for which reparations may be due are of recent vintage; they are well within living memory. Hence framing the issue as 'reparations for slavery' is a mistake. As Bittker ([1973], 2003: 9) has said, 'This preoccupation with slavery, in my opinion, has stultified the discussion of black reparations by implying that the only issue is the correction of an ancient injustice.'

Focusing on Jim Crow places the issue in a very different context. Jim Crow began to be dismantled only with the advent of the civil rights era, which we can date from the Supreme Court decision in *Brown* v. *Board of Education*. Brown was decided in 1954, meaning that the Jim Crow system, and all of the wrongs that it involved, is of more recent vintage than, for example, the many wrongs associated with World War II. Consider the payments by Germany to Jewish victims of the Holocaust, and to the state of Israel, or the payments by the American government to the victims of the Japanese American internment during the war. Few would suggest that these wrongs are too ancient to be addressed.

This focus also allows us to avoid many questions that have preoccupied some advocates (and critics) of black reparations. There has been much debate about how exactly the debt that is owed should be calculated. Some have suggested that unpaid wages for slave labor should be the starting point. Others have focused on the market value of slaves. Still others have focused on the unjust enrichment obtained by slave-owners, or the white population in general. All of these methods then rely on compounded interest to arrive at present-day estimates of the debt (see the citations in Valls 1999). One critic of black reparations has engaged in similar reasoning, but has argued that the value of benefits received by African Americans under slavery (food, shelter) must be subtracted from any estimate of what is owed—and of course the interest on these benefits must be compounded at the same rate (Schedler 1998). All of this is very tendentious. At each point in any of these arguments, objections can easily be raised against the assumptions being utilized. Also, the compounding of interest seems to assume that we can know with some certainty what would have happened over all of those decades if proper wages had been paid.

If we focus on more recent wrongs, and the inequalities that they have generated, these other issues simply become moot. The fact is that, while slavery is the beginning of the story of racial inequality in the United States, it is hardly the end. If reparations had been paid immediately after the Civil War, and measures had been taken to ensure full inclusion of freed slaves and their descendants in American society, this whole issue might not be salient today. But the fact is that these things did not take place, so the issue has been bequeathed, so to speak, to us. Racial inequality is clearly the result, not only of slavery, but of Jim Crow, and of the failure to confront this inequality even after Jim Crow. We have many very reliable measures of this inequality—differences in education, health, income, and—especially—wealth (see Oliver and Shapiro 1997). These are all we need as indicators of how we are doing in addressing the legacies of the wrongs of the past. Until the racial gaps on these measures close, the debt will not have been paid. And policies aimed at closing these gaps, I now want to suggest, should be thought of as part of a black reparations program.

5.2. PAYMENTS TO INDIVIDUALS?

As usually conceived, reparations—and other forms of compensation—involve payments to individuals for wrongs that they have suffered, and it is true that many reparations programs take this form. In the American context, for example, the reparations to Japanese American internees during World War II involved individual checks from the federal government for US$20,000. This reparations program has served as a common point of reference for advocates of black reparations since the passage of the Civil Liberties Act 1988, which provided for this compensation among other things—including an apology. If Japanese Americans are entitled to US$20,000 and an apology for a few years of unjust incarceration, the argument runs, why are African Americans entitled to no compensation, and no apology, for centuries of brutal oppression (see Verdun 1993; Matsuda 1995)?

Yet the disanalogies between the two cases provide opponents of black reparations plenty of ammunition as well: only those actually interned, not their descendants, were eligible for payments under the 1988 Act. This observation is sometimes the basis for a critique of black reparations. While the Japanese American internees could show individual harm, and were thus entitled to individual payments, most African Americans cannot make a similar showing. A proper reparations scheme, on this view, must involve direct payments to individuals who can show actual harm from wrongs that they directly suffered, and the implication of this is that reparations for slavery and Jim Crow are not appropriate (see Paul 1991).

It has been argued elsewhere that these individualist objections to black reparations can be overcome (see Valls 1999; Boxill 2003; McCarthy 2004). The point I wish to emphasize in the present context, however, is that reparations need not, and in the case of black reparations should not, take the form of payments to individuals. Indeed, there is plenty of precedent for reparations programs that do not involve payments to individuals who can demonstrate specific wrongs that they have directly suffered. The payments of the German government to Israel depart markedly from this sort of strict individualism. In the American context, the Indian Claims Commission was charged with compensating Native American tribes for the wrongs that they suffered at the hands of the federal government. Whatever shortcomings the ICC may have had—and they are many (see Brooks 1999: Part 5, and Rebecca Tsosie's chapter in this volume)—it at least stands as an acknowledgment by the federal government that compensation may be appropriate to members of current generations for harms originally suffered by previous generations. The conception of reparations as necessarily involving cash payments to individuals is far too narrow; reparations can include a wider array of measures than this (see Pablo de Greiff's chapter in this volume).

While we should avoid an overly narrow conception of reparations, at the same time we should also avoid an overly inclusive conception of them as encompassing all measures that attempt to address the legacies of the past. Minow (1998) has suggested that some purely symbolic gestures, such as an apology, should be considered a form of compensation. I believe that this stretches the notion of compensation too far, though Minow is right to point out that a symbolic measure can achieve some of the same results as compensation, as both convey an acknowledgment of past wrongs. Still, I suggest that the notion of compensation, or reparations, be restricted to material measures—those that seek to improve individuals' material well-being, but that it not be so restricted as to include only direct payments to individuals.

Indeed, as Brooks (1999: 8–9) has argued, reparations can take many forms. Brooks states that reparations can be either monetary or nonmonetary, and they can be directed either at individuals or at whole communities. He counts among the nonmonetary forms of reparations 'amnesty, affirmative action, and municipal services'. He calls reparations directed at whole communities 'rehabilitative', and says that these measures are intended 'to nurture the group's self-empowerment, or the community's cultural transformation, or at least to improve the conditions under which the victims live' (1999: 9). More recently, Brooks (2004) has distinguished two models of black reparations, the tort model and the atonement model. The tort model relies on litigation and seeks payments to individuals for specific wrongs that they have suffered, while the atonement model seeks racial reconciliation through more collective and democratic processes. Both are models of reparations, but Brooks favors the latter. He finds the tort model morally deficient, since it fails to include reconciliation as one of its main objectives, and because, given its adversarial nature, it can hardly achieve that objective. If part of the point of black reparations is to repair—and repair not just the victims but the society as a whole—then the tort model of individual payments cannot achieve this goal.

In a similar vein, I have argued elsewhere that black reparations should be part of an overall program of transitional justice in the United States (Valls 2003*a*). Drawing on models such as the transition from apartheid in South Africa, I have argued that a just transition from our own apartheid-like regime of Jim Crow must include both reparations and symbolic forms of acknowledgment (see also Valls 2003*b*). While the cultural and symbolic measures are not themselves forms of reparations, I argue, they are a necessary complement to the reparations if we are to properly remember the past and reaffirm both our rejection of racism and our commitment to racial equality. Reparations without acknowledgment, as Brooks emphasizes, may be seen as merely a payoff, while acknowledgment without reparations may be seen as an empty gesture. Reparations are necessary to address the material legacies of the past, and should be thought of as policies aimed at the material well-being of African Americans.

Conceived of in this way, black reparations need not involve payments to individuals. Indeed, as far as I know, no serious advocate of black reparations has urged that they take the form of checks to African American individuals. Instead, what advocates usually have in mind is a whole set of policies directed at addressing the large gap in material well-being between African Americans and the rest of American society. A number of commentators have suggested the notion of a 'domestic Marshall plan' on the model of the substantial resources that the United States poured into rebuilding Europe after World War II. A domestic Marshall Plan for African American communities could involve a large array of policies: affirmative action in education and employment, urban renewal, job training and other educational resources, favorable terms for loans for starting new businesses and buying homes, and favorable terms for government contracts—to name just a few. This broad program should be explicitly directed to closing the racial gaps in American society, gaps that are the direct result of our past, and of our failure up to now to address its harmful and unjust legacies (see Feagin 2000: ch. 8; and Brooks 2004: ch. 5).

5.3. A STRATEGIC MISTAKE?

Some writers who are concerned about inequality in general and racial inequality in particular have argued that focusing on race-specific issues such as black reparations is a strategic mistake. This argument suggests that what is needed to address inequality—including racial inequality—in American society is a united front that includes all those whose class position provides incentives for them to work together in pursuit of common goals. Focusing on race, this argument says, is divisive, and has the effect of dividing the poor and working classes along racial lines, making the achievement of common political goals difficult or impossible.

This 'strategic' way of thinking about racial justice is not distinctive to black reparations, but has precedent in arguments about affirmative action, among other issues. A case in point is William Julius Wilson's book, *The Bridge Over the Racial Divide* (1999). Although Wilson admits that racial discrimination still exists and that racial inequality is not reducible to class inequality, he nevertheless argues that the economic condition of African Americans is affected mainly by broad economic structures that have little to do specifically with race. Hence he suggests that addressing inequality in general and racial inequality in particular requires a broad-based political coalition among the poor and working classes across racial lines.

At the same time, Wilson argues that race-blind policies alone cannot address racial inequality. In the case of affirmative action, Wilson cites evidence that when specifically race-based affirmative action policies have been eliminated, even if they are replaced with similar class-based policies as in California's university system, racial and ethnic diversity plummets. This leads Wilson to conclude that race-based affirmative action continues to be necessary and justified, yet, for strategic reasons, he suggests that we stop using the phrase 'affirmative action' and start calling it 'affirmative opportunity'. In the conclusion of the book, he writes:

> ... [L]eaders of a progressive multiracial coalition could include affirmative action programs as a part of the coalition's agenda and prevent it from becoming a divisive racial issue. They could first of all emphasize the idea of affirmative opportunity,

> as opposed to numerical guidelines or quotas. They could also associate affirmative opportunity with the notion of flexible, merit-based criteria of evaluation to enlarge the pool of qualified candidates. In other words, they could implant the idea of using flexible, merit-based criteria to identify candidates who have real merit or potential to succeed, not those who are unqualified or lack the potential (Wilson 1999: 126–7).

What is striking about this set of suggestions is that Wilson wants to essentially maintain affirmative action as it has been practiced—it has never been about identifying persons with no merit or potential, and quotas have been illegal since the Bakke decision of 1978—while somehow softening the rhetoric so as to not offend white members of his progressive coalition. Wilson is privileging style and rhetoric over substance. Substantively, he wants to maintain race-based affirmative action. At the level of rhetoric, however, he wants to mute the emphasis on race and use words or phrases that are less likely to alienate whites.

How successful is this strategy likely to be? Not very, I suspect. While it is true that the use of certain words or phrases affect how people perceive and evaluate policies, the kind of shift Wilson is suggesting is unlikely to fool anyone. More importantly, however, the main objection to his strategy is that it sacrifices clarity for the sake of more attractive window-dressing. If one believes, as Wilson does, that race-based policies like affirmative action are justified, then surely there are advantages to stating that clearly, and providing the reasons behind the position. Even at a purely strategic level, there are surely serious costs to focusing on subtle changes in rhetoric in the hope of not alienating one's coalition partners. In other words, if one is in favor of race-based affirmative action but also aware that some whites with whom one hopes to form a coalition are opposed to this, then one faces a choice: either give up support of race-based affirmative action for the sake of the coalition, or attempt to convince members of the coalition that they should support it, too. But Wilson tries to have it both ways, to neither give it up nor to try to convince coalition partners to support it. Rather, he wants to maintain race-based affirmative action while playing with the rhetoric so that this does not split up the coalition.

The view that strategic considerations weigh against focusing on race-specific issues has led a number of observers to reject the idea of black reparations. For example, Carol Swain has written that

> talk about reparations at the present time is ill-advised and can be positively harmful in terms of improving race relations and garnering support for policies to help the truly distressed. Current reparations talk inflames the white electorate, undermines the bridge-building process across racial lines, fuels white nationalist sentiments, and is insufficiently targeted in its aims to help those members of minority groups who are most in need.... [T]he whole matter should be dropped (Swain 2002: 181).

Similarly, Adoph Reed has dismissed the idea of black reparations on the grounds that it is a 'political dead end' and is 'so obviously a nonstarter in American politics' (quoted in Torpey 2004: 178). Finally, Glenn Loury, in his contribution to this volume, has argued against the idea of black reparations on the grounds that 'a racial reform movement built around the theme of paying reparations to blacks is unlikely to engage these newcomers [immigrants], making the construction of political coalitions in support of progressive public policies that are essential for black flourishing less likely to occur' [page 88].

I would make two points about this 'strategic' line of thought. First, on strategic grounds there are advantages to speaking in terms of the past and in terms of race. The fact is that, without speaking about the past, the case for any race-conscious policies to address the legacies of racial injustice is weakened. The case for reparations, or any policy aimed at addressing racial inequality, is strengthened by pointing to the grave injustices of the past, and to the way that these injustices have led to current inequalities. If one believes that race-conscious policies called for by advocates of black reparations are necessary to address racial inequality, one needs a narrative of how these inequalities came about (McCarthy 2004). As Loury concedes, without such a narrative it is not clear why racial inequality per se is even a problem. Admittedly, there are probably strategic costs and benefits to either approach to addressing racial inequality: the focus on race and on the past risks alienating potential allies, but it has the advantage of offering an account of the origins of racial inequality in American society. On the other hand, focusing on present-day conditions and race-blind remedies may win over more allies, but has the effect of avoiding the issues when it comes to race, and may make it less likely that these issues will be addressed, even indirectly. This latter approach is likely to mean that race-conscious policies to address the legacies of the past will seem indefensible. On balance, strategic considerations may well favor the more straightforward approach that is not embarrassed to talk about race and the past in a direct and open manner.

Second, all of these strategic considerations are beside the point as far as the ethical argument is concerned. From a philosophical point of view, the political viability of the idea of black reparations is irrelevant to the issue of whether there is a good case for black reparations. Whether there is such a case depends on the wrongs that have been done, and the remedies that are available and appropriate under norms of justice. Of course, like all arguments, the arguments for black reparations are contestable, but whether they stand or fall does not depend on the political viability of the proposals, but on the premises, arguments, evidence, and conclusions that are offered. To think that strategic considerations can refute a philosophical argument is to make a category mistake. Like any other philosophical or ethical issue, whether black reparations are justified is not determined by public opinion polls, or political or strategic considerations. It must therefore be emphasized that Wilson, Swain, Reed, and (at least sometimes) Loury are not offering philosophical arguments but rather political advice. While I am inclined to disagree with their advice, the main point to be emphasized is that their arguments do not touch the substantive issue of whether black reparations are justified.

5.4. A PHILOSOPHICAL MISTAKE?

If strategic considerations are sometimes mistaken for philosophical or principled objections to black reparations, it is nevertheless true that there are genuinely philosophical arguments against the idea. I focus on two such arguments: the negative argument against the backward-looking, compensatory nature of reparations; and the positive argument that forward-looking, race-blind, egalitarian theories can accomplish what advocates of black reparations seek.

The negative argument against black reparations, and reparations programs in general, when they involve large-scale historic injustice, is that it is impossible to know what would have happened in the absence of these injustices, and hence it is impossible to know who is entitled to what under a reparations program. If compensation is supposed to return victims to a *status quo ante*, then this ideal—or even a reasonable approximation to it—is unknowable. The *locus classicus* of this argument, in the recent philosophical literature, is Waldron's '*Superseding Historic Injustice*' (1992), and the argument crops up in many guises. It is reflected, for example, in Glenn Loury's contribution to this volume when Loury raises the 'epistemological problems' that plague the idea of black reparations—that is, the problem of knowing 'how blacks would have fared but for the wrongs of the past'. I have attempted to address these worries elsewhere (see Valls 1999), but a couple of points bear emphasis here.

First, this objection presupposes what Brooks (2004) calls the 'tort model' of black reparations. That is, only if payments are to be made to individuals do we have to know how those individuals would have fared in the absence of past injustice. At the aggregate level, there is no question that the black–white gap in well-being is a product of past injustice and our failure to adequately address it. This seems to be all we need to justify, at least prima facie, policies directed toward closing that gap. The odd thing about Loury's position is that he recognizes the significance of past injustice and its effect on present disadvantage, but eschews talk of compensation. As discussed above, some of his concerns are strategic, but his principled objection to talk of compensation in this context presupposes an overly narrow view of compensation.

Second, even the most individualist model can accommodate the notion of black reparations. Nozick (1974), whose libertarian theory is as individualist a framework as one can imagine, recognized this. After developing his principles of justice in 'holdings', Nozick considers what justice requires when those principles are violated. He endorses a principle of rectification that requires that past violations of rights, when they have an impact on the present-day distribution of holdings, must be rectified by redistributing holdings to conform to our best estimate of the distribution that would have obtained in the absence of the violations. Nozick recognizes the epistemological problems involved here, but, rightly, he does not reject the idea of rectification on this basis. Rather, he endorses the use of 'rules of thumb' to estimate the counterfactual distribution. Nozick maintains that a greater injustice is done by not compensating at all for past injustices than by compensating, despite the imprecision involved in the latter. The one work to which Nozick refers as an example of the sort of thing he has in mind is Bittker's *The Case for Black Reparations* ([1973] 2003) (see Valls 1999).

So while the negative argument raises reasonable worries about the idea of black reparations, these are not insuperable. Reparations do not always require the strict individualism that the tort model involves, and even a very individualist view can accommodate and indeed endorse the idea.

The other argument against reparations in general and black reparations in particular focuses less on the problems with reparations than on the superiority of an alternative approach, namely, a forward-looking egalitarian theory of justice that would overcome racial inequality. This position maintains that, not just for strategic but for philosophical reasons we should focus on class rather than race, and that this will reach the same ends that advocates of black reparations seek. If we apply a color-blind egalitarian theory of justice, say, Rawls's, we will overcome the unjust legacies of the past.

I wish to make several points about this position. First, the forward-looking, egalitarian argument for overcoming racial inequality will only appeal to those who are already egalitarian liberals. I count myself in that camp, but not everyone does. There is, therefore, reason to rely on a backward-looking argument at least as a supplement to forward-looking egalitarian arguments. These two approaches may converge on some of the same conclusions, yet their respective premises may appeal to different audiences—say, Nozickean libertarians and Rawlsian liberals.

Second, the exclusive reliance on a forward-looking, egalitarian approach to racial injustice presupposes the soundness of the general theory of justice in which it is embedded. It ignores any problematic feature of this theory, even as it takes the problems with compensation as decisive against the compensatory approach. (This, at least, was the tenor of much of the discussion at the conference out of which this volume flows.) In short, the argument for the superiority of an egalitarian, forward-looking approach involves a comparison to the one recommended here, but the comparison often remains implicit, with the virtues of one view presupposed, and the problems with another view quickly taken as decisive against it. Are there no 'epistemological problems', for example, in determining when Rawls's difference principle has been satisfied?

Third, there is reason to doubt that an egalitarian theory of justice alone can adequately address racial inequality in the United States. Now at one level, the argument that I have been pressing is itself egalitarian. It assumes that each individual is of equal moral worth, with interests equally worthy of consideration. But it maintains that these egalitarian principles require attending to the way in which past injustices disadvantage present-day individuals. So while my premises are race-blind and egalitarian at the most abstract level, I maintain that race-conscious principles and policies are required by our basic moral equality, in light of our racist past. My position therefore departs from color-blind egalitarianism, which leaves open the possibility that, even if a preferred pattern of distribution is achieved, African Americans will continue to be overrepresented among the (relatively) poor. I would argue that even if a society conforms to some patterned principle of justice, say, Rawls's difference principle, if it remains the case that an historically disadvantaged group is overrepresented in the lower end of the distribution, then this is evidence of the unjust influence of past wrongs on present generations. The color-blind egalitarian, it would seem, would be unconcerned as long as the distribution conforms to her preferred pattern.

The alternative for the egalitarian liberal is to maintain that abstract egalitarian principles require color-conscious policies, but that such policies should not be thought of in compensatory terms. While in principle it is possible to have a purely present- and future-oriented justification of color-conscious policies, I suspect that such justification often silently relies on the way past injustices have produced the patterns that we see today. If those patterns of racial inequality had been produced through a large number of individual choices, unconstrained by the violation of rights, the argument for undermining those patterns would appear much weaker. Hence Loury's position, which recognizes the link between past and present injustice, but which eschews talk of compensation or reparation, seems in a precarious position. It relies on the past for much of its force, yet it denies that the rationale for race-conscious policies is (in part) to compensate for the effects of the past.

In addition to these considerations about taking the past and race into account for pursuing justice with regard to material distributions, the idea of black reparations performs a crucial symbolic and cultural, and perhaps a psychological, function as well. Reparations serve the function of not only providing material compensation but also of *acknowledging* the harms of the past, their wrongness, and the humanity, equality, and dignity of the victims (see Valls 2003*a*). Reparations are not the only way to do this, and indeed other symbolic measures of acknowledgment are necessary, lest the reparations alone be interpreted as a mere payoff, akin to a legal settlement where no wrongdoing is admitted (Brooks 1999: 8–9). Nevertheless, reparations—especially when coupled with other measures—can be an important means of acknowledgment.

The forward-looking, egalitarian approach to racial justice cannot play the role of acknowledging and rejecting the injustices of the past. If compensation is offered without acknowledgment, this may undermine the basis of the self-respect of victims and victim groups. If acknowledgment is offered without material repair, the symbolism is hollow and might reasonably be interpreted as insincere. Most important, if the material equivalent of compensation is offered, but it is not characterized as compensation but rather as a gift, or as the requirements of abstract principles of equality, then in this case too, something important is lost. In this case the material repair cannot convey the acknowledgment of the past that may be required to affirm the equal dignity of the members of a previously victimized group.

The idea of black reparations, then, is supported by the concern that the present-day material effects of past racial injustice be attacked directly, and that the message be thereby conveyed that the injustices of the past are rejected. As Elazar Barkan explains in his introduction to this volume, reparations do not bring closure, they create new relationships. It would be a mistake to view black reparations (either favorably or unfavorably) as a way for society at large to dispense with the obligations that the past imposes on it, once and for all. In conjunction with other measures, black reparations could help to create new and better relationships in a society that remains racially divided because of its past—and because of the way that past continues to shape the present.

5.5. CONCLUSION

In conclusion, allow me to make some observations on what I see as some promising (and some not-so-promising) developments related to the issue of black reparations and racial reconciliation.

The discussion in this chapter has implicitly assumed that the federal government is the proper agent to undertake a program of black reparations. It has assumed that the policies that would constitute this program would be federal policies, enacted on a nationwide scale. In this, the argument has been typical of the discourse on black reparations in general. And yet it may be the case that the most promising developments related to black reparations are not taking place in the arena of the federal government. Rather, two promising developments are taking place outside that arena.

The first development is that specific racial incidents of the past are being addressed, mostly at the local and state level. For example, a local commission looked into the Tulsa Race Riots of 1921 and issued a report in which it recommended reparations to the victims of the riot and their descendants (Milloy 2001). In Virginia, a scholarship fund has been created to compensate African Americans who were denied education when public schools were closed to avoid integration after the Brown decision (Janofsky 2005). The massacre in Rosewood, Florida in 1923 led to the passage of a state law in Florida in 1994, providing for reparations to the victims, among other measures (Barkan 2000: 296–9). In each of these cases reparations have been proposed or enacted for specific racial wrongs. While they fall well short of a general reparations program, they can be seen as steps in that direction. Where enacted, the reparations provide material compensation for some specific victims, and may also serve as a more general acknowledgment of the sorts of wrongs that occurred under Jim Crow.

The other development is efforts to address specific events outside of the purview of the state entirely, but rather in civil society. For example, the International Center for Transitional Justice, a nongovernmental organization that consults mostly with national governments making transitions to democracy, has been working with local groups in Greensboro, North Carolina. Their work focuses on an incident in 1979, where five protesters were killed and ten wounded when planning a march against the KKK. No one was ever convicted for the crimes. The Center is working with many constituents in the community to work toward reconciliation through an unofficial Greensboro Truth and Reconciliation Commission. Recently, spouses of some of the victims in the incident have asked prosecutors not to charge those implicated in testimony before the Greensboro TRC, in the interest of full disclosure about the events surrounding the massacre (*New York Times* 2005).

These developments in state and local government, and in civil society should, I think, be viewed positively by advocates of black reparations. They hold out the possibility of specific victories in attempting to achieve justice—or at least acknowledgment—for particular crimes. They also may play an important role in raising the consciousness of Americans about the brutality of our racial past, and may therefore be steps in the direction of a more comprehensive, national approach to black reparations.

There is another development that may serve a similar function, although it may also ultimately undermine a more comprehensive approach, and therefore should be viewed more ambivalently. I have in mind the many civil suits that have been filed against specific corporations for the profits that they derived through their involvement with slavery (Ogletree 2002). For example, Aetna Insurance has been shown to have profited from the policies it issued to protect slave-owners' investments in human chattel. While these suits have the same potential to raise awareness about our past as the developments discussed above, they may also carry another message: namely, that slavery, and Jim Crow, involved a series of individual wrongs, rather than systemic wrongs for which society as a whole bears responsibility. The suits shift the focus from the wrongs themselves to the profits derived from them (a misplacement of the proper emphasis, in my view) and conveys the impression that we can add up the individual profits from slavery (and Jim Crow)—if only we had the documentary evidence—and thereby rectify the legacies of that past. Also, by their focus on slavery, these suits carry the problematic message discussed above—making the wrongs for which black reparations are a remedy appear ancient indeed. Finally, it is not clear to whom reparations are due if Aetna and other corporations did profit from slavery. In short, the suits reflect what Brooks (2004) calls the tort model of reparations, and are subject to the limitations of that model that he identifies.

Whatever one makes of the issues discussed above, one thing seems clear. Current racial inequalities in American society are largely due to centuries of brutal oppression. The civil rights era brought an end to legalized racial subordination, but subsequent experience has made it clear that ceasing the active violation of rights is not enough. If they are not directly attacked, the inequalities created under the old regime are essentially continued under the new one. Whether one finds the language of reparations useful or one prefers to employ a different vocabulary, the basic point of the black reparations movement seems undeniable. African Americans continue to be disadvantaged in American society as a result of the legacies of our shared past. Basic fairness requires that something be done about this situation. I have tried to address what I take to be some misunderstandings about the issue, in an effort to clarify what advocates of black reparations are after, and why their claims are plausible. What seems most implausible is the idea that we need do nothing about the legacies of our past—or that it is permissible to continue to do as little as we are doing.

6

Further Trouble for Unsettled Waters: Attention to Gender in the Debate on Black Reparations

Carolyn Benson

6.1. INTRODUCTION

In a recent article on the history of the black reparations movement, Martha Biondi raises what would seem to be a straightforward question. Given the lack of discussion afforded to the particular exploitation suffered by black women under slavery and Jim Crow in the literature on reparations, she asks, will pending reparative policies address the realities of systemic sexual violence against women and the abuses of reproductive freedom during slavery and its legacy?[1] While straightforward in and of itself, however, this question seems to be grounded in a larger and ultimately more complex set of questions concerning the appropriateness of introducing gender and gender oppression as central categories of analysis in the discourse on black reparations. What would our vision of the harms suffered as a result of these racist institutions look like if attention to the relationship between gender oppression and racial oppression were more central to the theoretical framework underlying discussions on black reparations? How would we come to conceive the measures required by a substantive reparative project if attention to gender were to become a fundamental part of our way of thinking about these issues?

Reparations for slavery and Jim Crow are commonly cast as a matter of racial justice; in particular, the category of race has tended to structure our thinking about the transgressions that occurred in these contexts, who was made to suffer, and what ought to be done in order to effect the necessary repair. As Biondi suggests, reparations talk has been presented as offering an 'innovative and compelling' way to transcend the inadequacies of traditional civil rights discourse—an alternative means of revealing and dismantling the complex structures of white supremacy.[2] Although I would not quarrel with this general way of picturing the reparations movement, in this chapter I explore the extent to which a lack of attention to gender when it comes to questions of race and racial progress risks compromising the reparations project in ways that ought to concern us.

I begin, in Section 6.2, by considering how attention to gender might affect our understanding of the relevant harms experienced during slavery and Jim Crow, as well as the way in which certain expectations concerning the ontology of race- and gender-based oppression, if allowed to underlie our ways of thinking about reparations, risk effecting the subtle exclusion of many of the particular injustices suffered by black women. In Section 6.3, I turn to the significance of paying attention to gender and gender inequality when it comes to articulating the remedies required by historical justice. Given the complex differences at work within the communities who stand to benefit from reparations, my specific worry is that certain ways of thinking about racial justice and racial progress risk leading to the perpetration of further injustices against those who might lack the authority and the resources to define the nature of repair—a result that, from the standpoint of a movement that acts under the banner of justice, ought to be highly worrying. Finally, I conclude by raising and assessing what I take to be likely objections to my suggestion that gender must find a place as a category of analysis in the discourse on reparations.

Given the breadth of approaches to black reparations, and given the fact that these approaches are only beginning to be developed (at least in the context of mainstream political philosophy), my aim in raising questions about gender is to articulate concerns about the future directions that the reparations movement may or may not end up taking as a result of grounding itself in certain ways of thinking. As such, it is not my intention to provide an argument either supporting or condemning reparations for slavery and Jim Crow. In the observations to follow, I take as a starting point the fact that reparations talk, whether one supports it or not, is indeed a part of our political reality—one that is likely to have effects on our social situation. To this extent, it is important to ask serious questions about the analytic frameworks underlying this discourse: about what they now are, and, more importantly, about what they ought to be.

6.2. RACE, GENDER, AND THE IDENTIFICATION OF HARM

Why ought we to think that gender is relevant to discussions on the historic injustices characteristic of slavery and Jim Crow?[3] As I mention above, we tend generally to address the harms at issue in black reparations through the language of race, and this for good reason: both slavery and Jim Crow were unquestionably racist institutions, built on and in the interest of maintaining a race-based system of oppression.[4] It would certainly be strange to suggest that race ought not to serve as a central concept when dealing with these realities.

My concern, then, is not that we have gotten things altogether wrong in interpreting the injustices that reparations are meant to redress through the lens of 'race'. Rather, I worry that a certain way of thinking about racial oppression may obscure the extent to which slavery and Jim Crow were institutions realized in contexts where the operations of gender-based oppression were also at work—operations which contributed fundamentally to the shape of the racial injustices in question.[5] Put simply, the racialized subjects at the forefront of reparations talk were, and are, gendered subjects as well. This is not merely an interesting fact about the context in which slavery and Jim Crow took place. As I will suggest, an acknowledgment of the relationship between race and gender in this context is essential to an adequate understanding both of the harms at the center of the reparations debate and, perhaps more significantly, of the full extent of the measures required by a substantive reparative project.

6.2.1. Complicating the Ontology of Harm: Lessons from Feminist Theory

The above claim is sure to run against some people's intuitions about how we ought to structure the discourse on black reparations. Indeed, when it comes to articulating the injustices at issue, it would seem natural to conceive of the harms suffered by African Americans under slavery and Jim Crow as one sort of thing, in contrast to the sorts of harm normally taken to belong to the category of gender inequality. Both within and outside the context of reparations, for example, this underlying ontology is sometimes evidenced in a way of speaking and writing about the targets of racism as distinct from the targets of sexism: 'black people' on the one hand, 'women' on the other.[6] At other times, it is evidenced in a way of speaking about the injustices experienced by black women under these institutions that construes these realities as a 'double burden' of sorts.[7] When evaluated in light of this kind of rhetoric and the ontology that underlies it, the notion that we might want to introduce gender as a central category of analysis when discussing reparations is likely to seem misguided, a confusion of categories. What stands in need of explanation, it seems, is the idea that certain ways of conceiving the harms at stake in cases of systemic racism may be based on an oversimplified understanding and that gender ought to take a more central place in our reflection on racist institutions, including slavery and Jim Crow.

As a means of explaining this idea, it is useful to consider a strand of discussion in feminist philosophy, where attention to the practical and conceptual difficulties posed by sorting injustices into distinct kinds has received careful attention. As critics of certain feminist theorists have suggested, one of the guiding assumptions behind many of the theories of sexism that emerged in this century has been the notion that gender oppression is something that women experience 'as women'.[8] In the kinds of theory in question, sexism, conceived as one sort of thing, is contrasted to racism, conceived as a burden of a different sort. Each has its proper category of analysis—gender and race, respectively—and differences between women on the basis of the latter are largely construed as being irrelevant to questions about gender identity. In *The Second Sex*, for example, Simone de Beauvoir quite frequently compares 'women' (the subject of her analysis) to groups that have been oppressed along other axes of identity—including slaves. While at points she acknowledges that women make up part of this group, also recognizing that we live in situations characterized by many forms of oppression, de Beauvoir makes clear that her philosophical focus is on 'free women', effectively excluding as irrelevant to questions of gender oppression the experiences of black female slaves.[9]

Echoing de Beauvoir's approach, there is a tendency in strands of more recent feminist philosophy to construe sexism as having primarily to do with the injustices that a person experiences *because she is a woman* in a social context of a certain sort—of taking these experiences to be distinguishable in kind from those that a person experiences because she is a black person, or a white person, and so forth.[10] According to this kind of interpretive framework, the experiencing self is made up of separable 'bits' of identity that are also to be distinguished in kind: pieced together to constitute a whole person with feet planted in separable bits of the social world.[11] As Elizabeth Spelman argues, however, this way of thinking betrays a 'tootsie roll metaphysics': a vision of the self as consisting in separable identity 'pieces,' the significance of each unaffected by any other.[12] Yet to conceive of race and gender as isolable factors when assessing experience in complex social contexts is to get things seriously wrong. In circumstances such as these, 'man' and 'woman'—along with the symbols, limitations, privileges, and powers that accompany these categories—are not uniformly realized: for just *how* one is treated 'as a woman' or 'as a man' depends significantly on the nature of one's racial identity.[13] It is clearly not the case, for example, that the 'helpless maiden', the 'nurturing mother', or the 'precious commodity' are projections applied in practice to all women; when it comes to those forced to live in the shadow of the 'welfare queen', the 'sexual deviant', and the 'bad mother', the symbolics of womanhood are altogether different. Similarly, we cannot assume that the systemic injustices experienced by white upper-class women necessarily share something essential with those suffered by women of different races or classes. Consider, for instance, the mainstream feminist preoccupation with women's liberation from the home—an agenda that did not even nearly reflect the experiences and concerns of those women who had been selling their labor for years (often in other women's homes) in order to support themselves and their families.[14]

In one sense, the criticisms mounted against this ontology of race and gender reflect a concern to get things right—a concern about the theoretical adequacy of certain ways of thinking about systemic oppression and social categories. In another sense, however, these criticisms also reflect a more practical concern about the subtle forms of exclusion effected by this way of conceiving our social situation.[15] As many frustrated with certain strands of feminism have suggested, a collection of feminist theorists have tended to universalize the particular injustices experienced by white, middle-class women: that is, to understand them as the kind of oppression that all women experience as women. Because a white, middle-class woman does not suffer exploitation or discrimination on the basis of her race or class, it is assumed that her experiences sufficiently reflect the realities of sexism. As well as reflecting the mistaken assumptions that white women are not themselves racialized in contexts of racism, that the form of sexism experienced by white women is in no way shaped by their racial identities, and that racial oppression is something that black women suffer in addition to sexism, however, this way of thinking has historically tended to effect a systematic exclusion of black women's experiences from many discussions of gender oppression. In their failure both to consider the deep complexities of different people's experiences of sexism and racism and to acknowledge the significance of race to our understanding of the former, feminists who develop these kinds of theory have tended to theorize and to problematize the experiences of some women at the expense of others.[16]

What all of this suggests is that, rather than diverting our attention and needlessly complicating talk about gender, paying real attention to race may help feminists to gain a better and more inclusive understanding of the workings of systemic oppression and the complexities of identity. The self-critical move in feminist theory that began largely in the 1980s provides an example of a way of beginning to think about the connections between race- and gender-based oppression that, rather than obscuring our understanding of people's experiences in contexts of systemic injustice, allows the very real complexity of these experiences to come more fully into view. Nothing in this criticism entails the notion that categories such as 'race' and 'gender' are no longer useful, no longer able to capture the reality of our social lives; however, what this criticism does call for is a careful reexamination of what we mean when we use these categories, as well as a commitment to genuine self-consciousness when we do so.

6.2.2. Gender in the Context of Slavery and Jim Crow

Race matters when we talk about the harms of slavery and Jim Crow—as I have suggested, it matters fundamentally. If we are to take seriously the criticisms of mainstream feminist analysis outlined above, though, it seems important to consider the extent to which an adequate understanding of the injustices suffered by African Americans during slavery and Jim Crow may also require that we consider quite seriously the significance of gender to individuals' experiences under these institutions.

In quite general terms, paying attention to the workings of gender oppression in this context is necessary for a full understanding of many of the harms at the center of the reparations debate. For example, we cannot understand the racism that underpinned the systematically unjust persecution of black men for the rape of white women under these systems (both outside the courtroom and within) without understanding its relation to the sexism that grounded an anxiety about the threat of black male sexuality to the 'protection' and 'possession' of white women.[17] Although men within these systems were not the victims of sexism in the way that women were, the symbolic and ideological mechanisms of gender oppression still played a constitutive role in the shaping of men's relationships with each other. Similarly, and as may be more immediately obvious, we cannot understand the real nature of the dehumanization, exploitation, and domination of black women in these contexts without also considering how these harms were embedded in intersecting systems of racism and sexism.

Just how sexism affected the experiences of black men and women during slavery and Jim Crow is both complex and difficult to articulate, and we must be careful not to assume, simply, that the power relations at work between white men and women during these times were in any way universal. As Angela Davis suggests, the male supremacist structures operative in white communities during slavery could not become deeply or identically embedded in slave communities: given the fact that traditional (white) divisions of labor and privilege among gender lines were not applied to black men and women under slavery (creating what Davis calls a 'deformed equality' of sorts[18]), we must pay careful attention to the very specific ways and areas in which gender did or did not make a difference in slaves' lives when we engage in this kind of analysis. Although the period of Jim Crow may have evidenced a breaking down of this deformed equality between black men and women to some extent, an adequate understanding of the relationship between gender- and race-based oppression in this context would seem to require an equally careful consideration of the specific gender relations at work.

As in the context of feminist theory, however, the worry here is not simply that we risk getting the picture wrong in excluding gender as a category of analysis. More troubling is the possibility that, in doing so, we may fail both to recognize and to struggle against many of the harms that ought to matter to a truly inclusive reparative project. As the criticisms mounted against certain strands in feminist theory show, exclusion can be subtle and difficult to avoid. Part of the task at hand in the issue of reparations is the identification of harm, the wronged and the wrongdoers, yet there are sure to be significant ambiguities concerning just how we ought to classify the experiences of black men and women during slavery and Jim Crow and, as such, concerning what ought to count as a truly *relevant* injustice when it comes to this political issue. For instance, given the intersections of race- and gender-based oppression in this context, ought the systemic rape and sexual exploitation of black women by white men to be considered relevant to reparations for slavery and Jim Crow, alongside more straightforwardly acknowledged considerations such as forced labor, wrongful death, segregation, and the systemic denial of developmental resources?[19] Ought the forced sterilization of thousands of black women from the early twentieth century into the 1960s and 1970s to be considered relevant to black reparations as well?[20] For some, it will be tempting to understand these realities as properly belonging to the category of gender oppression—as matters for a different kind of redress. Yet the institutionalized sexual exploitation and denial of reproductive freedom to black women are realities that cannot be explained as *simply* falling under the category of gender. Indeed, just how these harms were realized depended in great part on the structure of white supremacy operative during these contexts, on anxieties about black sexuality, power, and population that also underpinned many of the harms more commonly addressed in reparations-talk. To this extent, they were just as central to the systemic workings of slavery and Jim Crow as mob lynchings, forced segregation, and economic exploitation.

My general point is that paying real attention to the connections between gender and race in these contexts—to the complex ways in which systemic male supremacy related to systemic white supremacy—may allow for the institutionalized sexual and reproductive violence during the periods of slavery and Jim Crow to be understood, at least in part, as a function of the very workings of these racist systems rather than problems that belong to another category of harm.[21] If our discussions betray an underlying assumption that what we are interested in are the specific harms inflicted upon black Americans simply *as* black Americans, and if what counts as an instance of injustice within these systems is limited to those experiences that have to do specifically with one's 'blackness', in isolation from one's gender, then it seems as though we risk treating some of the harms central to these systems as irrelevant (or at best peripheral) to the issue of black reparations.

In a sense, my worry here is anticipatory of trends that risk emerging as the discourse on reparations develops and becomes more concrete rather than a criticism of already explicit ways of framing things within the debate. It is a worry in response to a general lack of specific attention in the literature to black women's particular experiences and to the dominance of the blanketing categories of 'black Americans' and race, as well as to the rather general and abstract ways in which many theorists write about the entrenched harms and inequalities resulting from slavery and Jim Crow.[22] It is also a response to the occasional tendency of theorists to continue to refer to women and 'sexism' as categories in contrast to black Americans, 'slaves', and 'racism'[23] and to a more than occasional tendency to focus on statistics affecting black men alone, particularly when it comes to the matters of overrepresentation in prison and life expectancy.[24] This is not to suggest that there is a complete absence of theoretical attention to sexual slavery, the denial of reproductive education, rights and liberties, the forced displacement of black children from their families, and the widespread refusal on the part of the American legal system adequately to support black women's charges of rape in cases where the alleged perpetrators were white men. The challenge, however, is to begin to understand (and indeed to talk about) these harms as a part of the very mechanisms of slavery and Jim Crow, as a means of preventing the entrenchment of an implicit way of conceiving these realities as something that some people were made to suffer *in addition* to institutionalized racism.[25] To conceive of these harms in the way that I am suggesting is not to reduce gender oppression to racial oppression (or vice versa), as if the latter were somehow prior to the former. Instead, it is to understand them as inherently informed by the racism at work within slavery and Jim Crow, such that to separate one 'sort' of injustice from the other in particular cases no longer makes sense.

In a related way, acknowledging the relationship between race and gender in these contexts may also draw attention to issues concerning the construction of gender identity during slavery and its legacy. As many writing on reparations have suggested, attention to economic harms alone cannot be enough.[26] If reparative measures are to bring about the cultural respect and self-determination envisioned by many reparations advocates, attention must also be paid to the harms inflicted on black Americans at the symbolic level: to the destructive racial stereotypes and social meanings engendered during the periods in question and perpetuated in their legacy. While attention to economic harms is of course central to the reparations project, it is clear to many that real change must also involve an endeavor to address the far-reaching effects of the diminished and diminishing social meanings engendered by the construction of race that determine in large part what it *is* to be a black man or a black woman in America.[27] If a full treatment of these social meanings is what we are after, however, attention to the construction of black *masculinity* and *femininity* during slavery and Jim Crow ought to be understood as central to the reparative project rather than a matter better left for feminists to deal with. To be sure, black women activists and philosophers have long sought to bring the relevance of the construction of black masculinity and femininity, including the construction of black fatherhood and motherhood, to the forefront of discussions on racial justice.[28] I wish neither to underplay the vast extent of the work on these issues nor to underestimate the influence that these writers have had on our thinking about race and gender. With this said, these writers are often understood as contributing to the feminist project in particular rather than a broader project within critical race theory. As Cressida Heyes suggests, this illustrates a continuing tendency to treat issues about gender identity as fundamentally separate from issues of race and racial justice.[29]

Indeed, much of the philosophical attention given to this issue up until now has tended to focus on broader questions about whether there is a case to be made for reparations of this sort and about how we ought to conceive of the reasons and arguments in favor of developing and implementing reparative measures.[30] Substantive questions about just which harms are relevant and how, specifically, the legacy of slavery and Jim Crow ought to be redressed in the here and now are just beginning to receive concrete attention.[31] Understandably, these questions have not been met with anything that could coherently be described as a 'general' or 'common' way of dealing with the issue, and so, again, my worries are mainly anticipatory. Rather than constituting a reaction to clearly identifiable inadequacies in a preexisting body of work on reparations, then, what I have been arguing here reflects a concern for how the ways of thinking about gender and racial oppression that have been common to some strands of feminist theory may come to shape the more substantive accounts of reparative justice that are surely (and perhaps inevitably) to follow.

6.3. ATTENTION TO GENDER IN THE CONTEXT OF REPAIR

In addition to what I have said above, the category of gender would seem to be relevant when it comes to articulating the practical measures required by a substantive reparative project. In a sense, this point follows from what I have already been arguing: if, as reparations advocates quite reasonably argue, the nature of reparation policies must reflect the nature of the injuries suffered during slavery and Jim Crow, then attention to the relationship between race and gender in these contexts will be an important factor in assuring that certain harms are not excluded from our list of reckonings. This acknowledged, there are ways in which attention to gender inequalities in the here and now—in the very context of repair—may be appropriate, if not required, in order to ensure that reparative programmes do not themselves perpetuate further injustices. In what follows, I will focus on the significance of this point to two prospective modes of remedy commonly raised by supporters of the reparations movement.

6.3.1. History and Authority

Many reparations advocates acknowledge the extent to which repairing the dangerous social meanings engendered and perpetuated by slavery and Jim Crow may involve a concerted effort to reeducate Americans about the past through historical storytelling.[32] What is needed, some suggest, is the construction of a collective cultural narrative that is able both to reveal the truth about America's history of 'freedom', 'fairness' and 'equality', and to diffuse the dangerous myths about race and responsibility that continue to infect American consciousness.[33] Storytelling provides a powerful means of generating more appropriate social expectations; this insight is important, and it points toward a direction of thinking about how to address the deep-seated, symbolic legacy of slavery and Jim Crow where attention to economic redistribution on its own does not appear to be adequate. Again, however, there is a real risk that the narrative reconstructions of the injustices suffered during these periods will be grounded in a way of thinking about race and gender that conceives these realities as wholly separate, making it difficult to articulate many of the institutionalized harms experienced by black women as a genuine function of the systemic racism in question. To this extent, we must be conscious of the already functioning narratives that ground the stories we aim to construct through reparative retellings.

Even if we are to construct historical narratives that resist conceiving race and gender in isolation, however, attention to present-day gender inequalities in narrative authority and access to the means of communication may also be necessary in order to ensure that certain experiences are not excluded from projects of collective reinterpretation. Given very real and very present power differences along gender lines, both within black communities and in North American culture more generally, the authority to voice the past, to be acknowledged and *heard* as a legitimate storyteller when it comes to matters of history, has tended to be a privilege denied to women.[34] As such, we may have good reason to be concerned about the extent to which some people's stories have been, and will continue to be, excluded from the agreed-upon 'national narrative' that is meant to function as a means of redress. As Angela Davis points out, for example, attention to the particular situation of slave women was conspicuously absent from the literature on slavery that proliferated during the 1970s.[35] At this time, a guiding assumption seemed to be that historians could reveal the real workings of this institution without talking about women's experiences in any in-depth way and without ensuring that women were substantively included as participants in the project of historical reconstruction. To the extent that we risk perpetuating this kind of exclusion in our present-day projects, what seems to be called for is a conscious acknowledgment of the social and political barriers that black women face in adequately communicating their experiences, as well as the putting into effect of substantive measures to ensure the collective inclusion of their particular historical subnarratives.

6.3.2. 'Community' and the Redistribution of Resources

Rather than conceiving the material aspect of reparations as consisting in monetary payments to individuals, many advocates propose the establishment of a set of policies of redistribution directed at what is sometimes called 'the African American community'—policies including, but not limited to, the regeneration of urban areas, the infusion of resources related to employment, education, and the building of skills, the introduction of favorable terms for loans and contracts, the infusion of capital for access to the media, the implementation of greater political representation, and the assurance of more adequate health care facilities.[36] For many reasons, this is a more satisfying idea than the notion of handing out 'cheques to individuals'. Again, however, this kind of infusion of funds to black communities seems to risk dissolving into further injustice in the absence of an acknowledgment of (and action against) the power relations at work *within* these communities—relations that have historically resulted, and may continue to result, in the unequal distribution of social resources along gender lines.

As many critical of the masculinist nationalism informing many parts of the black liberation movement earlier on have argued, there was a time in the history of North America when one had good reason to worry about the conflation of the good of 'the black community' with the good of black men.[37] Reflecting on the nature of the power relations at work within radical groups in the sixties and seventies, some women writers have brought to light the ways in which the existence and strengthening of a deeply rooted misogynist strand both within and outside of the liberation movement resulted in the maldistribution of social and material gains, as well as the harsh self-sacrifice that many black women activists were compelled to suffer, in the name of 'race loyalty', for 'the cause'.[38] If they are to avoid the mistakes of past struggles for equality, it is clear that those who are in the position both to articulate and to effect the measures required by reparative justice must take into account the problematic gender hierarchies internal to black civil society when devising and implementing what is to be done in the name of dismantling white economic supremacy. In invoking the notion of a community, and in directing reparative measures at this kind of social reality, advocates and policymakers must take genuine care to ensure that the focus of reparations is the material and psychological effects of slavery and Jim Crow upon *all* who have suffered, not simply those who have enjoyed relative social and political privilege within these groups. What must be thoroughly kept in mind, in other words, is that both the historical institutions in question *and* the repairs to be realized occur in contexts of intersecting forms of systemic inequality.

It is often stated in the discourse on reparations that the material measures in need of implementation ought to have as their goal the bridging of a material 'gap' between black and white Americans. What is needed, many advocates suggest, is a 'catching up', a 'leveling of the playing field', when it comes to the well-being of black Americans compared with white Americans, in terms of wage averages, wealth levels, test scores, unemployment rates, incarceration statistics, health and mortality numbers, and so on.[39] When we encounter this way of speaking, however, we ought to ask questions about just what this means. Just which kinds of white Americans are black communities supposed, materially, to 'catch up' to? What does catching up mean, when the social group that is supposed to be caught up to is itself defined by internal inequalities? Given the material imbalances within white communities, would it be acceptable, within the framework of reparations, for this 'bridging' to result in a reflection within black communities of the material imbalances that exist between men and women (and indeed along class lines) in white civil society? One of the worries, here, is that the desired side of the 'racial gap'—the 'American Dream' of material success and economic power[40]—is left unquestioned. As with the context of the liberation struggles of the sixties and seventies, the worry is that, in the absence of an acknowledgment that gender inequality in the here and now is neither inevitable nor acceptable, what may be tacitly implied, or at least assumed, by this rhetoric is that black men ought to enjoy the powers and privileges afforded to white men—that *this* equals a successful bridging of the gap and leveling of the field along racial lines.

In truth, this worry reflects the difficulties of trying to address one kind of injustice within a system that is inherently unjust along many axes. Whatever the cause of this difficulty, however, the reality is that talk about catching up or 'bridging the economic gap' may, whether one means to or not, perpetuate the idea that reparations ought to be formulated as a matter of creating the conditions in which black communities are able to reflect the material situation of white America, which is itself left as unproblematic. But what if that which must be caught up to ought not to be as it is in the first place? What if quite radical change to our economic and social situations—a complete *transformation* of the playing field rather than its leveling—is necessary in order for genuine repair to be realized by all black Americans in the legacy of slavery and Jim Crow? As bell hooks quite importantly points out, both white women and black men have led liberation movements resulting in the further oppression of members of other groups; although the black men who participated in these struggles were victimized by racism, many nonetheless acted as oppressors and exploiters of women, just as many white feminist activists have come historically to aid in the exploitation and oppression of black people. As she suggests, '[a]s long as these two groups, or any group, defines liberation as gaining social equality with ruling-class white men, they have a vested interest in the continued exploitation and oppression of others'.[41] My particular worry, then, is that the problems that have arisen in past struggles for social justice might just repeat themselves in the context of the contemporary struggle for reparations.

Some may take the above as an indication of the unsuitability of the reparations movement to social situations such as ours.[42] Indeed, what I have been saying echoes Jeremy Waldron's concerns back in 1992, when he acknowledged the extent to which any justification for the redistribution of social resources based purely on a backward-looking notion of repayment and debt may dissolve quite drastically when present conditions are such that redistribution would result in the enactment or perpetuation of further injustices and inequalities.[43] Although we will have yet to see how things unfold, I believe in the possibility of both acknowledging and working to guard against the worries I have outlined above *and* engaging in a substantive reparative project that involves extensive economic redistribution (rather than mere symbolism). Rather than signalling the inappropriateness of reparations altogether, what these worries may suggest instead is that there are real moral constraints that must be put on reparative action, at least if we are to engage in such action from the standpoint of justice. Part of coming to articulate those constraints involves paying close attention to the unacceptable inequalities that exist along multiple axes in contemporary social situations; as I have been arguing, gender is a clear example of such an axis.

6.4. PROBLEMS

I expect that there will be many who will be made uncomfortable by my suggestion that gender ought to be introduced as a central category of analysis in the debate on reparations. To echo the words of one reparations theorist, bringing talk of gender into the picture is sure to be taken by some as the further troubling of already 'unsettled waters', and, as such, it may be viewed by quite a number of advocates as unwise.[44]

From the standpoint of a concern for strategy, for instance, one worry may be that a focus on differences along gender lines in the context of this debate divides black communities along gender lines where they ought to be unified. Moreover, there may be a worry here that talk about the complexities of things is sure to cause the reparations project to be unbearably demanding and difficult. It is hard enough to effect real progress in the struggle for reparations, some might say, without bringing gender difference into the picture.[45] With this acknowledged, I would like to raise two further points in defense of bringing greater specificity to the discourse on reparations. First, it would be misguided to suppose that talking about gender in and of itself is likely to create division within black communities along gender lines. As I have argued, whether or not we choose to talk about it, this kind of division already exists as the result of a long history of intersecting inequality. Second, part of the project of *creating* unity would seem to involve consciously addressing and actively repairing internal inequalities—and this would seem to involve paying real attention to the differences that gender makes in the context of reparation. Any unity that depends on the systematic exclusion of some people's voices at the expense of others—voices that ought to be included—would seem to be very hollow indeed.

Another objection may be grounded in the notion that bringing greater specificity to the reparations discourse causes the project to seem unbearably complicated. I agree that paying attention to gender when articulating harm and remedy is likely to be epistemologically challenging, involving the gathering of a broad range of stories, making difficult decisions about what ought to be included under the category of the effects of slavery and Jim Crow, and making informed projections about how reparative policies may affect relations within groups in the here and now. Again, however, any attempt to gloss over the complexity and demandingness of an acceptable reparations project would seem also to be a movement in the direction of a kind of willing blindness. Of course we *can* engage in more simple reparative projects, focusing on easily specified harms (perhaps those harms that fall most clearly under the category of slavery and Jim Crow), and, of course, we *can* choose to understand the task of paying attention to issues of present injustice involving axes of difference other than race as something that ought to be undertaken by other projects and social movements, such as feminism. Strategic simplicity of this sort is both intellectually and politically convenient. Yet I worry that, in doing so, the reparations measures in question are likely to lose their significance—as well as their ultimate justification. If it is the case that my suggestions trouble already unsettled waters, then I would hold that justice demands this troubling.

With all of this said, I do recognize that the reparations project must start somewhere, and the practical difficulties that my suggestions present may be very great indeed. Waiting for a full articulation of the harms at issue or for a comprehensive analysis of the extent to which proposed reparative measures exclude certain people is clearly unwise, at least from the standpoint of activism. In light of this, further thought may have to be given to the relationship between theory and practice within the framework of my argument, and this is something that I am willing to concede. In the end, my suggestions may be better construed as considerations that must be brought into reparations activism as it unfolds, constituting a goal and point of eventual normative assessment rather than a constraint on action in the here and now. Granting this point does not, however, imply that we could be justified in simplifying our theoretical conception of the project in the ways that I have been arguing against. While advocates must start somewhere, my suggestions would seem nevertheless to place normative constraints on where they may justifiably end up.

Even if we are able to draw acceptable distinctions between theory and practice in some cases, however, another, perhaps more serious objection to my argument might be grounded in the claim that the methodological turn that I am advocating rests on a misunderstanding of the real nature of reparations for slavery and Jim Crow as it ought to be conceived. In particular, some may worry that I extend the scope of reparative justice beyond its proper subject matter: the specific redress of very specific harms suffered by black Americans, *as black Americans*, under slavery and Jim Crow. Those harms that are relevant to reparations, some may argue, are precisely those that are identifiable solely along the lines of racial injustice; to include harms that occupy the territory of both race and gender oppression is to confuse the project, which has and ought to have a much narrower scope than my suggestions assume it to have. Likewise, some may hold that to saddle reparative projects with the task of attending to present day justice along axes of difference other than race is to confuse what reparations are properly meant to achieve.

This is an objection that I am, at least in some sense, willing to concede. In a sense, what I am suggesting implies an expansion of the boundaries of reparative justice for slavery and Jim Crow at its most basic form: a solely backward-looking, sharply delineated project of redress for discrete harms suffered by discrete individuals. However, this is not the conception of reparations that underlies many arguments in the contemporary literature. What has been called for, at least by many who engage in the debate, is a more complex, far-reaching project that is able to take into account the systemic and highly complex nature of the harms suffered under slavery and Jim Crow—a project that has as a part of its vision not only the straightforward compensation of past harms but also the achievement of meaningful equality and justice in the future. According to many advocates, the nature of the repairs required by justice ought to reflect the complex material and psychological harms effected by the historical institutions in question, but it is also generally allowed that this must be undertaken in a way that does not perpetuate further harm. Given the systemic nature of both past and present injustices, I would maintain that our reparative solutions ought to reflect a complexity of their own; as such, they must extend beyond the simple model of backward-looking monetary redistribution.[46]

Part of the motivation behind the contemporary surge of reparations talk has been a growing dissatisfaction with the limited achievements of recent black liberation movements, which until now have been unable to dismantle the complex, intersecting structures of inequality that enshrine white privilege. Given these goals, we may wish to call for an expansion of the notion of harm—a movement away from attention to discrete occurrences, toward a more systemic and holistic treatment of slavery and its legacy, including attention to harms that do not simply, solely, or explicitly fall under the category of the official policies realized during slavery and Jim Crow. Moreover, acknowledging the possibility that highly focused reparative action may result in further injustices, including the exclusion of some who ought to benefit from the race-specific policies in question, we have good reason to maintain that the legitimacy of the reparations project rests quite considerably on its ability to take into account the systemic inequalities that exist on axes other than race and that characterize the contemporary North American situation. To the extent that advocates are able to support this broader, more nuanced vision, it would seem that my suggestions find quite an appropriate place in the reparations movement.

6.5. CONCLUSION

If complexity in the discourse on reparations is what is called for, I would suggest that this is because it already exists as a fundamental part of the social contexts in question. Admittedly, the expanded project of repair outlined above may be inappropriately characterized as 'black reparations', at least if we are to maintain a more traditional understanding of this concept. This I am willing to grant, and I look forward to future discussions concerning just what this concept ought to capture and just how reparations ought to be implemented. In arguing for the importance of paying attention to the ways in which gender and gender oppression affect both the nature of the harms at stake in the reparations debate and the nature of the measures brought about in the name of their remedy, I have attempted to explore the extent to which certain ways of conceiving reparations may result in unacceptable limitations to the achievements envisioned by those advocates who strive for a more inclusive, complex reparative project. If reparations are undertaken in the name of moral progress, and if this progress is to be universally realized, then these are reflections that must be engaged with seriously. Given what we would seem to risk in refusing to complicate our ways of thinking, attention of this sort is not simply appropriate or justifiable—it is, from the standpoint of justice, quite substantially required.[47]

NOTES

1. Biondi (2003: 17).
2. Biondi (2003: 5). Although the centrality of race as a category of analysis in discussions on slavery, Jim Crow and reparations is usually implicitly maintained by theorists, its importance is made explicit in Robinson (2004: 143). For a very interesting discussion on the way in which racial identity affects perception and life prospects, see also Glenn Loury's contribution to this volume.
3. Given my interests in this chapter, I focus on the categories of race and gender in particular rather than explicitly considering the relationship between race and other identity categories (such as class, ability, sexual orientation, and so on). In doing so, I do not wish to underplay the significance of these other categories or the importance of paying attention to the ways in which they might complicate the debate on reparations. Moreover, I do not wish to set up the category of 'black women' in a way that betrays an underlying essentialism of the kind that I criticize in the argument to follow. I appeal to the significance of gender difference mainly because it has been taken by a collection of theorists on race and gender to make a great difference when it comes to people's experiences under slavery and Jim Crow—one that is underdiscussed in the literature on reparations. Although I cannot entertain this question here, I would fully support further analysis into how other axes of difference might also be relevant to this debate.
4. Although I appeal to the concept of oppression throughout this analysis, I am not unaware of its ambiguity. A full account of this concept is beyond the scope of this chapter, however. For my purposes here, I assume at least a general

understanding of what it means for a group to be oppressed, and I assume that my use of this concept in the context of thinking about reparations, while perhaps controversial, is not altogether problematic. For a helpful background on this concept, see 'Oppression' in Frye (1983). See also 'Five Faces of Oppression' in Young (1990).

5. I go on to describe these ways of thinking in the first part of the next section.
6. Although his is not a discussion of reparations in particular, a clear example of this way of conceiving of race- and gender-based oppression may be found in Laurence Thomas's article on sexism and racism, where he builds an analysis of these phenomena in large part from an understanding of the way in which each 'conceives of its object: women and blacks, respectively' (see Thomas 1980: 242). Thomas suggests that one outcome of sexist social meanings is the stereotype of men as benefactors of women: as those who are meant to 'protect women and to provide them with the comforts of life' (p. 244). Looking to the history of relations between black women and white men in America, however—to the strangeness of the thought that it was ever a part of white men's stereotypical role to 'protect' or to 'provide' for black women—it is clear that Thomas is really speaking about relations between men and women of the same race, relying on gender concepts in a way that erases the reality of the particular roles that white men have come to hold vis-à-vis black women. When thinking about his analysis of how women have come to be treated as a result of sexist social meanings, it is natural to ask where the particular experiences of black women fit in—if they are meant to fit in at all. As Elizabeth Spelman suggests, it is important to understand that, the moment that black women enter into this kind of analysis, Thomas's construal of the objects of sexism and racism as being *different* cannot possibly make sense (see Spelman 1988: 120–2).
7. In her analysis of women's experiences under slavery, for example, Gerda Lerner asserts that black women's 'work and duties were the same as that of the men, while childbearing and rearing fell upon them as an added burden' (Lerner 1973: 15; quoted in Spelman 1988: 123). Spelman calls this way of approaching racism and sexism an additive analysis of oppression: a way of thinking that treats 'the oppression of Black women in a society that is racist as well as sexist as if it were a further burden when, in fact, it is a different burden' (p. 123).
8. I am referring in particular, here, to certain theories developed from the 1970s to the 1990s. I will point out particular cases of this tendency in what follows.
9. Spelman (1988: 65). See de Beauvoir (1953: esp. 131, 454, 569). For a very interesting discussion of de Beauvoir's essentialist tendencies, to which I am much indebted here, see Spelman (1988: ch. 3).
10. Examples of feminists who have been criticized for isolating gender from other axes of identity and for focusing on gender relations largely in isolation from other forms of oppression when constructing theories of sexism include, e.g. Nancy Chodorow, usually in reference to her (1978); Kate Millett, in reference to the general strategy underlying her (1969); Catharine MacKinnon, in reference to her (1987) along with other works; Shulamith Firestone, largely

in reference to her (1970); and Carol Gilligan, in reference in particular to her earlier strategy in (1993). Although many of these contemporary philosophers do consider the relationship between gender oppression and other forms of oppression, their conceptions of sexism would seem to obscure some key aspects of both white and black women's experiences under intersecting forms of oppression. For interesting discussions on the essentialism at work in these theorists' conceptions of sexism and the specific criticisms brought against them, see Spelman (1988: chs. 4, 5) and Heyes (2000: esp. chs. 4, 5). For an interesting analysis of feminism and racism, see also 'On Being White: Toward a Feminist Understanding of Race and Race Supremacy,' in Frye (1983).

11. I am indebted to Elizabeth Spelman for the image of a whole person composed of 'separable units of identity' (see Spelman (1988: 158).
12. Spelman (1988: 136). For a comprehensive discussion of gender essentialism that treats many of these issues as well, see Heyes (2000: esp. ch. 1).
13. Spelman (1988: 55).
14. For a very interesting discussion of this reality, see Davis (1983: ch. 4, esp. 91–3).
15. For analyses of the exclusion of black women's experiences and opinions from mainstream (white) feminist theory, see hooks (2000: esp. ch. 1); Collins (1998: esp. chs. 2, 6).
16. Spelman (1988: 58).
17. As Spelman argues, '[t]he ideology according to which whites are superior to and ought to dominate Blacks is nested in the ideology according to which white men must protect their wives from attack by Black men and keep their race pure from pollution by miscegenation' (Spelman 1988: 106). As a side note, Spelman rightly acknowledges that white men of course 'gave the lie to this ideology in their failure to protect their wives from their own violence as well as in their enormous contribution to the mixed-race population' (106). For more on these themes, see also Angela Davis's 'Rape, Racism and the Myth of the Black Rapist,' in Davis (1983).
18. See 'Reflections on the Black Woman's Role in the Community of Slaves,' in Davis (1998: 117).
19. According to Angela Davis, attention to the specific kinds of mistreatment that black women experienced during these times (in particular, the use of rape as an instrument of white supremacist terror) has tended to be absent in the historical literature on slavery—although this is being remedied in more recent studies. As she notes, '[d]espite the testimony of slaves about the high incidence of rape and sexual coercion, the issue of sexual abuse has been all but glossed over in the traditional literature on slavery' (Davis 1983: 25). See also Davis (1983: ch. 11) and 'Reflections on the Black Woman's Role in the Community of Slaves' in Davis (1998).
20. For a discussion of this phenomenon, see Sinderband (2005).
21. In speaking of sexual violence, here, I do not wish to exclude the rape and castration of black men also documented in historical treatments of these contexts. This said, it seems to me that these experiences are more likely to be

understood as relating to white supremacy than is the sexual violence suffered by black women, which is often far more ambiguously categorized.

22. For instance, there is a tendency in the literature to refer generally to inequalities in health, income, wealth, education, and opportunity when it comes to black Americans as opposed to white Americans and almost no discussion at all of the ways in which these inequalities are distributed *within* black communities. See e.g. of this, Ogletree Jr. (2003: 284), Henry (2003: 133–4), Robinson (2004: 140, 146–7), and Hylton (2004: 34–6).
23. See, for instance, Ogletree (2003: 318) and Williams and Collins (2004: 980).
24. e.g. see Henry (2003: 134) and Dyson (1995: esp. 11). For worries on the lack of attention to the gender-specific effects of racial segregation, see Collins (1998: 17–23) and 'Reflections on Race', in Davis (1998: 308–9).
25. As I have mentioned above, this is a tendency that has already taken hold in the writings of quite a number of feminist theorists.
26. See especially Hall (2004) and Miller (2004: esp. 55–78).
27. See, for instance, Hall (2004: 8–12) and Zack (2003: 141–3). This issue is further explored in Glenn Loury's chapter in this volume, where he considers the significance of the social meanings attached to racial markers for individual perception. See especially Section 4.2 of his contribution.
28. For important examples of this, see Davis (1983: esp. 3, 92–3, 176) and Collins (1998: esp. 35–49).
29. Heyes (2000: 185).
30. For a comprehensive background on these questions and their treatment in the literature on reparations, see Ogletree (2003: 279–94)). See also Valls (1999, 2003*a*), Hall (2004: esp. 1–8), Biondi (2003), and Hylton (2004: 31–6).
31. To be sure, these substantive questions will have been addressed in the context of lawsuits and legislative initiatives recently undertaken in various state and federal courts (again, see Ogletree (2003: 279–94)). My observation is directed mainly at the philosophical literature on reparations, which, when addressing the issue of relevant harm and the shape of reparative measures, has tended to conceive of things in more general terms.
32. See, for instance, Ogletree (2003: esp. 317–20). Although I speak here about the construction of a unified cultural narrative, there is no reason to think that advocates could not also endorse a more pluralist vision of historical storytelling.
33. See, for instance, Miller (2004: esp. 72–8), McGary (2002: 103), and Brophy (2004: 131–6).
34. For an interesting discussion on this issue, see Code (1995). On the subtle and implicit ways in which certain kinds of people have been systematically excluded from political discussion—even when formally included in debate—see Young (1999).
35. See 'The Legacy of Slavery: Standards for a New Womanhood,' in Davis (1983).
36. See, for instance Balfour (2003: esp. 41) and Henry (2003: 149). See also Andrew Valls's contribution to this volume.

37. This issue is well discussed, e.g. in Davis (1998: 309).
38. For more on this phenomenon, see Collins (1998: esp. 26–9). To be sure, the deeply rooted patriarchal assumptions at work in the minds of white policymakers resulted in their being no better at identifying and attending to the needs and demands of black women during this time.
39. See, e.g. Hall (2004: 8–9), Robinson (2004: 154–6), and Andrew Valls's contribution to this volume.
40. According to Hall, '[t]he most compelling claim for reparations, centuries after the initial violation occurred, is made by those who are still locked out of this country's dream despite years of legislative initiatives' (see Hall 2004: 9).
41. hooks (2000: 16).
42. This point echoes some of Glenn Loury's points in his contribution to this book.
43. Waldron (1992).
44. Robinson (2004: 140).
45. As Patricia Hill Collins points out, e.g. efforts to articulate the particular issues confronting black women during the rights movement in the 1960s and 1970s were often discouraged in the name of solidarity and strength (see Collins 1998: 28–9).
46. See McGary (2002) and Miller (2004).
47. I am very grateful to Jon Miller for his very helpful suggestions on my chapter. Many thanks also to my teachers, Susan Babbitt, Rosemary Jolly, and Jacqueline Davies, for introducing me to many of the issues raised in this chapter. Finally, I am very much indebted to the Social Sciences and Humanities Research Council of Canada for their generous financial support throughout my graduate studies.

Part III

Reparations for Conflict

7

Justice and Reparations

Pablo de Greiff

While a great deal of attention has been paid to what countries that have undergone transitions to democracy have attempted to do by way of prosecutions, much less attention has been paid to these countries' attempts at reparations. Clearly, both kinds of efforts, the prosecutorial and the reparative, can be considered elements of justice, but the latter has not received sufficient systematic attention. Surprisingly, this is true despite the fact that most of the recent transitional processes have at least given some consideration to programs of reparations that seek to make up, in some way, for the harms endured by some members or sectors of society.[1]

It is worth emphasizing that from the standpoint of the victims, reparations programs occupy a special place in a transition to democracy. Reparations are, for them, the most tangible manifestation of the efforts of the state to remedy the harms they have suffered. Criminal justice—even if it were completely successful both in terms of the number of perpetrators accused (far from being the case in any transition) and in terms of results (which are always affected by the availability of evidence, and by the persistent weaknesses of judicial systems)—is, in the end, a struggle *against perpetrators* rather than an effort *on behalf of victims*. Something similar can be said with respect to other transitional justice measures; from truth-telling victims will obtain significant benefits that may include a sense of closure derived from knowing the fate of loved ones, and a sense of satisfaction from the official acknowledgment of that fate. But, in the absence of other positive and tangible manifestations truth, by itself, can easily be considered as an empty gesture, as cheap and inconsequential talk. Finally, institutional reform will always be a long-term project which affects the lives of the victims indirectly.

Hence, some systematic attention to the question of reparations under conditions of transitions is clearly called for. In this brief chapter I try to summarize the direction which I have taken in this area. Here I will start with a modest effort to establish some semantic clarity, at least by trying to distinguish between two different contexts of use of the term 'reparations'.

The semantic overflow from one sphere of use—the legal—into the other—the more political arena in which massive programs are designed—actually has some pernicious consequences. So it is important to distinguish the uses of the term (Section 7.1). I then proceed to a brief discussion of what justice in reparations may mean when the idea is to repair a large number of cases, as opposed to individual, isolated cases. I discuss some of the problems with taking the idea of compensation in proportion to harm as an unproblematic criterion of justice, and argue instead in favor of three goals which are intimately related to justice, namely, recognition, civic trust, and social solidarity (Section 7.2). Finally, without ever pretending that a blueprint for a program of reparations can be designed from a purely theoretical perspective, I offer some clarification of the basic trade-offs that accompany some of the choices that have to be made in the process of constructing a comprehensive and coherent reparations program (Section 7.3).

7.1. CONCEPTUAL CLARIFICATION: THE MEANING OF THE TERM

I start by concentrating on a fact that surprisingly has not received sufficient attention in discussions of reparations thus far, namely, that there are two different contexts of use of the term reparations (and that within each of them the term is used in different ways). The first context is the juridical one, particularly, the context of international law, in which the term is used in a wide sense to refer to all those measures that may be employed to give redress for the various types of harms that victims may have suffered as a consequence of certain crimes. The breadth of the meaning of the term reparations in this context can be seen by considering the diversity of forms reparations can take under international law. These include:

- *Restitution*, the object of which is to reestablish the victim's *status quo ante.* Depending on the circumstances of the case, this kind of reparation includes measures that seek to reestablish rights, such as liberty and citizenship, and conditions such as the victim's social situation and family life.
- *Compensation*, which is the essential and preferred component in reparations, especially at the international level. In the human rights field, every quantifiable harm should be compensated, be it economic, mental, or moral injury, whether the consequence of a violation of international human rights law or international humanitarian law.

- *Rehabilitation*, which includes measures such as necessary medical and psychological care, along with legal and social support services.
- *Satisfaction and Guarantees of Nonrecurrence*, especially broad categories that include such dissimilar measures as the cessation of violations, verification of facts, official apologies, and judicial rulings that establish the dignity and reputation of the victim, full public disclosure of the truth, searching for, identifying and turning over the remains of dead and disappeared persons, along with the application of judicial or administrative sanctions for perpetrators, and institutional reform.[2]

The other context in which the term reparations is frequently used is in the design of programs (i.e. more or less coordinated sets of reparative measures) with massive coverage. For example, Germany, Chile, and Argentina can be said to have established 'reparations programs'.[3] In this context, and despite the relations that each one of those programs may have with other efforts to achieve justice, the term is used in a narrower sense. Here reparations refers to the attempts to provide benefits directly to the victims of certain types of crimes. In this sense, programs of reparations do not take truth telling, criminal justice, or institutional reform, for example, as parts of reparations.

The categories used in the context of the design of programs in order to analyze reparations are different from those proposed by international law. In this context the two fundamental distinctions are between material and symbolic reparations, and between the individual and the collective distribution of either kind. Material and symbolic reparations can take different forms. Material reparations may assume the form of compensation, that is, of payments either in cash or negotiable instruments, or of service packages, which may in turn include provisions for education, health, and housing. Symbolic reparations may include, for example, official apologies, rehabilitation, the change of names of public spaces, the establishment of days of commemoration, the creation of museums, and parks dedicated to the memory of victims, etc.

There are, then, two different contexts of use of the term reparations, and they differ significantly from one another. In the sphere of definitions, the fundamental question is not so much about the correctness of a particular definition, but rather, about the relative advantages of understanding a term in a particular way. In the case at hand, the advantage of the breadth of the legal understanding of the term consists in the fact that it provides an incentive to design programs of reparations that cohere with other measures of justice, a topic to which I will return shortly. Nevertheless, the breadth of this understanding also carries a price: a program of reparations can hardly be designed from the beginning so as to include as parts of a single whole all the measures which international law takes to be forms of reparations.

The more restricted use of the term characteristic of discussions about the design of programs also has advantages and disadvantages. One of the advantages is that it suggests certain limits to the responsibilities of those in charge of designing such programs, which in principle makes their task satisfiable. However, this narrower use also poses the risk that the program of reparations will be completely unrelated to other justice measures. Although I insist on the importance of preserving the links between the program of reparations and other measures of justice in times of transition, I defend the use of the term reparations in the narrower sense described above, that is, to refer to measures that provide benefits to victims directly. This use contrasts with measures which may have reparative effects, and which may be very important (such as the punishment of perpetrators or institutional reforms), but which do not distribute a direct benefit to victims themselves.

7.2. NORMATIVE CONSIDERATIONS: THE AIMS OF REPARATIONS PROGRAMS

7.2.1. Reparations as a Political and not a Juridical Project

Now, the differences in use are of course motivated and not simply arbitrary. Part of the underlying motivation is functional in nature; in the juridical context, the meaning of the term is tied to the specific aim pursued in judicial settings, that is the achievement of justice for individuals, where the means of achieving justice, namely, the trial of isolated cases, has an impact on the concrete content of justice. This approach to the concept of justice differs significantly from that which those who are responsible for the design of reparations programs may and should adopt. Courts do not have an option but to consider each case in its own terms.[4] By contrast, whoever is in charge of designing a massive program of reparations has to respond to a much wider and more complex universe of victims, and has to employ, perforce, methods, and forms of reparation suitable to these circumstances.

Although reparations are well-established legal measures in different systems all over the world, in transitional periods reparations aim, in the last analysis, as most transitional measures do, to contribute to the reconstitution or the constitution of a new political community. In this sense also, they are best thought of as part of a political rather than a judicial project.[5]

There are two fundamental reasons that justify thinking about reparations politically rather than juridically. In the first place, and from a negative perspective, a massive program of reparations cannot reproduce the results which could be obtained in the legal system, because all legal systems work on the assumption that norm-breaking behavior is more or less exceptional. But this is not the case when programs of reparations are being designed, for such programs attempt to respond to violations that far from being infrequent or exceptional, are massive and systematic. The norms of the typical legal system are not devised for this sort of situation. It is worth pointing out that this problem is not limited to national jurisdictions. Most human rights treatises are conceived and configured to respond to violations in an individualized fashion, and not through massive programs.[6] General international law has not formulated clear norms or principles on this matter either. In any case, the capacity of the state to redress victims on a case-by-case basis is overtaken when the violations cease to be the exception and become very frequent. I will return to this point shortly.

In the second place, and from a positive perspective, to assume a political perspective on reparations opens up the possibility of pursuing ends through the reparations program that would be more difficult to pursue if the sole aim of the program were victims' redress in accordance with a legal formula. Some of these ends, as is argued below, have to do with a broad conception of justice that goes beyond the satisfaction of individual claims, and that involves recognition, civic trust, and social solidarity.[7]

7.2.2. Justice

The most general aim of a program of reparations is to do justice to victims. The question, of course is, what should victims in fairness receive?

Perhaps, rather than approaching the question in a vacuum, it would be easier to start by examining what international law and jurisprudence have to say about the issue. Needless to say, here I can only do so in the most cursory manner. There seems to be growing consensus among international lawyers that victims of human rights abuses are entitled to reparations. This emerging consensus is grounded, in part, on the general principle that all violations of international law entail some responsibilities. But responsibilities to do what? Here is what some international human rights instruments say: Article 8 of the Universal Declaration of Human Rights talks about 'effective remedies'.[8] Article 10 of the American Convention, about 'adequate compensation', Article 63 about 'fair compensation', and Article 68 talks about 'compensatory damages'.[9] Article 9 of the International Covenant on Civil and Political Rights includes vocabulary about 'an enforceable right to compensation',[10] Article 14 of the Convention against Torture speaks about 'fair and adequate compensation including the means for as full rehabilitation as possible',[11] and Article 50 of the European Convention about 'just satisfaction to the victim'.[12]

This, of course, does not settle the issue. What do the expressions effective remedies, 'fair and adequate compensation', and 'just satisfaction', mean, precisely? Once again, perhaps it is easier to approach the subject by examining what different bodies, responsible for interpreting these norms have said about the subject. Both the inter-American and the European human rights systems have dealt extensively with the issue, the courts in each system having decided well over one hundred cases each involving reparations. Although there are important differences between the decisions in the two systems, I will not deal with these here.[13] In general, it can be said that they agree on the following interpretation of fair and adequate compensation and other cognate terms: the ideal behind reparations is 'full restitution' (*restitutio in integrum*), that is, the restoration of the *status quo ante*. In cases where this is impossible, for example, when a death has occurred, compensation is required, and this means, for the inter-American Court, for example, that material and moral damages are called for. To pay material and moral damages means to cover 'any damages of economic value such as physical or mental damages, psychological pain or suffering, opportunity cost, loss of wages and the capacity to earn a living, reasonable medical and other expenses in rehabilitation, damages to goods and trade; including loss earnings; damages to reputation or dignity and reasonable expert fees'.[14] Procedurally, the Court has calculated these damages by projecting the victim's actual income, multiplying it by whatever was left of his or her professional life (based on national professional and life expectancy averages), and subtracting 25 per cent of this amount (assuming that this was the portion of income that the victim would have consumed for personal use, and therefore not available to relatives). In cases where it is difficult to estimate the victim's income, the Court has used national minimum wages, and in at least one case, where it determined that the national minimum wage was too low, it went as far as using the average of regional minimum wages.[15] To this amount, the inter-American Court then has added its calculation of subjective, or 'moral' damages, which try to compensate for pain and suffering. In sum, decisions by the Court have required payments of between $150,000 and $200,000 per victim.

Now, in an isolated case of a human rights violation, this ideal of complete reparation (*restitutio in integrum*) understood in terms of the restoration of the *status quo ante* or of compensation in proportion to the harm suffered, is unimpeachable. Its justification should be obvious: from the perspective of victims and survivors, it attempts to neutralize the consequences of the violation they have suffered. From another perspective the ideal hopes to prevent perpetrators from enjoying any benefit they may have derived from their criminal actions, or to obligate the state to take responsibility for having allowed, by act or omission, certain violations to occur.

But there are circumstances in which this ideal is unrealizable, either due to insurmountable constraints such as the impossibility of bringing someone back to life, or due to constraints that although not absolute, are still severe, such as real scarcity of resources of the sort that makes it unfeasible to satisfy, simultaneously, the claims of all victims and of other sectors of society that in fairness, also require the attention of the state.[16]

Let me illustrate with a concrete example some of the problems generated by the prevalent interpretation of adequate compensation. I want to say that it not only fails to provide guidance, but may actually have pernicious effects. I was involved with the Peruvian TRC on the formulation of its reparation plan. Before the final number of persons killed in the conflict was tallied (more than 69,000), the commission estimated that a potential reparations plan would have to provide benefits to 40,000 persons. If the plan aspired to follow the inter-American Court's procedures, assuming that it would give each of them the lower figure typically awarded by the Court (US$150,000), not counting any of the additional services that the Court usually requires, this would consume more than US$6 billion. Now, Peru's total yearly budget is US$9 billion. This is to say that this part of the reparations plan alone would consume two-thirds of the national budget. Clearly, this is completely unfeasible for the country, even if the costs could be spread over a number of years, and even if there had been total political support for the reparations plan (which there was not, for different reasons, including the generalized perception that the plan would give benefits to a large number of people who are deemed not to deserve them, namely former insurgents, people who do not have 'clean hands').

In a case such as this one, it is obvious that to insist on proportional compensation does not provide much guidance. But I made a stronger claim above: I said that to insist on the criteria may have pernicious effects. Why? As the Peruvian TRC discussed its reparations plan, the inter-American Commission and the Court kept deciding cases of torture and disappearances in the country, making the familiar sorts of awards. So the TRC's deliberations were taking place against this background, and this naturally awakened expectations that the reparations plan would do likewise. But it could not. The end result was that there was a very strong probability that given these expectations, whatever the TRC proposed it would have been a huge disappointment. And, given the impact that perceptions concerning reparations have in people's assessment of the success or failure of the *general* work of a truth commission, this is no insignificant matter. In South Africa, for example, the failure to implement the TRC's recommendations on reparations has affected the overall perception of its success, despite the fact that the South African TRC is not at all responsible for the implementation of the plan!

In a case such as this one, the state cannot simply ignore the claims of victims with the argument that there are no resources to cover the corresponding costs. This would be tantamount to acknowledging that it is in no position to sustain a fair regime. The state's responsibility consists in designing a program of reparations of which it might be said that it satisfies conditions of justice, even though its benefits are not the same as those that would be determined by a court resolving infrequent or at least isolated suits. But what is involved in 'satisfying conditions of justice' if one cannot rely on the standard of compensation in proportion to harm?[17]

Before addressing the question directly, it is worth making a preliminary remark. Mere disparities in the awards distributed by courts and by mass programs do not necessarily manifest a flaw, let alone a lack of fairness, in mass programs. For this reason, reparation programs need not to be considered simply as second-best alternatives to judicial procedures. Reparation programs at their best are administrative procedures that, among other things, obviate some of the difficulties and costs associated with litigation. These include long delays, high costs, the need to gather evidence that might withstand close scrutiny (which in some cases may be simply unavailable), the pain associated with cross-examination and with reliving sorrowful events, and finally, the very real risk of a contrary decision, which may prove to be devastating, adding insult to injury. A well-designed reparations program may distribute awards which are lower in absolute terms, but comparatively higher than those granted by courts, especially if the comparison factors in the faster results, lower costs, relaxed standards of evidence, nonadversarial procedures, and virtual certainty that accompanies the administrative nature of a reparations program.

In the second place, it is important to keep in mind that most programs of reparations are designed in the context of a transition to democracy.[18] This, in my mind has an impact on how justice—and the different measures applied to achieve it—should be understood. There are three specific aims, closely related to the notion of justice, but particularly salient during times of transition, that I think can help structure an answer to the question of what is fair in terms of reparations. These aims are simultaneously necessary conditions and consequences of justice.

7.2.3. Recognition

One of the main aims of transitional justice is to return (or, in some cases to establish anew) the status of citizens to individuals. To the extent that a reparations program aims to contribute to the achievement of justice, and that recognition is both a condition and a consequence of justice, this links reparations and recognition. In order to recognize individuals as citizens it is necessary to recognize them as *individuals* first. That is to say, it is necessary to recognize them not only as members of groups (as important as this might be), but also as irreplaceable and unsubstitutable human beings. Citizenship in a constitutional democracy is a condition that individuals grant to one another, each one of whom is conceived as having value on his or her own.

One of the ways of recognizing another person as an individual, in addition to recognizing the peculiarities of his or her chosen form of life (which is to recognize the person's *agency*) is to recognize the ways in which the person is affected by the environment, that is, to recognize that the person is not only the *subject* of his or her own actions, but the *object* of the actions of others. In other words, there is a form of injustice that consists, not in illegitimately preventing her from exercising her agency through, say, the deprivation of liberty, but that consists in depriving her of the sort of consideration which is owed to whoever is negatively and severely affected by the actions of others. A minimum condition for the attribution of moral standing, without which individuals cannot be recognized as such, is the acknowledgment that my actions impinge on them. The denial of this sort of standing, of this sort of consideration, reveals clearly that I have failed to recognize that I am dealing with individuals.[19]

As if this were not enough, in a constitutional democracy it matters that members recognize one another not only as individuals, but also as *citizens*. To withhold from victims the type of consideration we are talking about makes the mutual attribution of this status impossible. In a democracy, citizenship is a condition that rests on the equality of rights of those who enjoy such status. And this equality of rights determines that those whose rights have been violated deserve special treatment, treatment that tends toward the reestablishment of the conditions of equality.

From my standpoint, the various transitional mechanisms can be usefully seen through the lens of recognition. That is, all of them can be interpreted as efforts to institutionalize the recognition of individuals as citizens with equal rights. Thus, criminal justice can be interpreted as an attempt to reestablish equality between the criminal and his or her victim, after the criminal severed that relationship with an act that suggested his superiority over the victim.[20] Truth telling provides recognition in ways that are perfectly familiar, and which are still probably best articulated by the old difference proposed by Nagel between knowledge and acknowledgment, when he argued that although truth commissions rarely disclose facts that were previously unknown, they still make an indispensable contribution in acknowledging these facts.[21] The acknowledgment is important, precisely, because it constitutes a form of recognizing the significance and value of persons—again, as individuals, as citizens, and as victims. Finally, institutional reform is guided by the ideal of guaranteeing the conditions under which citizens can relate to one another and to the authorities as equals.

The exact way in which reparations contribute to justice is complex. On the one hand, it is one aspect of the close relationship that binds the different elements of transitional justice together, and specifically, of the ways in which reparations complement other transitional justice processes. Let me illustrate. Truth telling, in the absence of reparations, can be seen by victims as an empty gesture, as cheap talk. The relation holds in the opposite direction as well: reparations in the absence of truth telling can be seen by beneficiaries as the attempt, on the part of the state, to buy the silence or acquiescence of victims and their families, turning the benefits into 'blood money'. The same tight and bidirectional relationship may be observed between reparations and institutional reform, since a democratic reform that is not accompanied by any attempt to dignify citizens that were victimized can hardly be understood. By the same token, reparative benefits in the absence of reforms that diminish the probability of the repetition of violence are nothing more than payments whose utility and furthermore legitimacy are questionable. Finally, the same bidirectional relationship links criminal justice and reparations: from the standpoint of victims, especially once a possible moment of satisfaction derived from the punishment of perpetrators has passed, the punishment of a few perpetrators, without any effective effort to positively redress victims could be easily seen by victims as a form of more or less inconsequential revanchism. In summary, reparations contribute to justice not only because they complement transitional justice measures generally, but because they do so in a particular way, namely by helping to keep those other measures from fading into irrelevance for most victims.

On the other hand, reparations can play this 'supportive role' precisely because they constitute, in themselves, a form of recognition. They are, in a sense, the material form of the recognition *owed* to fellow citizens whose fundamental rights have been violated.

7.2.4. Civic Trust

Another legitimate aim of a program of reparations as an instrument of justice is the formation or the restoration of trust among citizens.

Needless to say, whether the hypothesis is reasonable, and testable, depends on what 'civic trust' means. Thus, some explanation is in order. First, let us start with a broad understanding of trust: trust in general, as a disposition that mediates social interactions, 'is an alternative to vigilance and reliance on the threat of sanctions, [and] trustworthiness . . . an alternative to constant watching to see what one can and cannot get away with, to recurrent recalculations of costs and benefits'.[22]

Now, the term 'civic' in civic trust, I understand basically as a limiting qualifier. In other words, my focus will be not on the sort of thick trust that develops among intimates, a disposition which is based on deep familiarity, long-term and repeated interactions, and which is therefore relatively (but only relatively) resistant to disappointment and also relatively (but only relatively) open to reconstruction. Civic trust, rather, I take to be the sort of disposition that can develop among citizens who are strangers to one another, and who are members of the same community only in the sense in which they are fellow members of the same *political* community. Thicker forms of trust can develop among members of other communities, even some large-scale ones, such as religious and in some circumstances, ethnic groups, but these thicker forms, usually accompanied by bonds of solidarity, will not be the focus of my concern. I have a more modest phenomenon in mind. If we take as one further general description of trust the notion that it implies the 'presumption of generally benign or at least nonhostile intentions on the part of partners in interaction'[23], *civic* trust I take to be best (although not exhaustively or exclusively) described by the second, rather than the first, characterization in this description. Fellow citizens need not attribute to one another substantively benign intentions. For the most part, in complex societies, we can get by *as citizens* attributing to one another merely nonhostile intentions. In contrast to trust among intimates, then, civic trust is thin, brittle, and even more difficult to rebuild than in personal relations.

Just as recognition, civic trust is at one and the same time a condition and a consequence of justice. There are myriad ways in which a legal system relies on the trust of citizens. At the broadest level, a legal system works only on the basis of the citizens' generalized norm-compliance. In other words, the legal system can cope with norm-breaking behavior only when it is exceptional. This means that most social interactions are not directly mediated by law, but rather, at some level, by trust between citizens. Closer to home, however, all legal systems rely not just in the trust that citizens have toward one another but on the trust that they have in the systems themselves. In the absence of total(itarian) surveillance, criminal legal systems must rely on the citizens' willingness to report both crimes that they witness and crimes that they suffer.[24] And this willingness to report, of course, rests on their trust that the system will reliably produce the expected outcomes. This is actually a complex sort of trust: in police investigations, in the efficiency of the court systems, in the honesty of judges, in the independence of the judiciary (and therefore on the executive's willingness to protect and promote that independence), in the at least minimal wisdom of the legislature, and in the strictness (but perhaps also the simultaneous humaneness) of the prison system, etc. Needless to say, each of these objects of trust can be further analyzed.

On the other hand, it is not just that legal systems rely on the trust of citizens both between themselves and in the system itself. Legal systems, when they operate well, also catalyze trust, once again, both among citizens themselves, and in the system itself. Indeed, Rawls takes the rule of law's ability to generate social trust—which he understands in terms of the reliability of expectations—as a definitional aspect of the rule of law:

> A legal system is a coercive order of public rules addressed to rational persons for the purpose of regulating their conduct and providing the framework for social cooperation. When these rules are just they establish a basis for legitimate expectations. They constitute grounds upon which persons can *rely on one another* and rightly object when their expectations are not fulfilled.[25]

To the extent that law helps to stabilize expectations, and that it helps to diminish the risks involved in trusting others, especially strangers, it contributes to the generation of trust among citizens.

As for the catalytic role of law in generating trust in legal institutions, the underlying argument should be clear: legal institutions, insofar as they are reliable, provide further reasons for citizens to rely on them for the resolution of their conflicts. This simply follows from the fact that trust is something that is earned, rather than arbitrarily bestowed, and this is true just as much for institutions as it is for individuals. The easier way of seeing this is by noticing attitudes toward law in societies where the legal system is perceived as inaccessible or otherwise unreliable.

The fundamental point, of course, is to clarify the relationship between reparations and civic trust. Again, for victims, reparations constitute a manifestation of the seriousness of the state and of their fellow citizens in their efforts to reestablish relations of equality and respect. In the absence of reparations, victims will always have reasons to suspect that even if the other transitional mechanisms are applied with some degree of sincerity, the 'new' democratic society is one that is being constructed on their shoulders, ignoring their justified claims. By contrast, if even under conditions of scarcity funds are allocated for former victims, a strong message is sent to them and others about their (perhaps new) inclusion in the political community. Former victims of abuse are given a material manifestation of the fact that they are now living among a group of fellow citizens and under institutions that aspire to be trustworthy. Reparations, in summary, can be seen as a method to achieve one of the aims of a just state, namely inclusiveness, in the sense that all citizens are equal participants in a common political project.

7.2.5. Solidarity

Finally, another legitimate aim of a program of reparations, considered once again as one of the forms of promoting justice, may be the strengthening or the generation of another attitude which—like recognition and civic trust—is also a condition and a consequence of justice. This is the attitude of social solidarity.

Just as civic trust, solidarity also comes in different types and degrees. Social solidarity is the type of empathy characteristic of those who have the disposition and the willingness to put themselves in the place of others. That this attitude is a condition of justice may be seen in the following way: an impartial perspective, an indispensable requisite of justice, is not achievable unless the person that judges is prepared to assume the place of the contesting parties. Moreover, in a democratic system which distinguishes legitimacy from mere balances of power, the only way to assure that the legitimacy of a law has been attained is by making sure that the law incorporates the interests of all that are affected by it. And this implies having an interest in the interests of others.[26] This is, precisely, what social solidarity is.

Reparations can be seen as an expression of this type of interest, and, at the same time, as generators of this form of solidarity. In societies divided and stratified by the differences between the urban and the rural, by ethnic, cultural, class, and gender factors, reparations manifest the interest of the traditionally most advantaged in the interests of the least favored. Although it cannot be assumed that the former will immediately support a reparations program, this is a point at which the relations between reparations and other transitional mechanisms, especially truth telling, may play an important role, for historical clarification can awaken empathy with victims. On the other hand, to the extent that victims feel that a new 'social contract' in which their dignity and their interests are amply recognized is being offered, they will have reasons to take an interest in common interests, contributing in this way to the strengthening of the basis of a just society.

Notice, to conclude this section, three additional advantages of thinking about the aims of reparations in these explicitly political terms rather than in the more judicial terms of compensation in proportion to harm: first, this way of thinking about reparations, although based on principled normative considerations, permits crafting reparations in a way that attends contextual features in two important senses: as I have pointed out before, it suits the peculiarities and the needs of transitional situations, taking advantage of the aspects of such contexts that call for a 'constitutional moment'. However, it is not just that in thinking about the aims of reparations in terms of recognition and the reconstitution of civic trust and social solidarity important transitional goals are explicitly assumed as guides for the design of an important transitional tool, thereby helping to guarantee the success of both the reparations program and the transitional policy, but that taking these as the main goals of the reparations program gives it a beneficial forward-looking character. One of the main sources of dissatisfaction with most reparations awards is the fact that beneficiaries frequently consider them insufficient compensation. In this, they are usually correct, independently of the magnitude of the award, for reasons that have to do with the difficulty—and ultimately, the impossibility—of quantifying great harm; there is no amount of money that can make up for the loss of a parent, a child, a spouse. There is no amount of money that can adequately compensate for the nightmare and the trauma of torture. In my view, reparation programs, not least because of the financial difficulties that arise in cases with massive numbers of claimants, should not even try, and should always avoid using the vocabulary of proportional compensation. There should not be anything in a reparation program that invites either their designers, or their beneficiaries, to interpret them as an effort to put a price on the life of victims or on the experiences of horror. Rather, they should be interpreted as making a contribution to the quality of life of survivors. Thinking about reparations in terms of recognition and of the promotion of civic trust and social solidarity invite the assumption of this forward-looking perspective.

Second, there is another sense in which taking the more political aims of granting recognition, and promoting civic trust and social solidarity allows for a healthy form of contextualism: for example, what, in a given society is sufficient to provide adequate recognition to victims is largely a matter of context. What US citizens expect by way of recognition may differ widely from what the potential beneficiaries in different contexts may expect. And satisfying those different expectations, despite their differences, is obviously not a bad thing.

Another advantage of thinking about reparations in explicitly political terms, rather than in terms of judicial considerations is that it places another thorny issue in the design of reparations programs in its proper context. I am talking about the question of finances. A political perspective on reparations introduces some clarity in discussions about financing strategies. Basically, this happens because it takes the question of finances out of the exclusive domain of technicians and lawyers and returns it where it should properly lie, namely, in the domain of competing social priorities. Most governments respond to recommendations concerning reparations with one or two responses. Either 'reparations are too expensive and we cannot afford them', or, 'if we repair, let us do it collectively'. To the first response, the adequate reaction is to point out that questions about what can and cannot be afforded at public expense are always questions about priorities. Perhaps, unless there is a budget surplus, nothing can be afforded leaving everything else untouched. The question is about what is deemed urgent, and this is always a matter of politics.[27] To the second response, which usually accompanies the preference of governments for folding reparations into development programs, the proper reaction is to point out that the bias in favor of the collective is nothing more than that; the collective can be quite expensive, more expensive than the individual (in fact, given the generally dismal record of development programs, these, in particular can be very expensive).[28]

7.3. STRUCTURAL CONSIDERATIONS

7.3.1. Integrity or Coherence

Up to this point I have said virtually nothing about the characteristics of reparations programs. Part of the reason is that, needless to say, I do not think that their design follows deductively from matters of principle. Nevertheless, I am prepared to make two general points.

The first is a remark about a desirable characteristic that I think all programs should have. Reparations programs should display what I call integrity or coherence, which I analyze into two different dimensions, internal and external. *External* coherence expresses the requirement that the reparations program be designed in such a way as to bear a close relationship with the other transitional mechanisms, that is, with criminal justice, truth telling, and institutional reform. This requirement is both pragmatic and conceptual. The relationship increases the likelihood that each of these mechanisms be perceived as successful (despite the inevitable limitations that accompany each of them), and, more importantly, that the transitional efforts, on the whole, satisfy the expectations of citizens. But beyond this pragmatic advantage, it may be argued (although I will not spell out the argument here but in another document), that the requirement flows from the relations of complementarity between the mechanisms that I sketched before.

But reparation programs ought to display integrity or coherence in another dimension: a program of reparations, if it is to attain its proper goals, must always be a complex program that distributes different benefits, and the different components of the plan ought to be mutually coherent. That is, the program ought to be *internally* coherent. Most reparations programs distribute more than one kind of benefit. These may include symbolic as well as material reparations, and each of these categories may include different measures and be distributed individually or collectively. Obviously, in order to reach the desired aims, it is important that benefits be part of a plan whose elements internally support one another.

The second set of points about the structure of reparations programs that can be safely made from a relatively abstract perspective is the following. Although the final details of a program for a particular country will depend on heeding many contextual features, the trade-offs between different measures can be clarified in very general terms. So although I do not think that theorists can properly get in the business of writing up blueprints of such programs—at least not in their capacity of mere theorists—there is a great deal of work that can be done in the clarification of the advantages and disadvantages that may accompany different design choices. The following scheme illustrates the basic orientation:

1. *Symbolic Measures*
   (*a*) *Individual* (personal letters of apology, copies of Truth Commission reports, proper burial for the victims, etc.)
      (i) *Advantages*
         - Constitute a way to show respect for individuals.
         - Express recognition for the harm suffered.
         - Low cost.
      (ii) *Disadvantages*
         - May create the impression that by themselves they constitute sufficient reparations for the victims.
   (*b*) *Collective* (public acts of atonement, commemorative days, establishment of museums, changing of street names and other public places, etc.)
      (i) *Advantages*
         - Promote the development of:
           —Collective memory;
           —Social solidarity; and
           —A critical stance toward, and oversight of, State institutions.
      (ii) *Disadvantages*
         - May be socially divisive.
         - In societies or social sectors with a proclivity toward feeling victimized, this feeling may be heightened.

- May create the impression that they alone constitute sufficient reparations for the victims.

2. *Service Packages*
   (*a*) Service packages may include medical, educational, and housing assistance, etc.
   (i) *Advantages*
   - Satisfy real needs.
   - May have a positive effect in terms of equal treatment.
   - May be cost effective if already existing institutions are used.
   - May stimulate the development of social institutions.

   (ii) *Disadvantages*
   - Do not maximize personal autonomy.
   - May reflect paternalistic attitudes.
   - Quality of benefits will depend on the services provided by current institutions.
   - The more the program concentrates on a basic service package, the less force the reparations will have, as citizens will naturally think that the benefits being distributed are ones they have a right to as citizens, not as victims.

3. *Individual Grants*
   (*a*) *Advantages*
   - Respect personal autonomy.
   - Satisfy perceived needs and preferences.
   - Promote the recognition of individuals.
   - May improve the quality of life for the beneficiaries.
   - May be easier to administer than alternative distribution methods.

   (*b*) *Disadvantages*
   - If they are perceived solely as a way of quantifying the harm, they will always be viewed as unsatisfactory and inadequate.
   - If the payments fall under a certain level, they will not significantly affect the quality of life of the victims.
   - This method of distributing benefits presupposes a certain institutional structure. (The payments can satisfy needs only if institutions exist to 'sell' the services that citizens wish to purchase.)
   - If they are not made within a comprehensive framework of reparations, these measures may be viewed as a way to 'buy' the silence and acquiescence of the victims.
   - Politically difficult to bring about, as the payments would compete with other urgently needed programs, may be costly, and may be controversial as they would probably include ex-combatants from both sides as beneficiaries.

There are those who think that reparations can also take the shape of development programs. I do not agree with that option, but to complete the analysis, the following may be said.

4. *Development and Social Investment*
   (*a*) *Apparent Advantages*
   - Gives the appearance of being directed toward the underlying causes of the violence.
   - Would appear to allow due recognition to be given to entire communities.
   - Gives the impression of making it possible to reach goals of justice as well as development.
   - Politically attractive.

   (*b*) *Disadvantages*
   - Has very low reparative capacity, as the development measures are too inclusive (are not directed toward the victims) and they are normally focused on basic and urgent needs, which make the beneficiaries perceive them as a matter of right and not as a response to their situation as a victim.
   - In places characterized by a fragmented citizenry, these measures do nothing to promote respect for individuals rather than as members of marginal groups.
   - Uncertain success: development programs are complex and long-term programs. This threatens the success of the institutions responsible for making recommendations regarding reparations, which may lead to questions regarding the seriousness of the transitional measures in general.
   - Development plans easily become the victims of partisan politics.

In principle, there is no conflict at all between the distribution of symbolic and material reparations. In fact, ideally, these benefits can lend mutual support to each other, something that will be especially important in contexts characterized by scarce resources, where symbolic reparations will surely play a particularly visible role. Nor is there any conflict at all, in principle, between individual and collective measures. As long as there is a substantial individual component, the exact balance between the two kinds of measures should be established taking into consideration, among other factors, the kind of violence sought to be redressed. In those places where the violence was predominantly collective, it makes sense to design a program that also places special emphasis on these kinds of methods.

Having said this, it should be obvious from considerations under point (4), above, that I am skeptical of the effort to turn a program of reparations into the means of solving structural problems of poverty and inequality.

Strictly speaking, a development program is not a program of reparations. In fact, development programs have a very low reparative capacity, for they do not target victims specifically, and what they normally try to achieve is to satisfy basic and urgent needs, which makes their beneficiaries perceive such programs, correctly, as ones that distribute goods to which they have rights as citizens, and not necessarily as victims. In the second place, development programs are affected by a very high degree of uncertainty, for development aims are both complex and long-term. This threatens the success of the institutions responsible for making recommendations concerning reparations, and may raise questions about the seriousness of the transitional process in general. Given the importance of reparations in a transitional process, to propose a program with a very uncertain or very extended horizon of success could generate questions about the commitment to democratic renewal.

Here it is worth distinguishing between reparations in their strict sense, and the reparative effects of other programs. Development, just as criminal justice, for example, may have reparative effects. Nevertheless, this does not make either of them part of the domain of responsibility of those who design programs of reparation. Naturally, we may reiterate here that the latter must cohere with other aspects of the transitional policy. That is to say, the program must be internally and externally coherent, and it must avoid reproducing and perpetuating unjust social structures. In the last analysis, a transitional government in a poor country will most likely propose a development plan, and ideally, the program of reparations must also cohere with that plan. But the point I have emphasized is that it is important to set boundaries of responsibilities between different policies, for strictly speaking, the responsibilities of a program of reparations are not the same as that of a development or social investment plan.

7.4. CONCLUSION

My work on reparations takes as its starting point the difference between the requirements of fairness in isolated cases, versus those requirements in the design of massive programs. It has tried to spell out both some legitimate aims and the limitations of reparations programs. It has emphasized the political nature of reparations programs. It has insisted on the importance of individual reparations, allowing, all the while that there are situations in which a collective dimension is perfectly proper. It has defended both the differentiation of benefits and the need for both external and internal coherence.

One of the incidental aims of my chapter, as I hope it has become obvious, is to show that reparations is a topic to which we, political theorists, could actually make an important contribution. I say this for two main reasons: first, this is an area that suffers from a great deal of semantic disorder. The concept of reparations itself, even if one holds the view that it is impossible to draw hard and fast borders between concepts, is still one that could be neatened up quite a bit. This, I take it, is one of the tasks of political philosophy. Second, as all issues having to do with public policy, reparations is a topic that involves substantive normative considerations. Moreover, given that reparations are supposed to make up for past wrongs, that the issue normally (although not always cf. Germany) arises in contexts of great scarcity, and that the success or failure of reparations programs depends at least in part on whether they satisfy the *normative* expectations of beneficiaries and others, discussions about reparations are such that connections with questions of justice are inevitable. Hence, even more opportunities for our contributing to the area. It is always nice to know that (sometimes despite ourselves) our work need not be totally irrelevant in the social world.

NOTES

1. It is not just transitional societies that are considering or have actually implemented programs of reparations. Many nontransitional societies are dealing with the issue. A recent 'best seller' on the topic talks about 'a new international morality' characterized by 'the willingness of the perpetrators to engage and accommodate the victims' demands'. What the author finds especially noteworthy about some of these cases is that they 'involve no coercion but rather evolve from the perpetrators' willingness to acknowledge, and choice to compensate, their victims or their descendants' (Barkan (2000: ix).
2. See, e.g. van Boven (1983). More recent updates have not changed the categories.
3. In my chapter in Villa-Vicenzio and Doxtader (forthcoming), however, I distinguish between 'reparations efforts' and reparations programs more precisely.
4. Except, of course, when dealing with mass claims. There are interesting parallels between mass claims and reparations programs, including a similar shift in the understanding of what is fair to particular claimants. I cannot pursue the parallels here.
5. When it is claimed that reparations are part of a political project it is assumed that the 'political' refers to, among other things, the (ideally deliberative) exercise of power in the distribution of public goods and benefits for the good of all, rather than to the partisan exercise of power for the good of a few. A strong

defender of the constitutive role of truth commissions and their recommendations is André du Toit (2001).

6. See Tomuschat (1999).
7. This explains some of my initial reservations concerning the tendency to juridify discussions about reparations. The discussion about reparations for African Americans in the United States is part of a long series that demonstrates the increasing tendency to juridify political issues and not just in that country. Of course, the motivation to do so is unobjectionable, especially considering the obstacles that would have to be overcome in order to gain a political solution to this issue. Nevertheless, the case both illustrates and entrenches what in the end is a suspicious attitude about politics. The future of democracy looks grim indeed—for this reason also.
8. Universal Declaration of Human Rights, UN Doc. A/RES/217A (III) of December 10, 1948.
9. American Convention on Human Rights, O.A.S. Treaty Series No. 36, 1144 U.N.T.S 123 entered into force July 18, 1978, reprinted in *Basic Documents Pertaining to Human Rights in the Inter-American System*, OEA/Ser.L.V/II.82 doc.6 rev.1 at 25 (1992).
10. International Covenant on Civil and Political Rights, UN Doc. A/RES/2200A (XXI) of December 16, 1966.
11. Convention against Torture and Other Cruel, Inhuman or Degrading Treatment or Punishment, UN Doc. A/RES/39/46 of December 10, 1984.
12. The European Convention on Human Rights, Council of Europe, Rome November 4, 1950.
13. For a useful but under-theorized survey, see Shelton (1999).
14. Rodríguez Rescia (1999: 594).
15. See the following cases: *El Amparo, Panel Blanca, Castillo Paéz, Niños de la Calle, Ricardo Baena, Bámaca Velásquez, Barrios Altos*. In *Neira Alegria* the Court decided to use the average of Latin American wages, considering the Peruvian minimum wage too low.
16. This elides another very real problem, namely, the quantification of harm. The ideal of making victims whole assumes harms can be measured in some reliable way. It should be obvious that this is not so easy. To illustrate, one of the relevant questions here is how to assign values to different sorts of harms: what is more 'costly': the loss of a limb, or of an eye, e.g. or the psychological trauma of torture? How can the relative costs of physical and psychological harms be compared? And those stemming from the loss of a relative? How can these 'costs' be sensibly assessed? An additional challenge arises from difficulties stemming from interpersonal comparisons. This challenge comes about, ultimately, because there is a fundamental difference between losses and harms; two persons who suffer the same loss are not necessarily equally harmed, for harms depend, to some degree on the individual's reactions to circumstances. e.g. not everyone who loses a hand reacts in the same way. Even if having both hands is equally important for two persons—say, because both are manual

laborers—it is possible that the experience will sink one of them into depression, while the other may live the experience as a challenge, a painful one of course, but one that she is determined to overcome. Finally, in order to show that even seemingly precise reparations based on calculations of past income and earning potential have some degree of arbitrariness to them, consider that they must rely both on generalizations and on questionable assumptions; the generalization, of course, refers to calculations about average projected incomes for different professions, which are notoriously sensitive to, e.g. geographical location. The most questionable assumption refers to the assumption that the world remains in a steady state; when a lifetime income is calculated, a whole host of assumptions is made, including the assumption that there will be no sharp economic cycles, that the demand for professionals in a given career will remain steady, that the person in question would not have died before the expected average age, that she or he would not have become an alcoholic, a failure, etc. I cannot deal with these difficulties here. But they are certainly worth flagging. In her chapter in this volume, Debra Satz illustrates the last set of complications.

17. Some people defend the idea that for massive cases, at least, international law should not try to set criteria for determining *the size of awards*, but rather criteria should be selected that would have to be satisfied by the processes used to articulate the criteria for determining the size of awards. More concretely, the idea is to give some impetus to deliberative, consultative processes at the national level, processes that would lead to the choice of awards levels. This presumably, would consist mainly in assuring that victims and victim groups have a say in the determination of award levels. See, e.g. Heidi Rombouts, 'Reparation for Victims of Human Rights Violations: A Socio-Political Approach' (presented at the Expert Seminar on Reparation for Victims of Gross and Systematic Human Rights Violations in the Context of Political Transitions, Katholieke Universteit, Leuven, Belgium, March 10, 2002). In general, I am supportive of this idea, but with the following cautionary note. In the end, and for reasons that are very easy to understand, victims will always want more benefits. Although I do not mean this derogatorily at all, victim groups will in the end behave like other interest groups—this one with a cause, that is particularly compelling to me. In order for this proposal to make sense, one would have to include victim groups not just in discussions about the reparations plan, but about the national budget, so that they have an adequate perception of the other legitimate projects (such as health, education, justice, and development, to mention only a few) reparations always competes with.
18. There are of course important exceptions. Some so-called 'well-established democracies' have instituted reparations programs. These include the United States (for Japanese American internees during World War II), Canada (for mistreatment of indigenous groups), Australia (for Aborigines), etc.
19. See Onora O'Neill's attractive account of moral standing *Towards Justice and Virtue* (1996: ch. 4).

20. See Hampton (1981, 1991), as well as her essays in Murphy and Hampton (1988).
21. Thomas Nagel argues that there is 'a difference between knowledge and *ac*knowledgment. It is what happens and can only happen to knowledge when it becomes officially sanctioned, when it is made part of the public cognitive scene'. Quoted in Wescheler (1989).
22. Annette Baier, 'Trust and its Vulnerabilities' *Moral Prejudices* (1994: 133).
23. Offe (1999: 44).
24. From the perspective of well-ordered societies, it is hard to conceive of circumstances in which people would not bother reporting even serious crimes like murder. But this indeed happens. In Colombia, e.g. more than 35% of murders are never even reported. See Rubio (1999).
25. Rawls (1972: 235). My emphasis.
26. See Habermas (1990), and Rehg (1994).
27. Perhaps the best illustration of this point comes from South Africa where efforts to restart the stalled discussions of reparations at one point were taking place with the government arguing that there was no money for the program while at the same time, it was proposing the purchase of two new submarines. See CSVR Report XXX.
28. Of course, placing reparations in the political arena rather than in the judicial sphere puts a premium on an effective strategy of effective coalition building in favor of reparations.

8

Countering the Wrongs of the Past: The Role of Compensation[1]

Debra Satz

8.1. INTRODUCTION

Demands for repair can sound in different registers. Think of a mundane case of harm, concerning harm to one person's property, occurring in the present. If A intentionally damages B's car, B can ask A: to provide monetary compensation; to restore (if possible) her car to its undamaged state; to apologize or perhaps even to make a public acknowledgment of his responsibility. B can seek to have A prosecuted under law for his acts, seek mediation, or attempt to settle things on her own without third-party involvement. What B asks of A can reflect what B cares about, what she thinks she is likely to receive, or what she thinks she is owed. Different individuals in the same circumstances as B might ask for and accept different measures of repair. And different individuals in the same circumstances as A might respond to these demands in different ways.

This example involves a simple case of a single individual who suffers damage in the present to her property from a single individual who is directly (and intentionally) responsible. But even here, demands for repair can vary, and responses that might be appropriate in one situation might not be appropriate in another. Varying the relations between A and B, for example, might make apology seem especially important in one case, and monetary compensation sufficient in another. If through negligence I break my son's favorite toy, it will seem heartless to offer him its cash equivalent while showing him absolutely no remorse or regret. In other cases it can be difficult to know, when you have hurt someone, what response to his pain is appropriate, and what, if anything, you can and should do if that response fails to repair.[2]

It is not easy to move from this simple example to the large-scale contexts in which demands for repair have recently been made: the contexts of Majdanek and Treblinka, the disappeared of Argentina and victims of Pinochet, the large-scale expropriations of Eastern Europe, the destruction of Aboriginal homelands, American slavery and Jim Crow. It is not only that these large-scale evils are difficult to contemplate and to understand, and that they have caused losses that seem impossible to repair, it is also that they extend into the past and encompass many victims and perpetrators who are no longer alive. How can repair actually occur in these contexts?

Efforts to respond to and repair the wrongs of the past raise both practical and philosophical concerns. Such concerns include not only the questions related to identifying those who are the appropriate recipients of reparation and those who are obligated to bear the costs, but also questions about the appropriate goal of programs aimed at countering wrongs (is it compensation, reconciliation, or punishment, for example) and the best means for meeting that goal (is it money, apology, land redistribution, changes in law, or something else altogether?) Is there even a single best form, or should the form vary from case to case and, if so, is there any basis for choosing between forms of remedy?

In this chapter, I explore the role of compensation in repairing historical wrongs. I focus on the standard welfare economist's view of compensation since this seems to be the one that is most often appealed to in philosophical and legal discussions of compensation. Furthermore, the default position in such discussions, as in American tort law, is that cash is the best form of compensation, a view that accords well with the economic conception of compensation. But while cash compensation is a part of many claims of reparative justice, victims often focus on other demands. Are there good reasons for preferring other responses to historical wrongs, and if so, what are those reasons? What role, if any, should compensation play in countering the wrongs of the past?

8.2. COUNTERING WRONGS IN TERMS OF COMPENSATION

Victims of grave injustices or their descendants sometimes argue for compensation for the losses that they have suffered. Indeed, reparations in the form of financial compensation have been a part of many programs in which states are trying to remedy past harms.[3] In this section, I examine a common meaning of 'compensation'. However, I want to register two initial caveats to the idea of repair understood in terms of compensation. First, victims of large-scale injustices most often seek compensation as part of a larger set of goals. These include the goals of coming to terms with their pasts, receiving acknowledgment of the harms that were done to them, attempting to regain a way of life that was lost, and punishing the perpetrators. Second, the societies involved in reparative efforts also usually have larger goals than simply compensating losses. This is in part because projects of repair have a special place in societies undergoing transitions to democracy. Compensation, in this context, is the most tangible manifestation of the efforts of the new state to remedy the harms that these victims have suffered, and to reinstill a sense of trust and social solidarity. Compensation claims can also arise between states, as in the recent cases before the International Court of Justice. In these cases, states are also seeking compliance with international rules and a cessation of violations.[4] These caveats are meant to underscore the fact that compensation does not usually stand alone as a means of repair and that compensatory demands themselves may involve aims of retribution or deterrence.

How should we understand the term compensation? The term is familiarly seen as a form of payment for a loss or disadvantage. Judith Thomson develops the idea that compensation is a debt we owe someone when we have wronged him, a way of making up for what we have done.[5] This debt can be viewed in cash terms, or at least in terms of material goods, the provision of which is seen as making up for some loss of goods that has occurred by providing other goods in the same or another category. It can also be understood in terms of less tangible goods such as apology and the public expression of responsibility.[6] Restitution is often defined as a subcategory of compensation where the good to be made up is precisely the good that was lost.[7]

Unfortunately, the idea of 'making up for' a loss is imprecise, especially if we consider the cases in which restitution is impossible.

Welfare economists give us a more tractable interpretation of compensation: agent X compensates agent Y for his loss if and only if receiving this compensation leaves Y at least as high on an indifference curve as he would have been without receiving it but also without suffering the loss.[8] On this view, an agent is completely compensated for a loss when he is indifferent between his life as it was before the loss and his life as it is now after the loss but with additional goods. The agent has no reason to prefer his past situation before his losses to his current situation after the loss has occurred. More expansively, this idea of compensation can be applied to the agent's overall lifetime satisfaction: an agent is completely compensated when he receives the same lifetime sum of happiness that he could have expected to receive given his circumstances before experiencing the loss.

The goal of this view of compensation might be accomplished in any number of ways, although money is frequently the form such compensation takes, since money can be directed to the satisfaction of a wide range of an agent's preferences and satisfactions. Money is, or appears to be, an all-purpose means.[9]

This way of understanding compensation is only one of several possibilities: as I mentioned, understanding compensation in terms of restitution is another. Compensation as restitution is on the other end of the continuum from the economic idea of compensation as establishing an equal level of preference satisfaction because in the case of restitution there is no equivalent for the loss; only the restoration of the very thing lost will accomplish the work of repair. Between these polar points, we can also imagine views of compensation that restrict to some degree the scope of either the aim or means of compensation. For example, affirmative action has been defended as a means for making up for the educational opportunities (and not for other losses) that African Americans were previously denied.

While those who have different understandings of the appropriate goals of or means for compensation may converge on a specific policy proposal, they will have very different rationales. Someone who cares only about returning victims to a prior level of satisfaction might eschew money as a means of compensation in favor of an in-kind payment, but she will have only contingent reasons for preferring the in-kind payment. For example, Eric Posner and Adrian Vermeule argue that a payment of cash compensation to members of a Native American tribe who suffer from high rates of alcoholism, due largely to the original injustices suffered by the tribe, might serve only to exacerbate the effects of those injustices.[10]

There are three important points to note about what I am calling the economic view of compensation. First, it seems to presuppose a theory in which the only thing that matters (at least from the standpoint of public policy) is overall preference satisfaction: compensation aims to render an individual as satisfied after as before a loss. Second, it suggests that all such satisfactions can be put on a single scale and aggregated into an overall utility function. Third and finally, it suggests that the basis of a claim to compensation arises from the losses to a person's level of satisfaction, and not the need to redress a particular wrong.

The goal of compensation understood in this sense appears reasonable in many contexts, and it is not my point to argue against it in all circumstances. Still, there are contexts in which people find compensation of this sort to be partly or wholly inappropriate. Before turning to the cases of historical injustices, I want to consider the three features of this view of compensation to see if we can understand why this is so.

8.2.1. Compensation as Equal Preference Satisfaction

Consider the following example, which I adapt from a chapter by Jo Wolff.[11] African American children in the United States receive, on average, an education inferior to whites. This inferior education effectively excludes many of them from even the possibility of attending a selective four-year college. It is a reasonable assumption that under more just social circumstances many of these children would have had a much better chance of attending a good university. Most of us would agree, further, that it is unfair that such children did not have such a chance. At the very least, such unequal chances violate the American dream. Suppose that we conclude that children who were effectively excluded from higher education, on the basis of their inferior education as children, now have a claim as adults to some form of redress. What form should this redress take?

Imagine a proposal to offer all African American children who have attended inferior schools when they reach the age at which they would have graduated university, a lump sum cash payment. Imagine further that the African American adults to whom this payment was made would be satisfied with this payment and that society was willing to go on making such payments in compensation for its unequal schooling.

It is doubtful that many of us would feel that this payment really 'made up for' the losses that these young adults suffered. Nor would we think that it was an appropriate response to the initial (and continuing) injustice. Why?

First, we might doubt that the uneducated adult really knows what he has missed by not attending college. Like John Stuart Mill, we might be tempted by the thought that the value of certain goods can only be grasped through experiencing those goods. People's preferences reflect their experiences. Further, using preferences as a basis of compensation in cases where people have little opportunity could lead to too little compensation since many people adjust their desires to their opportunities (the problem of adaptive preferences).

Second, we might reflect on what it is a person loses when she receives an inferior education. On our list would undoubtedly be future earnings, and the chance to pursue many high-paying and interesting career options that are only possible for someone with a good education. But we would likely also include the chance of a person to develop her capabilities.[12] The development of a person's capabilities can enrich the whole of her life. It changes the way she thinks about herself and perhaps even the way she thinks, enabling her to make her choices in a more informed way. This development of a person's capabilities may be valued for its income earning dimensions, but such development is also valued by people on independent grounds.

A third and perhaps a deeper reason for rejecting this proposal is that we might think that by focusing only on the losses to an individual's level of satisfaction, the proposal fails to counter the central wrong: society's objectionable norms and practices that led to so few African American children attending selective colleges. Improvements in a person's subjective preferences do not make up for disadvantages that have been publicly and unjustly imposed on them. If a person finds happiness in her life despite being oppressed by others, this hardly serves to justify (or undo, or otherwise erase) the oppression.

In the case of cash compensation to African Americans who have been effectively excluded from higher education, the form of remedy in terms of financial compensation seems jarring because it does not match the type of harm it is being used to counter, the unjust foreshortening of their opportunities for development. This is also the reason why many people view cash compensation for past injustices to African Americans as misguided.[13] Nevertheless, as I will discuss below, this lack of fit between wrong and remedy does not demolish the case for cash compensation, even in cases such as this one. In some circumstances, cash may be in fact the only reasonable option practically available. Perhaps it is too late, in the case of many of these adults, to return them to education and ultimately to college. In such cases, we need to ask whether a rough justice is better than no justice.[14]

8.2.2. Aggregation of Preferences into a Single Scale

A second assumption of full compensation is that we can aggregate all of an individual's satisfactions into a single scale, an overall utility function. But sometimes people view what they care about as incommensurable with other goods. In cases where restitution is being demanded, for example, an individual wants a particular good returned to her, such as a home, a homeland, or a particular family heirloom. In such cases, many people reject the idea that money can somehow compensate them for their loss. For example, eight Sioux tribes have refused to accept a US$122 million payment awarded to them in a 1980 US Supreme Court case as compensation for the lands seized from them in the Black Hills.[15] They insist that the Black Hills belongs to them and that no settlement is acceptable that does not include its return.

In other cases, people reject cash payment as insulting or demeaning; in their rejection, they say things like they do not want to be 'bought off'. When the Prime Minister of Japan offered a letter of apology and monetary compensation to some 500 survivors of the 200,000 'comfort women' exploited as sexual slaves during World War II, only six women accepted the offer. Most of the women rejected the offer because the fund came from private sources rather than the government and was unaccompanied by any official apology.[16]

Different forms of compensation send different and nonequivalent messages. If I cheat on my partner and then offer him money as compensation, he may surmise that I have not really understood the harm I have caused him. After all, I betrayed him; I did not merely cause him to suffer a tangible decline in his level of preference satisfaction. Repairing a betrayal takes a lot of emotional effort, time, and mutual understanding. In cases where past injustices have damaged not only people's possessions but also their self-esteem and trust, limited their options, and treated them with contempt, money can communicate that we think that these are just tangible losses that can be paid off.

The examples of some of the most emotionally powerful claims for repair, claims that emerge in the face of humanity's worst abuses—genocide, ethnic cleansing, torture, colonial domination, and enslavement—point to a similar problem with the assumption of commensurability. How can we possibly find an equivalent to compensate for these wrongs? When damages are offered as rectification for atrocities, no level of compensation seems sufficient—there is no payment that can wipe the slate clean. As one critic of the compensation paradigm for reparations puts it: 'No market exists for the value of living an ordinary life, without nightmares or survivor guilt. Valuing the losses from torture and murder strains the imagination'.[17]

While such difficulties with compensation do not rule out the possibility that cash payment may have an appropriate role (we do, after all, compensate accident victims or entertain wrongful death suits), they suggest that not all payments are equivalent and that different losses may be incommensurable with one another, and that in some contexts money will be inappropriate.

8.2.3. The Obligation to Compensate is Disconnected from the Wrong Done and from the Wrongdoer

The economic view of compensation does not specify the relationship between the compensator and compensated. In theory, if an individual has suffered a loss, anyone can make up for the loss. But clearly this is not true of all kinds of losses. Suppose that my friend has lied to me. Her cousin cannot meaningfully apologize to me for her lie to me; only she (the liar) can do that. The Korean comfort women could accept reparation only from the government that had wronged them, and not from anyone else. The very ability to compensate is in such cases a relational property.

Some philosophers writing about reparations, such as Bernard Boxill and Martha Minow, have argued that compensation cannot be the right paradigm for understanding what reparative justice means.[18] Reparative justice in the context of historical wrongs is by its nature concerned with repairing the moral relationships between victim and perpetrator: it is necessarily relational. By contrast, an agent may owe compensation even when he has done nothing wrong.

An example might help to draw out the distinction these critics of the compensation paradigm have in mind.[19] Suppose that your father steals my bicycle and gives it to you. You are unaware that the bicycle was stolen. I die, but my son eventually finds out about the theft. Even though you are an innocent third party, you arguably still have a compensatory duty to return the bicycle. But you have no duty to restore a relationship with my son for you have done nothing to damage it.

Reparatory duties thus differ from compensatory duties. But we have to be careful about the conclusion we draw from this. Compensation might itself be a way of repairing relationships, and even if is not a sufficient means for doing so, it might sometimes be a necessary one. People often say that 'talk is cheap' and that you should 'put your money where your mouth is'. President Clinton's exploration of an apology to slave's descendants, unaccompanied by compensation, met with a great lack of enthusiasm. Moreover, sometimes victims are not interested in healing their moral relationships with the perpetrators. Even if compensation cannot be the whole of repairing the past, it might be (and often has been) a significant part. Indeed, until quite recently, most demands for repair following historical injustice were primarily financial.

However, the critics are correct in pointing out that the idea of countering a wrong is central to the case of reparations for historical injustices. In some cases, wrongs will not show up as losses in satisfaction. If our obligation to act is in response to the fact that we are in some way complicit in a wrong, then focusing on preference satisfaction is misleading. For even if there were no effects on an agent's preferences, an obligation to counter wrong can persist, especially to the extent that the wrong continues to have effects through society's norms and practices.

In sum, I have argued that there are three considerations relevant to determining the kind of compensation that is appropriate in response to a wrong:

- compensation should be targeted (where possible) to the wrong it is meant to redress;
- compensation should respect the different varied harms that victims have suffered and not try to reduce these harms to a common currency;
- compensation should be understood relationally and should make sense in light of the basis of our obligation to repair.

These considerations do not show that the economic view of compensation is always inappropriate, but I believe that they do help explain why we have strong intuitions that it is inappropriate in certain cases. In particular, it seems partly or wholly inappropriate in cases in which we think that the specific injustice centrally involves something other than a loss to welfare, in cases where the lost objects are irreplaceable, in cases where problematic social practices and norms serve to perpetuate the original injustice, and in cases in which we think that the losses can only be 'made up' in very specific ways.

The examples of the Korean comfort women and the demands of the Sioux tribes suggest the need for a more case-specific view of the appropriate metric of compensation, a view that ties compensation more closely to the particular harm that is being compensated for.[20]

8.3. COUNTERING WRONGS OF THE PAST IN TERMS OF COMPENSATION

In some ways, compensation claims for past injustices resemble ordinary claims of corrective justice. But they differ in three important respects. First, in ordinary cases, the perpetrator has harmed the victim and is now obligated to do something to make up for the harm (or at least benefit the victim.) But in compensation for historical injustices, the class of victims and the class of those held responsible for compensation can include people who were not direct victims as well as people who were not directly responsible for the wrongs done. Many philosophers have argued that the descendants of original victims were not harmed by those injustices, given a plausible conception of harm.

Second, and related, claims based on past wrongs can range over multiple generations and across very different circumstances. In the case of a piece of property for example, unjustly expropriated in the past, there are likely to have been intervening owners, some of whom have built their lives around this property.

Third, the harms of slavery and other historical injustices were systematic rather than discrete. This makes their causal effects on current disadvantages almost impossible to determine.

Even if the economic conception of compensation is appropriate in theory, it seems to face four serious philosophical worries in the context of repairing the wrongs of the past that stretch back in time and have multiple dimensions.

First, some theorists argue that injustices affect not only how people fare, but also what people there are. Present claimants have no basis on which to make their claims of harm since, but for the injustice, they would not have been born.

Second, even if this problem can somehow be addressed, it has been argued that the descendants of injustice were not themselves victims of that injustice. In the case of slavery, contemporary descendants were not enslaved.

Third, critics argue that the original claims that people have to property or possession fade with time. In particular, these claims can be 'superseded' by changing circumstances as well as the claims of intermediary owners. Jeremy Waldron, in making this argument, questions whether some aboriginal claims to land—which originated in contexts when land was plentiful—are still valid when land is scarce.[21]

Fourth, there are significant problems of calculation, even if we exclude the complex (and perhaps unanswerable) questions of how to put value on those losses due to torture, the expropriation of slave labor, the destruction of families and cultures, and genocide. Even ascertaining the valuation of more ordinary property losses may be impossible when those losses occurred in the distant past. What would the value of land or other property seized over two hundred years ago be to current beneficiaries? If we think of the problem primarily in terms of the economic valuation of the original asset, we are likely to be plagued with counterfactual problems (would the original owners have been good stewards of the resource or would they or subsequent generations have gambled it away?)[22] as well as calculation problems (what rate of compounding should we use to calculate the assets' net worth?)[23] While over a relatively short time period such questions might be given straightforward (if not altogether uncontroversial) answers, it is nearly impossible to provide clear answers over longer-time periods. It is not simply that moving away from the parties directly harmed to consider descendants complicates the evaluation problems. Rather, it is that there is simply no clear fact of the matter about what full compensation for wrongs committed far in the past requires.

Some of these worries can be addressed in specific reparative contexts: for example, the worry about nonexistent beneficiaries seems less compelling in cases where claims are being put forward on behalf of a tribe or ethnic/cultural group that has retained its identity over time. It might also be noted that the original victims themselves sometimes bring forth claims of compensation. Finally, some of these concerns can be answered to the extent that less individualistic views of responsibility for wrongdoing are persuasive.[24]

In the end, however, these objections seem to many to be beside the point. For these objections can be acknowledged without entailing that the case for compensation is completely demolished. For the case for compensation for historical injustices primarily rests on the mutual recognition of a wrong, and even those who disagree about the quantitative extent of the wrong might nevertheless agree that there needs to be some response to the commission of a wrong. Even if we cannot determine the exact level of compensation that descendants are owed, we might be able to show that if not for the wrong, they (or any other descendants who happened to have been born) would plausibly be better off than they are now.[25] So understood, compensation would take on a different goal than that of literally making up for historical violations. I believe that indeed, this is the significant underlying purpose of compensation in intergenerational contexts: its role is to help reestablish relations of trust and mutual respect in the context of a torn past.

8.4. A RESPONSE: COMPENSATION REMADE

A plausible strategy for countering some of the objections to using compensation in cases of historical injustice would be to attempt to shift the focus away from the ties between people and possessions to the ties between people and their descendants. The tie between people and their children is stronger than the tie they have to many other things and might explain why intergenerational compensation makes sense even when the original victims are dead. In her *Taking Responsibility for the Past*, Janna Thompson develops a theory of reparative compensation in terms of a theory of intergenerational ties and obligations.[26] Since I believe that this theory is quite promising, I want to spend some time discussing its strengths and weaknesses.

On Thompson's view, at least when the original victims are dead and the wrongs are in the past, the loss to be compensated is not best conceived of as a loss of external goods to be measured in terms of financial compensation. Rather, the loss is to be conceived of in terms of intergenerational relationships. Insofar as societies are intergenerational communities, she argues, they depend for their moral and political integrity on their members 'accepting transgenerational obligations and honoring historical entitlements'.[27] Historical obligations belong in the first instance to members of structured intergenerational communities and it is also such communities whose members can bring claims of repair. Thompson's primary example is that of Australian aboriginal communities and their claims for the restitution of ancient homelands. The dependence of a community on the economic and cultural resources of their national territory gives immediate descendants a right of repossession. Their ancestors were engaged in transgenerational projects and activities associated with their way of life, and it was their way of life that they hoped to pass on to their children. She writes,

> ...when a nation is dispossessed, this is not only a great evil to existing members; it harms their successors, robbing them of the inheritance to which they are entitled, and by so doing disrupts their ability to carry on their common life. Nothing but the return of their national territory counts as appropriate reparation for this wrong.[28]

In the case of individuals who are not members of communities, the basis for their claims for compensation rests with the fact that they stand in specific relations to the victims of past injustice (that is, they are their descendants).[29]

Recognizing the value of family relations and national communities makes it reasonable for the state to support a presumption of inheritance, even when we do not know in fact that a given individual would have passed assets to their children. If we think that parents express their love and ties to their children by passing certain assets to them, and that such expression is valuable and legitimate, then we have reason to uphold a presumption of intergenerational transmission of assets, especially with respect to goods that have special meaning to the family members.[30]

For Thompson the wrong of many past injustices is not loss of property (although it can also be that) so much as the loss of an inheritance from one generation to the other. A society owes it to its past generations to honor their wishes and to respect the ties that they had to their descendants, as much as it owes its descendants compensation for having unjustly interfered with those ties.

Thompson's theory thus conceives of a legitimate claim for compensation as stemming from the moral duty a society has to respect the interests of its members in passing on an inheritance to their children. The theory derives its force from the fact that claims of compensation do seem stronger when the good to be compensated has a special meaning in the life of a family or community. To see this, it is helpful to consult your intuitions about the strength of the claims stemming from two different cases of expropriation: the loss of a piece of real estate and the loss of a farm that has been in the family for generations. Insofar as the family farm is tied to an ongoing way of life, invested with identity and memory, the case for restoring it seems stronger than the case of restoring a capital investment. Family farms can have an ongoing connection to the lives of people in a multigenerational family that a piece of commercial real estate does not. Thompson is therefore right to emphasize that within the life of a family, or more expansively, a people, some goods play a special role in sustaining the identity of that family and peoples over time. They are rightly conceived of as parts of an intergenerational project. This then allows a partial answer to Waldron's superseding worry: it is harder to supersede claims that play an important role in a community's or family's life. The ties between people and their children are stronger than the ties they have with their property. If we assume that most people strongly desire to see their descendants participate in carrying on the family line, then it is not unreasonable to suppose that they would have passed on their assets to them. Honoring the relationships that people have with their children entails that certain property rights not be so easily superseded.

But we must be careful not to exaggerate the implications of Thompson's idea: the ties between generations are thickest in the cases of direct descendants, and we may suspect that those ties weaken with time. In the case of historical title to land, less immediate successors grow up in new places and adjust their expectations and adapt to new environments. More generally, in the case of individuals far removed from the victims of injustice, the claims for inheritance are weakened, since we assume that people pass on their assets to those that they love and know. However, there may be some heirlooms that have been in a family for so many generations that even remote descendants might plausibly have a claim to them.

Thompson's theory focuses on the central problem of time and its effects on compensation claims but shifts the discussion away from what happens to property over time to what happens to the descendants of victims of injustice. To the extent that the goods of inheritance are specific—land, home, family heirlooms—it lies closer to the restitution view of compensation than to the economist's view of compensation as equal preference satisfaction.

Can Thompson's view of reparative compensation replace the economist's view of compensation and other alternatives in illuminating the basis of the claims for countering the wrongs of the past across generations? While her view is illuminating in some specific contexts (and probably the contexts in which people think the case for intergenerational compensation is most plausible) I do not think it makes sense of all such cases. It cannot therefore replace the economic view, although it can supplement it in particular instances.

Consider the example of reparations paid to victims of the Holocaust and their descendants. Jews who were sent to concentration camps were robbed of many goods, but this is hardly the worst of the injustices they suffered. The outright denial of their most basic human rights, the fact that they were treated worse than animals, the cruelty and humiliation they suffered, the rapes, beatings and forced labor—these were more serious than the theft of material goods. And it was these harms—as well as the ultimate harm of extermination—that form the basis for claims by descendants, and not the loss of an 'inheritance', unless we understand that term so capaciously that it includes a world that was lost. An analogous argument can be made with respect to the case for reparations for slavery.

These examples suggest that while Thompson's theory provides a plausible basis for compensatory reparations, and is perhaps the most compelling theory of intergenerational compensation we have, it is limited in its applications. There is more than one true justification for compensation across generations. In practice we recognize many different kinds of claims as relevant considerations for intergenerational compensation: theft, assaults on dignity and humiliation, the infliction of severe mental and physical injury, violations of reciprocity, loss of inheritance, destruction of property, and unjust killing.

To the extent that we find demands for compensation for past injustices like the Holocaust, slavery, apartheid, and genocidal killings, plausible, I suspect that this is because we understand such claims fundamentally as means to reestablish relationships of mutual respect among persons and groups whose relationships have been severely damaged by past denials of that respect. The relevant relationship here is not between a person and their descendants, but between each of us now as an inheritor of the legacies of an unjust past. The question that gives compensation for these past wrongs its point in this case is: what we can do now, in light of our past wrongs, to appropriately express the social value of mutual respect and trust that we want to characterize our society? As Tom Hill writes in defense of affirmative action, 'We cannot change our racist and sexist past, but we can also not express full respect for those present individuals who live in its aftermaths if we ignore it'.[31]

Hill argues that affirmative action is best understood as a means to convey a message, sincerely and effectively. In the absence of concrete action, talk of repair can seem empty. The message of affirmative action for Hill is that we as a society are willing to bear some costs to win back the trust of African Americans who regard their society with suspicion and resentment. Even if we cannot precisely quantify the degree of harm done to blacks, we cannot ignore the past and its role in shaping opportunities and relations. We may not be able to achieve full justice to victims and descendants, but doing nothing is usually worse than doing something imperfect.[32] In some cases of intergenerational compensation repair, then, the message sent by compensation can be more important than its tangible effects.

8.5. PRACTICAL OBJECTIONS TO COMPENSATION

Even if compensation is an appropriate response to historical injustice in some contexts, and even if it can sometimes be an important component of repair, there are serious limitations to its usefulness in practice. Most countries simply lack the financial resources to offer full compensation to victims, in cases in which the victims number in the thousands or even millions.[33] It is a challenge in many cases even to respond to the massive number of victims and large range of violations, as well as to overcome the disparities that are evident in isolated judicial remedies. In such contexts, the very idea of compensation in proportion to harm raises challenges. Being fair to all the victims may mean that full compensation for their losses, even if it could be calculated, is impossible. Besides which, there are competing and sometimes more urgent needs in many of the contexts in which demands for reparatory compensation are made.

Given the total funds available, and the presence of competing contemporary aims, governments have typically chosen an allocation to victims that involves less than full compensation. But less than full compensation raises problems of its own.[34] As a compromise it seems less attractive, and on less sure conceptual foundations, than the case for full compensation. And it runs the risk that as a partial payment it will not heal but only open wounds.

This means that practically speaking, financial compensation programs will need to be coupled with other forms of countering past wrongs that serve to reinforce the dignity of victims, repair the broken relationships and promote civic trust. Many reparations programs have emphasized not monetary compensation but truth-seeking, prosecutions, memorials of victims and resisters to injustices in monuments, national museums dedicated to public education about past injustices, and apologies.[35]

8.6. CONCLUSION

Successor governments sometimes undertake obligations to redress the victims of their predecessor regime and such obligations are often assumed under the passage of time. Different forms of redress seem more appropriate in different circumstances and in this chapter I have been concerned to understand why. Is compensation a plausible form of reparation? While some worries about the usefulness of compensation in the context of historical injustice are well founded they yield no persuasive general challenge to compensation. Indeed, many of those who ask for compensation are under no illusion that there is any payment that can bring back what they have lost. As Jon Elster observes, life has no 'undo button'.[36] Instead, victims are seeking a second-best and rough form of justice. For this reason, economic compensation remains a form of redress that belongs in the toolbox of those seeking to counter the crimes of the past. While it is imperfect and unlikely to admit of precision, it can be the best alternative available to victims. However, I have argued that the applicability of that form of compensation is limited: by principle and by practice. In principle, it is inappropriate in contexts in which claimants seek to repossess a particular good that has been wrongfully taken from them. This has especially been the case with land, ancestral remains, works of art, and other property claims.[37] In other cases, what is needed is primarily to reestablish relations of respect among groups and individuals that have been badly frayed by injustice. Compensation serves, in this case, less as the dutiful payment of a debt incurred in the past, but more as a means of expressing sincerity and regret, and reestablishing relationships based on mutual respect. Compensation in this case may take the form of apology, reform of institutions, and measures aimed to restore trust. Still, in other cases, the type of harm that was done may call for a specific form of response. In practice, economic compensation must compete with other aims and needs.

There is no single best form of compensation and no single justification for offering it. Instead, philosophers writing on compensation should pay close attention to the specific circumstances in which such demands arise, as well as the way particular programs are implemented. Given how difficult it can often be, even in simple cases, to repair a hurt, we should not be surprised that those who offer compensation sometimes get it wrong.

NOTES

1. A version of this chapter is also forthcoming in a *Nomos* volume on Transitional Justice. Thanks to Gary Bass and Adrian Vermeule who provided helpful comments on this chapter for a panel organized by the editors of the *Nomos* volume, Melissa Williams and Jon Elster. Thanks also to Rahul Kumar for his comments on an earlier draft, and to Rahul and Jon Miller for helpful prodding and inordinate patience.
2. Avishai Margalit discusses some of the dilemmas of forgiving and asking for forgiveness in *The Ethics of Memory*.
3. Examples include US payment to Japanese Americans interned in World War II, US payment to victims of the Tuskegee syphilis experiments, German payment to Holocaust survivors, Czech payment to those whose property was confiscated by the Communist government, and Canadian payment to Aboriginals for the forced assimilation of their children.
4. Some recent cases involving requests for reparations include Armed Activities on the Territory of the Congo (*Congo* v. *Uganda*; *Congo* v. *Rwanda*; *Congo* v. *Burundi*); Aerial Incident of August 10, 1999 (*Pakistan* v. *India*); Convention on the Prevention and Punishment of the Crime of Genocide (*Bosn&Herz.* v. *Yugo.*)
5. Thomson (1977).
6. Note that the Greek verb for forgiveness (*aphinmai*) means the cancelling of a debt.
7. See Thompson (2002).
8. See, e.g. Robert Nozick's formulation (1974: 57).
9. Rawls refers to income and wealth as primary goods, all-purpose means to an agent's ends.
10. See Posner and Vermeule (2003).
11. Wolff (2002).
12. Wolff (2002: 207–8).
13. In Randall Robinson's reparations for slavery proposal payments would go for educational scholarships to black children and youth, aiming to redress directly the effects of past injustice on educational opportunity.
14. The phrase 'rough justice' comes from Adrian Vermeule's comments on my paper at APSA.
15. *U.S.* v. *Sioux Nation of Indians*, 448 U.S. 371 (1980). This is discussed in detail in Rebecca Tsosie's contribution to this volume.
16. Cited in Minow (1998: 105).
17. Minow (1998: 104).

18. Boxill (1972). Minow writes that 'social and religious meaning rather than economic values lies at the heart of reparations' (Minow (1998: 110).
19. I adapt this example from Boxill (1972).
20. Notwithstanding these objections, compensation in the form of cash could be defended in many cases as a second best, where other more attractive alternatives are not feasible. So even if these objections are right in theory, their implications depend on the array of viable alternative options.
21. Waldron (1992). See also Waldron's contribution to this volume.
22. See Waldron (1992).
23. Tyler Cowan points out the extreme importance of compounding decisions to economic valuation. If we are trying to decide on compensation for a US $1 billion loss suffered 100 years ago, if we choose to compound at 1% per year, the assets will be valued at US$2.7 billion; if we compound at 3% per year, the assets will be worth US$19.2 billion; if we compound at 5%, the assets will be worth US $131.5 billion. See Cowan (1997).
24. See Kutz (2000).
25. Glenn Loury argues for an 'interpretive' justification for targeted compensation for African Americans. He claims that given the overlapping nature of generations, parents inevitably influence the lives of their children, in part through the transmission of social capital and wealth. Thus, it is plausible to assume that African Americans today still suffer from disadvantages associated with slavery, even if we cannot say precisely how much. See Loury (2002) and his contribution to this volume.
26. She also develops a theory of how current generations can bear responsibility for past injustices done by their predecessors. See also her contribution to this volume.
27. Thompson (2002: xviii).
28. Thompson (2002: 61).
29. However, she notes that they can only bring such claims forward if there is an institutional structure that bears responsibility for honoring their ancestors' wishes to see their children flourish.
30. Thompson (2002: esp. 123–32).
31. Hill (1991*a*: 206).
32. Note that I write 'usually' and not 'always'.
33. e.g. in Brazil, The Black Consciousness Center at the University of Sao Paolo has presented a demand for compensation for US$6 trillion, the equivalent of twelve years of Brazil's GNP.
34. There are also complicated questions related to determining the full compensation value of seized property.
35. Examples include Peru, South Africa, Sierra Leone, and Congo. Some of these are discussed in de Greiff (2006).
36. Elster (2004: 167).
37. It may sometimes be a second best when there are reasons why such goods cannot be recovered or current title transferred.

9

Justice and Reparations in World Politics

Catherine Lu

> Somebody must suffer for the consequences of the war. Is it to be Germany, or only the peoples she has wronged?[1]

9.1. INTRODUCTION

War and other forms of political violence, at domestic and international levels, tear or stain the fabric of individual lives, as well as the moral, political, and social fabrics of communities. Such depictions of the consequences of war naturally invoke the image of repair. The project of moral regeneration can be understood to entail numerous kinds of repair. One might, for example, characterize the aim of moral regeneration as the repair of morally defective or damaged norms, institutions, and social relationships. Effecting 'reparation' so understood could entail several components, including recognition, retribution, and restitution, since moral repair might require a public accounting of events, punishment of the guilty, material compensation for losses suffered by victims, public acknowledgment and remembrance of the wrong, and legal and other institutional transformations to legitimize a new political, social, and economic order. Used in this way, the concept of repair or reparation is basically synonymous with the entire project of moral regeneration.[2]

The term reparation in contemporary political discourse is often understood in a narrower sense, to refer to monetary or material payments, as well as other symbolic acts such as apologies and commemorations, made by the state and/or offending parties to victims of recognized moral wrongs. In this chapter, I focus specifically on the use of monetary or material reparations as a strategy of moral regeneration, especially after war. Since material reparative claims are essentially moral claims for transfers of material resources from one party to another, it is useful to ask what moral interests or purposes related to the larger project of moral regeneration can ground these claims.

Contemporary theorists typically conceive of material reparations as elemental to notions of 'restorative', 'reparatory', or 'reparative' justice that are formulated as distinct from classical retributive justice. Janna Thompson, for example, understands reparative justice as conceptually distinct from retributive justice and distributive justice. While reparative 'justice concerns itself with what ought to be done in reparation for injustice, and the obligation of wrongdoers, or their descendants or successors, for making this repair', retributive justice concerns itself with 'the punishment of wrongdoers', and distributive justice with equity, or the question of 'how goods should be distributed among individuals or how members of a society should share its benefits and burdens'.[3] Martha Minow locates her discussion of material reparations entirely within the framework of restorative justice, which, unlike retributive justice, she asserts, 'emphasizes the humanity of both offenders and victims. It seeks repair of social connections and peace rather than retribution against the offenders'. Put in this way, reparations sound more like measures to promote social rehabilitation or reconciliation rather than accountability-based justice. In another passage, however, Minow seems to place reparations back into a framework of justice when she writes, 'The core idea behind reparations stems from the compensatory theory of justice. Injuries can and must be compensated. Wrongdoers should pay victims for losses. Afterward, the slate can be wiped clean. Or at least a kind of justice has been done'.[4] Under this view, reparations can contribute to the achievement of justice as accountability because they redistribute benefits and burdens according to the moral merit of the parties.

Although most theorists locate material reparations within the framework of reparative justice, I argue that in some contexts, material reparations may also serve as retribution and therefore fit into the moral logic of retributive justice. More generally, it seems that the moral functions of monetary or material reparations may be quite diverse, including acknowledgment of injustice and victims' suffering, accountability of perpetrators, and their atonement for wrongdoing. These tasks highlight the moral debts owed by perpetrators to repair the moral damages suffered by their victims. At the same time, political violence and war typically result in considerable material burdens on victims, their families, and communities. The moral impetus to provide reparations to victims and their communities stems in part from an evaluation of the negative material legacies of these acts and conditions, and the desire to deliver victims from those negative effects. If it is the rehabilitation of victims that is the guiding aim behind material reparations, rather than the accountability of perpetrators, however, the obligation of repair may extend beyond perpetrators to the wider communities involved. The justice of allocating material reparations to victims then must also involve notions of distributive justice that raise questions about how claims for material reparations by victim groups are to be assessed in relation to wider societal obligations to the generally disadvantaged. Although conceptually distinct, then, retributive, reparative, and distributive justice may be very much interrelated. In this chapter, I hope to clarify the diverse moral functions and justifications for material reparations, and examine their implications for determining the moral appropriateness of various reparative schemes, as well as for assessing the moral obligations of perpetrators and others to pay the costs of acknowledged wrongdoing.

9.2. REPARATIONS, RETRIBUTION, AND JUSTICE AS ACCOUNTABILITY

The concept of reparations in international politics has acquired a bad reputation, as the demand for reparations after World War I is commonly thought to have contributed to unleashing a more devastating World War only twenty years later. Revisionist history after World War II blamed the architects of Versailles for pursuing 'victor's justice' and 'vengeance' rather than a 'peace of justice'.[5] In particular the idea of exacting material reparations from defeated states after international war was widely condemned as a mechanism of moral and social regeneration. John Maynard Keynes, for example, argued that 'the policy of reducing Germany to servitude for a generation, of degrading the lives of millions of human beings, and of depriving a whole nation of happiness should be abhorrent and detestable ... even if it were possible, even if it enriched ourselves, even if it did not sow the decay of the whole civilised life of Europe'.[6] George Kennan, in a slightly different critique, considered it 'foolish' of the victors to attempt 'to draw the blood of reparations and war debts from the veins of the exhausted peoples of the continent'.[7] As Elazar Barkan has noted, Allied leaders took this lesson from Versailles and, rather than impose harsh reparations on Germany in 1945, embarked on the Marshall Plan: 'Rather than hold to a moral right to exploit enemy resources, as had been done previously, the victor underscored future reconciliation and assisted its defeated enemies to reestablish themselves. In hindsight the policy is widely celebrated'.[8] Contemporary historical scholarship on Versailles, however, shows that Germany did not pay excessively harsh reparations.[9] Sally Marks has observed that contrary to public memory, 'In the end, the victors paid the bills'.[10] Eugene White notes that reparations were not a new phenomenon, but 'have a long and varied history', and were a common part of the financial settlements following major wars.[11] Despite the bad reputation of post-World War I reparations, they continue to be a common part of peace settlements after interstate war. What moral and political functions are reparations supposed to serve in such contexts?

Historically, payment for damages caused by war has been guided by the outcome of the military contest, with the loser incurring the obligation to pay the victor, whatever the moral merits of their justifications for engaging in war. In the 1871 Treaty of Frankfurt that concluded the Franco-Prussian war, for example, a defeated France had to pay huge 'indemnities' to a victorious Germany, despite the fact that the Prussian Chancellor Otto von Bismarck was the main aggressor who pushed the French into declaring war.[12] The term 'indemnity' refers to material goods or resources exacted by the victor against defeated parties in war. Paying indemnities was the cost of making war and losing, but did not necessarily signify any moral judgment of the losers. In such a framework, material transfers are not guided by considerations of justice between victors and vanquished, but by considerations of relative power advantage, so that 'they that have odds of power exact as much as they can, and the weak yield to such conditions as they can get'.[13] In the aftermath of the Franco-Prussian war, German victory on the battlefield allowed it to force material transfers, including the annexation of Alsace and parts of Lorraine that served the purposes of boosting German national pride and compounding French national humiliation. Although the practice of paying indemnities may have served the moral function of deterring potential aggressors from initiating wars that they were uncertain of winning, it also provided a material incentive to aggressors who were confident of their military superiority.

In different contexts, the payment of indemnities could also serve moral and political functions other than the self-aggrandizement of the victors. The determination of French reparations after the Napoleonic wars was based on the prudential judgment that a 'stable, moderately strong France' was necessary to effect a 'just equilibrium' or enduring balance of power in Europe after French hegemony. Initially, in the 1814 Treaty of Paris, the victorious Allies—Britain, Austria, Russia, and Prussia—agreed to waive all Allied claims to war damages. This strategy of restraint was well articulated earlier by Thucydides who highlighted its prudential value:

> great hatred is most safely cancelled not when one that have beaten his enemy and gotten much the better in the war brings him through necessity to take an oath and to make peace on unequal terms, but when having it in his power lawfully so to do if he please, he overcome him likewise in goodness, and contrary to what he expects, be reconciled to him on moderate conditions. For in this case, his enemy being obliged not to seek revenge as one that had been forced, but to requite his goodness, will, for shame, be the more inclined to the conditions agreed on.[14]

After Napoleon's escape from imprisonment, military remobilization, his 'Hundred Days', and subsequent recapture, however, prudence suggested that the Allies should be less forgiving in the Second Treaty of Paris. They exiled Napoleon far away from France, left an army of occupation of 1.2 million on French soil, took more territory away from France, and imposed war reparations for the Hundred Days, as well as for the cost of the occupation, and wartime damages to allied nationals. According to White, 'Reparations now became part of a tougher peace package, assessing a penalty for threatening the new European order and a deterrent against future ventures. Payment of reparations was also an incentive, whose fulfilment would allow France to resume its role as a Great Power in the management of European affairs'.[15]

The moral and political functions of reparations can thus be quite diverse. In the aftermath of the Napoleonic wars, reparations aimed to serve justice by holding the French accountable for rallying to Napoleon in the Hundred Days, contribute to the prevention of future aggressions through deterrence, and provide a basis for future reconciliation that involved the reintegration of France into the European balance of power. In serving the ends of accountability-based justice, deterrence and reconciliation, reparations, like retribution, may find their moral and political justifications in the ends of moral regeneration.

In the aftermath of moral transgressions, justice as accountability provides a typical normative framework for assigning rights and responsibilities to victims and perpetrators. Justice as accountability demands that moral agents exercise their agency in accordance with established community norms; when violations of those norms occur, justice demands that those who intentionally committed the violations are held accountable in some way. Typically, punishment is the means by which violators are held accountable for moral wrongdoing. According to Jean Hampton, retributive justice aims to establish the good in a negative fashion by repudiating moral wrongs, thereby contributing to the reassertion of moral truths that have been denied or violated by a wrongful act. Retribution effects 'the defeat of the wrongdoer at the hands of the victim (either directly or indirectly through an agent of the victim's, e.g. the state) that symbolizes the correct relative value of wrongdoer and victim'.[16] Retribution aims at redeeming the good by making the wicked pay for their wickedness through some kind of deprivation. Theories of retributive justice are anchored in the notion of justice as accountability; they are primarily concerned with affirming the connection between agency and accountability, so that only those who intentionally perpetrate a wrong deserve to be punished for it.

In the aftermath of World War I, leaders of the Allied and Associated powers premised the legitimacy of exacting reparations from Germany on their judgment of Germany's moral guilt and responsibility for the war, and it is in the framework of justice as accountability that we may understand their argument at Versailles that 'reparation for wrongs inflicted is of the essence of justice'.[17] In a speech on September 18, 1919, for example, US President Wilson supported a punitive policy against Germany: 'I hear that this treaty is very hard on Germany. When an individual has committed a criminal act, the punishment is hard, but the punishment is not unjust. The nation permitted itself, through unscrupulous governors, to commit a criminal act against mankind, and it is to undergo the punishment... it must pay for the wrong it has done'.[18] Earlier in August 1918, British Prime Minister Lloyd George characterized reparations as a punitive deterrent, arguing that 'Germany had committed a great crime... and it was necessary to make it impossible that anyone should be tempted to repeat that offence. The Terms of Peace must be tantamount to some penalty for the offence'.[19] Under Versailles, reparations constituted a means of holding accountable German leaders and the German people for throwing the world into the abyss of a fifty-one-month long war that claimed ten million lives.

When theorists contrast reparations with retribution as alternative responses to moral violations that also imply alternative conceptions of justice, they obscure the fact that both measures may share a common justificatory framework of justice as accountability. Thus, the use of material reparations may not indicate adherence to an alternative conception of justice, but may actually fit neatly into a retributive model of justice, especially if they are legitimated as a punitive measure to condemn the offender's conduct. In this vein, Gary Bass has argued, 'War crimes trials can never punish all the guilty, since the Nazis and Hutu Power *genocidaires* relied on vast numbers of killers, collaborators, bureaucrats, and bystanders; so reparations offer another way of punishing those who, while perhaps not criminally guilty, bear some responsibility for abetting a genocide'.[20] Reparations, under this interpretation, do not constitute an alternative to punishment, but serve only as an alternative means of exacting retribution, the moral purpose of which is to condemn wrongful conduct by holding perpetrators accountable for their moral transgressions.

The punitive use of reparations is grounded in the notion of justice as accountability, and is quite familiar in other contexts. For example, in 2004 US federal district judge H. Russel Holland of Anchorage, Alaska imposed US$4.5 billion worth of punitive damages against the Exxon Mobil Corporation for an oil spill that devastated Prince William Sound fifteen years earlier. The judge based the amount on 'the degree of reprehensibility' of the oil company officials' conduct, and viewed the purpose of punitive damages as 'retribution and deterrence', in contrast to the aim of compensatory damages, which is to help victims recover their losses resulting from the oil spill.[21] Such reparations can be considered retributive to the extent that they are directed against the culpable agent for the purpose of expressing disapproval of the wrongful conduct and holding that agent accountable for violating communal norms.

Institutionally, such accountability mechanisms may be an important aspect of repairing the moral order, by validating the connection between the moral agency and responsibility of corporate agents, institutions, and collectives, and by effecting the repudiation of moral falsehoods and the reassertion of moral truths violated by the wrongdoing. Seen in this light, the distinction between retributive and reparative justice is blurred or, at least, the two are united by a common notion of justice as accountability, since the imposition of retribution and reparations against perpetrators both respond to the question of 'what ought to be done in reparation for injustice' that focuses primarily on 'the obligation of wrongdoers, or their descendants or successors, for making this repair'.[22]

The moral efficacy of reparations as a mechanism of accountability after war clearly depends on several critical factors. For one thing, the imposition of reparations against defeated parties can easily look like self-aggrandizement or a continuation of forceful domination if exacted by the victors in the absence of an authoritative and institutionalized normative framework that reflects a wider communal judgment of the moral entitlements and responsibilities of the victors and the vanquished. This is to say that in international relations, the viability of justifying reparations as a measure of justice as accountability depends on authoritative judgments of justice and injustice, and authoritative determinations of the guilt and innocence, and moral entitlements and responsibilities of the parties involved. Military victory is not enough to justify the imposition of reparations on the defeated, although the military incapacitation of perpetrator parties may be necessary to enforce compliance with accountability mechanisms.

In the aftermath of World War I, the 1918 armistice, prompted by Germany's military defeat on the Western front, provided the political conditions on which the Allied and Associated powers were able to construct the terms of peace. Why did the mechanisms by which the victorious powers attempted to hold Germany accountable for the war fail? One problem was that key segments of the German political, military, and industrial elite did not accept the assignment of war guilt, and became preoccupied with expressing their rejection rather than acknowledgment of responsibility. The German sense of grievance against the judgment of their moral culpability for the war was compounded by the Versailles treaty process. No direct oral discussions were admitted between the Allied and German delegations, and at the signing of the treaty, the two German delegates, denied seats at the table, were 'ushered in and out of the hall like criminals escorted to and from the dock'.[23] E. H. Carr wrote of the 'unnecessary humiliations' of the process, which 'fixed in the consciousness of the German people the conception of a "dictated peace"; and they helped to create the belief, which became universal in Germany and was tacitly accepted by a large body of opinion in other countries, that the signature extorted from Germany in these conditions was not morally binding on her'. Carr condemned this arrogant and self-defeating use of power, arguing, 'Historical truth cannot be established by international treaty—least of all by a treaty imposed by victors on vanquished. The Allied governments, in the passion of the moment, failed to realize that this extorted admission of guilt could prove nothing, and must excite bitter resentment in German minds'.[24] The treaty process, in its obvious contempt for the German delegation, did not help to induce Germany to acknowledge its responsibilities for the war and its obligations to make amends; on the contrary, the German elite, feeling victimized at Versailles, actively sought to thwart the mechanisms of accountability set out by the treaty.

With regards to reparations, although Article 235 of the Versailles Treaty required Germany to pay 20 billion gold marks by May 1, 1921, Germany 'only "paid" about 8, approximately half of which was the credit granted for her purchases of food and raw material'.[25] The historical evidence suggests that influential members of the German business elite expressed their resentment of the moral judgment against Germany by effectively resisting compliance with the reparation demands. Germany's economic recovery in the 1920s might also have been delayed by its political leaders who intentionally mismanaged Germany's economic affairs 'in hopes of obtaining substantial reductions in reparations'.[26] Furthermore, the architects of Versailles enabled German denial of responsibility to persist and intensify when they failed to maintain moral and political solidarity to enforce their moral judgment. For example, the lack of substantial payment of reparations could be explained in one of two ways: either Germany was unable to pay, or it was unwilling to do so. The British were more persuaded by German claims of inability to pay, while the French viewed the lack of payment as an indication that 'defeat and revolution had not really transformed the German spirit'.[27] The mechanisms of accountability thus lacked authoritativeness not only in the eyes of Germans, but also among some of the victorious powers and their populations. This combination of factors meant that the mechanisms of moral accounting laid out in the Treaty of Versailles—trials and reparations—were largely ineffectual, rather than overly harsh in their effects on Germany. Indeed, the incongruence between the punitive terms of Versailles and their lack of punitive effects on Germany is striking.

The use of reparations as an accountability mechanism was complicated by the revolution in Germany that issued in the Weimar Republic. Bass has noted with respect to war crimes trials, that leaders, such as Lloyd George, were worried that the fledgling regime would fall if too many Germans were subjected to the trials: he 'only wanted to make an example. Trying very large numbers would create great difficulties for the German Government, which he believed to be better than either a Bolshevist Government or a Militarist Government'.[28] Similarly, concern for the stability of the political transition in Germany led Lloyd George 'to take an indulgent attitude toward Germany [on the issue of reparations], to be flexible regarding the treaty, to be generous in allowing time for compliance'. While French leaders were not willing to be indulgent, they lacked the means to enforce compliance. Jacques Seydoux for the French Foreign Ministry concluded, 'Through threats alone, France had been unable to force Germany to make a serious effort; on the other hand, to go in and reorganize all of Germany, he later wrote, was "beyond our power" '.[29] As Jacobson has put the dilemma, 'The potential cost of the fulfilment of the Versailles Treaty . . . was either the end of democratic conditions in Germany or its loss of economic and territorial sovereignty'.[30] In a world exhausted by war and increasingly reluctant to employ force to obtain compliance, a militarily defeated but unrepentant Germany effectively evaded moral accountability.

9.3. REPARATIONS AND JUSTICE AS RESTORATION

The use of material reparations as punitive mechanisms of accountability after war encounters several dangers. Bass has warned that the restraint necessary to construct a morally defensible reparations scheme 'often falters in the face of war's devastations. Economic obligations can easily become harshly punitive'.[31] Indeed, what amount of material reparations would constitute adequate punishment for waging aggressive war, or for wrongs such as genocide, slavery, and other crimes against humanity? Another way to employ reparations as mechanisms of justice is not as retributive measures, but as compensatory measures. On this view, the moral focus of reparations is not on the need to make offenders suffer some deprivation for their wrongful conduct, but on the need of victims to have the damages they have suffered repaired. Reparations serve what Aristotle termed 'rectificatory justice', the rectification of wrong done to an injured party by restoring the *status quo ante*.[32] Justice is done, not by making perpetrators suffer like their victims, but by restoring victims to their previous condition.

The restitutive or remedial function of reparations is recognized in international law. According to the Chorzow Factory judgment of the Permanent Court of International Justice, dealing with a claim by Poland against Germany in 1949,

The essential principle contained in the actual notion of an illegal act... is that reparation must, so far as possible, wipe-out all the consequences of the illegal act and re-establish the situation which would, in all probability, have existed if that act had not been committed. Restitution in kind, or, if this is not possible, payment of a sum corresponding to the value which a restitution in kind would bear; the award, if need be, of damages for loss sustained which would not be covered by restitution in kind or payment in place of it—such are the principles which should serve to determine the amount of compensation due for an act contrary to international law.[33]

Similarly, in the 'Draft Articles on State Responsibility', Article 31 obliges states responsible for internationally wrongful acts to make 'full reparation' for the injury caused.[34] Reparations are tied to rectificatory justice, so that the aim and extent of reparations is limited to remedial measures, and excludes the use of economic sanctions or penalties such as punitive damages.[35]

One might think that locating reparations in a restitutive or compensatory, rather than retributive, framework would help to limit excessive claims. Restorative or compensatory accounts of reparations, however, suffer from similar problems as their retributive counterparts. Especially in contexts of war and other political violence, it is impossible to cancel out the losses and suffering of victims, or to restore lives to the way they were before, and the idea that one can do so is perverse. What amount of material reparations would constitute adequate compensation for the death of one's husband or children, and what price can be put on the injuries suffered by victims of rape or torture? The problem with the moral evils endemic to war and violence is their fundamental irreparability, and the inescapable inadequacy and arbitrariness of any amount of material compensation.

Although full or pure restitution to a preexisting state of affairs may not be possible in most cases, material reparations may still fulfill an accountability function if they involve perpetrators taking some responsibility for improving the lives of victims. Michael Ridge has thus characterized reparative obligations in the following way: 'reparations are owed when (a) one party, the "perpetrator", has wronged another party, the "victim", (b) the perpetrator has thereby harmed the victim, and (c) the perpetrator now can do something to benefit the victim'.[36] Wars and other similar kinds of political catastrophes typically yield not just significant moral damage but also widespread material losses and devastation. In this vein, Bass has argued that, 'Since the task of postwar economic restoration must be undertaken, surely it is better that the perpetrators pay than the victims'.[37] Indeed, it offends our notions of justice as accountability and as fairness to know that victims continue to suffer from the negative material effects of their victimization, especially if perpetrators seem to have done better. The late historian Iris Chang relies on these moral sentiments in her criticisms of the failure of the Japanese government to pay reparations to elderly survivors of the Nanking massacre, perpetrated by Japanese troops after they took over the city in December 1937. Chang observed of the survivors, 'Most lived in dark, squalid apartments cluttered with the debris of poverty and heavy with mildew and humidity. I learned that during the massacre some had received physical injuries so severe they had been prevented from making a decent living for decades. Most lived in poverty so crushing that even a minimal amount of financial compensation from Japan could have greatly improved the conditions of their lives. Even US$100 in reparations from the Japanese to buy an air conditioner could have made a world of difference for many of them'.[38]

Viewing the moral entitlements and obligations of victims and perpetrators through the framework of justice as accountability highlights the right of victims to material compensation or restitution and the obligation of perpetrators to pay, but tends to obscure the possibility that perpetrators may themselves become materially diminished by their own actions, or that perpetrators may have some legitimate entitlements despite their culpability. These issues, however, significantly affect the moral legitimacy of victims' reparative claims. We may accept that victims have a prima facie entitlement to *some* compensation for their losses, and that perpetrators have a prima facie obligation to provide such compensation, but the determination of exactly how much benefit is owed to victims by perpetrators depends on various other moral considerations beyond the assessment of victims' damages and perpetrators' culpability.

In the case of World War I, although strict accountability-based justice might have dictated that Germany as the aggressor nation should pay to rebuild the areas it had devastated, French leaders were aware that this 'would completely crush [Germany] and reduce her to a state of economic bondage which would strip away from humanity all hope of a lasting peace'. French Premier Georges Clemenceau recognized that while the function of reparations was to hold Germany accountable for the war, they could not be designed with the aim or outcome of destroying Germany: 'Crushing Germany was out of the question—a powerful nation could not be destroyed, and ultimately France and Germany had to live together'. French leaders even thought that French security would best be achieved through 'economic collaboration' with Germany, and that 'the surest way of re-establishing between the two countries a peace worthy of the name is by working to join together their material interests'.[39] No matter how horrible the consequences of war, the appropriateness of victims' reparative claims may be limited, not only practically but also morally, by considerations such as future peace and reconciliation.

Furthermore, the extent of a perpetrator state's reparative obligations to victim parties, whether they are individuals, corporations, or states, must also be balanced with the obligations of perpetrator states to provide for their own populations. Indeed, nothing may justify a level of material reparations that would incapacitate a state from fulfilling its domestic obligations of ensuring domestic security, the effective administration of justice, the provision of a basic and universal level of health care and education, and viable economic structures that can support a basic standard of economic welfare to its population. The 'Articles on State Responsibility', while insisting on the obligation of full reparation for international wrongdoing, provide for some limitation of reparations through the concepts of proportionality and equity. Thus, Dinah Shelton observes that reparative obligations of wrongdoers are to be determined not only by the claims of injured parties but also by wider community interests.[40]

These wider moral considerations came to be acknowledged in the design of the United Nations Compensation Commission (UNCC) and Compensation Fund, created through Resolution 692 by the UN Security Council in 1992, following the First Gulf War that was ignited by Iraq's invasion of Kuwait. The UN Security Council started from the assumption that Iraqi responsibility was already established 'under international law' and therefore created the UNCC with the primary purposes of 'examining claims, verifying their validity, evaluating losses [and] assessing payments'.[41] The UNCC constituted an innovative institution of moral regeneration in international politics as it replaced 'the traditional loose pattern of cooperation between the victorious powers with a highly institutionalized framework provided by the UN, in order better to reach a settlement which satisfactorily achieves the imperatives of principle and policy'. Unlike the Inter-Allied Reparation Commission formed under Versailles, which was not connected to the League of Nations system, the UNCC is a creature of the UN system, with the implication that it 'does not represent the interests of a single state, for example Kuwait, nor of the coalition of states which fought for the liberation of Kuwait, but rather of the whole international community'. Andrea Gattini also observes that as a reparative regime, the UNCC did not only efficiently process the entitlements of victims of Iraqi aggression, but it also took into account 'the needs of Iraq's people. Until now, it has not been sufficiently noted that the UN management of Iraqi war reparations is as much a guarantee of Iraq's interests as those of the claimants, in that it deals with masses of potentially disruptive claims in an impartial and orderly manner'.[42]

More substantively, in its decisions, the UNCC limited the reparative obligations of Iraq in various ways. For example, the Allied coalition forces were not eligible for compensation for the cost of the forces or their military operations against Iraq, and with some exceptions, members of the Allied coalition force were ineligible for compensation for loss or injury sustained in the course of military operations against Iraq. The UNCC's decisions also ranked the urgency of different types of claims, creating a hierarchy of victims that privileged individual over corporate and governmental claims. In its first decision, the UNCC assigned priority to the reparative claims made by individuals for losses not exceeding US$100,000, over claims by corporations and governments. Of the 2.6 million claims submitted, for 'death, injury, loss of or damage to property, commercial claims and claims for environmental damage resulting from Iraq's unlawful invasion and occupation of Kuwait in 1991', the UNCC had resolved all but about 25,000 by December 2004.[43] It has awarded as of January 2005, approximately US$51.8 billion out of a total amount claimed of over US$300 billion.[44] Gattini observes that in its efficient and feasible processing of reparative claims, the UNCC will 'have the chance to be remembered in the history of international law not as an isolated case of stern, uncompromising retribution, but as the first successful model of a collective relief system organized by the international community in response to an aggression'.[45]

To fund the payment of reparations, the UNCC was assured a 30 percent (reduced to 25% in December 2000 and to 5% in May 2003) allocation of the revenues from Iraqi export sales of Iraqi oil, petroleum products, and natural gas that were authorized through the UN 'oil-for-food' scheme.[46] In many contemporary cases of violent political conflict, however, the parties or countries involved are not only politically dysfunctional, but also economically disadvantaged, and already unable to meet the material needs of their own populations.[47] Of course, both the cases of Germany after World War I, and Iraq after the First Gulf War, reveal that perpetrator states, in an attempt to evade moral accountability, can use and even create the hardships of their own populations in order to claim economic incapacity and be relieved of their reparative obligations. But there are cases of genuine economic incapacity, such as post-genocide Rwanda. If only perpetrators are obligated to pay reparations for the harms suffered by their victims, then in contexts of widespread deprivation and economic dysfunctionality, many victims will continue to bear the material burdens of their victimization. For this reason, it is unfortunate that the newly established International Criminal Court (ICC) proposes to pay reparations to its acknowledged victims through a victims' Trust Fund that will consist only of fines and assets seized or collected from convicted perpetrators.[48] In the case of Rwanda, for example, with the military victory of the Tutsi-dominated Rwandan Patriotic Front in the civil war, many perpetrators fled to neighboring states and became refugees themselves. Even some of the architects of the genocide, undergoing criminal prosecution at the International Criminal Tribunal for Rwanda, have insufficient funds to pay for their own defence, much less to contribute to a victims' compensation fund.

Victims are not likely to receive adequate resources for rebuilding their lives if only perpetrators, who are often as destitute as the victims, are obligated to pay reparations. This means that if we are concerned with the plight of victims of the Rwandan genocide and with the achievement of justice as victim restoration (as opposed to justice as perpetrator accountability), some international effort will be needed to provide sufficient remedy.

9.4. REPARATIONS, RECONSTRUCTION, AND DISTRIBUTIVE JUSTICE

Locating material reparations in an accountability-based justice framework highlights the obligation of perpetrators to pay for the damage suffered by victims. If, however, we are concerned mainly with repairing the ability of victims to exercise effective political, social, and moral agency that has been significantly diminished by their victimization, it may not only be perpetrators that bear reparative obligations. The wider communities in which victims can claim membership may also bear some moral obligation to assist victims. State compensation schemes for victims of crime points to an acknowledgment of communal responsibilities to help victims recover some of the costs of suffering injustice. Societies that fail to provide special assistance to victims may be guilty of 'passive injustice', compounding the original injustice committed by perpetrators.[49] In case of the survivors of the Nanking massacre, for example, is it only the Japanese government bears moral responsibility for the dire straits of the survivors? Does not the government of the People's Republic of China bear some responsibility for their continued deprivation? In cases where both victim and perpetrator communities lack the economic conditions for guaranteeing effective political, social, and moral agency to any or most of its members, what ought to be the moral weight of victims' reparative claims against the distributive claims of their generally economically disadvantaged or burdened societies? Such questions naturally lead to questions of distributive justice between victims and their fellow citizens, and between victim communities.[50]

In the aftermath of World War I, with an unrepentant Germany stalling on reparation payments, the political necessity of reconstructing the devastated areas and resolving the payment of general war costs raised the problem of distributive justice between the victorious victims of the war. Although the framework of justice as accountability might demand that Germany pay for postwar reconstruction, an alternative framework that focused on justice as victim restoration might have generated a moral duty of the international community as a whole to restore areas devastated by Germany. On this view,

Germany was not the only state that had obligations to help the victims of the war. This is indeed how the French hoped to recover economically from the war: 'French leaders looked not to Germany but to their allies for a solution'. The French Minister of Commerce in 1918, Etienne Clémentel, envisaged a global fund to restore the ravaged areas, the creation of an Allied economic bloc strong enough to restrain German ambitions, and the eventual development of an 'economic union of free peoples' into which Germans could ultimately be integrated.[51] Unfortunately, the 'community of sacrifice' that had been forged in war failed to persist in peace.

The history of the reparations negotiations between the Allied and Associated powers reveals little sense of communal obligation between them. The United States remained aloof from its European allies, and while it contributed militarily to Germany's defeat and was willing to fund the Allied war effort through loans, 'America expected to be paid back'. Instead of exhibiting economic confidence in its allies and promoting economic solidarity, American officials were motivated by mistrust of European economic management skills, and by a sense of Anglo-American economic rivalry. American abandonment of the wartime system of economic cooperation meant a denial of the French view of distributive justice during the period of economic reconstruction, which involved the pooling of war costs, and the reapportionment of inter-Allied debt, with 'each nation paying according to its ability'.[52] Without American cooperation with these proposals, the economic recovery of the European belligerents came to rely more on the payments that could be extracted from Germany.

German obligations to make reparations to the Allies were premised on a condition of the armistice, which required Germany to pay 'for all damage done to the civilian population of the Allies and their property by the aggression of Germany by land, by sea and from the air'. During the Paris Peace Conference, the payment of reparations referred specifically to the 'restoration of the devastated areas', and especially of Belgium and northern France, which were ravaged by German forces. As Marc Trachtenberg has shown, German troops destroyed important French coal mines while retreating in 1918, an act that had no military purpose, but served the economic one of crippling French competition in order to ensure 'a postwar market for German exports'. Reparations thus constituted only a subset of the total 'war costs'.[53]

While France suffered the most direct devastation, Britain had assumed the greatest war costs. France favored privileging reparation payments over war costs, but this meant that it could claim the greatest share of German reparation payments, and Britain the least, since Britain suffered little direct civilian damage. Britain succeeded in enlarging the portion of the reparation pie that it was due by insisting on the inclusion of pensions and separation allowances as part of civilian damages; but whatever increases it received would be at the expense of France, since 'inclusion of pensions and allowances increased the British share of the pie but did not enlarge the pie'.[54] France initially claimed 70 percent of German payments, with Britain receiving 20 percent, and the rest going to Belgium, Italy, and Serbia. The British proposed in April 1919 a proportion of 56:28. Negotiations over these percentages continued until 1920, when it was finally agreed that the French–British ratio of German payments would be 52:28.[55] Ultimately, disagreements about how to distribute the financial burdens and benefits of the war made it impossible to fix a final sum for the treaty, heightening German fears, often manipulated for political reasons, that the 'German people would thus be condemned to perpetual slave labor'.[56] The conflicts between the Allies about reparations and war debts did not so much poison their relations as reveal the tenuous nature of their solidarity.

Jacobson has described well the impact of failures in Allied cooperation after the war:

> The breakdown of Allied economic cooperation was significant because the potential benefits of a postwar stabilization based on continued Allied solidarity would have been ... far-reaching. A redistribution of war costs in 1919 might not only have removed a source of division among the Allies but also have made possible an early compromise reparations settlement, eliminating a major obstacle to Franco-German reconciliation and precluding the Ruhr invasion. Monetary stabilization might have been accomplished earlier and prevented hyperinflation in Germany in 1923 and the fall of the franc in 1924–26. The sharing of raw materials, a prompt settlement of war debts and reparations, and immediate American loans to Europe might have facilitated the rapid economic reconstruction of the Continent. A recovering German economy might have been reintegrated into a system of Allied economy unity without dominating it; failing that, a permanent Allied economic bloc might have been strong enough to counterbalance German power. In either case, the German threat to the peace and stability of Europe would have been substantially lessened.[57]

The economic regeneration of France and Belgium, and a strong Allied economic union could have protected everyone even from an unrepentant Germany, and in time may have provided the material basis for moral reconciliation based on mutual interest and acknowledgment of war responsibility. Instead, 'the net effect of World War I and the peace settlement was the effective enhancement of Germany's relative strength in Europe, particularly in regard to her immediate neighbours'.[58]

In the case of World War I, the United States, Britain, and France founded a sense of community through war, but such communities ultimately prove too weak to sustain the far more demanding claims of distributive justice. Their divisions on the issue of reparations reveal the interconnection between retributive, reparative and distributive justice, and the relationship between problems of justice and problems of community in international relations.

9.5. CONCLUSION: RECONCILIATION AND THE PROBLEM OF DISGRACE

Although superficially, claims for material reparations may seem concerned primarily with delivering the goods, rather than the good, it is clear from this discussion that the good is fundamental even to this narrow understanding of reparation, since material transfers are characterized as reparation only when made in response to harms caused by an acknowledged moral wrong. If this moral evaluation is inappropriate, then the notion of reparations is also inappropriate. To take a simple example, if my friend Brian voluntarily lends me $10 and I return the amount one week later, the transfer of money cannot be termed reparation, since there was no moral wrong involved in the initial transaction. If, however, I steal ten dollars from his wallet, and am found out, then it would be intelligible to think of my repayment to him as an act of restitution or reparation. In fulfilling my obligation to make material reparation to Brian, I have settled the moral debt I owed him; one could say that justice has been done.

Doing justice even in this simple case, however, does not mean that reconciliation has been achieved or is achievable. I may return the money grudgingly or only under compulsion, without repairing the demonstration of disrespect my act exhibited toward Brian. Paying the debt, voluntarily or involuntarily, also may not necessarily resolve the problem of moral disgrace that I incurred by my initial wrongdoing. The removal of moral disgrace, rather than of moral debt, however, may be key to achieving reconciliation.

Some argue that reparative approaches 'aim to help victims move beyond anger and a sense of powerlessness ... [and] also attempt to reintegrate offenders into the community'.[59] On this view, making perpetrators pay reparations may be important for achieving justice as accountability and as victim restoration, but it is also important for fostering social reconciliation between victims and perpetrators and their respective groups. Perpetrators may pay reparations not only as a way of being held accountable for their wrongdoing; they may also pay as a way to atone for their wrongdoing, creating a moral basis for reconciliation of the specific victim–perpetrator relationship.

In the case of World War I, the architects of Versailles wagered that by paying reparations, a morally disgraced Germany would convey its acknowledgment of guilt and responsibility, a condition of its rehabilitation and reintegration into the European family of nations. This understanding of the connection between accountability-based justice and reconciliation was especially clear in French reparation policy. Such reconciliation depended on a morally transformed Germany, and France measured the progress of that transformation by the efforts that Germany made to comply with the Treaty of Versailles. The reconciliation of victors and vanquished thus depended on the acknowledgment of moral guilt by the vanquished.

Although Germany did pay some reparations, it did so reluctantly, and in such cases, the payment of reparations may do little to promote social reconciliation. Reparations may be a more effective tool for reconciliation only when perpetrators voluntarily accept to undertake the task of meeting their reparative obligations to their victims. Such a voluntary acceptance would convey not only an acknowledgment of moral responsibility, but also a transformation of spirit that may be necessary to lift at least partially the stain of moral disgrace from perpetrators. The project of moral regeneration, in its pursuit of the moral repair of social relationships, cannot aim for total erasure of the tears and stains of injustice on victims and perpetrators alike. In this sense, moral regeneration is focused less on restoring a (perhaps nonexistent) tearless or stainless social fabric, and more on transforming an existing stained and torn fabric of social relationships toward a new pattern of social relationships founded on mutual moral respect and reconciliation. In this sense the project of moral regeneration after war entails great transformations.

NOTES

1. US Department of State (1947: 48).
2. I first discussed the idea of moral regeneration in Lu (2002).
3. Thompson (2002: xi).
4. Minow (1998: 92, 104).
5. Both Germany and the Allies claimed to seek a 'peace of justice'. See 'German Observations on the Conditions of Peace,' May 28, 1919, and 'Reply of the Allied and Associated Powers,' June 16, 1919, in US Department of State (1947: 39, 49).
6. Keynes (1963: 17–18).
7. Kennan (1996: 16).
8. Barkan (2000: xxiii).
9. See Trachtenberg (1980: 205) and Marks (1978: 233).
10. Marks (1978: 233).
11. White (2001).
12. Howard (1962).
13. Thucydides (1989: Book V, paragraph 89).
14. Thucydides (1989: Book IV, paragraph 19).
15. White (2001: 339).

16. Hampton (1988: 125).
17. From 'Reply of the Allied and Associated Powers', in US Department of State (1947: 48).
18. Quoted in Trachtenberg (1980: 51).
19. Quoted in Trachtenberg (1980: 48).
20. Bass (2004: 409). Even though activities such as war and genocide occur between groups, the appropriateness of collectivizing responsibility remains to be determined. In the case of war waged by governments, collectivizing responsibility for war damages through reparations may be more just in the case of aggressive democracies than in the case of aggressive authoritarian, dictatorial, or totalitarian regimes.
21. See Liptak, '$4.5 Billion Award Set for Spill of Exxon Valdez,' The *New York Times*, January 29, 2004. Judge Holland awarded the 32,000 fishers and residents of Prince William Sound $513 million in compensatory damages, and although he acknowledged that Exxon had already spent over $2 billion to clean up the spill, he did not consider that amount penalty enough.
22. Thompson (2002: xi).
23. Welch (1993: 128).
24. Carr (1965: 5, 46). On June 23 the German government, 'yielding to superior force and without renouncing in the meantime its own view of the unheard of injustice of the peace conditions... declares that it is ready to accept and sign the peace conditions imposed' (Finch 1919: 554). Finch was assistant technical adviser to the American delegation at the peace conference.
25. Trachtenberg (1980: 205). Sally Marks notes that '20 billion marks is approximately what Germany paid during the entire history of reparations' (Marks 1978: 233).
26. According to Marks, the German government delayed tax reform and currency stabilization measures (see Marks 1978: 239). Jon Jacobson argues, however, that the German government did not pursue 'a contrived and coordinated policy of deliberately promoting inflation to avoid reparation payment.... Internal political and economic weakness rather than foreign ambition determined German reparation policy'. See Jacobson (1983: 638).
27. Trachtenberg (1980: 99).
28. See Bass (2002: 79).
29. Trachtenberg (1980: 103, 273).
30. Jacobson (1983: 638).
31. Bass (2004: 409).
32. *Nicomachean Ethics*, Book 5.5 (Irwin trans.).
33. Quoted in Shelton (2002: 835).
34. Gattini (2002: 162). The forms of reparation, listed in Article 34, are restitution, compensation, and satisfaction, singly or in combination. See Shelton (2002: 845).
35. Shelton (2002: 838).
36. Ridge (2003: 39).

37. Bass (2004: 411).
38. Chang (1997: 183).
39. Trachtenberg (1980: 18, 100, 158).
40. Shelton (2002: 838).
41. Paragraph 16 of UN Security Council Resolution 687 stated, 'Iraq is liable under international law for any direct loss, damage, including environmental damage and the depletion of natural resources, or injuries to foreign governments, nationals and corporations, as a result of Iraq's unlawful invasion and occupation of Kuwait'. Gattini (2002: note 27).
42. Gattini (2002: 167, 165, 164).
43. The outstanding cases comprise claims of individuals for losses over $100,000, environmental damage claims, and 'late filed' claims by Palestinians.
44. As of the end of 2004, approximately US$19 billion has been paid to successful claimants via their governments or international organizations. See the UNCC Web site, the UNCC at a glance, http://www2.unog.ch/uncc/ataglance.htm, and January 26, 2005 press release, http://www2.unog.ch/uncc/pressrel/pr_12sp.pdf
45. Gattini (2002: 166, 181).
46. See the UNCC Web site, January 26, 2005 press release, http://www2.unog.ch/uncc/pressrel/pr_12sp.pdf
47. See Mani (2002).
48. See Article 79 of the *Rome Statute of the International Criminal Court*, July 17, 1998, UN Doc. A/CONF. 183/9, 2187 U.N.T.S. 90, reprinted in *International Legal Materials* 37, no. 5 (1998): 1002. For a lengthier discussion, see Lu (2006).
49. On passive injustice, see Shklar (1990).
50. For an account of reparative obligations of contemporary democratic states and citizens for historical injustice, see Lu (2005).
51. Trachtenberg (1980: 1, 17).
52. Trachtenberg (1980: 21, 54). Albert Rathbone, an Assistant Secretary of the US Treasury wrote in a letter of March 1919, 'the Treasury... will not assent to any discussion at the peace conference, or elsewhere, of any plan or arrangement for the release, consolidation or reapportionment of the obligations of foreign governments held by the United States. The Treasury would discontinue advances to any government that supported such schemes' (54–5).
53. Trachtenberg (1980: 43).
54. Marks (1978: 232).
55. MacMillan (2001: 192). Trachtenberg claims that the percentage set at the Spa Conference in mid-1920 was 52:22 (Trachtenberg 1980: 72).
56. MacMillan (2001: 192).
57. Jacobson (1983: 633).
58. Marks (1978: 255).
59. Minow (1998: 92).

Part IV

Reparations for Colonialism

10

How Should We Respond to the Cultural Injustices of Colonialism?

Rajeev Bhargava

Colonialism has been a recurrent feature of human history. Everywhere in the past, lands have been conquered and new settlements have emerged brutally. Marauders who came to new lands to plunder wealth stayed on after killing the original inhabitants and stealing their goods. All brutal invasions were unjust even when they were not recognized to be so but in most such cases of past injustices, circumstances have changed so drastically as to supersede them. The possible historic injustice inflicted on the people of parts of north India by the Mughal conquest in the early sixteenth century has certainly been superseded first because of the common suffering inflicted on both Muslims and Hindus by British colonialism and second by the birth of political democracy in India. These past injustices of conquest and ancient colonialisms that have long ceased are not the concern of the chapter.[1]

Rather, I attend in this chapter first to injustices that started in the somewhat distant past, mostly in the early modern era, but are still continuing. Many examples of such continuing injustices exist. The plight of the blacks or the Indians in America and the suffering and marginalization of the native inhabitants of Australia and New Zealand are all a result of colonization. Arguably, the dalits in India have suffered injustice as a result of a long process of internal colonialism that persists to this day. Among continuing injustices, I deal more specifically with the injustices of modern European colonialism whose impact was felt by almost all non-Western peoples. Although my chapter has a larger theoretical concern, my focus is still narrower and I concentrate largely, though not wholly, on the Indian experience of colonialism.

Modern colonialism went beyond physical violence, forcible occupation of lands or extraction of tribute and wealth. It forcibly established a relationship between the lands of the colonizers and the colonized and inaugurated a flow of human and natural resources that continually fed the economy of the colonizers and impoverished the colonized. As the early protagonists of the movement of Indian independence from British rule argued, there was a ceaseless drain of wealth from the colony to the metropolis. This economic injustice was accompanied by political injustice. The maintenance of economic asymmetries between the colony and the metropolis required that the latter kept a near absolute political control of the former. Neither economic nor political control could have been sustained without the pervasive belief in the cultural superiority of the colonizers. In order to establish this superiority, it was important to conquer not only the land and goods of the colonized but also their culture and mind. Colonization therefore involved not just economic and political injustice but also *cultural* injustice.[2] The primary focus of my chapter is the *continuing* cultural injustice of modern colonialism. This injustice has neither ceased nor is present with the same force and vividness as in the past. Though somewhat faded, it has not evaporated completely, however. How do we respond to these injustices? What is the requirement of justice when the culture and the mind of a people are severely damaged by another people?

We can respond to colonial and other forms of injustices in different ways. For killing, rape, torture, and abduction, legal prosecution and punishment is appropriate, even when it is not always possible. Contemporary societies have sought to prosecute perpetrators of atrocity and sometimes even those who benefited from the repression of communities. Less aggressive forms of retributive punishment can also be tried. For example, Czechoslovakia removed those civil servants from public office who were implicated in the old regime. But retribution is not the only response to grave injustice. If goods are stolen and lands occupied, then justice minimally requires not only that the offender be punished but that they be restored to original owners. Similarly, if the reins of a community have been wrongly usurped by members of another community, then justice, at the very least requires that the members of the wronged community begin to rule themselves again. And if retribution and restoration are either not possible or are morally unsustainable, then justice requires some form of compensation to the victims. This is as true of individuals as it is of groups. Many societies have attempted alternative reparative responses. In Canada, First Nation groups were recompensed with land grants. In India, jobs in the government and seats in educational institutions are reserved for dalits to compensate for gross economic injustice in the past.

Other forms of reparations have also been attempted. After the overthrow of repressive communist regimes, East Germany allowed public access to secret police files. In Chile and Argentina, commissions of enquiry were set up to recover the bitter truth of mass disappearance. The South African TRC too combined different reparative strategies that included a search for truth and sociopsychological healing. In a sense, these are all restorative strategies to give back dignity and self-respect to those from whom they were snatched. Indeed, affirmative action programs in India were introduced for dalits to compensate for systematic exclusion from the political sphere. Implicit in these policies, however, was an acknowledgment that a wrong against them had been committed by the rest of the community for which it was now prepared to offer an apology. Which of these responses is appropriate, if at all, for cultural injustice?[3] Can perpetrators be punished for inflicting cultural injustice? Does justice require the restoration of cultures and the healing of injured minds? Is this even possible? If not, what other reparations are in order? I undertake three tasks in this chapter. First, to specify what I mean by cultural injustice and to identify the different forms of cultural injustice in colonialism. Second, I delineate three diverse perspectives on cultural injustices of colonialism. I offer a brief evaluation of each and specify which of these is more suited to India and related countries and why. Third, I try to explore a response to this injustice, one which goes beyond silence and denial but rules out retaliatory violence against or forcible exclusion of cultures of former colonizers. I argue that though both victims and perpetrators must work out their own separate and distinctive responses, the rectification of cultural injustice also requires a common response from both.

10.1. CULTURAL INJUSTICE

What is cultural injustice? I take it that all of us are equally entitled to make choices about how to live our lives and that it is wrong, indeed unjust to interfere with these choices. To make these choices, we must first be able to make sense of and evaluate the situations within which they are made. This activity of interpreting and evaluating situations and choices is partly group-dependent because it depends on collectively generated and sustained systems of meanings and significances. The group in question involves not just all contemporary members but their predecessors and successors as well. Thus the generation and sustenance of this system of meanings, interpretations, and significances are historical. Culture, then, is a historically generated, collectively sustained system of meanings and significance by reference to which a group understands and regulates its individual and collective life.[4]

Being a system of meanings, culture is reflected in our conceptual framework, and in our language. Since culture is also a system of evaluation concerning our own life and the lives of others, our action and that of others, an inextricable link exists between culture and ethics. Since religion and ethics are frequently tied to one another and culture is the overarching structure of all meanings, culture is also tied to religion. Thus culture is embodied in the collective memories and future visions of a group, in the group's myths, rituals, rules, norms, and customs. Since all of these—conceptual framework, language, collective memory, future visions, rules, norms and customs, myths and rituals, morality and religion, provide a sense of who we are and our self-worth, culture is inextricably linked to individual and collective identity.[5] Given its importance, every group must have access to its own systems of meanings, interpretations and values, to its tradition and heritage, to its cultures. If members of a group are denied access to their own culture then they suffer cultural injustice. This happens when they are born into the practices of a society that prevent them from having a knowledge of the historical and cultural traditions of their own ethnic or cultural group. Thomas calls this natal alienation.[6] If natal alienation occurs because of the forcible destruction of their culture, then there is grave cultural injustice.

Anything that is generated and sustained over time cannot remain static. Since cultures are historical, they must change over time. However, wherever humanly possible, members of a cultural community must be able to change their culture by their own light, by their self-understandings, in terms of a set of reasons with which they identify and which they have more or less worked out themselves. When the culture of a group changes behind their backs, by acts of another group of people in terms that it does not understand, then the group loses cultural autonomy, which is another form of cultural injustice.

A culture is sustained when there is an uninterrupted transfer of cultural goods and resources from one generation to another. Just as individuals care about their children and grandchildren and are predisposed to accept a collective obligation to save and pass on resources to their descendants, just so members of a cultural community care about future generations and are predisposed to accept a collective obligation to transfer cultural resources to their descendants.[7] To be sure, this transfer cannot be entirely free of interruption but nor must the interruption last too long or go too deep. If that were to happen, the fundamental ways in which a group frames its experience and thinks about, individuates and understands the world—what I call the *basic cultural forms* of a group—can undergo a fundamental change. Even if this were to happen, it would not constitute a cultural injustice where this occurs on its own or by the group's own mistaken actions. Cultural injustice occurs when the basic cultural forms of a group are altered by the arbitrary or deliberate actions of another powerful or dominant group. An individual may appear to live her life autonomously if she acts on reasons (beliefs, desires) that she chooses or endorses but the group to which she belongs may not be autonomous if the framework within which it conceives, understands, and interprets these reasons is not collectively chosen or endorsed. A forcible alteration in the basic cultural form affects cultural autonomy in this deeper sense. Finally, cultures are sustained by groups whose individual members possess the capacity to do so. If this capacity to sustain cultures is damaged by the deliberate or arbitrary actions of members of another cultural group, then here too there has been cultural injustice.[8] Indeed, this loss of capacity has grave consequences. If part of the culture of a people is lost or damaged but their collective capacity to repair or reinvent it is intact, then the wrong of a cultural injustice can be undone relatively easily. However, if the collective capacity of a group is itself lost or badly damaged, then the harm is particularly grave. I shall call this a grave psychocultural injustice.

10.2. THREE PERSPECTIVES ON CULTURAL INJUSTICE

10.2.1. Fanon, Cesaire, Memmi: The Extreme Negative Perspective

Allow me to now examine the first view on the cultural injustice of colonialism: grave cultural injustice and frequently, grave psychocultural injustice is an integral feature of the system of domination that has come to be associated with modern colonialism. Without detracting from the truth or importance of this claim, I shall call this the extreme negative perspective on cultural colonialism.

The African writers Aime Cesaire, Franz Fanon, and Albert Memmi passionately argued that the main consequence of colonialism was not the mere exploitation but the objectification and dehumanization of the colonized subject. Fanon declared that colonialism had so crushingly annihilated the self of the black African that after this experience 'the black man is not a man'.[9] But what does it mean to lose one's self? Is this even a coherent idea? It is possible to make sense of what Fanon is trying to get at. At the very least, it means that as a result of colonization, the black man has lost a complete sense of self-respect. But Fanon draws our attention to something even more fundamental. A person whose self has been annihilated is one who is almost entirely what the other makes of her and one whose attributes could not have been constituted by her own conception and agency for the simple reason that she has no conception or agency of her own. Such a person cannot function as a human agent because she has lost the most crucial and fundamental relation a person can have with herself. She is devoid of basic self-confidence.[10] Those who have undergone extreme experiences of physical violation such as rape and torture are known to have been deprived of the ability to access their needs as their own and to express them without fear or anxiety. It follows that if they lose their self-confidence, the colonized must have been subjected to severe repression. They are subjected to coercion of the body, to physical violence and severe restriction of physical movement. They are also subjected to coercion of the will by punishment or by the threat of it. Moreover, this coercive, interfering action by the colonizer is done with impunity and at will. Because he can hardly ever be penalized, the colonizer interferes with impunity. He interferes at will because he never waits for an independent legitimating circumstance or motive. Only the power of his own capricious will restricts his own behavior.[11] This arbitrary but persistent and coercive interference ultimately breaks the spirit of the colonized resulting in the loss of basic self-confidence. This confirms the central point of Fanon's claim that '... de-humanization enters the psyche and subjectivity of the colonized people'.

A person without basic self-confidence lacks the fundamental capacity to contribute to the sustenance and growth of his culture. Such a person is condemned to lose his memory for memory is not purely a mental phenomenon. It rests on its institutions. However, once the institutions of the colonized are demolished or petrified, he also loses a proper memory of the past.[12] From then on, 'the memory assigned to him is not that of his own people. The history he has been taught is not his own. Everything seems to have taken place out of his country. Everything exists only with reference what he is not'. Such a person who has been forced to turn away from his own culture and tradition suffers from natal alienation. The colonized is natally alienated because he is born into the practices of a society that prevent him from participating in or having a secure knowledge of the historical and cultural traditions of his own ethnic or cultural group. A colonized group that suffers natal alienation and whose members have no common memory or basic self-confidence and show signs of self-hatred and pathetic mimicry of the colonizers are victims of grave psychocultural injustice at the hands of the colonized.

A person who suffers from natal alienation and has lost basic self-confidence develops grave moral defects, the principal deficiency being a permanent propensity to be servile. Given the relationship between culture and identity, it is not surprising that the attributes of natal alienation and servility are frequently found in the same people. Thomas Hill's fictional Uncle Tom almost wholly echoes what Fanon and others have in mind.[13] Uncle Tom steps aside for white men, does not complain when less qualified whites take over his job, displays the symbols of deference to whites, always with a bowed stance and a ready 'sir' and 'ma'am'. He accepts without question the idea that as a black he is owed less than whites, his desires are worth nothing and those of the white man are worth their weight in gold. In short, he believes in the intrinsic superiority of the white man and because this belief affects his character and action, he betrays complete absence of any self-respect or self-worth.

To escape their colonized condition, victims of grave psychocultural injustice make an earnest attempt to resemble the colonizer to the point of 'disappearing in him'.[14] Hoping that the colonizer would make them one of his own, they endeavor to forget the past, change collective habits and adopt Western language, culture, and customs. His desperate need for approval and acceptance from the colonizer goes hand-in-hand with his rejection of his true self. As he adopts the colonizer's values, he also embraces his own condemnation. 'In order to free himself, he agrees to destroy himself'.[15] His love for the colonizer is 'subtended by a complex of feelings ranging from shame to self-hate'.[16] When Negro women try desperately to uncurl their hair, which keeps curling back or torture their skin to make it a little lighter or when bourgeois women prefer a mediocre jewel from Europe to the purest jewel of their tradition, they succumb to the most superficial Europeanization. Superficiality is the achievement of the colonized and mimicry the process by which it is accomplished.

10.2.2. The Contact-Zone Perspective: Denial of Cultural Injustice

The most direct opposition to this extreme negative perspective on cultural colonialism comes from those who argue that while colonialism involved economic and political injustice, it generally refrained from interfering in the cultures of the exploited people.[17] Colonial empires, they argue, are known to have given the colonized a great degree of cultural autonomy. Over time, cultural interchange and diversity was an inevitable by-product of colonial empires and a synthesis or what has come to be called hybridity was a natural outcome of this encounter. If so, it might even be denied that cultural injustice was a feature of colonialism.

There is some evidence to support this view, particularly if it is used selectively. Undoubtedly, despite ideological pronouncements of cultural difference, colonialism brought together different groups of people in intimate contact with one another. Disparate cultures met each other in a 'contact zone' where they grappled with the other's way of looking at the world.[18] Borrowing and lending were commonplace in these social spaces and therefore, the distinction between the cultures of the colonizer and of the colonized began to blur. For example, there is ample evidence to show that in the early part of the East India Company's foray into India, colonial settlers willingly embraced large chunks of Indian culture in order to feel at home. They lived like Indians at home and in the office, wore Indian dress and observed Indian customs and religious practices. A number of them married Indian women. 'White Mughals' are clearly a case of crossover. Such crossovers came from the opposite direction when as a by-product of colonial rule or as a result of colonial policies, Indian immigrants reached the metropolis and non-Indian colonies of the empire. Over a period of time, a degree of synthesis simply had to come about no matter who imitated whom in the initial stages of colonial encounter. If so, far from freezing identities, colonialism destabilized and made them fluid. Second, colonial belief systems could hardly have formed without negotiation with and incorporation of indigenous ideas. Frequently, the colonizer depended on the native for access to vital information without which colonial rule would collapse. Much evidence exists to show that without local knowledge it would have been impossible for the colonizer to build dams, bridges, and irrigation systems or to collect revenue. Land management would have been impossible without traditional knowledge governing the relationship with peasants, landlords, and the state.[19] Moreover, even as Western ideas were brought to colonized lands, their successful realization would not have been possible had local experts not grafted them onto their traditional analogs. For example, the idiom of order could not have functioned without the Indian idiom of *Danda* (an ensemble of power, authority, and punishment emphasizing force and fear as the fundamental principles of politics). Likewise, the civilizing mission of the British required the idiom of improvement which depended for its realization on the Indian idiom of *Dharma*, understood broadly as 'virtue, the moral duty'.[20] Similarly, travelers and conquerors were frequently dependent on the services of translators and relied on them for understanding almost everything about the natives. These translations into a suitable vernacular vocabulary were never pure or perfect; some synthesis was therefore inevitable. In such situations of dynamic cultural interaction and ambivalence, is it not hard to sustain the claim of cultural injustice?

Claims of cultural injustice can be disputed in other ways too. First, it can easily be argued that directly in the midst of economic exploitation and political despotism, there was one arena where the colonized continued to exercise near absolute sovereignty. For example, in India elites began to resist cultural colonization by dividing the world into a material, outside sphere constituted of the economy, statecraft, science and ideology, and a spiritual, inner-domain of culture which includes religion, customs, and the family.[21] The colonized elites asserted their claim over their mother tongue and set up instruments for their dissemination. They conceded the supremacy of the West in the material world, but claimed the spiritual-cultural world for themselves and made it the essential feature of nationality, one that must be protected and defended. The state may have been given over to the colonizers but culture and the private sphere remained in the hands of the colonized. So the colonized exercised the right to their own culture and were permitted by the colonial state. If that be the case, then, so the argument might go, no matter how unjust colonial rule was from the economic and political view point, surely there was no cultural injustice inflicted by it.

Second, colonialism anyway was not an unambiguous, unmitigated disaster for the colonized. It was a civilizing force. Had not the Raj interjected liberal Western values and helped thereby to foster social reform, combat superstition, and raise the level of indigenous culture? In particular, colonial culture was a modern culture that directly challenged the filth in indigenous traditions. Elites and people from the lower strata both benefited from modernity. Thus, westernization was adopted for purely instrumental reasons. As early as in the late eighteenth century, shocked by the murky excesses of their own traditions, Calcuttan youth 'openly adopted an aggressive attitude to everything Hindu and openly defied the canons of their inherited religion, . . . while some of them offended public opinion by their youthful exuberance, such as drinking to excess, flinging beef-bones into the houses of the orthodox and parading the streets shouting "we have eaten Musalman bread".'[22] In short, hyper-Westernization became a form of protest against the filth in one's own traditions, something started by Ram Mohan Roy and continued to this day by dalits. (The statue of Ambedkar in a blue suit, with spectacles and polished shoes, Constitution in hand, is an apt reminder.) Quite possibly, changes in society necessitated certain functions to be performed and, in the absence of functional analogs within existing cultural systems, this role could be fulfilled only by elements within Western modernity. This explains the painless, rather smooth acceptance in India of modern educational and legal systems. As early as 1841, 'it was noticed that the Chamars, despised untouchables of northern India were not afraid to bring suits against their more powerful and privileged landlords'.[23] If the colonial modern culture served the interests of the colonized, how can the claim of cultural injustice be upheld?

Not only did the colonized benefit from colonial culture but arguably, the colonizers were harmed by it. This goes against folk wisdom for which the only sufferers of colonialism are the subject communities. However, as the Indian writer, Ashis Nandy points out, 'what Cesaire calls the decivilization of the colonizers is not an impotent fantasy but rather an empirical reality'.[24] For Nandy, colonialism is a cultural code shared by both the rulers and the ruled, the main function of which is to alter the cultural priorities on *both* sides and bring to the center of the colonized culture subcultures previously dormant and removes from the center of the colonizing culture that which might have been salient earlier. For example, parts of British culture which were least tender and humane became prominent. The 'softer, feminine side' of human nature was made irrelevant to the public sphere and in the name of the values of competition, achievement, control and productivity, new forms of institutionalized violence and ruthless social Darwinism was sanctified. Nandy claims that 'the tragedy of colonialism was also the tragedy of the younger sons, women, and all the etc. and so forths of Britain'. Nandy goes on to argue that the ideology of colonialism produced an 'undeveloped heart' and encouraged the colonizers to falsely impute to themselves magical feelings of omnipotence and permanence. A culture that harmed the victor as much as the victim surely obliterates the distinction between the two and this makes it difficult to hold on to one's claim of the cultural injustice of the colonialism.

Finally, it might be argued that even if there was cultural injustice in the colonial encounter, it was possibly due to larger social forces that even without direct political rule would have negatively affected cultures. If so, cultural injustice was incidental, not necessary to colonialism. On this view, colonization was only one form assumed by an expanding capitalism and a liberal democratic ethos that usually accompanies it. An emphasis on equality, individual freedom, and the resulting conception of justice would sooner rather than later have challenged the collective, hierarchical mode of thinking that characterizes non-Western traditional cultures. That it did so with the help of brutal colonial politics is no doubt unfortunate but modern culture would have come to traditional societies even without colonialism. More to the point, regardless of the consequence of political conquest, the colonizers were as much in the grip of this culture as the colonized and therefore, nobody can really be held morally responsible for the results. Given the ambivalent character of the colonial encounter, the most reasonable conclusion then can only be that colonialism generated at best minor cultural injustices, for which some regret can be expressed but nothing more.

How seriously do we take the claim that denies cultural injustices of colonialism? For a start, the importance of crossovers and hybridity must not be exaggerated. The number of colonized who crossed over was very small. Those who crossed over tended, at least in the initial but long period, to virtually surrender to colonial culture. More importantly, the much larger number of colonized peoples had no contact with their colonial rulers. Though their lives were surrounded and deeply affected by the empire, the vast majority of Indians never saw the English administrator. They were excluded from colonial modernity and its benefits, partly by the nature of its cultural form to which they insufficiently attuned but also deliberately by those very natives who had crossed over. Second, the assertion that Indian elites affirmed their originality in the private, cultural sphere is overstated. It fails to grasp the crucial point that the urgently felt need to be formally educated in one's own native language was itself a symptom of Western, colonial influence. Under conditions of modernity, access to a shared literate high culture had become the most important possession of a person.[25] Because it gave him employment, wealth, social status, and citizenship, he had a head start if this culture was shaped by his mother tongue. A sense of importance of one's mother tongue prefigured the realization that it could bring great economic and political benefits. There was nothing particularly original in this, for it replicated the trajectory of European nationalism. Third, the proud deployment of one's mother tongue did little to prevent a deeper split between the public and the private. The Indian intelligentsia became increasing concerned with social reform in public life and continued to nurture oppressive and hierarchical values within the four walls of their homes. Thus, they managed at the very best to stitch together a patchwork of the colonial modern and the traditional 'feudal' and lived in this world with an unacknowledged schizophrenia.[26]

Fourth, claims concerning the civilizing force of colonial rule understate the failure of colonial liberalism to overcome the resistance of oppressive customs and hierarchical belief systems and the many compromises imposed by these on attempts at social reform. It fails to recognize the pressing need felt by those unaffected by Western influence to effect transformation in their social practices. It also underestimates the real motivation behind the introduction of modern ideas and the distorted form they assumed. This motivation had less to do with social reform or revolution and more with the maintenance of colonial rule. Much of the justification to maintain this rule came from European values and institutions. However, colonial rule also necessitated that values and institutions prevalent in colonized societies were not entirely displaced. This meant that modern values were introduced partially and half-heartedly. Colonial rule both introduced and held back the flow of new ideas and institutions. Many of them therefore took a mediocre, stunted form. As Ranajit Guha puts it, 'ideas which were political dynamite in Europe had their critical charge doused and defused by colonialism'.[27] This might be overstating the case but not entirely wrong for at least some ideas with emancipatory intent.

But can anyone seriously contest that the colonized benefited from colonialism? Would not denying that they did be plainly wrong? However, it is hard to tell if the same benefits and many more would not have accrued without the mediation of colonialism. The historical geographer J. M. Blaut has argued that prior to 1492, 'the progress toward modernization and capitalism which was taking place in parts of Europe was also taking place in parts of Asia and Africa'.[28] European colonialism, in his view, probably thwarted these developments in other parts of the world and the wealth obtained from non-Europe was a necessary and important basis for the continued development of European modernity and capitalism.[29] Therefore, the view that Europe brought progress to the rest of the world is, quite simply, the colonizer's version of what happened. It is a Eurocentric picture that offers 'the colonizer's model of the world'. In any case, benefits of modernity to the colonized and its harm to the colonizer miss the point of the critic because the crux of the matter here is cultural autonomy, not gains and losses. After all, the liberty of persons and groups has frequently been impeded on the ground that such interference is for their own good, in their own real interests. When American Indian children were taken from their parents, sent to boarding school and educated in white ways, the goal was not to harm but to benefit them, 'to kill the backward Indian and to save the man'. No consent was obtained from their parents. No matter how beneficial modernity is to the colonized, the real issue is whether or not he and other members of his group are authors of the conceptual and cultural frame that gives their life meaning and significance. Colonial cultural modernity can be seen at best as a case of cultural paternalism.

The truth is that it is hard to ignore the historical fact that the meeting of disparate cultures took place in highly asymmetrical relations of domination and subordination, and though the ambivalence of colonial relations may not have been a product of pure imperial duplicity nor can it be construed as an outgrowth of an innocent encounter between equals. Not that all those who draw attention to these ambivalences espouse this myth but quite a few, in the name of restoring agency, deliberative capacity and crucial self-consciousness to victims, and to register the voice of native informants end up viewing the construction of colonial cultures and ideology as the joint product of a dialogue between the colonizers and the colonized.[30] This is far from the bitter truth. In short, it is hard to deny the cultural injustice of colonialism.

Does this mean that the extremist view is correct after all? This does not follow. This perspective is useful for some societies (African), for some elites of many colonized societies and for most elites of such societies in an important middle phase of colonialism. What is questionable in this view is not that colonialism took this coercive form and generated grave psychocultural injustice or that it threatened to bring grave cultural injustice about but that this happened everywhere, all the time. In short, the disputable feature of this view is that it makes pure coercion, a necessary and grave cultural or psychocultural injustice, a constitutive feature of colonial rule. This is not so for societies such as India. It is of course true that large sections of Indian elites were virtually forced or seduced into breaking away from their own identities and that they submitted to colonial modernity but this happened in one phase of colonialism. In another phase, a sustained critical examination of this self-surrender began to develop. The rebirth of self-questioning implies that even when there was a sustained assault on their indigenous culture, their collective *capacity* to reconstruct it was never damaged. On the whole, Indian elites were not victims of grave psychocultural injustice and Indian society did not suffer from grave cultural injustice.

10.2.3. The Moderately Negative View on Cultural Injustice

The perspective which denies that grave psychocultural justice was not a pervasive feature of colonialism, but admits that a variety of systematic cultural injustices were constitutive of it and therefore which challenges the extremism of both the first and the second perspectives may be called the moderately negative perspective on the cultural injustice of colonialism. For this perspective, it is important that we see that colonial rule operated with different mechanisms. In particular, that some of the more effective mechanisms of colonial rule have depended on voluntary and contrived consent of culturally co-opted elites and the cultural exclusion of the masses. In short, colonial regimes achieved their domination by creating partial consent. This consent was partial, first in the sense that the threat of coercion always surrounded it and secondly, in that it was given only by those incorporated within the regime, not by those excluded from it. Incorporation and exclusion were two intrinsic features of colonial cultural modernity.[31]

How was incorporation of elites achieved? Initially, assimilation was sought by a deliberate attempt to intellectually destroy the culture and history of the colonized on intellectual and moral grounds. As Ranajit Guha explains, colonial historians tried to do this in India so that they could then go on to fill the void with their own civilizational ideas. The substitution of Indian by colonial culture was meant to be completed in two successive phases. In the first, the historic culture of the Hindus was to be demolished by showing that it was superseded by the culture of Muslims and then the culture of Muslims was itself to be shown as inferior. Taken together, these two movements were to result in the virtual deletion of the entire precolonial past of our people who were then to be 'compensated for that loss by the gift of a new history—a fore-shortened history with the colonial state as its subject'.[32]

Had they succeeded in wholly destroying India's past and its culture or in demolishing their ability to resist and rebuild them, the extremist perspective would have got it just right. Fortunately this did not happen. However, colonialism did succeed for long periods in partially destroying the self-respect and confidence of elites in almost every colonized society. This happened in India too. This is the grain of truth in the extremist claim. This is why it is hard to accept the blanket assertion that 'there was no rupture with the past' or that 'traditional identities were not disrupted' or that 'colonialism introduced no more than one new idiom, one new strand in the complex mosaic of the societies subjected to it'. Or finally that 'the alleged schizophrenia induced by the conflict between traditional and modern identities did not quite exist'.[33] As I have mentioned, sections of the Indian elite in at least one phase of colonialism and to some degree, experienced some rupture with the past, a great deal of disruption of their own received identities, some form of schizophrenia and that the colonial modern was not merely one among several but the dominant idiom of self-understanding and the understanding of societies. Colonial society as a whole escaped this fate because a majority of its people were excluded from colonial culture and therefore also escaped many defects it created in the elites.

If cultural destruction did not succeed as a strategy of incorporation, by what mechanism were Indian elites incorporated into the colonial system? Incorporation was achieved by shaping the beliefs and desires of the elite and altering their identity. Fundamental to this alternative strategy was to get the colonized to believe in the worthlessness and inferiority of their own culture.[34] In the nineteenth century, many Indian things began to be denigrated. For example, the architect of early Indian liberalism, Raja Ram Mohan Roy felt that the government policy of support to Sanskrit and Arabic-Persian education would only serve to keep India in darkness.

The inferiorization of indigenous cultures, necessary for the exercise of colonial power, was effected by the generation of colonial discourse by Western political theorists, advisers to colonial governments, colonial administrators, official historians, and teachers of English literature. Following Edward Said, several scholars have argued that colonial power functioned by producing a discourse about the Orient, crucial to European self-understanding, premised on a binary opposition between the West and the non-West and that quite fundamentally misrepresented and traduced the latter. Thus, in the writings of apologists of colonialism such as James Mill, Indian history was assimilated into the history of Great Britain and used to mark a major difference between the people of two countries. One constituted the white-rulers, materially prosperous, much better civilized with a superior religion and belief system. The other were the ruled, ethnically black, vastly underdeveloped at a much lower level of civilization and inferior religion and belief system.[35] The colonizers had their own explanation for this superiority. By keeping their sexual appetite under control and working hard, European produced a mature, morally complex civilization. The Orient was lazy and barbaric and at best, primitive, childish, and morally simple, lacking the psychological growth of the European.[36] Similarly, the irrationality of the colonized was contrasted with rational Europeans. In the primitive mind, thought and reflection were largely absent and instinct predominated. Delayed gratification of desire was unknown to the non-European.[37] This made it hard for them to be rational.

Cultural colonialism then was largely a project of the inferiorization of colonized cultures whose members were seen by it in the image of a child, if not exactly treated as barbaric.[38] Two things followed, once this inferiorization was in place. First, since it generated a loss of self-esteem and self-respect, those among the elites who could escape their own 'inferior culture' did so and became 'more British than the British' in those spheres of societies that really mattered. They became, as Fanon puts it, 'people with black skin and white masks'. They did not entirely leave the whole of their culture but became uncomfortable with almost every one of its features. This discomfort with different aspects of their culture and tradition was indiscriminate and pervasive among Indian elites in one long phase of the colonial period. Second, those who could not or did not wish to escape their culture were condemned to be treated as inferior by their own, precisely those elites who had forsaken it. This led to new cultural divisions and to a system of graded inequality.[39]

This needs further explanation. No matter how much the colonized elites emulated their colonial masters, they were not accepted by them as their equals. (Hence the schizophrenia, the resentment and later the resistance.[40]) Not that the colonizer discouraged the elites to mimic him but nor did he entirely permit them to attain a European identity. In the last instance, their emulation was met with disdain. The colonized elites could not escape being culturally victimized. However, the more inferior they felt vis-à-vis the colonial masters, the more they tried to inferiorize their own people from whom, by virtue of their adoption of colonial culture, they increasingly became culturally estranged. In his writings, Ashis Nandy has made this point differently. He agrees that a colonial system perpetuates itself by forcing the colonized to accept new social norms and cognitive categories by a system of socio-economic rewards and punishments.[41] But, for him, it does this even more so with the help of a more dangerous and permanent system of inner rewards and punishments, the unconscious, secondary psychological gains and losses from suffering and submission under colonialism.[42] Over time the victim begins to identify with the aggressor and develops an inner resistance to even recognize what colonialism does to him.[43]

Colonial education played a major part in encouraging the emulation of the colonial masters. It taught Indian elites 'to appreciate colonial conquest as a triumph and achievement, when triumph meant their own defeat and achievement the loss of independence'.[44] Moreover, colonial education displaced popular Indian traditions. Once English became constitutive of thought itself, it cut the elites off from their own tradition. This was noted by the famous Bengali thinker, Bankim Chandra Chatterjee, who said that 'the term *sikshita* has now become the usual designation for those who have been educated in the Western mode', and is antonymous to *vidya*. Those who were *sikshita* were naturally alienated from traditional learning, entirely unacquainted with the systems of ancient Indian thought. One major consequence of colonialism then was this: it opened a wide schism between a Westernized colonial modernity and Indian tradition and this made it impossible for the new generation of the educated to communicate with the older generation of traditional scholars.

To sum up: colonialism did not destroy every indigenous culture. Nor did it objectify and dehumanize every colonial subject or treat him as barbaric. It did not even annihilate the basic self-confidence of all colonial subjects. However, by interfering in other cultures, colonialism began to distort them. It did so by shoving into margins hitherto central strands of indigenous culture and by pushing to the center those of its elements that were dormant or peripheral. This displacement often continued till elements centrally organizing the experience of the colonized people began to survive only as memory and were displaced by facets that were considered by them to be insignificant and worthless. This is how I understand Nandy's claim that colonial culture altered the cultural priorities of the colonized culture. Now this movement of elements from the center to the periphery and vice versa and change, more generally, is common to all cultures. It occurs partly because culture is a complex and unsystematized whole without a coordinating authority. So it is not change as such that is morally objectionable. Nor is the marginalization of once dominant strands. Rather, disapproval stems from the fact that this change is partly orchestrated by an authority with enormous political and economic power, which did not have the capacity to live the indigenous culture from the inside, and that forcibly changed the direction of indigenous cultures—bringing about changes in them almost wholly behind their backs. Ironically, the agents of this change were usually colonized elites themselves and only sometimes their white masters themselves.

Of the many examples Nandy furnishes, I mention one. Colonialism, he says, produced a cultural consensus in which political and social power symbolized the dominance of men and masculinity over women and femininity. Both androgyny and psychological bisexuality in Indian men were obscured marginalized and dislodged by middle-class European sexual stereotypes. These stereotypes were soon internalized by Indians who slowly resurrected the ideology of martial races latent in the traditional Indian concept of state craft and made them central to their experience and thinking. Henceforth, kshatriyahood became the indicator of authentic Indianness. Precolonial Indian culture, Nandy tells us, made subtle distinctions between different forms of androgyny and subjected them to evaluation. Some forms of androgyny were good and some others damaging. Colonialism lumped all these forms together, devalued them and opposed this crude diminished form to an undifferentiated, newly valorized form of masculinity. For example, the

Bengali writer Madhusudan Dutt rewrote the Ramayana and reversed the value hierarchy between Rama and Ravana. From Dutt's point of view, and in keeping with the cultural elevation of masculinity, the original Ramayana began to seem like a tragedy of sorts in which Ravana who was masculine, courageous, proud, competitive, achievement-oriented, and technologically superior was defeated by a feminine, weak-kneed, self-abnegating, and technologically inferior God, Rama. After the colonial transvaluation of values, Madhusudan Dutt grafts this masculinity to Rama himself. Rama now becomes a modern kshatriya king competing with and defeating another kshatriya king, who is alien but shares the same cultural codes. So in keeping with colonial ideology, a recessive feature of traditional Indian culture was now made salient.

I have so far spoken of two kinds of cultural injustice. First, the inferiorization of indigenous cultures. Second, the enforced marginalization of elements of indigenous culture by the colonizers. But there is a third kind in which the basic cultural form of indigenous cultures is transformed by the intentional and unintended acts of the colonizers. Let me give three examples of this transformative process. First, in colonial cultures, group classification became more important than individualization. Albert Memmi reminds us that very often the mark of the plural was a sign of the depersonalization of the colonized. 'The colonized is never characterized in an individual manner; he is entitled only to drown in an anonymous collectivity'.[45] This is not uncommon when a group encounters strangers. It sees them only as an undifferentiated mass, through a crude stereotype, as if they are all the same, each merely instantiating the broad features shared equally by all. Individuation and individuality is frequently denied to the unfamiliar. Colonialism institutionalized this and evolved policies based on the idea that the conception of an individual was simply absent among the colonized and only group identities mattered in their traditions.

Second, related to the first, is the invention in India of a new conception of caste and its elevation as the central symbol of Indian society. Precolonial India had multiple social identities and their relations and trajectories could be understood only as part of a complex and dynamic social and political context. An individual could be a member of a temple community, territorial group, family unit, occupational reference group, agricultural or trading associations, faith networks and so on. He was also a member of a jati (also translated as caste), which was only one category among others, one way of organizing and representing identity. Not much evidence exists that the people of precolonial India ever used a single term to express the diverse forms of identity and community in their own life worlds. Colonialism displaced the idea of jati with varna—the classification of all castes into four hierarchical orders with the Brahmin on top—gave it the sanction of religious scripture, thereby making caste a matter of a person's religious identity and finally turned it into the central, pervasive, and centralizing feature of Indian society and Hindu religion.[46]

The colonial encounter more than just gave salience to groups in general and caste in particular. It transformed how people conceived of their faiths. The great scholar of comparative religions Wilfred Cantwell Smith has reminded us that religion as a demarcated system of doctrines—scriptures—beliefs is an early modern European invention and begins its existence in and through the theological disputes of the sixteenth and seventeenth centuries.[47] Under the impact of colonialism, this category came to India and obliged Indians to think of themselves as members of one exclusive religious community, not just different from but opposed to others.[48] It is of course true that Gods and Goddesses, ethical norms and prescriptions, even rituals and practices that we now associate with Hinduism did exist in some form in the past. But that is not at issue here. Rather the point is that these were not all thought to be part of one single entity so that those who owed allegiance to any one of these set of practices did not think of themselves as belonging to a single system of belief and doctrine in competition with and opposition to all others. Elements that were later seen to be integral to Hinduism were not a reified ideological entity with the potential of being mobilized for political purposes, for instance, for the nationalist cause. It was cultural colonialism which made this possible. This alteration has played a central part in reshaping modern lives as we now live them.

It might be argued that if the colonial modern culture gave the colonized a robust but oppressive sense of collective identity and an equally restrictive sense of a unified belief system, it also gave them a cultural technology to escape from them—a technology that included conceptions of individual freedom and social justice. But this argument misses the point here. It concedes that the basic cultural form of indigenous cultures has been altered, bypassing their own understanding and reasoning. And this is a loss of cultural autonomy in a very deep sense. If so, it is a major cultural injustice. Besides, once older conceptions of individuation, multiple belongings and fluid selves as well as notions of faith are displaced or lost, there is a narrowing of reasonable options for the colonized to choose from. This too is loss of cultural freedom and therefore a definite cultural injustice.

Allow me to summarize. The extreme negative perspective is useful as an interpretative and explanatory tool for several African societies. It has great value for the understanding of internal colonialism. However, it is only of partial relevance to the understanding of European colonialism in societies such as India. The contact-zone perspective offers some insights, but overshoots its point. It is true that new contact zones emerged between hitherto disconnected cultures and that this resulted in synthesis and crossovers. Yet, all this happened within an overall context of asymmetries of power and knowledge. The third relatively moderate perspective on cultural injustice goes to the heart of the matter and reflects features found in all forms of colonial rule. Always and everywhere and at the very least, colonialism displaced, distorted and inferiorized cultures and altered the basic cultural forms of indigenous peoples. By forcefully interjecting a wholly new knowledge system, it not only violated the cultural autonomy of the colonized but generated new sociocultural divisions among them. All this was and continues to be unjust. My concern in the remaining part of the chapter is with claims of the moderate view and focuses therefore on how we must respond to the specific injustices to which it draws our attention. Since the cases of cultural injustice dealt with here involve special kinds of perpetrators, namely those who misrepresent, calumniate and inferiorize the common life or culture of other peoples, I shall call these perpetrators, traducers. I shall call victims of misrepresentation, calumny, and deliberate falsification, sufferers. These are terms of art designed to name perpetrators and victims of cultural injustices, used here to distinguish them from perpetrators and victims of other graver injustices, including cultural and psychocultural injustices to which I have referred above.

10.2.4. Cultural Injustice as Historic Injustice

So far I have assumed that the cultural injustice of colonialism is continuous over time. But this assumption can be challenged. It might be objected by some that colonialism is a thing of the past. It did, at one time, inflict injustices, including cultural injustice on the colonized, but now, the objection goes, the era of colonialism is over. In instances of historic injustice, there is no clear or determinate way of correcting past wrongs. After several generations have passed, some wrongs are simply not worth correcting.[49] If so, we should let bygones be bygones, and forget and forgive the colonizers. No further response is required. At any rate, a situation of a dialogic encounter between cultures may not have existed under conditions of colonialism but it does exist today. If so, the claim that something needs to be done now by way of correcting those wrongs need not be addressed because historic injustice has been superseded. Any action now may result in some other cultural injustice.

I offer three points against this claim. First, Jeremy Waldron, one of the principal protagonists of the idea of the supersession of historical injustice, admits that his thesis does not pertain to communally owned, nonmaterial goods. Even material goods such as land are not covered by his thesis when the disposed subject is a tribe or community and where the land holding of which it has been dispossessed is particularly important for its sense of identity.[50] If his thesis of supersession of historic injustice is not relevant to material goods with symbolic significance to the community, surely it cannot be valid for irreducibly social cultural goods. Finally, Waldron's thesis of supersession of reparative entitlements holds only if it is replaced by a proper theory of prospective justice. If one can show that no sustained effort is forthcoming to rectify current global cultural injustices, then there is no case for the supersession of historic injustice.

Second, this objection is premised on the view that cultural injustice ended with the cessation of colonial rule. But has it? Arguably, cultural injustice may have become more acute since the demise of formal and direct colonial rule. Several scholars point out that the colonialism of thought and categories may not only have survived the demise of empires but intensified. For example, Nandy claims that proper cultural colonialism began in India in 1947 and that the inner supports of colonial culture were resurrected just as its outer supports were being removed.[51] Others claim that the experience of colonialism is a continuing psychic experience that would have to be dealt with long after the actual colonial situation formally ends.[52] In some form, the anxiety and schizophrenia generated by a sudden break from one's own culture and knowledge systems persists among elites even today. Generally, those who have written of the cultural injustice of colonialism maintain that it is a continuing injustice. For example, the world over, those who express their protest in nonmasculine ways are treated with contempt. Since recognizable forms of protest must have a masculine character, protest is not even acknowledged as such when it does not have a masculine form. The hegemonic ideal of contemporary masculinity, a product of colonialism, continues to be sustained by a wide variety of social and cultural practices. For example, inspired by colonial role models of masculinity, Hinduism continues to grow more aggressive and intolerant because it is inspired by colonial role models of masculinity.

In northern India, those unable to speak English continue to feel inferior and are treated as such. Similarly, given the organization of research programs and the structural design of modern universities, ancient Indian manuscripts gather dust as there is no incentive to properly examine them. Sanskrit, which ought to be recognized as an appropriate research tool, is artificially and farcically revived as a 'living language' in news broadcasts that few people understand or care about. It is probably better nurtured in Kyoto or Jerusalem than in Indian universities. In fact, entire intellectual traditions that were once alive in Sanskrit or for that matter in Persian have been forgotten to such an extent that they are barely objects even of historic research. Courses on the history of social and political thought begin with the Greeks and end with Mill and Marx without a single reference to Indian thought. This happens predictably in all Western universities but also surprisingly in Indian universities. There is an occasional urge to do a history of Indian concepts but material for such work is either unavailable or cannot be properly understood. Scholars do not have an inkling of how to dredge up concepts that began life much earlier but are still embedded in social, political, and cultural practices. A creative use of ancient traditions for contemporary purposes is virtually nonexistent. In short, whole traditions of intellectual enquiry are virtually dead for modern Indian scholars today. Indeed, the gap between traditional pundits and modern scholars has probably grown after political independence. It would be fair to say that some degree of natal alienation is still present in the formerly colonized elites. Thus it is precisely because cultural distortions and unequal relations of colonial rule are reinscribed in current practices of postcolonial societies and in contemporary imbalances between first and third world countries, that we need to think today of some response to this injustice.

Critics may still not be satisfied. They may agree that the cases mentioned above are instances of cultural injustice but then add that these are all newly born injustices. They may require rectification but to drag European colonialism into their discussion is normatively irrelevant. For how can we be sure that psychological injuries (inferiority complex, etc.), the displacement of basic cultural forms, and the loss of communication between Western, modern and older, local systems of beliefs and knowledges are connected in a causally relevant way to past injustice? A person has a reparative obligation only if he is responsible for the injustice. He is responsible only if he has intentionally brought about the harm which constitutes injustice. How can a reparative demand be made on people who are not intentionally responsible for the injustice? Consider the case of a young unruly adolescent who drives without a licence and kills an innocent bystander. Surely, he is responsible for the death of the person. But in a sense, his parents too must share responsibility. After all, the child was brought up in their care and it was their business to make him rule abiding, and to ensure that he did not drive without a licence. In modern societies, such reparations must be the responsibility of the family. But what if the parents point a finger at the company their child keeps, at the school, even at the larger social environment in which he lives that is neither morally sensitive nor rule abiding? Must the demand for reparation be directed then at all these other agents, at society at large? Or consider another possibility. What if after his death, the family of the victim is destitute and his son, angered by his condition, robs a bank and gravely injures the bank manager? Is the family of the unruly adolescent at least partly responsible for the injury to the bank manager? Must they pay damages to him? This seems counterintuitive.

It is true that the killing of an innocent bystander is an injustice. It is also true that the injury to the bank manager is a new injustice. But how are the two injustices linked to one another? If they are not, then how can reparative obligations for both injustices, the old and the new, be imposed on the family of the unruly adolescent? Similarly, the current cultural disadvantage of a people may be a result of several disconnected historical injustices and the people responsible for them may be too many, existing at different points of time in a very long period between the initial injustice and the present harmful condition.[53] How can reparative obligations be imposed on all of them for each of the disconnected injustices?

A number of assumptions implicit in these questions must be made explicit. First, that we are responsible only for our intentional acts. Second, that these intentions are properties of individuals, not collectivities. Third, that injustices which appear to be disconnected *are* indeed disconnected and further that there is only one account of the way injustices are connected or disconnected. Each of these assumptions can be challenged. To do so, allow me to begin with what Bernard Williams has suggested are 'universal banalities'. When human beings act their actions cause things to happen, sometimes intentionally and sometimes not. What is brought about is sometimes celebrated and sometimes regretted or deplored, by the agent himself or by the beneficiaries or victims of the act or by both. Regret or its opposite, say a feeling of satisfaction or elation are not the only responses, however. For example, if a bad result is generated by virtue of something that a person did and therefore for which he is retrospectively responsible, then it becomes his prospective responsibility to repair the damage, and make amends. Such a demand that the retrospectively responsible person make up for the bad state of affairs produced by him may come from the agent himself or his victims or from both. This is self-evident when the damage is caused by an intentional act. If my rash driving causes an accident damaging the other person's car, then the entire responsibility for repairing or replacing it falls on me. My offer to make amends and the expectation of the injured party that I do so are both appropriate. But I may have to make amends even when a bad state of affairs ensues without my intentionally causing it. For example, if I lose a book that I borrowed from a friend, it is only proper that I offer to replace it and for my friend to expect that I do so. Both responses are equally legitimate, no matter how I lost it. I could not have *lost* it intentionally, but this may have happened either because I am a careless person who is prone to losing things or because my life had gone so wrong on that particular day that the unusually preoccupied state of my mind induced me to forget it on the bus that brought me home. This shows that I am responsible and can be blamed for acts I did not even intend. As Williams puts it, 'the responsibilities we have to recognize extend in many ways beyond our normal purposes and what we intentionally do'.[54] Again, he says 'those who have been hurt need a response; simply what has happened to them may give them a right to seek it, and where can they look more appropriately than to you, the cause'.[55]

This is true not only for acts which I perform on my own but also for those I perform jointly with others.[56] A group has collective responsibility for the suffering its acts cause to others, whether or not its members intend them. Going back to the example mentioned above, we all must share responsibility, though in different degrees, for the death of the innocent bystander because we all have contributed to generating and sustaining a morally insensitive environment in which people break the law with impunity. Moreover, this collective responsibility may spread not just horizontally but also vertically. We may be responsible for the current harm to persons even if we unintentionally contribute to practices that cause the suffering and which were initiated much before we were born. Those of us who do nothing to prevent the culture of lawlessness that we only inherited but did not create are still at least partly responsible for the action of the unruly kid who ran over his innocent victim. The entire case for reparations for injustices committed in the past is based on a notion of collective responsibility that stretches over time and is distributed among persons who live at different times. Thus, it is neither true that we are responsible only for our intended acts nor that responsibility is the property of individuals.

But what about the argument that there is no connection between one injustice in the past and another or injustices in the past and a current injustice? I am persuaded by Janna Thompson's response to this objection. According to her, injustices that happen over a period of time can be linked to one another. Consider the policies toward Aboriginals adopted by different Australian governments over a long period of time. These policies may have changed and may have been differently unjust but they all had in common the assumption that Aborigines were racially and culturally inferior. Thus, the injustices of each of the policies, seen from one point of view, are disconnected from one another but they can also be seen as 'interdependent components of a history of disrespect'. It is this history, according to her, that is relevant to reparative claims.[57] Past injustices 'often belong to an interconnected history of wrongs that ought to be treated as a whole for purposes of reparation', a point not fully appreciated by those who claim that reparation is warranted only for the automatic effects of the initial wrong act.[58] Thus, it is clear that in the complex historical processes of injustices, a plausible narrative can be built of continuing injustice. It would not then be a case of the earlier injustice having been superseded and a new injustice requiring rectification but rather a matter of a continuing injustice requiring a holistic reparative policy. In any case, if the roots of a current injustice lie in the past, then it is hardly likely that it can be rectified without acknowledging the past injustice.[59]

10.3. RESPONSES TO CULTURAL INJUSTICE

10.3.1. Traducer-Response and Sufferer-Response

I have spoken above of two responses. The first is demanded by the victim from the perpetrator. The second is a requirement imposed by the perpetrator on himself. Because these are both responses demanded of the perpetrator, let me call them perpetrator-responses and since we are concerned here with particular kinds of cultural injustice inflicted by traducers, let these be called traducer-response. A reparative response may be demanded not only of the perpetrator/traducer, however. It may come from the victim as what she owes to herself. No matter who caused the damage, we all have some responsibility to repair our own broken life. The victim has some obligation to bring himself back from the dead, even if there is no response from others, including from the person who caused the harm. Let me call this victim-response and in the context of cultural injustice, sufferer-response. Both perpetrator/traducer-response and victim/sufferer-response are necessary in situations of injustice and something is amiss when one or the other is absent. A situation in which the victim demands a response from the perpetrator/traducer but the latter, not acknowledging responsibility, makes no demands on himself goes ineluctably toward the growth of the unjustified belief that by generating a blame culture, victims are unduly perpetrating a new wrong. Nor will a situation of injustice be fully rectified if perpetrator/traducer-response is not accompanied by victim-response. A pure victim-response will also not take us very far. If former perpetrators do not participate in their rectification, then old injustices may continue or new injustices may be created. If our objective is to eliminate injustice, then we must ensure both kinds of responses in an appropriate form.

Postcolonial literature has made an important contribution to our understanding of cultural injustices. However, it appears to pay insufficient attention to responses. When it does attend to them, it focuses purely on sufferer-response. This sufferer-response is dominated by a rhetoric of resistance that excludes the traducer from any strategy of liberation and therefore, asks practically nothing from him. This suits the traducer fine because it helps him to continue living his life as if no wrong has been done. There is no expression of agent-regret at the cultural injustices of colonialism. Nor does he have a sense that in the aftermath of colonialism, it might be morally required of him to contribute to repairing damaged selves and cultures and to restoring the self-confidence and self-respect of the colonized. There is a widespread belief shared by everyone, by both the colonized and the colonizers, that after the transfer of political power, justice is fully restored. The colonized believe that the sole responsibility for restoring self-confidence and self-respect in themselves is their own. So do the colonizers.

There are many reasons for the belief of ordinary people that colonizing countries bear no responsibility for continuing injustices. This belief is due first because of a common sense morality according to which we are answerable only for actions that we intentionally perform. If the misery of a person is caused by our unintended acts, then that suffering is his or her personal misfortune—a case of pure bad luck. Since few people intentionally cause harm to the cultures of the formerly colonized people, no one can be held responsible for their continuing distress. Even if this continuing cultural disadvantage is recognized as a form of injustice inflicted by actions of members of one's community in the distant past, how can people today be held responsible for past actions? And if they are not responsible, then why should they be asked to make amends? Second, it may still be a moral requirement that the personal misfortune of human beings not be left entirely unattended. But the relevant agent who must do this attending, so modern sensibility tells us, is the state. The state, however, is meant to ameliorate suffering not of people generally but that of its own citizens. If so, the cultural injustice of communities must be remedied by their own state, not by the state of others. Third, most modern colonizing cultures on the one hand, make a special thing of some ethical emotions recognized separately as guilt and on the other, make relatively less of the reactions they recognize as shame.[60] This is unfortunate because though guilt directs us toward victims, it continues to restrict our attention to voluntary and intentional acts. I am believed to be guilty only if my intentional and wrong actions have caused suffering to others. And only under these conditions may the wronged person demand reparations from me. Otherwise not. Why, if I am not guilty, should the victim direct his anger at me or demand that I make amends? Now, since guilt explores the relation between intentional acts and the wrongs they cause, it pays insufficient attention to those unintended acts which flow from the kind of people we are and the harms they cause. Generally, it is other ethical emotions such as shame that push us to examine the moral defects of our character. Ideologies that over emphasize guilt over shame are unable to guide the attention of the perpetrator to himself and his deficiencies. Guilt does not quite reach the self-related depth to which shame does and this failure successfully blocks the acknowledgment of some responsibility where it is due. This puts former colonizers in a situation where they feel neither adequate guilt nor adequate shame at continuing injustice.

But what if the colonized publicly identified the role of the colonizers in sustaining cultural injustices? What if they tried to shame them: 'look this precisely is your role in the perpetuation of injustice. You must own up to responsibility for what you have done and for being the kind of person who could do such wrong things?' The basic experience of shame, Williams tells us, is that of being seen, inappropriately by the wrong people in the wrong act or condition.[61] When this happens, the natural reaction is to hide oneself, for example to be embarrassed because in being seen by others, one's sense of self is diminished. Are the colonizers ever embarrassed and diminished when told that the colonized have finally caught them in the wrong act in perpetuating cultural injustice? Very rarely.

Shame is not just a matter of being seen by any odd observer. But rather of being seen by an observer of a certain kind with a particular type of view.[62] The observer in question must be someone you respect and be one who, as a result of having seen you in the wrong act or condition, has a poor view of who you are. We feel ashamed only if poorly viewed by an observer whose opinions carry weight with us, not by those who do not matter. The colonizer feels no shame because the colonized still does not carry enough social weight in his moral life. The poor opinion of the colonized makes no difference to him.[63] Sufferers fail to induce the appropriate traducer-response: no agent-regret or remorse is seen or heard.

In a context where colonizers do not experience appropriate ethical emotions or acknowledge responsibility, they feel no moral need for reparation either. Over time, even sufferers give up demanding a response from traducers. Beyond a point, it is useless to look for any remedial action from the traducer. Therefore, it is no surprise that sufferer-responses abound and they take the form that they do: a persistent and shrill rhetoric of isolated, monologic resistance. Underlying it are motives of revenge: to defeat the colonizer by violence or by deceit and manipulation or else a tit-for-tat strategy of inferiorization. Thus one familiar response is to lump cultural injustice together with other injustices and to have the same crude solution for all of them, vengeful counterviolence. This is manifesting today in what is believed to be anticolonial, counter-hegemonic terrorism, though elements of it are also found in Fanon's radicalism. A second response is also inspired by Fanon. Algerian women must veil themselves to frustrate the colonizer, he had announced, so that they can see without being seen.[64] The veil, he said, was historically dynamic because its use can be changed strategically, according to circumstance. The cultural meaning of the veil must be read within the social space of those who wear them. It is about privacy, identity, rank, class, and kinship status and not necessarily about the subordination and oppression of women. The colonizer must be defeated by the cunning deployment of local cultural meanings that he can never fully understand. A third form of sufferer-response is to impose on one's own society an iron curtain, for example by banning 'foreign culture'—films, TV, books and so on. This sufferer-response uncritically accepts the idea of discrete cultures that interact with one another only as a zero-sum game. This fiercely parochial stance indiscriminately views all outsiders as cultural aggressors and forces them to lay off. It then tries to build a cultural and intellectual world in reaction to and isolation from the colonizing West—a pure, uncontaminated, original world radically decolonized and dewesternized. It further branches out into two different kinds. The first tries to establish its own superiority vis-à-vis the culture of the colonizer. The second seeks neither to be exploited nor to exploit. Since cultural interaction must make one either the traducer or the sufferer, the only escape from a relation of domination is to not interact at all. Rather, it is to discover the authentic sources of one's own culture and live by them in isolated splendor. To these three typical responses, we may add one more: to deny cultural injustice, to pretend that it does not exist.

10.3.2. Reparations for Cultural Injustice

None of these responses can, in the long run, really address the cultural injustices of colonialism. Is another response possible then between violence and forcible exclusion on the one hand and silence and denial on the other? What possibly could this response be? How should we respond to continuing cultural injustice? What should the sufferer demand from the traducer or from himself? I take it as given that prosecution is an absurd remedy for cultural injustice. If any morally adequate response is appropriate, then it must take some form of reparation. Why so? And what should be the content of such reparative claims?

Recall the attributes of cultural injustice: (*a*) the displacement and dislocation of indigenous cultures and the loss of their basic cultural forms. (*b*) The generation of damaged selves and schizophrenia in the colonized.[65] (*c*) The imposition on the colonized of the position of a perpetual chaser of the colonizer. Because he is cast as an imitator, he is forever condemned to be behind the colonizer, always pursuing purposes not of his own making. Such a situation leaves no scope for alternating and reciprocal leadership. (*d*) The inferiorization of the culture of the colonized. (*e*) Given to inferiorizing the colonized for long, the colonizer develops grave indifference to the fate of the colonized. He is morally deadened to the vulnerable and the estranged—a massive moral defect. In sum, at the deepest level, colonialism not only gravely damages colonized cultures and selves but also relations between the colonized and the colonizer.[66]

How are damaged cultures and broken relationships to be mended? Should the colonizers financially compensate for the damage and dislocation they caused to the cultures of the colonized? It is hard to calculate the monetary value of cultures and anyway inappropriate to do so. Therefore, like prosecution, this too seems an absurd requirement. What then should be the content of such reparative claims? A significant cause of broken relationship between the colonized and the colonizer is the failure on the part of the colonizer to extend the principle of moral equality to the colonized. How can moral indifference be replaced by an attitude that grants equal moral standing and worth to people of formerly colonized cultures? How can the basic attitude of the colonizer be changed? How can the circulation of crude stereotypes about other cultures be stopped? This is related to other questions. How can asymmetries of cultural power be transformed into relations of cultural equality? How can monologic interactions become dialogic? Two reparative strategies are relevant here, if we have traducer-response in mind. First, an apology for past wrongs. Apologies, as Martha Minow reminds us 'acknowledge the fact of harms, accept some degree of responsibility, avow sincere regret, and promise not to repeat the offence'.[67] Sincere apologies depend on experiencing shame and then making a positive use of this emotion to improve oneself and to reconstruct the world in which one has to live, a relevant traducer-response is to feel shame.

The promise not to repeat the offence is as difficult as, and presupposes, the acknowledgment of harms and the acceptance of responsibility. Because if the promise is to be fulfilled, it must be accompanied by a genuine cognitive resolve to change the ways in which the colonizers have viewed the colonized. This entails a major transformation on the way in which Western knowledge systems have been organized and regulated. It is also linked to the second reparative strategy: truth telling. Thus, stories of empire building, colonialism and imperialism and the cultural and cognitive damage they caused must be constructed. History, social science, humanities, the arts, and the media more generally each have a role to play in dismantling these powerful intellectual-cum-cultural colonizing systems and showing the collusion between belief-systems and colonialism. Coming to terms with the past is not only a political but a powerful cultural and intellectual act of truth telling. Such truth telling must be inspired by a persistent and engaging search for ethnocentric biases. New theoretical structures and strategies of perception are required to contest the previous dominant Western ways of saying things. Once upon a time, every single story was told from the standpoint of the colonizer. The colonized were included as a mere object, never as a subject. Changing this requires a major conceptual re-orientation toward the needs of the non-Western world.[68] Let me give an example from my own experience. Indian universities generally tend to be lukewarm to social and political philosophy. This is partly because of a lack of interest among academics in normative issues but also because of certain features of political philosophy itself. Its content may well be universal but its form is certainly parochial, no doubt partly because there are few non-Western scholars who take it up. Much of academic political philosophy takes little inspiration from non-Western societies, makes hardly any references to the problems they face and takes little notice of how cross-cultural issues acquire a distinct inflection in their cultures. Most of the examples discussed in political philosophy have no immediate relation to these societies. Besides, there are few non-Western philosophers who could become a role model for Indian students. No wonder that political scientists in India take virtually no interest in political philosophy. All this makes the task of a political philosopher in India very difficult. These difficulties are compounded by the unavailability of journals all of which are published abroad. It is hardly surprising therefore, that Indian students though enthused by political philosophy, do not display a great deal of self-confidence or competence in doing it. Changing all this means literally turning the world upside down. 'It means looking from the other side of the photograph, experiencing how differently things look when you live in Baghdad rather than in Boston and understanding why. It means realizing that when the West looks at the non-Western world, what it sees is often more a mirror image of itself and its assumptions than what the non-West is really like and how non-Western people actually feel and perceive themselves'.[69] This requires sustained intellectual commitment framed by a larger moral commitment to equal consideration and respect for all including the vulnerable and the stranger and a resolve to build common spaces where different cultures can enter into dialog with one another on equal terms. It also requires building a larger culture that allows ordinary people in colonizing countries to morally disassociate themselves from those practices of their governments and multinational corporations that perpetuate injustice.[70]

This resolve may also carry financial implications. The rectification of intellectual blunders committed in the past may be possible only by the institutionalization of systematic learning about other cultures and civilizations. This may require more than a token gesture of setting up an area studies program or a research institute. It may involve setting aside huge sums of money for research and education, educational scholarships, and the hiring of people with knowledge and understanding about these cultures. It would most certainly require correcting imbalances in the media by instituting more scrupulous policies of selecting the right people for the job and for ensuring adequate and culturally sensitive coverage of events in former colonies.

I have spoken above of traducer-response. Let me turn my attention once again to sufferer-response. What is an appropriate sufferer-response? I believe it too must change its character. Monological resistance may well be justifiable as a temporary act of defiance. But in the long run, sufferer-responses must cease to be restricted only to sufferers and must encompass the traducer. Surely, to rectify continuing cultural injustice, we need not monadic, isolated and disengaged responses but those which, though separate, are mutually engaged. This mutual engagement is mandatory for another important reason. I have hitherto spoken of colonizers and colonized and assumed that all colonizers are traducers and all colonized are sufferers. This is incorrect for two reasons. First, those descendants of colonizers who have unambiguously dissociated themselves from the acts of the colonial state and colonizers should be included, if at all, with the greatest of caution. The mere fact of being a white man or a white woman does not make one a traducer. Second, those among the colonized who had begun to collaborate and had benefited from colonization and those of their descendants who have still failed to morally dissociate themselves from the process of colonization can barely be counted among the sufferers. The mere fact of being, say, an Indian does not make one into an unambiguous victim or sufferer. I do not mean to suggest that colonizers and the colonized elite share equal responsibility for the suffering of the colonized people. However, the colonized elite has some responsibility, if not for their own initial suffering, then at least for the contribution they made toward the suffering of others in the reproduction of cultural injustices. Such people were surely morally tainted. It is no longer possible then, as it once might have been, to identify all perpetrators of injustice as Western and all victims as non-Western. The historical responsibility for the continuing cultural injustice of colonialism is distributed among both the colonizers and at least a part of the colonized elite. From here on, therefore, when I speak of traducers, I exclude some descendants of the colonizers and include some descendants of the colonized. Likewise, when I speak of sufferers, I do not mean to imply that every colonized person was a victim of cultural injustice to the same degree. These points must be kept in mind when we are thinking of appropriate responses to cultural injustices. If what is mentioned above is correct, then within the larger plot of working out a better understanding and reconciliation between colonial traducers and colonized sufferers is the subplot of better mutual understanding and reconciliation between colonized traducers and colonized sufferers. The colonizers have an obligation to the colonized. Among the colonized, the elites too have special obligation toward the colonized sufferers. The collaborative nature of the colonial enterprise at least in its middle phase implies that a proper response to it must also be worked out jointly.[71] An intellectual coming to terms with the past, a proper acknowledgment and telling of the truth about cultural colonialism must be the result of a joint effort of Western and non-Western intelligentsia.

However, this is easier said than done. No matter how complicitous the non-Western elites were or are in the production of cultural injustice, there is no getting away from the fact that huge asymmetries of knowledge and power still remain intact. We must reckon with the fact that Western people including those who have dissociated themselves from colonialism continue to function with little knowledge of the non-Western world. This is not the case with non-Western intellectuals. Indeed, it is impossible for them to function as intellectuals without a great deal of knowledge about Western intellectual traditions. I do not here mean merely that there are inequities of empirical knowledge of each other. I have in mind something deeper. The very assumptions and presuppositions underlying our enquiries into our own world are shot through with categories derived from Western experience. It is self-evident by now that the categories of Western thought are inadequate for our experience and lifeworld. Yet, it is these categories with which we cannot help but begin. We recognize that they should be neither the starting point of our investigations nor its finished product. Yet, this is an ever-present danger of our enquiries. We know for example that contemporary political theory is useful for our societies but we know better still that it is a product of a context that has practically no relation to our own. In short, the deep problem today for the sufferers of cultural injustice is that Western categories have both an undeniable universal potential and that they are fully intermingled with the specificity of Western practices and, worse, possess a deep imprint of Western domination and hegemony. We can neither ignore Western ideas nor fully show how they can be rescued from the pernicious effects of their own imperial imprint.[72] Western thought to non-Western people is both recognizably their own *and* alien.

It appears then that apart from working jointly with their western counterparts, the sufferers of cultural injustice also have to work on their own and work out their own distinctive responses. To begin with, they must know which responses to eschew. First, they should not yield to the temptation of 'postcolonial revenge'.[73] They should not retreat from anything Western merely on the ground that it is Western. They should neither blindly reject nor accept it. Second, they should avoid the pitfalls of a naive and dangerous nativism or an intellectually impoverished cultural nationalism. Third, as already implied above, the elites among the formerly colonized should not behave as if they had no hand whatsoever in their own victimization or in the victimization of their fellow citizens. Indeed, they should more openly acknowledge their active role in the neglect or inferiorization of their own tradition and culture.

What then should they do? First, sufferers of cultural injustice must turn their biculturalism into a strength rather than perpetually view it as a sign of their subjection. As they identify the eurocentrism and parochialism of Western categories, they should also see in this an invitation for the creative renewal of a potentially common tradition—that is one among many and yet shared. This can be done only if it is reinvigorated by non-Western peoples with their own outlook and interests in mind. Western traditions were also frozen by the impact of colonialism or by the sheer intellectual lethargy of its inheritors. It needs 'outsiders' to rejuvenate it. This is already happening with concepts such as secularism and democracy.

However, the renewal of Western traditions by non-Western people is not possible unless they are committed to a focused, collective effort to retrieve their own forgotten and neglected traditions. This entails the examination of texts that have so far been gathering dust in unknown sites. But can these indigenous traditions ever be recovered? Can cultures of the colonized be restored to a state in which they were before colonization? Can they be relocated where they were before their displacement by colonialism? Can basic cultural forms be recovered? It is doubtful if 'original cultural forms' can ever be recovered. There is a sense in which there is no going back to pure indigenous cultures because every rediscovery is at least partly a reinvention. We know that every revival of tradition has turned out to be its reinvention. Restoration may be possible for cultural artifacts that are physically embodied but for artifacts such as conceptual frameworks that are largely disembodied, this is extremely difficult. Yet the slow painstaking process of a part recovery of the voice and history of the colonized can begin by putting together and reinterpreting traces of evidence and meaning present in largely forgotten texts.

Retrieving intellectual traditions is not, of course, just a matter of locating texts and reading them creatively. It also means connecting with those people who escaped the deep impact of colonial modernity and who, therefore, are still steeped in traditions from which elites are themselves cut off. It is this collaborative effort between modern scholars, traditional pundits, organic intellectuals, and people on the ground that will help to rebuild forgotten cultural and intellectual traditions. This would also help articulate concepts embedded in social and cultural practices so that they are available as a resource for creative use. Only thus might the sufferers of colonialism be able to construct alternative modernities that are shaped by the experience of interacting cultures on an egalitarian basis and which respect the autonomy of all participants.

This is not as hopeless a task as might seem at first sight. In a way, it has been happening less self-consciously during much of the colonial encounter. In any encounter between cultures, some lending and borrowing is inevitable. This certainly is the grain of truth in the contact-zone perspective. In the making of the modern Bengali novel, modern and traditional conventions were mixed freely. Bankim drew freely from conventions of classical Sanskrit drama and epic poetry for describing nature, on Vaishnav lyrics for the representation of sexuality and eroticism. On folk comedy for farcical effects, on oral literature like the ballad for direct address to the reader, on Hindu mythology for prophesies and other forms of providential intervention.[74] Anticolonial movements reworked local resources to mobilize for decolonization.[75] Gandhi's movement for swaraj built on local resources in its methods at the same time as it borrowed from Western authors such as Tolstoy and Emerson.

One version of this attempt is already present in Gandhi's response. He took it on himself not only to liberate the non-Western peoples but also the West from the history and psychology of British colonialism.[76] For example, Gandhi believed that he could use the resources of androgyny available both in the east and in the repressed, marginalized Western traditions to challenge the hypermasculine worldview of colonialism. In his view, activism and courage could be liberated from aggressiveness and made compatible with the feminine principle.

Gandhi identified with the marginalized traditions of the West and made them his own. For him, 'India held in trusteeship aspects of the West lost to the West itself'.[77] Borrowing from the West was never for him a problem by itself. Choosing to borrow an object or an idea to suit one's own purposes is very different from being forced or manipulated into having it. Indeed, Gandhi freely acknowledged that the idea of nonviolence had its roots not in the sacred texts of India but in the Sermon on the Mount.[78] Yet, it was important for Gandhi to make sense of the West in Indian terms. This entailed grasping that the modern West offered one possible lifestyle among many, which unfortunately for both the West and India became cancerous, so Gandhi thought, by virtue of its disproportionate spread and power. In the end, however, it was not enough for Gandhi to make sense of the West in Indian terms but also to have a genuine place for it within Indian civilization. This was the very least he also expected from the best proponents of Western civilization.

The general point that emerges from Gandhi's project is this: what we have hitherto believed as universals is only one particular masquerading as such. These are false, abstract universals. If we are to arrive at genuine, concrete, transcultural universals, then we must first accept that we are different, unfamiliar, and strange. There are no easy and neat shortcuts to communication across cultures. Once we accept the difficulty and messiness of translation across cultures as also the initial circle of prejudice that surrounds us, we may be able to find a morally acceptable place for each other in our respective cultures. Then we can also hope for a richer, greater commonness.

NOTES

1. I am concerned with modern colonialism in this chapter but not with its most recent instances. It is arguable that the American invasion of Iraq and more broadly, the emergence of new forces of globalization led by the United States and its allies—transnational companies, financial and media institutions—betray the beginnings if not the return of a colonial empire. Whether or not this is the case, such instances of a possible, newly emerging imperial system are also not the concern of this chapter.
2. In this book, Kok-Chor Tan discusses all the three forms of injustices and argues that rectification of these injustices can be framed both in terms of arguments from global egalitarian justice and in terms of reparation. My focus is narrower, on cultural injustice and my own framing of the issue of rectification avoids an appeal to global egalitarian justice and relies on a broad idea of reparation.
3. This is not an issue that has been much addressed. Hitherto, focus has remained on socioeconomic and political injustice in both national and international contexts. More recently, attention has shifted to the exploration of responses to mass atrocities and cultural injustice within the nation-state. But there is a form of global cultural injustice which has been around for centuries. Much has been written on the injustice of cultural colonialism but not enough attempt has been made to construct a proper moral response to it.
4. See Parekh (2000: ch. 5).
5. See Raz (1994*b*).
6. See Sterba (1996).
7. Members are not always aware of these concerns nor do they necessarily acknowledge them but such concerns are presupposed by a number of things they do. It is also institutionalized in the educational system sustained by teachers and educators and is part of what parents expect from the teachers of their children.
8. Similarly, if colonial settlers and missionaries undermine the ability of indigenous people to govern themselves according to their own law, then there is grave political injustice. This precisely appears to have happened in Australia with the Aboriginal nations. On this, see Thompson (2002: 73). Similarly, the Canadian state had launched a systematic cultural assault on Aboriginal communities of Canada by promulgating the Indian Act that banned their cherished customs. The entire act presupposed the cultural backwardness and the incapacity for self-rule of these people. On this, see Cairns (2003: 78).
9. Fanon, *Black Skin, White Masks*, in Loomba (1998: 8).
10. See Honneth (1996: 118).

11. See Pettit (1996).
12. Memmi (1965: 103).
13. See Hill (1991*a*: 19).
14. Memmi (1965: 120).
15. Ibid. 121.
16. Ibid.
17. Gellner (1994: 62, 78). Gellner says 'Rulers of dynastic states and empires were not concerned with whether their boundaries transgressed the so-to-speak ethno-graphic limits or even whether they reached them. They were interested in the tribute and labour potential of their subjects, not in their culture'.
18. Mary Pratt quoted in Loomba (1998).
19. Guha (1998: 158–64).
20. Ibid. 24–39.
21. Chatterjee (1998).
22. Charles Heimsath quoted in Singh (1988: 89).
23. O'Malley quoted in ibid. 100.
24. Nandy (1983).
25. See Gellner (1994: 62).
26. On the cultural phenomenon of patchwork, see Bhargava (2001: 9–26).
27. Guha (1998: 169).
28. Blaut (1993: 152).
29. Ibid. 10.
30. On this, see Dirks (2002).
31. Incorporation is necessary because 'it is an essential feature of colonization to try to create an institutionally complete society'. This requires that 'natives adjust to the language, pattern of work and mental habits of the colonizers, if they had any hope of survival leave alone flourishing'. See Kymlicka (1995).
32. Guha (1998: 75–80).
33. Pieterse and Parekh (1997: 2–3).
34. Fanon understood this well. For him, 'the colonized people are not simply those whose labor has been appropriated but those in whose soul an inferiority complex has been created by the death and burial of its local cultural originality'.
35. See Guha (1998: 3).
36. See Mehta (1999), Sterba (1996), Nandy (1983), and Viswanathan (1998).
37. See Mehta (1999).
38. As Mehta (1999) points out, childhood is a theme that runs through the writings of British liberals on India. For these liberals, 'India is a child for which the empire offers the prospect of legitimate and progressive parentage and toward which Britain, as a parent, is similarly obligated and competent' (32).
39. This term was used by Ambedkar, the great leader of the so-called 'untouchables' of India.
40. This is what Tagore had to say, 'we had just graduated and undertaken to translate such foreign phrases as equality, liberty, fraternity, etc. into Bangla, we thought that Europe, with all its physical prowess, acknowledged the weak as its

equal in terms of human right. We, the recent graduates, were absolutely overwhelmed and looked upon them as gods whom we could go on worshipping for all time and who would go on helping us for ever with their beneficence . . . The point I want to make is that an idea is fast gaining ground in India as well as in England itself that European principles are meant for Europe alone. Indians are so very different that the principles of civilization are not fully suitable for their needs' (quoted in Guha (1998: 68–71). Thus, even the most eminent of Indian liberals—one who believed in the universality of culture more than many of his contemporaries—was finally not deceived by the universalist claim of English liberalism.

41. To transform Indians into white men was a conscious colonial policy of the British after mid-19th cent. Lord Macaulay famously evolved a strategy guided by the need 'To form a class of persons, Indians in blood and color, but English in taste, in opinions, in morals, and in intellect' (quoted in Mehta 1999: 15).
42. See Nandy (1983).
43. Nandy (1983: xiv). Indeed, a colonial culture is one in which the ruled are constantly tempted to fight their rulers within the psychological limits set by the latter. e.g. even anticolonial protest is modeled on this new valorized image of masculinity. For Nandy, it is no surprise that the West has produced not only its servile imitators and admirers but also its circus-tamed opponents and its tragic counter players performing their last gladiator-like acts of courage in front of appreciative Caesars, Nandy claims that the standard opponents of the West have been integrated within the dominant consciousness as 'ornamental dissenters'.
44. Guha (1998: 171).
45. Quoted in Loomba (1998: 70).
46. See Dirks (2002: 13–14), and Sheth in de Souza (2000: 237–63).
47. Smith (1991, original edn. 1962).
48. There is no word for religion in most Indian languages. The Sanskrit word 'dharma' into which it is usually translated is not adequate for this purpose.
49. See Waldron (1992).
50. Waldron, ibid.
51. Nandy (1983).
52. George Lamming cited in Hulme (1993).
53. See Thompson (2001).
54. Williams (1993: 74). On this and related points also see Swinburne (1989) as well as the discussion of these issues in Thompson (2002: 44–6).
55. Williams (1993: 70).
56. On a defense of the idea of collective responsibility, see the essays by David Cooper, Joel Feinberg, Howard McGary, and Larry May in May and Hoffman (1991).
57. Thompson (2002: 82).
58. For this point, see Thompson (2002: 79).
59. For discussion of this point, see Kok-Chor Tan in this book.

60. Williams (1993: 91).
61. Williams (1993: 78).
62. Williams (1993).
63. On these and related issues concerning imperial indifference on the opinion others hold of the actions of superpowers, see Bhargava (2002).
64. Fanon (1970).
65. As Fanon put it, 'colonialism forces the people it dominates to ask themselves the question constantly: "In reality, who am I"' Frantz Fanon, quoted in Young (2001: 139).
66. Janna Thompson has helpfully made distinction between two theories of reparations which she calls 'reparation as restoration' and 'reparation as reconciliation'. I locate my own perspective on reparation within the second theory, i.e. as part of a broader theory of reconciliation. On my own perspective on reconciliation, see Bhargava (2000).
67. Minow (1998: 112).
68. See Young (2001).
69. Young, ibid. 2.
70. On moral disassociation, see Sterba (1996).
71. This point was important also because reparative claims presuppose that we have properly identified both the claimants who are entitled to reparation as well as those who have the obligation to provide it. On these points, see Thompson (2002: ch. 3).
72. Some of these issues are also raised by Chakrabarty (2000), and Pieterse and Parekh (1997).
73. I borrow this phrase from Gandhi (1998: x).
74. See Guha (1998: 179).
75. On this, see Pieterse and Parekh (1997: 6).
76. See Gandhi *Hind Swaraj* in, e.g. Gandhi (1997). For an illuminating discussion of these issues, see Nandy (1983).
77. Nandy (1983: 74).
78. Nandy, ibid.

11

Reparations as Symbol: Narratives of Resistance, Reticence, and Possibility in South Africa[1]

Brandon Hamber

In South Africa there is clearly the need to address its history of colonialism, labor exploitation akin to slavery, internal oppression largely by the white minority, as well as a litany of human rights violations committed during the struggle for independence. This task, however, cannot only be backward-looking or simply about recognizing past hurts; it needs to reckon simultaneously with a legacy of profound racially based socioeconomic inequalities that continue to weigh heavily on the present. This chapter considers the place for reparations in this task. In considering this, however, several questions are immediately apparent. For example, when thinking about reparations in South Africa are we talking about reparations for direct violations of human rights committed under apartheid, or for systematic oppression, or both? In terms of the structural and systematic oppression, are we presupposing that reparations are a useful vehicle for achieving economic and social justice? Are we conflating reparations with socioeconomic development? And finally, are reparations the most effective vehicle for mending relationships between the oppressed and former oppressors especially in a context such as South Africa where former oppressors and oppressed continue to live side-by-side following a negotiated transition?

Much has happened to date concerning reparations in South Africa, but equally the debate is in its infancy. This chapter, which is a developing exploration of reparations in the South Africa context post-1994, begins by outlining the parameters of the reparations debate in South Africa. This is discussed in three parts, that is individual reparations, apartheid reparations, and what is termed 'community reparations'. Some reflections as well as some questions and considerations that are emerging in these debates are then highlighted. The chapter concludes by discussing the symbolic meaning of reparations in the so-called new South Africa, and the importance of acknowledgment in the process of reparations.

Of course, it is difficult to discuss the issue of reparations in South Africa without contextualizing this within the changes that have taken place both socially and politically over the last decade. Within the limits of this chapter, however, it is not possible to do justice to the complex set of developments that have taken place. Suffice to say, South Africa has undergone a rapid process of change in the last ten years. In structural terms, a significant proportion of postapartheid South Africa is the same as it was prior to 1994. Voting still continues largely along racial lines (although not exclusively) and most of the poor remain black. Whites, although a minority, continue to wield the majority of economic power. That said, economic control and the influence of black South Africans across the spectrum in the country has changed dramatically. Political power has irreversibly changed hands and the African National Congress (ANC) government has made significant strides in attempting to deal with some of the socioeconomic legacies of apartheid,[2] although appalling inequality still exists.[3]

Nevertheless the old class structures, which were previously based on race, are changing. Although still wholly unequal in terms of overall economic distribution between blacks and white South Africans, a new black middle class is emerging. In less than a decade the number of black households' earning as much as the white household income has risen from 1,000 to 1,200,000; 43 percent of those in the top income bracket are now black and it is predicted that in 5 years they will be the majority.[4] It is now estimated that interblack inequality is greater than between blacks and whites,[5] indicating rapid socioeconomic advancement of a section of black South Africa. Journalist Allister Sparks concludes that broadly:

> These developments which to a degree make nonsense of President Mbeki's contention that South Africa consists of two nations,[6] one white and rich, the other black and poor. That there are two nations is indisputable, but the rich one is no longer entirely white. It is increasingly multiracial... It is not that nothing has changed, but that things have not changed for enough people.[7]

Since the advent of democracy in 1994, South Africa, unlike some of its neighbors, has managed to avoid large-scale internal civil strife in the first decade of its new dispensation. Many would argue this is a direct product of the approach to nation building which emerged from the 1990–4 negotiations, that is an approach to governance predicated on compromise, consensus, and reconciliation. It is within this context and the changing political and social landscape that issue of reparations has emerged on a number of different fronts. To date, three types of reparation processes have broadly been taking place in South Africa. These are interlinked in some ways, but are dealt with separately below, that is individual reparations, apartheid reparations, and community reparations.

11.1. INDIVIDUAL REPARATIONS

The debate concerning individual reparations has largely focused on so-called gross violations of human rights, such as murder and torture, and has mainly been linked with the TRC process. Space does not permit a thorough evaluation of the TRC,[8] and for this chapter I have chosen, in terms of the TRC, to only focus on the issues of reparations. Before doing that, however, it might be worthwhile summarizing some basic facts about the TRC.

The South African TRC process began in December 1995 and ended, at least in terms of documenting and receiving victim statements, when the Commission handed the first five volumes of its report to then President Mandela in October 1998. The amnesty hearings dragged into 2002, and the final two volumes of the report focusing on amnesty were published in March 2003. In total, about 20,000 people came forward and gave statements concerning the gross violations of human rights they suffered to the TRC, of which about 1,800 were heard in public. At the end of the process 7,094 people had applied for amnesty, and 1,160 of these individuals received amnesty or immunity from prosecution for their political crimes, which included murder, attempted murder, abduction or 'disappearance,' and torture. Essentially, the approach adopted traded truth for justice, that is amnesty was conditional on perpetrators disclosing fully all the details of the act for which they sought amnesty.[9] If amnesty was granted, all civil and criminal liability fell away.

In terms of reparations, the process technically fell within the remit of the least well-publicized of the three TRC Committees, namely the R&R Committee.[10] Unlike the Amnesty Committee[11] and the Human Rights Violations Committee,[12] it did not hold public hearings for either perpetrators or victims. Based on the findings of the other two Committees, the R&R Committee was mandated to design a policy of how best to assist those found to be victims, that is the direct survivors, family members and/or dependants of someone who had suffered a politically motivated gross violation of human rights associated with a killing, abduction, torture, or severe ill-treatment. The R&R Committee was obligated to make recommendations to 'reparate' these victims for the damages they had undergone in the conflicts of the past. According to the Promotion of National Unity and Reconciliation Act (hereafter the TRC Act) that set up the Commission, the TRC had to make recommendations to the President with regard to:

> The policy which should be followed or measures which should be taken with regard to the granting of reparation to victims or the taking of other measures aimed at rehabilitating and restoring the human and civil dignity of victims.[13]

The R&R Committee made such recommendations in its final reports. According to the TRC Act the policy could recommend any reparation measures in the form of compensation, ex gratia payment, restitution, rehabilitation, or recognition. The TRC final report makes a number of suggestions that utilize most of these measures. The President and Parliament was then to decide how, or whether, the policy would be implemented.

The TRC opted, in its final policy,[14] for an approach that did not utilize a means test for each victim. Seemingly, this was dismissed owing to cost, and the resources necessary for grading the psychological and physical injuries of the approximately 20,000 victims. The policy states that relatively equitable urgent and individual financial grants for each person 'found to be a victim' should be made available through the government.

A call for other reparations strategies was also included in the policy. These strategies included the need for symbolic reparations (e.g. erecting headstones, building memorials, renaming public facilities, a day of remembrance and so on), legal and administrative interventions (e.g. expunging criminal records, issuing declarations of death and so on), and the need for exhumations, reburials, and ceremonies. A number of community rehabilitation programmes were also recommended, and it was noted that these should form part of the general initiative to transform service provision in South Africa. These included, among others, establishing local treatment centers for survivors of gross violations of human rights, rehabilitation systems for perpetrators and their families, establishing self-sustaining community-based survivor support groups, as well as more broadly based recommendations such as setting up community colleges, establishing of housing projects and the rebuilding of demolished schools. A range of institutional reform measures designed to prevent the recurrence of human rights abuses are made. These form part of the wider recommendations of the TRC.

In line with the demands of the TRC Act, the TRC also had to consider granting *urgent interim reparations* (UIR). The R&R Committee proposed that the financial component of reparation be distributed in two phases. First, those found to be victims would be given an urgent one-off payment ranging from a baseline of approximately R2,000 (about US$325[15]) up to R6,000 (US$980) in exceptional circumstances.[16] The government has already paid out more than R50-million (about US$8 million) to 16,500 of the 18,800 victims identified by the TRC as needing so-called urgent relief. It is interesting to note that this only accounted for about 17 percent of the funds originally set aside for this purpose by the South African government.[17]

Regulations allowing for 'urgent' relief were only promulgated in April of 1998 despite the TRC beginning in December 1995. So-called urgent payment began in the July of 1998 about two-and-half years after the TRC began, and only months before the TRC officially ended its victim work and submitted its first five volumes of the final Report. Space does not permit a thorough evaluation of this process. Research with those who received this initial money has shown that:

> Urgent interim reparation (UIR) must be considered a token compensation or symbolic reparation in that it satisfied the recipients' material needs only briefly, and in that only those recipients who perceived the UIR as symbolic seemed to benefit from it. UIR has not in and of itself made a meaningful and substantial impact on the lives of recipients and cannot, therefore, be considered a significant or even an adequate attempt at reparations.[18]

The UIR scheme was intended to be complementary to a longer-term individual financial grant scheme proposed by the TRC. The TRC proposed a so-called long-term reparations scheme in its final report. It proposed that some 22,000 survivors should each roughly receive 17,000–24,000 (roughly US$2,750–US$3,950) each over a six-year period,[19] that is R477,400,000 million (US$78 million) per year. This is the equivalent of about 0.2 percent of government expenditure in total (based on 2000–1 figures). This would have meant paying out approximately R2,864,400,000 (roughly US$460 million) over a six-year period. These payouts were, in turn according to the TRC, to be complemented by the other symbolic, reparative, and rehabilitative measures mentioned above.

In February 2001 the government set aside a further R500 million (US$80 million at the current rate) for final reparations. This was added to the roughly R250 million already allocated and not used for UIR. Despite some announcements thereafter that a reparations programme was being designed, little happened. In June 2002 additional pressure was applied by victims' groups, using the Promotion of Access to Information Act. They applied to the Cape High Court for an order that would compel the government to make available to them the draft policy, or if one was not available, to provide a date when it would be. A court date was set for August 2003.

Finally, in April 15, 2003 (over seven years since the TRC began and over 4 years after the government received the TRC's first set of recommendations on reparations), South African President, Thabo Mbeki, announced that victims of apartheid who testified before the TRC would receive a one-off final reparations grant of R30,000 (US$4,900). A total of US$80 million would be paid to 19,000 victims, substantially less than the US$460 million recommended by the TRC, and fundamentally different in structure to a quasi-pension scheme approach spread over 6 years. Payments have begun.

The response from victims to the governments' eventual offer of reparations from victims was predicable given the delays and disparities between it and the TRC recommendations. Although some seem satisfied most seemed unhappy. Victims were quoted as saying that President Mbeki's words stung like salt in a wound, and Ntombi Mosikare, coordinator of the Khulumani Support Group added 'we only want the country to acknowledge us. What they are giving us is too little'.[20] Others referred to the grants as 'peanuts' and, in some cases, insufficient to cover medical expenses.[21]

These responses cannot be divorced from the acrimonious relationship between victim groups and the government that has developed over time. The relationship has not only been aggravated by delays and avoidance by government (and high expectations from victims), but also by direct and scathing comments. Some government statements have tried to reduce victim claims effectively to monetary gain. President Mbeki has, for example, undermined claims for reparations by victims from the TRC by saying: 'Did our people engage in a gigantic struggle, with some deciding to lay down their lives, with the prospect of financial reward in their minds? I have said, and I will say again, that any such suggestion is an insult to them and to all of us who now enjoy the freedom that they fought for'.[22]

To make matters worse President Mbeki reiterated the sentiment in his announcement that long-term reparations were to be granted.[23] Such comments have served to fuel the resentment many victims bore toward the government's seeming reticence in responding to the TRC's recommendations on reparation. This is one reason victim groups have sought alternative redress, albeit from a different source and fundamentally distinct in nature, through what have become known as the apartheid reparations.

11.2. APARTHEID REPARATIONS

On November 11, 2002, the Khulumani Victim Support Group (a group of victims of past political violence in South Africa)[24] filed a lawsuit in its name, as well as that of 85 of its 33,000 members, in the New York Eastern District Court against 21 multinational corporations and leading international banks for helping prop up the apartheid state.[25]

Khulumani, which has also been the group instrumental in lobbying for individual reparations, is supported internationally by a group known as the Apartheid Debt and Reparations Campaign (ADRC), an international umbrella body campaigning for the scrapping of developing-world debt and furthering the cause of reparations. This organizational alliance has seen the confluence of two different, and at times, competing but also complementary agendas. On the one hand, many of those who testified before the TRC probably have a more individualized view of reparations given their personal suffering following direct violations such as the murder of a loved one. On the other, some anti-debt campaigners invariably have a more politicized approach steeped in a strong anti-globalization ideology that can seemingly accommodate a more individualized approach. Most protagonists would also hold the view that given the profits gleaned by companies during apartheid, and the imposed financial exploitation, that it is just that some form of compensation and reparation is made by them.

In practical terms, the Khulumani claims are supported by US-based attorneys, Cohen, Milstein, Hausfeld, and Toll[26] who have adopted a strategy of citing each of the individual members of the Khulumani Support Group affected to avoid the necessity of having to go through class certification.[27] The lawsuits are based on the Alien Tort Claims Act[28] and common law principles of liability. Cohen et al. and complainants seek 'to hold those *businesses that aided and abetted the apartheid regime* responsible for the wrongs they made possible. For example: IBM and ICL provided the computers that enabled South Africa to create the hated pass book system and to control the black South African population. Car manufacturers provided the armored vehicles that were used to patrol the townships. Arms manufacturers violated the embargoes on sales to South Africa as did the oil companies. The Banks provided the funding that enabled South Africa to expand its police and security apparatus'.[29] Figures of anywhere between US$50 billion and US$100 billion have been mentioned.

As such the Cohen et al. led case, which is by far the most prominent case, is not a class action. That said there are other cases too and these have adopted the class action lawsuit approach modelled on compensation claims by Holocaust survivors.[30]

In the main, the South African government does not support the litigations. In fact, the government has dismissed the lawsuits out of hand. It is worth quoting President Mbeki on the issue as it highlights the government's unequivocal position:

> In the recent past, the issue of litigation and civil suits against corporations that benefited from the apartheid system has sharply arisen. In this regard, we wish to reiterate that the South African Government is not and will not be party to such

litigation. In addition, we consider it completely unacceptable that matters that are central to the future of our country should be adjudicated in foreign courts which bear no responsibility for the well-being of our country and the observance of the perspective contained in our constitution of the promotion of national reconciliation.[31]

Former President Mandela also holds the view that reparations is a domestic matter.[32] In June 2003, the South African Minister of Justice, Penuell Maduna, took the process one step forward by writing to the US District Judge John Sprizzo who was presiding over the cases asking him to dismiss them.[33] In the nine-page affidavit the Minister reiterates the government is opposed to the lawsuits; sees the issues they concern as being about sovereign domain of South Africa; notes the various achievements made by the government in terms of development; and dismisses the victims' actions as akin to wanting to set up 'a surrogate government'.

In November 2003, as a result of several companies named in the lawsuits filing a motion to dismiss, the cases were brought before the New York courts to decide if they would be allowed to continue. In December 2003, Desmond Tutu, former Chair of TRC, responded to South African Minister of Justice, Penuell Maduna's letter, by arguing for apartheid reparations in an affidavit Tutu then submitted to the US Courts. In his response Tutu notes:

> ... the very different character and objectives of the TRC process on the one hand, and potential civil litigation, on the other, make it clear that the assertion that adjudication of these Lawsuits would be at odds with the TRC, or otherwise undermine reconciliation in South Africa, is a *non-sequitur*. To the contrary, the obtaining of *compensation* for victims of apartheid, to supplement the very modest amount per victim to be awarded as *reparations* under the TRC process, could promote reconciliation, by addressing the needs of those apartheid victims dissatisfied with the small monetary value of TRC.

In September 2004 an amicus curiae or friends of the court was submitted to the US Court, this outlined the support for the case by international organizations, human rights groups, and TRC Commissioners.[34] However, on November 29, 2004 the judge dismissed the 'apartheid lawsuits'. Although the judge expressed the opinion that companies doing business with the apartheid regime may have been 'morally suspect or embarrassing', he said he could not see how the actions by US corporations had directly caused human rights violations such as murder or torture. The case is now on appeal.

Following the legal setbacks the Khulumani Support Group launched the 'Say Yes to Redress' Campaign which took place from 16 December 2004 to 16 December 2005. This campaign called on businesses to take the moral high ground and acknowledge that they conducted business in South Africa despite calls for restrictions on trade with the apartheid regime and sanctions, and that they profited from an unjust system. It also advocated for corporations to contribute voluntarily to a rehabilitation fund.[35] It remains to be seen if this will result in any action from corporations.

11.3. COMMUNITY REPARATIONS

A third type of reparations that has entered the domestic debate in South Africa is the notion of community reparations. One definition is that community reparations are strategies to provide broad access to some form of collective service for a large but select group of individuals said to have jointly suffered in some way. One example cited in the international literature is providing better and more accessible health services to previously oppressed minorities in remote areas.[36]

In South Africa, community reparations is a concept that is often alluded to, but has not been adequately defined. For example, when President Mbeki made his announcement about final TRC reparations, he noted these should be: 'Combined with *community reparations*, and assistance through opportunities and services'.[37] He did not fully define what he meant by community reparations. Based on the context of his statement, however, it seems as if he means actions that would benefit whole communities in some way. He adds services to his list of reparations as distinct from community reparations, so presumably he means general social upliftment when he talks of community reparations. This is in line with the general debate about reparations in South Africa, in which community reparations have a wider meaning, that is community development, social upliftment, and reconstruction more broadly (e.g. building schools and providing access to water). These may be targeted at specific communities that experienced high levels of violence. No 'reparations' have been granted in this way so far, or more to the point no development programme has officially been called reparations.

Such an approach, at least in theory, makes pragmatic sense and may even make egalitarian sense, that is if whole swathes of individuals were disadvantaged by apartheid, surely whole swathes of individuals should benefit from reparations.

But how does this approach intersect with questions of acknowledgment for past wrongs? And how is the role of those deemed responsible for such wrongs integrated into this approach? I shall return to these debates later in the chapter.

11.4. REFLECTIONS, QUESTIONS, AND CONSIDERATIONS

In South Africa one naturally cannot separate the debate concerning reparations (especially reparations for apartheid more generally) from the democratic transition that took place in 1994. The government is already engaged in programmes aimed at social development and upliftment. The South African ANC-led government with its massive majority and political power sees itself, through the use of state resources at its disposal and partnership with private sector, as the most legitimate and likely vehicle for reversing the oppression of the past.

That said, most readers of this brief history of the reparations debate in South Africa will probably be struck by the seemingly resistant attitude of new South African government to both individual and apartheid reparation campaigns. This approach is difficult to fathom—after all it is a government that has strong populist support and is ostensibly deeply committed to redressing the imbalances created by the apartheid past. Having said that, the government's resistance to the reparations process as it is currently framed by campaigners also makes perfect sense for the same reason.

The South African government *sees itself* as democratically elected (which they are with an enormous two-thirds majority) and fundamentally committed to transformation, a process which they have initiated and begun in earnest. To address this legacy the South African government has largely adopted a conciliatory and reformist approach—one that sees the business community as central to addressing these issues in a voluntary capacity and through structured institutional programmes. Such programmes have ranged from a Land's Claim process through to various economic policy initiatives.

The ANC-led government has squarely rejected any ideas of a wealth tax (as proposed by the TRC) and remains reluctant to demand any specific contributions from the business community other than through various business development funds that have already been set up. In terms of business it is keen to point out that a Business Trust partnership has been established. The Business Trust is an initiative of 145 companies in South Africa that work in partnership with government to undertake job creation and capacity building.[38]

One can only surmise that from the South African government's perspective, and assuming they feel they have now dealt with individual reparations for gross violations through the grants of 2003, accepting calls for apartheid reparations is tacit acceptance that the developmental plans they have put in place for transformation and redistribution are not working. Having made a moderate contribution to individual TRC reparations, community reparations in the broadest sense seem to be their preferred route at this stage for any further engagement with the reparations issue. Reparations (community reparations) should come in the form of development, which should benefit as many people as possible as President Mbeki has noted:

> An integrated and comprehensive response to the TRC Report should be about the continuing challenge of reconstruction and development: deepening democracy and the culture of human rights, ensuring good governance and transparency, intensifying economic growth and social programmes, improving citizens' safety and security and contributing to the building of a humane and just world order.[39]

At a broad level this is a persuasive argument, unless of course, one has doubts about the government's policy approach to development and if one considers it inappropriate to link reparations and development in the first place.

Many would oppose the government approach to reparations or more specifically economic development as reparations, because of policy difference; this is the case for most of those involved in the apartheid reparations campaign and certainly those coming from a more antiglobalization perspective. They are not alone, of course, and there is much internal criticism of the current governmental economic and development policy.[40] Space does not permit an analysis of this and it is not the focus of this chapter, but it is important to highlight the fact that the new government, as alluded to above, sees reconstruction unequivocally as a 'co-operative and voluntary partnership'.[41] They see local and international business as partners in this process, and wish to court them as such. Although the South African government suffers the pressure of having to toe the global international economic line, no doubt the mainstream of government now accepts much of the Western global thinking toward economic development—they are not merely victims of globalization but largely willing collaborators.[42]

In essence, the business community, despite being tied to necessary fairer employment practice and principles such as those of equity and affirmative action, has been allowed to continue without large-scale governmental intervention or redistribution. This made the earlier policies (and rhetoric) of the liberation movement with regards to redistribution and nationalization slip from the agenda, while facilitating greater white 'buy-in' into the process. The ANC, according to Allister Sparks,[43] has undergone an astonishing U-turn in the formulation of its economic policy—they have embraced free-market orthodoxy that involves large-scale privatization. To this end, there is a surprising degree of convergence between the economic thinking of government, business, and labor.[44] This convergence of thinking, certainly between business and government, is evident in the governmental response to the international reparations lawsuits and community reparations.

However, in terms of this chapter, one needs to ask how the concept of reparations fits with the question of economic development. Are reparations really about development in the first place? Are reparations the vehicle for altering large-scale economic policies? Does the debate about making South African society more equitable not lie more comfortably with a debate about economic policy and political priority rather than the issue of reparations?[45]

11.5. REPARATIONS AND DEVELOPMENT

Although reparations clearly need to have a collective dimension there seems to be a conflation of the language of social reconstruction and development with reparations in South Africa. As Roht-Arriaza has put it, two separate obligations of government are being conflated, that is their obligation to make reparation for past wrongs and provide services to the population.[46] She writes, 'Why should government be able to do what it is already obligated to do in its capacity as tax-receiver and public works provider, slap a reparations label on it, and get off cheaply?'[47] For most people in South Africa, upgrading their communities is considered a right, and is expected anyway, regardless of the reparations debate; reparations I would contend is about a much wider issue (this is discussed below in relation to acknowledgment).[48]

Having said that, it is difficult to reconcile the developments with regards to individual, community, and apartheid reparations within the frame of one dominant or even several dominant narratives or approaches. Not only is government conflating the reparations debate with development, campaigners too have different approaches that cause these complicated issues to overlap. Even from those calling for reparations several different ideologies and approaches are identifiable. Some individual victims might have fairly modest desires such as personal redress or even personal compensation for harms they directly suffered whether through perpetrators who appeared before the TRC or from various companies *aiding and abetting* the apartheid regime. At the individual level for victims of direct gross violations of human rights, social reconstruction as a form of reparation will have a limited psychological impact, especially for those seeking individual reparations. Individuals who suffered the brunt of the *direct* brutality of apartheid violence will probably need more. At an individual level, substituting social reconstruction for individual reparations will probably not work because for reparation to be psychologically restorative it has to be personalized.[49]

Although the broader system may have been responsible for creating a context conducive to human rights violations, and the system itself may have caused additional structural violations, individuals primarily experience violence through their personal universe. The consequences of political violence are interpersonal, social, and cultural. Although socioeconomic development (social reconstruction) is necessary, the physical and psychological impact of violence has to be simultaneously addressed directly and individually. There may be some hope if collective approaches to reparations were personalized, for example those tortured receiving specific personalized and free counselling services.[50] However, it is unlikely that such an approach in itself would carry sufficient acknowledgment and recognition at a political level or contain the symbolic capital needed to evoke sufficient meaning to the individual.

However, for some within the apartheid reparations campaign, although they acknowledge that reparations is about individual redress and recognition by the business community of their complicity in apartheid and forcing poverty on millions, they frame reparations as being about a much wider objective. From this perspective reparations are one vehicle to radical global and domestic economic change. As the Jubilee South Africa Chairperson has noted:

> A constant theme emerging through the debates in recent years is that the struggle for reparations is an important component in strengthening the broader struggle against neoliberalism and globalisation and that this broader struggle, in turn, must address reparations to move beyond the current system.[51]

Yet still for others the lawsuits are aimed at trying merely to improve international standards for corporate responsibility (perhaps a more reformist approach). Others have framed the debate somewhat more narrowly, but certainly wider than simply considering reparations for those who went before the TRC. For example, the Black Sash[52] has supported calls for introducing a Basic Income Grant in South Africa as a logical counterbalance to paying reparations to a limited number of victims.[53]

The major unions in South Africa recognize that the government has not done enough in forcing the business community to make a substantial contribution to redressing the past, but remain skeptical about the legal route as the best option for achieving reparations. As such, the Congress of South African Trade Unions (COSATU):

> Has not taken a position on the current court cases for reparations in the U.S. But as unions, we are not comfortable to rely on legal processes alone. This is a choice we often face when we are defending workers, and our experience is that it is better for all of us, in the long run, to use power and solidarity rather than legal action. Sometimes the law is the obvious choice, but it doesn't in itself empower our people or encourage them to mobilise and build solidarity.[54]

Clearly, therefore, in South Africa, there are different views of what reparations at the level of making amends for structural apartheid injustice really are and what they can achieve.

In addition, the notion of reparations has taken on some symbolic meaning in and of itself in South Africa, that is as a concept, certainly when spoken about outside individual reparations cases for gross violations, it represents a deep desire for social transformation and is inextricably linked with questions of economic progress. It is not confined simply to concerns about a range of individual acts of redress. As COSATU has put it, 'the reparations cases ultimately reflect frustrations with the failure of the business community, in particular, to recognise the need for more far-reaching and urgent measures to overcome the legacies of apartheid'.[55]

If this is correct, then why use the term reparations for essentially a conflict over the lack of delivery of social equity or distributive justice? Focusing on reparations in this way could distract attention from the real issues of injustice as Glenn Loury suggests in this volume.[56] But symbolically the struggle for reparations, I would argue, extends beyond representing the frustrations with economic progress; they are also about symbolically mending relationships between the so-called oppressed and oppressors (or reconciliation if one interprets this in a narrow sense as being about building or rebuilding relationships). It is at this level the reparations debate has to be taken seriously.

To expand: Kok-Chor Tan in this volume argues that demands for reparations can be useful in a struggle for what he calls global equality (or we could say distributive justice in the South African case), because (*a*) they can motivate action more than abstract arguments about global equality can; (*b*) they can be useful if the argument from equality is resisted; and (*c*) they may be necessary for repairing relationships necessary to deliver equality.

Arguably, in the South African case, the issue of apartheid reparations is being used in the first two ways Tan outlines. Reparations are being used as a rallying cry to raise the voices of those who remain impoverished in the South African context, hence the support from international anti-debt and other campaigners, as well as local unions such as COSATU. Reparations are also being used as a way of highlighting the moral injustices of the past and are used to present a moral argument as to why business particularly should contribute to narrowing inequality rather than exacerbating it.

However, it is Tan's view that reparations can build relationships necessary to deliver distributive justice that is the most interesting to consider in the South African case. To this end, I would argue, the issue of the relationship between the business sector and those impoverished through the apartheid system (even at a broad abstract level) is at the heart of the debate concerning reparations in South Africa. This has been profoundly affected by the discourse and limited approach of the TRC to questions of structural violations of human rights.[57]

11.6. ACKNOWLEDGMENT AND BUILDING RELATIONSHIPS

The TRC through its reconciliation agenda placed relationships and acknowledgment of past wrongs at the core of its work and hence the post-1994 transition period. In relation to the business sector it established a separate hearing 'to examine the role of business and labor in the period covered by our mandate 1960 to 1994 with specific reference to the context and circumstances in which human rights violations took place'.[58] It saw these hearings as contributing to (*a*) a better understanding of the conflicts of the past; (*b*) laying the foundations for a more just and equitable society; and (*c*) helping develop recommendations to the President on reparation and rehabilitation.[59] The TRC noted at the time:

> The hearing is not a witchhunt. It is not the forum for details of individual human rights abuses these have been aired at other hearings. It is an attempt to understand past conflicts, to prevent a recurrence of human rights violations, to contribute towards the documentation of South Africa's history and to look ahead.[60]

Based on the general ethos of the Commission, which stressed the importance of acknowledgment of wrongdoing as a way of promoting reconciliation or building future relationships, we can assume that the TRC understood the process of uncovering of the past role of business as instrumental in documenting and recognizing their role in the past (presumably in an exploitative sense) and this being able to be used as a way to 'look forward' and work in partnership to address the legacy of apartheid. In its final Report it notes: 'It will be impossible to create a meaningful human rights culture without high priority being given to economic justice by the public and private sectors. Recognizing that it is impossible for the public sector alone to find the resources required to expedite the goal of economic justice, the Commission urges the private sector in particular to consider a special initiative in terms of a fund for training, empowerment, and opportunities for the disadvantaged and dispossessed in South Africa'.[61] The TRC also argued for a wealth tax as noted earlier.

On the whole, however, the response from the business community has been minimal and certainly at the level the TRC had hoped, specifically with regards to the Commission general finding that the business sector largely benefited from the apartheid context.[62] As Yasmin Sooka, former TRC Commissioner has noted:

> The commission made findings in respect of the role played by business during the apartheid period, nine years into the transition, business has not only failed to acknowledge the role that they played during the apartheid era: in not only supporting the policies of the apartheid government; but also in acknowledging how they benefited from apartheid laws and profited from their collusion with the apartheid government.[63]

The business community see their contribution as one focused on the future through institutions such as the Business Trust or corporate social responsibility programmes (which are of course important), but this is not matched by their unequivocal acknowledgment of their role in the past. This was startlingly evident in a meeting between the Business Trust and government in 2003. At the meeting the Business Trust continued to pledge a further five-year term of support for development in a range of areas. However, the condition to the support from business was the programme had to be referred to as 'nation-building' and not community reparations.[64]

Thus reparations itself has become symbolic of much deeper questions that stand outside the debate concerning frustrations with economic progress alone. This has both a backward-looking and forward-looking dimension. Many reparations campaigners would undoubtedly agree that despite the TRC's condemnation of the business community and those who supported apartheid, there has been insufficient acknowledgment of the benefits reaped through the system by the business community and white South Africans on the whole. This is evidenced by the attitude of business to reparations on the whole. Saki Macazoma of Standard Bank commented recently, while publicly dismissing outright an invitation to a round-table discussion with apartheid victims on reparations, 'I just want to say this categorically, once... forget about this (dialog). There is no business that will admit a liability indirectly by actually getting into any reparations process'.[65]

Although broadly white attitudes have changed much over the last decade, a reticence with regard to accepting any form of direct responsibility for the past remains.[66] Recent survey data has found that only 20 percent of whites feel that national reconciliation requires material compensation for victims of apartheid, and only half of the adult (18 years and older) white population claim they are willing to contribute to nation-building in South Africa.[67] The acknowledgment that many black South Africans want (whatever this means in practice) remains elusive.

Certainly among many poor largely black South Africans you would not have to look very hard to find those that feel that the current government is steadily abandoning them and will not be fulfilling their expectations. This is implicit, for example, in a recent speech by Archbishop Ndungane when he commented:

> Much that is admirable has been achieved and our government—which took over the reins with empty State coffers and the insidious legacy of apartheid—is deserving of praise and respect. This makes the present situation regarding reparations all the more uncomfortable. How can this nation, which became a beacon of hope for the world because it consciously opted for restorative justice over retributive justice, fail those most in need of restoration?[68]

As such, two issues lurk below the surface of the reparations debate in South Africa. To state these plainly, firstly, masses of black South Africans fear that 'whites' (in the collective and essentialist sense) and the business community will 'get away with it' and never really make amends for decades of exploitation. In this context, the apartheid lawsuits make sense as they are targeted at these groups directly. They are not about the South African government. Within this there are many different voices, from those who see themselves as directly violated (in a physical violent sense) to those who see themselves as victims of wider structural exploitation, or both. Furthermore, unlike many other reparations claims, in the South African case claims are not wholly targeted at second-generation beneficiaries or those separate from the group responsible for injustices. Many of the beneficiaries of the apartheid system both domestically and internationally are alive, and who continue to benefit from its legacy just as many of those harmed by it are also living and in fact first generation reparations claimants.

Secondly, there is a growing concern by masses of black South Africans that they are steadily being abandoned by the government—a government which they equate with the ANC and as a result see as *their* government. In essence, and to state it bluntly, they fear being let down and sold out. To make matters worse they fear 'their own' government is colluding with the selfsame people who exploited them before and who continue to benefit from the system. This is captured by the words of Dumisa Ntsebenza[69] making reference to the business community in South Africa:

> They fit the classical bill of those who proverbially hunt with the hounds and flee with the hares. During the apartheid era, they hunted with the apartheid state in its internationally recognised violations such as extra-judicial killings, torture, genocide, arbitrary detention . . . During democracy, they have suddenly become hares who run and seek refuge under the welcoming petticoats of our democratic government in the face of lawsuits.[70]

Thus, although the apartheid lawsuits, individual reparations, and community reparations are seemingly different processes, we can see how for many in South Africa they intersect. Individual reparations represent the thin edge of the wedge and apartheid litigations the thick end, community reparations rest somewhere in the middle symptomatic of the government's approach to the issue of reparations as a whole.

There are those who see reparations as a struggle to take on local and global capital and perhaps it will eventually evolve into this or a political opposition in South Africa. However, I would contend, at this stage at least, most calling for reparations have more modest goals. Still influenced by the discourses of cooperation and reconciliation, they seek partnerships (as the government does) to redress past imbalances and guarantee nonrepetition in the future (for apartheid reparations this means assuring an end to socioeconomic exploitation and equal opportunity in the future).

However, unlike the government (who most reparations campaigners would probably agree are sheltering corporations under their 'welcoming petticoats' as Ntsebeza argues), it is likely that many of those calling for reparations feel this partnership cannot be built and guarantees on nonrepetition ensured if there is no trust, that is not only between government and the private sector, but between the majority of the poor, the private sector, and government. An analysis of the various statements made by reparations campaigners reveals that acknowledgment by the business community specifically and white South Africans more generally that they benefited from the system is the key to (re)building this trust.[71]

Currently one of the central problems in the debate about social development in South Africa and its relationship to reparation (or dealing with the past) is that it is presently almost exclusively forward-looking in its approach. Although various initiatives are underway to address the socioeconomic legacy of apartheid, without a more contrite acknowledgment by business (and white South Africans, others would contend) of the TRC's findings concerning the business community's complicity with the apartheid state, it is unlikely that community reparations will be accepted or have a significant enough impact or the ability to subdue any larger apartheid reparations claims. Without acknowledgment of past wrongs it appears as if confidence between different players such as victims (and most of those impoverished by the past) and business and government remains undermined. In this sense, the debate about reparations in South Africa is serving to undermine relationships (certainly between government, business and reparations campaigners) rather than to build them. Arguably a historical opportunity to mend some of the damage done in the past and rebuild relationships necessary to build a just and equitable future is being missed.

11.7. CONCLUSION

In conclusion, I would like make a distinction between the term *reparation* (the singular) and the plural *reparations*.[72] I define *reparations* (plural) as the acts or objects associated with attempts to make amends, for example compensation payments, building a memorial. *Reparations* can also be representational in form or intent, such as the act of stating an apology. Simply put reparations are the things done or given as an attempt to deal with the consequences of political violence or for the subject matter of this chapter the consequences of social and economic injustice.

From an *individual* psychological perspective it is helpful to think about the aim of *reparations*, as obvious as it may sound on first reading, as being about making *reparation*, or from the Klienian perspective to 'make good' psychologically for what has been damaged, lost, or destroyed.[73] At the individual level the victim is generally seeking through the granting of *reparations* some sort of *reparation*, that is a psychological state in which they will feel that adequate amends have been made for a wrong committed. Those granting reparations may aspire (or at least hope) that their reparations programme will be broadly satisfying to victims in this way.[74] That said, whether reparation has taken place for an individual is difficult to measure, if not impossible to satisfy—reparations are trying to repair the irreparable.[75]

Using the distinction between *reparations* and *reparation*, I would argue that in South Africa, as obvious as it sounds, what is missing is adequate *reparation*. As a result, a number of individuals have engaged in a process of seeking various acts of *reparations*. Campaigners want (whether consciously or unconsciously) these reparations (through courts, the government or the beneficiaries of apartheid) to be somehow translated into or moved toward a greater sense of reparation.[76]

However, it appears, that South African government is hoping that by offering limited individual reparations and redefining social development as (community) reparations this will translate into deeper symbolic and psychological reparation.[77] But from a psychosocial perspective how the process of *reparations* is structured, set up, publicly spoken about, and dealt with is one of the factors that psychologically communicates to victims how their plight is understood in the wider social context. The process of granting reparations is one of the factors that can contribute to reparation.[78] The reparations process in South Africa has been particularly fraught from the outset. The government's failure to act promptly on individual reparations for gross violations and to attend to apartheid reparations claims as potentially viable, as well as the business communities and largely white South Africa's lack of engagement with the issue, has, at least in part, turned the debate about individual reparations into a struggle over amounts of money rather than symbolic gestures.[79] The lack of validation of the importance of reparations and willingness to engage with the debate constructively has also turned some of the debate internationally and to the courts. This has hardened resolve between campaigners and those in a position to meet some reparations demands. This in turn has undermined the prospect for partnerships aimed at addressing the economic legacy left by apartheid—a situation which could never be addressed by reparations alone.

In South Africa, a link needs to be made in discourse, process, and action between the physical act of giving reparations (or demanding it through a court case) with the deeper psychological and symbolic needs and desires implicit within a call or drive to achieve reparation. This can only be done through dialog between all parties and acknowledgment (which could be financial or symbolic)[80] that is judged and felt to be genuine, particularly and at least initially at the domestic level.

Sadly, in South Africa, one wonders if the time to make symbolic gestures, such as an apology from various companies and classes of individuals that benefited from the apartheid system coupled with limited reparations,[81] has passed. An acrimonious process between government, campaigners, and apartheid beneficiaries—as well as a lack of conceptual clarity on what reparations are—has left the notion of reparations deeply intertwined with many black South Africans' general frustrations about the lack of economic progress for the poor despite governmental efforts to deal with it. The process of economic development designed to meet the needs of the poorest of the electorate as a governmental responsibility and the issue of reparations should be separated out.[82] Hiding, what is perceived by reparations campaigners, as a lack of acknowledgment and any form of direct compensation from the beneficiaries of apartheid behind the label of broad economic development, no matter how successful this development is, obscures the picture. It underestimates the aspiration by those who feel wronged for some sense of genuine remorse and acknowledgment, as well as demonstrable atonement (perhaps through reparations) by those they perceive as having wronged them. The symbolic power of reparations is being missed.

That said, at best, reparations—whether individual, community, or broader—can reframe the debate in terms of how hurts are recognized and attempts at redress made, deal with some material and psychological needs of those who see themselves as victims, and assist in recreating a sense of citizenship and belonging for recipients.[83] The collapsing of reparations with social development, rather than seeing reparations *as potentially one aspect* of social development, has made this even more difficult.

In South Africa, as noted earlier, many of those who have suffered and those deemed responsible from injustices are still living, and this places a greater imperative on addressing the issue now as a way of potentially minimizing the second generation claims. With second generation claims meaningful acknowledgment and recompense will be even more difficult to achieve. That said, the physical acts of reparations whether concrete in form such as money or representational in form or intent such as the act of stating an apology, and the psychological and symbolic needs underlying a desire for them, can never completely overlap. Reparations cannot meet all the demands implicit within the need for reparation, but this gap can be narrowed. It is here the role of acknowledgment and limited and clearly targeted reparations of past wrongs could be valuable. Without that tensions and confusions will endure, and for all involved, the process will remain deeply unsatisfying leaving the door wide open for an ongoing litany of reparations claims well into the future.

NOTES

1. My thanks to Matt James for his comments on the chapter and subsequent drafts of my work on reparations. The author of this chapter is also a Board member of the Khulumani Victim Support Group. The views expressed here are solely those of the author and not necessarily those of the Khulumani Victim Support Group.
2. Racism and discrimination have been outlawed, and large-scale socioeconomic development is under way. Since 1994, 3.5 million people have received electricity; 1.2 million houses have been built; and 34,365 land restitution claims affecting about 394,442 beneficiaries have been settled with 505,606 hectares of land restored. In 1994, only 2% of management posts in the civil service were filled by black South Africans, by 1996 it was 30%. Source: Government and Communication and Information Services, *South Africa Yearbook 2002/2003* (Yeoville, South Africa: STE Publishers, 2002). Figures at September 2002.
3. e.g. unemployment figures in the nonagriculture sector are estimated to be as high as 37.6%, and in 2001, 45% of South Africans lived in households in which adults earn R352 a month (about US$45). Currently, about 61% of black South Africans are considered to be 'poor' as opposed to 1% of white South Africans. Source: Government and Communication and Information Services, *South Africa Yearbook 2002/2003* (Yeoville, South Africa: STE Publishers, 2002). Figures at September 2002.
4. Sparks (2003).
5. Government and Communication and Information Services (2002).
6. This refers to a statement made by Thabo Mbeki on May 29, 1998 at the opening of the debate on reconciliation and nation-building in the National Assembly.
7. Sparks (2003: 44).

8. Elsewhere I have evaluated aspects of the TRC. See Hamber (1998, 2001, and 2002*a*).
9. It is important to note that it was criteria-driven and this differentiates South Africa from countries such as Chile, Zimbabwe, or Argentina, where amnesty was blanket. Although a provision for amnesty was made in the postamble to the Interim Constitution it was vague enough to allow a rather liberal interpretation of it in the legislation that gave birth to the TRC. Space does not permit an exploration of this complex issue, but it is important to bear in mind that the amnesty process was highly individualized. Individuals had to apply for amnesty for each and every act they thought they might be eligible for. Each act was then individually weighed up against a set of criteria set out in the Promotion of National Unity and Reconciliation Act that established the TRC.
10. For more detail on the full mandate of the R&R Committee see the full text of the Promotion of National Unity and Reconciliation Act, No. 34 of 1995 at http://www.doj.gov.za/trc/. There were also several amendments to the Act that ensured the extension of the amnesty cutoff dates and the life of the TRC, as well as the ongoing work of the Amnesty Committee. For more detail on this see the Promotion of National Unity and Reconciliation Amendment Act, No. 87 of 1995; Promotion of National Unity and Reconciliation Amendment Act, No. 18 of 1997; and Promotion of National Unity and Reconciliation Second Amendment Act, No. 84 of 1997.
11. The Committee responsible for organizing public hearings of amnesty applicants and adjudicating amnesty applications.
12. The Committee responsible for hearing and taking victim testimony and statements.
13. Promotion of National Unity and Reconciliation Act 1995, Section 40-f.
14. See South African Truth and Reconciliation Commission (1998*a*), vol. 5, for the full Reparation and Rehabilitation Policy. For information on earlier drafts and an analysis of the TRC's developmental thinking in this regard see, South African Truth and Reconciliation Commission (1998*b*). Also see Government Gazette No. 1654, Vol. 394, No. 18822, which outlines provisions for Urgent Interim Reparation. Information on proposed reparations and compensations was published by the TRC in their proposed Rehabilitation and Reparation Policies Document on September 9, 1997. Early summaries of this were also reported in the newspaper; see 'For Apartheid Pain TRC Calls for Pay-outs to Victims of Abuses' at http://www.africanews.org. This chapter does not give a detailed summary of the TRC Reparation and Rehabilitation Policy. It is suggested that this chapter be read in conjunction with the policy recommendations in the TRC final Report to understand the specific details of the formula used by the TRC to calculate the amounts that are proposed as payable to survivors and the families of victims.
15. All figures based on exchange rates in April 2005. These can fluctuate somewhat given market trends.

16. The grants vary as the TRC has factored in variance related to the number of people living in the 'victim's' house or whether the survivor or family member of a victim lives in a rural or urban area. This was done because services in rural areas, for example, are more costly than in urban areas.
17. In July 1998 then President Mandela set up the President's Fund and an initial R300 million was allocated to it.
18. Crawford-Pinnerup (2000).
19. It should be noted that direct currency translations probably do not match the spending power of Rands in South Africa. The average annual household income can provide some relative way of assessing the possible impact in South Africa of the suggested amounts for material reparation. In 1997 the average annual household income was R21,700. This was used as a benchmark by the TRC in the design of the monetary package. The Final Reparations Policy notes that, 'The poverty line of R15,600 per annum was rejected as a benchmark, as this would be condemning victims to a life of near poverty, rather than one of minimum dignity' (*Report of the South African Truth and Reconciliation Commission*, 1998, 5(5), 69). These amounts are not comparable to what a survivor might have received in a civil claim which would be substantially greater. A civil claim, however, would not be guaranteed in most cases.
20. *South Africa to Pay $3,900 to Each Family of Apartheid Victims*, *N.Y. Times*, Int'l, Apr. 16, 2003, at A5.
21. 'Victims Reject Reparation Grant' on News24. See http://www.finance24.com/articles/default/display_article.asp?Nav=ns&ArticleID=1518-25_1348751
22. President Thabo Mbeki, May 2000, Parliament.
23. See the Statement to the National Houses of Parliament and the Nation, at the tabling of the Report of the Truth and Reconciliation Commission, April 15, 2003 by Thabo Mbeki when he notes: 'We do so with some apprehension, for as the TRC itself has underlined, no one can attach monetary value to life and suffering. Nor can an argument be sustained that the efforts of millions of South Africans to liberate themselves were for monetary gain. We are convinced that, to the millions who spared neither life nor limb in struggle, there is no bigger prize than freedom itself, and a continuing struggle to build a better life for all'.
24. Khulumani (Zulu for 'speaking out') was set up in early 1995 to assist those testifying before the TRC in preparing for the hearings. Khulumani has become a powerful support mechanism and advocacy organization, lobbying for ongoing reparations and justice for survivors of apartheid violence.
25. The companies and banks named in the lawsuit are: Citigroup, JP Morgan Chase, Exxon Mobil, Caltex Petroleum, Fluor Corporation, Ford, General Motors, and IBM in the United States; German-based Commerzbank, Deutsche Bank, Dresdner Bank, DaimlerChrysler, and Rheinmetall; Credit Suisse and UBS in Switzerland; Barclays Bank; British Petroleum, Rio Tinto and Fujitsu ICL in the United Kingdom; Total-Fina-Elf from France and Royal Dutch Shell

from the Netherlands. The case was later moved to the Southern New York Eastern District Court.

26. See http://www.cmht.com
27. Cited at www.khulumani.net at http://www.khulumani.net/index.php?option=com_content&task=view&id=16&Itemid=1
28. This grants US courts jurisdiction over certain violations of international law, regardless of where they occur.
29. Extract from http://www.cmht.com/casewatch/cases/cwapartheid4.html
30. This case was initially brought and initiated by US lawyer Ed Fagan. However, shortly before the hearings in November 2003 he was allegedly dismissed from the case by the families. The case continues through John Ngcebetsha, the South African instructing attorney for the group. The ADRC, which initially supported the claim, has distanced itself from these lawsuits as has the Khulumani Victim Support Group.
31. Extract from Statement to the National Houses of Parliament and the Nation, at the tabling of the Report of the Truth and Reconciliation Commission, April 15, 2003 by Thabo Mbeki.
32. 'Mandela criticizes apartheid lawsuits,' August 25, 2003, available at http://iafrica.com/news/sa/265317.htm
33. Business Day, see http://www.bday.co.za/bday/content/direct/1,3523,1478932-6078-0,00.html
34. Available at http://www.apartheid-reparations.ch/documents/reparationen/e_2004-09_amcur.PDF
35. See Khulumani Support Group Press Statement entitled 'Reconciliation Day 2004: Call on international corporations' available at www.khulumani.net
36. Vandeginste (2003).
37. Extract from Statement to the National Houses of Parliament and the Nation, at the tabling of the Report of the Truth and Reconciliation Commission, April 15, 2003 by Thabo Mbeki.
38. See http://www.btrust.org.za/
39. Statement to the National Houses of Parliament and the Nation, at the tabling of the Report of the Truth and Reconciliation Commission, April 15, 2003 by Thabo Mbeki.
40. See, Marais (2000: 95).
41. Statement to the National Houses of Parliament and the Nation, at the tabling of the Report of the Truth and Reconciliation Commission, April 15, 2003 by Thabo Mbeki.
42. Sparks (2003).
43. Sparks (2003).
44. Sparks (2003: 197).
45. Kok-Chor Tan discusses similar issues with direct reference to African American calls for reparations for slavery. He wonders whether introducing the notion of reparations to global justice might distract and confuse the discussion unnecessarily moving it away from what is really at stake, namely appealing

to egalitarian principles which can assist the development process of poorer nations. This process of fostering global development and justice could stand outside of reparations as such.

46. Roht-Arriaza (2004*a*).
47. Roht-Arriaza (2004*a*: 188).
48. The theme of reparations and development is also a major theme developed by Pablo de Greiff in the global study being carried out by the Institute for Transitional Justice (http://www.ictj.org) on reparations, the results of which have been published by Oxford University Press (see de Greiff 2006). Roht-Arriaza also discussed this issue at length; see Roht-Arriaza (2004*a*).
49. I elaborate on the concept of personalizing reparations in Hamber (2006).
50. Vandeginste (2003).
51. M. P. Giyose, Jubilee, Reparations and the Lawsuits against Economic and Financial Backers of Apartheid. Paper presented at the Civil Society Conference on Reparations, Randburg, August 27, 2003.
52. A women's antiapartheid movement founded in 1955, which continues to try to ensure the recognition of human rights for all in South Africa. See http://www.blacksash.org.za/
53. Black Sash, Statement on Government's Response to TRC recommendations, presented as a paper at the Civil Society Conference on Reparations, Randburg, August 27, 2003.
54. Willie Madisha, Address of the President of COSATU on Reparations, presented at the Civil Society Conference on Reparations, Randburg, August 27, 2003.
55. Willie Madisha, Address of the President of COSATU on Reparations, presented at the Civil Society Conference on Reparations, Randburg, August 27, 2003.
56. Glenn Loury in this volume makes this point with regards to demands for reparations for African American slavery arguing that by focusing on the past slavery claims the real issues of injustice in the present are underemphasized.
57. Space does not permit a thorough exploration of the issue of the TRC approach to structural violations. Here I merely treat it from the perspective of what they did, i.e. hearings on certain thematic issues such as the role of business in apartheid. There is a much bigger debate on the issue of how the TRC dealt with structural issues. Mamdani, e.g. asserts that the TRC failed to provide a more racialized and structural economic analysis in its hearings (see Mamdani 1996). Rather, the TRC chose to define victims narrowly, that is, as the direct victims of gross human rights violations such as murder, torture, abduction, and disappearance. From this perspective, the TRC has failed sufficiently to make the link between the structural violations of apartheid (e.g. systematic poverty or inequality in access to services) and the direct human rights violations suffered by those who testified. Victimization was defined as stemming from a direct act of political violence, while those who suffered the ravages of apartheid through forced removals, pass laws, malnutrition, or poor education were not asked to testify. Neither were they directly categorized as victims.

58. Statement by Dr Alex Boraine, acting chairperson, TRC on Commission hearing on the role of business, July 31, 1997 available at http://www.info.gov.za/speeches/1997/08010W01697.htm
59. Statement by Dr Alex Boraine, acting chairperson, TRC on Commission hearing on the role of business, July 31, 1997 available at http://www.info.gov.za/speeches/1997/08010W01697.htm
60. Statement by Dr Alex Boraine, acting chairperson, TRC on Commission hearing on the role of business, September 4, 1997 available at http://www.info.gov.za/speeches/1997/09250X19297.htm
61. South African Truth and Reconciliation Commission (1998*a*), vol. 5, chapter 8, p. 14.
62. The TRC found that, 'Business was central to the economy that sustained the South African state during the apartheid years. Certain businesses, especially the mining industry, were involved in helping to design and implement apartheid policies. Other businesses benefited from co-operating with the security structures of the former state. Most businesses benefited from operating in a racially structured context' (South African Truth and Reconciliation Commission (1998*a*: vol. 4, ch. 2, p. 106).
63. Yasmin Sooka, 'South Africa, its past, human rights and reparations'. Keynote address at the Public Seminar on Reparations—International, social, legal, economic dimensions, Wits Institute for Social and Economic Research, July 6, 2004. Available at http://www.apartheid-reparations.ch/documents/reparationen/e_2004-08_RedeSooka.pdf
64. *Cape Argus*, November 14, 2003.
65. *Cape Argus*, November 14, 2003.
66. It is difficult to assess exactly why this is the case, but it is probably linked to two key factors. The first is fear, i.e. acknowledging or apologizing for complicity for apartheid could cause a backlash from the black majority. The second is about the diffusion of responsibility, i.e. given the apartheid system was structural and hierarchical there is often a feeling (whether right or wrong) among many whites that they were not personally responsible for the system or the violations caused by it.
67. *Cape Argus*, October 2, 2000. See the Web site of Institute for Justice and Reconciliation (http://www.ijr.org.za/) for a more detailed analysis and published results.
68. Njongonkulu Ndungane, Opening Address, Paper presented at the Civil Society Conference on Reparations, Randburg, August 27, 2003.
69. A prominent South African lawyer initially involved with one of the Ed Fagan apartheid litigations. He was also a truth commissioner.
70. South African Press Association (SAPA), 'Business has moral, legal duty to pay reparations: Ntsebeza,' October 10, 2003.
71. Pablo de Greiff argues in his chapter in this book that reparations can lead, at the individual level, to greater feelings of recognition by the state and increase levels of civic trust. This is also a major theme developed by de Greiff in the

global study on reparations being carried out by the Institute for Transitional Justice and published as de Greiff (2006*a*).

72. I elaborate on the use making such a distinction in Hamber (2006).
73. The term reparation also has a specific meaning in psychology, and particularly in psychoanalytic thinking. Historically it is mostly closely associated with the work of Melanie Klein (see Klein and Riviere 1964). Space does not permit a thorough examination of this, but suffice to say that in psychoanalytic thinking, reparation generally deals with internal psychic processes. It is closely associated with intrapsychic guilt, i.e. the profound (psychological) urge to make good for injuries done to others.
74. My focus here is on the individual impact of reparations rather than what they might mean at a collective, political, or social level.
75. From the perspective of direct victims of political violence, and even at times from the collective perspective, acknowledgment, apology, recognition, and even substantial material assistance do not 'bring back the dead' nor are they guaranteed to converge with, and ameliorate, all the levels of psychological pain suffered. No matter what the motive, all reparations strategies face this intractable problem of trying to repair the irreparable. The idea of repairing the irreparable is noted in Hamber (2002*b*) and later by Martha Minow (2002).
76. Of course there are those that see the struggle for reparations in much wider frame, i.e. a political strategy to move toward a new a different domestic and global sociopolitical order, but I restrict my comments here to those who have more modest goals.
77. Of course, one could argue that it is possible for social development to translate into deeper symbolic and psychological reparation. This may to a degree be possible. However, I would be less sure of this for reasons outlined earlier in the chapter, namely, that social development does not have the symbolic capital a dedicated reparations process has because social development is generally associated with ordinary rights and the expected role of a government to provide development for its citizens. In addition, reparations have a unique ability to contain both individual and collective elements (e.g. a monument which has names on it or compensation payments as part of a collective process of acknowledging a wrong). This I argue in Hamber (2006) is what gives reparations their unique ability to promote reparation.
78. This is not to say that I think that the outcomes of a reparations process are not important. I discuss the importance of process in the reparations elsewhere. See Hamber (2005).
79. There is also a practical reality to this debate, namely that many are severely impoverished in the country; money can and would make a difference to their lives.
80. Rajeev Bhargava in his chapter in this book adds an interesting concept to the idea of acknowledgment and taking responsibility, i.e. a genuine cognitive resolve to change the way the colonizers view the colonized. This has particular relevance in the South African context with regards to ongoing discussions

about racism and whether racist views have in fact changed. One view in South Africa would be that acknowledgment of complicity in the apartheid system by beneficiaries of it is not forthcoming because they still hold racist views and the 'cognitive resolve' to change or demonstrate change is not visible from beneficiaries of the apartheid system. Reparations could be a way to demonstrate this cognitive resolve.

81. Financial reparations are generally themselves only symbolic even if they have a material edge, i.e. they can only ever be nominal as all the losses associated with apartheid could not be completely calculated or compensated for financially.
82. I think the same could be said of talking about cancelling debt as a form of reparations. I think the issue of cancelling debt has sufficient merit morally to stand on its own. Reparations, if they are to move toward making reparation, or have any symbolic value and be used to build relationships, should be about making genuine, direct, and targeted amends for specific wrongs. That said, there is a much bigger debate on this issue and this chapter has not focused on debt cancellation as reparations.
83. Space does not permit a discussion on this, but the idea of reparations contributing to social belonging for the recipients of reparations is important especially when dealing with 'extreme' political trauma, which is considered to undermine an individual's sense of belonging to society (see Becker 2001; Becker et al. 1997). Traumatic events destroy the bonds between the individual and the community (Herman 1992). This could also be understood in another way, i.e. as a direct consequence of colonialism (exploitation) individuals can be alienated or marginalized from their own culture in different ways as Rajeev Bhargava discusses in his chapter in this book. De Grieff also writes about the value of reparations (although he largely considers reparations for gross violations of human rights) as being instrumental in creating civic trust and building recognition in societies in transition. See de Greiff (2006*a*).

12

Colonialism, Reparations, and Global Justice

Kok-Chor Tan

Paragraph 116 of the draft declaration prepared by the Group of 21 for the 2001 World Conference against Racism proposed that:

> ... reparations to victims of slavery, the slave trade, and colonialism and their descendants should be in the form of enhanced policies, programmes and measures at the national and international levels to be contributed to by States, companies and individuals who benefited materially from these practices, in order to compensate, and repair, the economic, cultural and political damage which has been inflicted on the affected communities and peoples, through inter alia, the creation of a special development fund, the improvement of access to international markets of products from developing countries affected by these practices, the cancellation or substantial reduction of their foreign debt and a programme to return art objects, historical goods and documents to the countries of origin.[1]

Predictably, this proposal for reparations for the injustices of slavery and colonialism did not make the final version of the Resolution that was adopted at the Durban conference.[2] In this exploratory chapter, I want to examine the moral basis of these demands for reparations with regard to colonialism. Specifically, I am interested in the kinds of claims that independent sovereign nations have on account of their past colonial subjection. The claims of formerly colonized nations are quite distinct from the claims for reparations by indigenous peoples who have been colonized. The reparations demanded by indigenous peoples often involve repatriation of territory or compensation of some form for the loss of territory, as well as demands for greater political self-determination. The reparative claims that are made by formerly colonized countries normally do not involve territory and formal political autonomy (which were largely restored when these countries were granted independence) but involve claims of the sorts identified in paragraph 116 noted above. They include financial compensation for the economic exploitation of colonialism in the form of debt relief, improved access to global markets, and development assistance. They also include claims for cultural restoration in the form of restitution of cultural objects removed during colonial rule, as suggested by the draft declaration. Other claims commonly made in the name of cultural restoration include the granting of special cultural rights to formerly colonized peoples, in the form of exempting cultural products from free trade agreements in order to enable the revitalization of local cultural industries and the special protection of local cultural (tangible and intangible) goods through international organizations such as UNESCO and so on. For this reason, it is worth examining the demands for reparations for colonialism as it applies to independent countries separately from that of reparations for indigenous peoples even though the latter are victims of colonization as well.[3]

I begin by recalling some common remarks about the injustice of colonialism (Section 12.1). Given that the demands made in the name of reparations presented in paragraph 116 of the Draft Resolution are also demands that arguably could be made in the name of global distributive equality, it might be thought that arguments from reparations are superfluous and that arguments from equality can do all the justificatory work. I will suggest, however, that reparative arguments can supplement arguments from equality; that they may even be necessary if egalitarian justice is to be realized; and that they can substitute for egalitarian arguments when the latter are resisted (Section 12.2). I then ask if the case for colonial reparations can satisfy the central philosophical issues that any account of reparations must confront (Section 12.3).

12.1. THE INJUSTICE OF COLONIALISM

It is generally taken for granted that colonialism was an injustice because, among other things, it violated the self-determination rights of nations, that it economically exploited the colonized peoples, and that it undermined their cultural identity. The history of colonialism is, of course, a highly complex one. There is no denying that colonized peoples have also benefited in different ways from their encounter with the colonizing power. Some commentators consider the global dominance of the English language as a positive legacy of British colonialism. As Salman Rushdie writes, 'peoples who were once colonized by the [English] language are now rapidly remaking it, domesticating it, becoming more and more relaxed about the way they use it.... The children of independent India seem not to think of English as being irredeemably tainted by its colonial provenance. They use it as an Indian language, as one of the tools they have to hand'.[4] It has also been suggested in some quarters that Britain's gift to its colonies includes the introduction of parliamentary democracy and the idea of common law, as well as more tangible contributions to the economic infrastructure of colonized countries (such as the railway system in India).

But there is also no denying that the loss to the colonized nations is also significant. Colonial intervention disrupted the economic development and thwarted the industrialization of colonized nations. It also undermined, even destroying in the cases of many indigenous groups, the local cultures of colonized societies, thus eroding one of the bases of self-respect of persons. As Fanon argues, the economic exploitation of the colonial powers was assisted by a policy of 'cultural estrangement'. The cultures of colonized peoples were degraded and devalued and it was 'consciously' driven into 'the natives' heads... that if the settlers were to leave, they would at once fall back into barbarism, degradation and bestiality'. The result is a sense of cultural inferiority among colonized subjects, says Fanon, especially among the local elites who have been schooled in the ways of their colonial rulers. The sense in which the effects of cultural estrangement of colonialism is 'conscious' can be further debated, but Fanon does not exaggerate when he says that one of the central struggles of postcolonialism is the rehabilitation and revitalization of local national cultures that have been eroded by colonialism.[5] And while colonialism often introduced new forms of government to the colonized peoples, some commentators rebut that this was at the price of disrupting and transplanting local political organizations and practices.

It is sometimes argued that colonialism improved the material and economic conditions of the lives of colonized peoples and hence colonialism could not on the whole be an injustice because it introduced more good than harm. Even if the historical premise is true, however, the argument assumes a consequentialist framework of sorts in which the injustice of a practice is determined by whether it generates more harm than good. On other moral conceptions, the denial of self-determination, the imposition of an economic order on a people, and the supplanting of its culture and language could count as wrongs in themselves whether or not accompanied by greater material gains for the subjugated group. If colonized peoples indeed had good reasons to oppose their colonization, that they (possibly) gained in other ways from it does not mitigate the wrongness of it. Indeed, recognizing the damage of colonialism to be more than just economic can help reveal why colonialism could be an injustice even if it (as is commonly argued) improved the economic conditions of peoples. As mentioned in paragraph 116, the damages for which reparations are sought are not just economic damages but also cultural and political. Because of these cultural and political ramifications, the injustice of colonialism remains even if colonialism introduced economic benefits. Be that as it may, I take the injustice of colonialism as a given for the purpose of this chapter. The challenging question for my purpose is whether reparations are owed by former colonial powers because of this presumed injustice.

What does require more clarifying for my purpose, however, are the different kinds of harms that colonialism inflicted. Colonialism was not only an injustice against individuals but also an injustice against a community or *a people*. While individuals who were discriminated against and denied, say, educational and economic opportunities were certainly directly and personally harmed at the time of colonial rule, these practices also harmed the collective by undermining its cultural, political and economic practices and structures of a people. Denying a colonial subject the option of education in her own language (or of higher education opportunities) is a personal wrong in that it deprived that individual of certain opportunities; but the loss of a community's language that this resulted in is a wrong against a people. Or, to take another example, denying a person the right of political participation is a violation of her basic political liberties, but the undermining of a people's right to self-determination that results in a wrong not just against persons but against the collective. To put this point in a way that I will explicate in some detail later on, some kinds of harm are harms against a collective in that they are not simply the aggregate of the harms inflicted on individuals. The loss of a community's language, for example, is not reducible to the sum of the loss to each potential language user. It is a loss that, if we like, transcends the lives and interests of each individual even as this loss is also felt by them personally (or even when it is not). This distinction between *harms against persons* and *harms against a collective* is important because, as I try to argue below, the moral force for reparations for colonial injustices is better appreciated if we do not neglect the collective harms of colonialism.[6]

12.2. WHY MAKE REPARATIVE ARGUMENTS?

Some philosophers have argued that debt relief, development assistance, greater or at least equal access for developing countries to global markets can be advanced on principles of global distributive justice.[7] Even special cultural rights for some nations, such as allowing developing countries to exempt cultural products from free trade agreements, the return of cultural artifacts to their countries of origin, and the establishment of international organizations to sustain and support cultural activities and practices of formerly colonized nations, can be defended by appeals to what global justice here and now requires. A theory of minority rights along the lines of the one developed by Will Kymlicka can, potentially, be modified and extended to the global domain, by showing that certain nations, even though politically independent, face unfair disadvantages with regard to their cultural development and protection due to the inequalities of the global cultural marketplace.[8] So, like minorities within a single state, some independent nations are entitled to certain cultural rights so as to rectify the unfair cultural disadvantages they are facing.[9]

In short, the specific demands for economic and cultural rights as forwarded in paragraph 116 and elsewhere can possibly be made on the basis of what it means to treat contemporary individuals with equal respect and concern. On this approach, a global arrangement that does not support the right to development, that treats the foreign debt of developing countries as acceptable market outcomes, that allows governments of developed countries to subsidize certain industries and agricultural products (thereby blocking off these markets from producers in developing countries), and that does not recognize the cultural rights of peoples fails to live up to the ideal of treating individuals with equal respect and concern. The call for development assistance, improved or equal market access, debt relief, and cultural rights can be grounded on the duty of global justice to treat all persons equally. For simplicity, I will call this the argument from global equality or the egalitarian argument.[10]

If these claims—for debt relief, development assistance, access to markets and so on—are claims that could be made in the name of global equality, why, one might ask, obscure and complicate the matter by introducing arguments from reparation? If the disadvantages that some people are now facing are *unjust* disadvantages that cannot be condoned under some defensible criteria of global equality, then these disadvantages should be criticized under these criteria, whether or not they are due to past injustices. Justice *here and now*, rather than injustice *then*, demands the rectification of these disadvantages. It is not the fact that individuals have been wronged in the past that is calling for greater global redistribution, but the fact that they are being wronged now. They are being wronged now because of the imposition of unjust global arrangements on them, that is, arrangements that fail to treat them with equal respect and concern, independently of whether or not they were also wronged in the past.

To be sure, a present unjust distributive arrangement can be the result of unjust events of the past. As Janna Thompson has put it nicely, injustice can 'cast a very long shadow'.[11] Past injustices can spillover into the present and can have effects that can *unjustly* harm people now. That is, unjust events of the past can be responsible for bringing about a present arrangement that violates the requirements of egalitarian justice. This is not the case of a past injustice persisting into the present, as when my stolen car is never returned to me (to use Jeremy Waldron's example), but that of a past injustice creating *new and present* social, economic, and political relations that are in turn unjust.[12] For example, it might be thought that the present unjust disadvantages faced by many African Americans, disadvantages that offend against the ideal of equality, are the result of the great evil of slavery and other forms of racial injustice continuing beyond the abolition of slavery in the United States.

But in this situation, reference to past injustices, while useful as a *diagnosis* of a present injustice, is not necessary as a *remedy* for the injustice. Or to put it more exactly, the fact of past injustices is not a necessary condition for our having a reason to remedy a present injustice. If a current distributive arrangement offends against the prevailing standards of egalitarian justice, there is a reason of justice to take action and to rectify the situation, independently of how the arrangement came about. Talk of the past may help us understand how the present unjust arrangement came about, but it plays no necessary justificatory role with respect to why we should do something about the current situation. There can be reasons independent of any past injustice to mitigate the disadvantages faced by persons if these disadvantages are unjust on other terms.

Many of the economic and social disadvantages that many African Americans face are objectionable on most defensible criteria of egalitarian justice, regardless of the origin of these disadvantages. This is not to deny that reparative claims with regard to slavery can be made in addition to that of egalitarian justice here and now. My point is that many of the social and economic disadvantages that African Americans currently face can also be criticized on forward-looking terms, by reference to what egalitarian justice now requires. There is no need to invoke the past wrong of slavery to show why these current disadvantages are unacceptable. For this reason, Glenn Loury rejects demands for reparations for African American slavery, stressing that it is the problem of gross present injustices against African Americans that should receive our attention.[13]

In other words, supposing that it is true that the current economic disadvantages faced by individuals in the developing world can be traced to the injustice of colonialism, if these disadvantages are also unjust according to principles of global equality, then the fact that these economic disadvantages have their roots in the history of colonialism is *normatively irrelevant* in a sense. References to a country's colonial past can contribute to a causal explanation as to why it had to borrow a massive amount of money to (re)build its economic infrastructure or why its economic development is lagging behind that of more developed economies. But invoking its colonial past is not necessary for the purpose of *justifying* why we now have a duty of justice to forgive its debt, or to assist in its development. If there is a duty based on egalitarian justice on the part of the better-off to assist the less well-off to develop their respective economies, then the foreign loans that poor countries have received should be seen not as a debt to be serviced and repaid, but as an entitlement based on distributive justice.

So it might be thought that reparative arguments are superfluous in the context of global injustice. The demands being made in the name of colonial reparations—the demands for development assistance, for debt relief, etc.—can be defended by appealing to egalitarian principles. Drawing attention to the injustice of colonialism seems to do no extra normative work as far as forwarding these specific demands goes. Indeed, it might be thought that introducing the notion of reparations to the debate on global justice will only distract and confuse the discussion unnecessarily.

I find the argument from equality very persuasive, and would support the view that egalitarian considerations can ground many of the global proposals made in paragraph 116 (for debt relief, development assistance and so on).[14] However, I want to offer some reasons why reparative arguments can be useful even if the demands for greater global redistribution of resources from rich to poor countries can be justified on global egalitarian grounds. Reparative arguments can complement and motivate egalitarian arguments in different ways, and so, I will argue, merit serious consideration in their own right.

First, arguments about reparation can supplement arguments about global equality by providing additional motivation for compliance with the demands of egalitarian justice. While reparation claims often face some difficult philosophical issues (as we see in Section 12.3), it is nonetheless the case that the core moral principle behind the idea of reparation speaks more immediately to the moral sensibility of most individuals, and hence is better able to move them to action, than the claim that one has positive duties of justice to assist strangers. This is because reparations appeal to a moral intuition that most persons hold, namely, that if we wrong another, we can be rightly asked to make amends. The positive action that is required in the making of amends is an action to make up for our (past) failure to avoid harming others, and so is strictly speaking a belated fulfillment of a negative duty. There is no need to invoke claims about positive duties, but only the noncontentious claim that we have a negative duty not to inflict harm, and the duty to make up for the harm that we do inflict. The positive duty (to make repairs) is ultimately 'a debt of honor' (to borrow Kant's phrase). It is a (positive) duty we have because we have not previously complied with our negative duty not to harm others.

So supplementing arguments from equality with arguments from reparation for colonialism can help motivate compliance with the demands of egalitarian justice. It appeals more directly to people's moral intuitions that individuals must take responsibility for their wrongdoing. The sentiment associated with the principle that one ought to return what you have wrongly taken from another is stronger than that associated with the principle that one ought to assist a stranger in need. Most ordinary and well-meaning people are more likely to take action to correct their past transgressions than to act as required by egalitarian justice (even if they are convinced of the demands of equality). The former is, I think, less vulnerable to problems of weakness of will. In this respect, reparative arguments have a practical advantage over egalitarian arguments.

A second reason for introducing reparative arguments is this: While a current arrangement may be unjust on terms defined independently of the past, the fact that the present injustice has roots in a past injustice may mean that the present injustice cannot be corrected without acknowledging and making some amends (even if only symbolically) for the past injustice. Relations based on justice require mutual respect and trust, and reasonableness on the part of the parties concerned. A relationship based on justice would require that both sides be willing to make only reasonable demands on each other and to respect each other's reasonable demands. Accordingly, parties in a just relationship must also be willing to make concessions on their own demands (i.e. to adjust one's claim against the legitimate entitlements of others), and to meet each other part way where necessary.

Historical injustices can have spillover unjust effects in an indirect way, then, by tainting present relations that make justice between the affected parties difficult to achieve.[15] Failure to acknowledge a grave historical wrong on the part of the unjust and to show remorse can be interpreted as a lack of respect for their (former) victims. As Kumar and Silver observe, one legacy of past injustice is that it can have the effect of taking present individuals (belonging to the group that was wronged) 'to be *deserving* of an inferior social, political, and legal status'.[16] Indeed, in this sense, past injustice can have ongoing harmful effects on present persons who were not themselves personally wronged by inculcating social attitudes that continue to accord them less than equal respect. In turn, the victims of the past injustice will not be in a position to trust their former aggressors. Sufferers of grave but unacknowledged wrong may also find it hard to be reasonable and to make concessions to those who have wronged them, even if the demands that their former violators are now making are reasonable on other criteria. Unacknowledged past wrongs not only distort parties' perception of each other, but can also infect their self-perception. Victims may internalize the morally inferior status they have in the eyes of their aggressors, while violators may come to have a distorted sense of their own moral superiority, furthering the asymmetry in relationship that makes a just relationship impossible.

So, even if the present global arrangement is objectionable by reference to justice here and now, it is arguable that international justice is in fact unachievable until a certain level of mutual trust and respect between different nations is attained, and the realization of this must require, among other things, an acknowledgment, by the perpetrators, of the great injustices in recent human history, including that of colonialism, and the making of reparations for these injustices in some form. So long as the relationship between formerly colonized peoples and their former rulers remain on unequal terms that are characterized by distrust and suspicion because of the failure on the part of the latter to acknowledge and make reparations for their past deed, justice here and now may not be realizable.[17] Past injustices can cast a very long shadow, then, because of their corrosive effects on human relationships that can make justice now, and into the future, difficult to achieve.

Arguments from reparation, on this reasoning, have more than a supplementary role in the quest for global justice. It will have the important function of helping to repair the kind of human relationship that global justice is dependent on. Justice is a relationship between equals, and the aim of reparations is to restore the moral equilibrium between the wrongdoer and the wronged.[18] In this regard, reparative arguments are not just supplementary to arguments for global equality; reparations are necessary if we want to achieve real justice.[19]

A third reason for invoking claims of reparation to support demands for debt relief, development assistance, improved access to global markets, and so on, is already suggested above. While specific claims of reparations are sometimes shrouded by controversy concerning the question of *who* is to compensate *whom* (as we will discuss in more detail later), it seems to me that the fundamental principle informing the idea of reparation is less controversial in the minds of most people than the idea of global egalitarianism. As mentioned, the underlying idea behind reparative claims, that one should make amends for the wrongs that one has committed is intuitively more obvious than the idea that one has a positive duty to assist strangers in need. Arguments from reparations for colonialism (as suggested in the paragraph 116) can therefore be invoked to justify greater global redistribution of resources, when arguments from global equality are met with skepticism (as they often are in the real world). In this regard, reparative arguments can serve as an alternative to global egalitarian arguments where necessary.

Not all present disadvantages are unjust. There can be disadvantages that a person faces that are not necessarily unjust on egalitarian grounds. For example, these disadvantages might be due to the person's free choice taken within an institutional scheme that satisfied egalitarian principles. Critics of global egalitarianism might think, then, that if the foreign debt incurred by debtor nations has been freely and fairly assumed in a global marketplace that is fair, there is no reason of justice why this debt should be forgiven. On this reasoning, that some countries are severely hobbled by their heavy foreign debt is not itself an injustice. Or critics might think that there is no right to development, and so there is no duty of assistance to provide aid to developing countries. The fact that some countries are economically underdeveloped, regrettable as it is, is itself not a matter of injustice because countries have to take responsibility for their own development and the choices that they have collectively made in this regard as self-determining nations.

Arguments from reparations offer alternative reasons for global redistribution that do not appeal to global egalitarianism, and so can avoid these anti-egalitarian objections. Even if it is conceded that the present disadvantages that some nations are currently facing are not unjust disadvantages by reference to egalitarian criteria, the fact that the disadvantages that they are facing are due to unmitigated past injustice presents a reason of justice for ameliorating these existing disadvantages. The argument from reparation will explain why a current arrangement that is not objectionable on account of egalitarian justice is nonetheless morally unacceptable because the disadvantages that some are facing under this arrangement are due to uncorrected historical injustices.[20]

In the case of the demands made in paragraph 116, an argument from reparation can say that *even if* the debt burden of developing countries cannot be objected to in terms of global egalitarian justice, this debt should nonetheless be forgiven as a form of compensation for colonial exploitation, particularly in cases where the debtor and creditor have a past colonial relationship. Or, to take another example, the duty of some developed countries to provide assistance to some developing countries for economic development can be explained not as a duty of egalitarian justice but as a duty to make amends for their past colonial exploitation.

Reparative arguments for special cultural rights can also work in lieu of arguments based on minority rights when the latter are contested. Indeed, in contemporary philosophy, minority cultural rights arguments face even more resistance than arguments for economic justice. Cultural rights and the rights of peoples are commonly associated with the so-called 'third generation' of human rights, which is presumably a more advanced and less accepted phase in the development of the concept and practice of human rights, than the so-called 'second generation' rights that include social and economic rights. Basing the call for special cultural provisions on the form of reparations for the culturally destructive consequences of colonialism—for example, the loss of cultural self-respect, the undermining of local languages, and the loss of tangible cultural objects—can be a useful argumentative strategy when arguments about global inequality and its impact on the cultural identities of some peoples fail to persuade. Indeed, Fanon's point about the culturally destructive and degrading aspects of colonialism can provide forceful reasons why former colonized peoples are entitled to special support and provisions to help with the rehabilitation and revival of their respective cultures, either directly in the form of special assistance from their former colonial rulers or indirectly through international organizations such as UNESCO that former colonial powers are especially obligated to support.

Thus, reparative arguments, if successful, can provide an alternative defense of global distributive justice that appeals only to moral principles that are widely shared. This general strategy is typified by Thomas Pogge in his defense of the moral responsibilities the global rich have toward the global poor. Beginning from morally modest premises, that our moral duties are simply the negative duties not to do harm, Pogge argues that the global rich have nonetheless failed to live up to their negative duties through their imposition of harmful global institutions on the poor. Thus the responsibility the rich have to protect the global poor, that can include global distributive commitments, derives from the duty they have to make good the harm that they are inflicting on the poor.[21] Pogge's claim, in short, is that he can derive morally robust demands regarding the global poor from relatively uncontroversial moral principles. In a similar spirit, reparative arguments for global redistribution and cultural rights, unlike arguments based on global equality, have the advantage in that they can begin from minimalist and widely shared moral commitments.[22]

To sum: arguments from reparation can be useful in three ways even though arguments from global equality can also ground many of the demands that have been made in the name of reparations. One, they are better able to motivate action than more abstract arguments about global equality. Two, they may be necessary for repairing the kinds of international relationships that are necessary for global egalitarian justice to be realized. And, third, they can step in when the argument from equality is resisted.

If it is correct that reparative arguments for colonialism are not redundant, the next thing to do is to see if such arguments can be philosophically defended. But before moving on to see whether the demands for reparation for colonialism can resist some of the common philosophical concerns commonly raised against the idea of reparative justice, it is worth noting some important qualifications implicit in the above discussion. Reparative arguments should be understood in the context of global egalitarian justice. Some former colonies may be doing better than countries that have not been colonized (compare, say, Singapore and Thailand), and it would be perverse to argue that the former should be the beneficiary of global redistribution but not the latter. Therefore, reparative arguments for debt relief, economic assistance and so on are to be understood within the parameters of global egalitarian justice. The demands of global justice will set limits on the kinds of reparations that may be demanded and who may demand them. Nonetheless, reparative arguments are not necessarily superfluous as I have suggested. Situating reparative claims within the larger context of global justice also helps assuage the worry that invoking reparative arguments may distract efforts from present and urgent matters like ongoing global injustices. Reparations should be seen only as one of the many steps toward real global justice and not its entirety. Indeed one of my arguments above is that reparative arguments can provide alternative routes toward the goals also shared by global egalitarians; and having multiple arguments for the same conclusion need not be distracting but can indeed allow for a productive division of labor among individuals, organizations etc. of different expertise, knowledge, skills, and inclinations.[23] Given the complementariness of egalitarian and reparative goals, reparative and egalitarian arguments do not undercut each other.

12.3. REPARATIONS FOR COLONIALISM: WHY, WHOM, WHO, AND WHAT

Is there a right to reparation for the injustice of colonialism? To answer this question, one must first identity the moral basis underlying the idea of reparation. This is the question (*a*) Why reparations? The answer to this, as most readers will agree, is quite straightforward. But identifying the moral basis of reparation is not sufficient to justify any particular reparative demand. Any claim for reparation has to fulfill the following conditions. It has to (*b*) identify the claimant who is entitled to reparation—to whom are reparations owed, (*c*) identify the agent who has the obligation to provide the reparation—who owes reparations, and (*d*) show that the reparations demanded can be offered without incurring further injustices—what kinds of reparations are owed. If there are no identifiable agents or claimants relative to any reparative claim, then the claim is quite meaningless. If the reparative actions demanded will themselves bring about further injustices (to third parties or even to the parties that can be reasonably called on to make repairs of some form), the reparative demands may not be satisfiable. I will elaborate on these points in turn.

(1) The fundamental moral basis of the idea of reparation is rather straightforward, and already alluded to several times above: One has the duty to make good the wrong one does; and, conversely, a person has the right to demand repairs of sorts from a person who has harmed her. The principle of righting one's wrong is present in our ordinary conception of morality.[24]

But identifying the moral basis for reparations alone is not sufficient for grounding any specific claim of reparation. The formulation above presupposes that there is an identifiable victim, and an identifiable responsible agent of reparation. A reparative claim could not be meaningfully made otherwise. It would be odd to make a claim of reparative justice if either of the parties—the victim or aggressor—is indeterminate. Indeed, the formulation as stated suggests that it is the *wrongdoer* who has to make good the wrong done, and that it is the *victim* who has the right to demand reparation. But for many interesting cases of reparations, the situation is more complex. The wrongdoers are often no longer present to bear the burdens of reparation; similarly the victims of the past injustice are often no longer present to personally demand and to benefit from the reparations.

Indeed, the most challenging and pressing questions of reparations involve cases where few, if any, of the past antagonists are still around to make demands of and to bear the costs of these demands. Demands for reparations for slavery in America and for the cruelty against indigenous peoples by European settlers in America and Australia (just to take common examples) involve assessing claims of wrongdoing and injury between persons that are not identical to the persons currently making reparative demands and the persons expected to bear the burdens of such demands. The situation is less extreme with regard to colonialism, for many individuals on both sides of the colonial experience are still alive. Still the demands for reparations for colonialism are not generally seen as compensations for the *individual victims* of colonialism, but as compensation for the colonized *nation as a whole*, for what it had suffered as a collectivity. They are effectively demands that a country's present and future citizens be compensated for their country's past colonial exploitation, even though these individuals themselves need not have been alive during colonial rule. And the cost of reparation is not to be necessarily borne by the actual individual participants and beneficiaries of colonialism, but by the former colonial country as a whole and this is a burden that those not directly involved in the colonizing, including its future citizens, are asked to accept. Hence the demand for reparations for colonialism faces the same philosophical challenges as demands for reparations for African American slavery and indigenous peoples: it implies that individuals who did not personally suffer an injustice are nonetheless entitled to some form of reparation, and that individuals who did not personally do harm are nonetheless responsible for making good this past injustice. Like claims for reparations for slavery, the prospective beneficiaries and agents of reparations are not the same persons as the perpetrators and victims of injustice but their successors.

In short, what makes the case for reparation challenging is that in many instances, the demands for reparation are made by individuals distinct from those who had personally suffered, and the burdens of reparation are expected to be shouldered by individuals distinct from those who had personally carried out the injustice. An argument for reparations in which the original parties to the past conflict are no longer present must be able to show how and in what sense the burden of past wrongs can pass across generations to visit the present, that one is not responsible only for the harm that one has personally caused but also for the harm carried out by one's predecessors. Conversely, it has to show also that individuals have a right to demand compensation for harms done not just against their own persons but against their predecessors.

(2) To whom, then, are reparations owed? In the colonial context, it is the current members of the colonized countries who are demanding repairs for colonialism. There is no implication here that the current members are restricted to the biological descendants of colonized individuals. All current members of the nation, including first-generation immigrants from other nations, are presumably entitled to the benefits of reparation. If, say, India, is to receive development assistance as a reparation for its past colonial exploitation, the fact that some of its citizens are new immigrants (who themselves and whose ancestors were not subjected to colonial exploitation) will not affect their actual enjoyment of the benefits of the assistance. But if those who are entitled to claims of reparations include all current members of a nation, it also excludes former members who have emigrated. Thus biological descendants of Indian subjects of colonial India who now live in, say, the United Kingdom are not in any position to enjoy and benefit from the development assistance given to India. Biological membership is thus neither necessary nor sufficient for identifying who has the right to reparations for colonial exploitation. It is one's current status as a member of a formerly colonized nation that gives one this entitlement.

The effective beneficiaries of the reparative demands as expressed in paragraph 116, then, are the *participating* members of the nation. It is participation in the cultural life of a nation, broadly construed, that determines membership, not ethnicity or biological descent. But why should present participating members of a nation have a right to reparations for injustices that are not necessarily carried out against them in person? And, conversely, why should those who have personally suffered the injustice of colonialism during the colonization of their country not be entitled to reparations if they choose to participate in the life of another nation? One way of responding to this question is to see the harm of colonialism not as a harm done against individuals but as a harm done against a nation or a people, and so it is to the nation as a corporate entity that reparation is now owed. That is, the reparative demand is a demand of a corporate group and not a demand of individuals as such.

Colonialism interfered with, and in some cases severely undermined, the cultural, economic, and political self-determination of a nation. While this interference clearly inflicted harm on individuals (and whether individuals who were personally affected by colonial exploitation have a right to be compensated is a different though serious question), it was also a harm done against a nation as a whole. Colonialism compromised the cultural, economic, and political structure of a people. These are wrongs not against persons as such but wrongs against the corporate entity to which individuals belong. The corporate group as a whole was harmed by the injustice of colonialism and in as far as the corporate group remains in existence, it has a right to demand reparations. To repeat an example made earlier in the chapter, the denial of educational opportunities to an individual during colonialism is a wrong against the person; but the resulting loss of the intellectual and cultural tradition of the person's community is a wrong against the collective, and is a wrong that extends beyond the life of the person individually denied the opportunity. Of course individuals have to make this demand for redress for wrongs against a collective, but the demand is normatively grounded on the harm that the group has suffered, and is made by individuals *on behalf of the group*. It is the harm against the nation as a corporate entity that is generating the demand for reparations. This is, I believe, how the demands for reparations expressed in paragraph 116 are to be understood. The demands presuppose a wrong done to a group rather than wrongs done to individuals as such.

One might object that it is just bad metaphysics to attribute the state of being harmed to groups. Ultimately, only individual human beings feel pain and hurt. Groups are not the sorts of things to experience pain. But the point about a group being harmed does not absurdly presume that a group is able to sense pain and to suffer; rather the point is that a group can be harmed in a way that is more than the aggregate of the harm against its individual members taken one by one. The loss of a language, for example, is of course ultimately a loss that only individual human beings can experience. Yet the harm to the nation that has lost its language is not simply the sum of the loss to its individuals; it is a loss that is not reducible to the loss experienced by individuals. We can take a loss of a language to be reducible to the sum of the loss felt by the individual users of that language only if we erroneously take the entirety of a language to be the collection of its individual users. To the extent that we accept a national identity to be nonreducible to the identities of the individuals making up the nation, to this extent any assault or insult against a national identity is not merely the sum of the felt experience of individuals. Rather than assuming an unlikely ontology of groups, speaking of groups being harmed allows us to acknowledge the fact of harms to a community of persons that are not simply the sum of the harm against each one of its members taken one by one.

Margalit and Raz refer to nations as 'encompassing groups' in that, among other things, individual well-being is 'bound up with' the prosperity of their nation and how well it is respected and regarded by others. So we care about how a group is faring because how well it is doing affects the well-being of individuals of the group. But taking groups to be morally important, because it is ultimately individuals that matter, is consistent with the idea that a group can be harmed in a way that is not reducible to the harm felt by its individual members. As Margalit and Raz write, 'Group interests cannot be reduced to individual interests. It makes sense to talk of a group's prospering or declining, of actions and policies as serving the group's interest or of harming it, without having to cash this in terms of individual interests. Group interests,' they go on to say, 'are conceptually connected to the interests of their members but such connections are nonreductive and generally indirect.'[25] What this means is that while groups have interests only because individuals have interests, these group interests need not be the sum of individual interests added up one by one. To put it in a different way, we may perhaps say that group interests supervene on the interests of individuals but they are not identical to these interests.

It is of course true that groups like nations are not the sort of things that can make demands on their own; only individuals can make demands. But the demands made by individuals for colonial injustices are demands that are made on behalf of their groups. It is the wrong against the nation that is being appealed to, and it is the nation as a whole that is making the claim for reparation even if individuals are voicing these demands. A nation can have a moral identity that is more than the sum of its individual members, and thus may be the subject of moral wrong that is not reducible to the harm against its individuals.

If we accept that not only individual persons but corporate entities may be harmed, we can avoid the problem of transferring occurred harms across generations or different individuals. The harm of colonialism is not being unwarrantedly distributed and shared across individuals if the harm is understood as harm against a corporate entity. Indeed, looking at the injustice of colonialism in terms of an injustice against a corporate group avoids a serious problem that an individualistic approach to reparations faces—that of showing how current individuals are continuing to be harmed by the wrong against their ancestors or predecessors. An approach that takes individuals to be the only kinds of things that can be harmed will have to show that the disadvantages that some individuals are now facing are due to past injustices against others. That is, an individualist approach will have to show that current individuals are being harmed, to wit made worse off, because of a past wrong. This is an argument based on counterfactuals. It says that if the historical injustice did not happen, then present individuals would not be experiencing the present harm. But as Waldron has argued, arguments based on counterfactuals are too indeterminate to have a decisive role in deliberations about reparative justice. How can we be certain that these individuals would not be in the same (unfortunate) situation had the injustice not occurred?[26] The more distant the past injustice the greater the number of intervening causal factors on a given state of affairs, and the more uncertain counterfactual arguments are.

But if we treat the harm against a nation as a harm against a corporate entity that is not reducible to the harm against individuals, we can sidestep Waldron's indeterminacy objection. What the argument from corporate agency says is that the nation was unjustly harmed, and its members are now demanding compensation for this harm against it. There is no mention of how agents could otherwise be faring were it not for the past injustice. It is the wrong against the group that is being complained about, not that some persons are currently worse off putatively because of an uncorrected past wrong.

Some countries came into existence only after and arguably because of colonialism. So, one might be tempted to say that because a country did not exist during colonialism, and in fact would not have existed were it not for colonialism, that it cannot demand compensation for colonialism. That is, one can accept that moral identity is not restricted to persons, but say still that a continuous identity is a minimal condition for continuing moral agency. But it is important not to confuse a nation with sovereign state. It is the 'historic community', to adopt Walzer's phrase, underlying the state that is taken to be the corporate moral entity and the subject that is harmed.[27]

(3) Who should bear the burdens of reparations? Just as it is a feature of ordinary morality that moral agents make good the wrongs they do, it is also central to most ordinary moral conceptions (especially those that take normative individualism seriously) that moral culpability does not travel across agencies. Passing the burden of reparative justice from the generation guilty of an injustice to another that is innocent seems to violate this basic moral dictum. If reparations for colonialism have the effect of imposing some costs on present citizens of former colonial powers, this seems to be an unfair imposition of the burdens of justice if present citizens were not themselves the perpetrators of the injustices of colonialism.

One way of responding to this problem of unfair burdens, as I will call it, is to show that present citizens of former colonial powers are continuing to benefit from the effects of colonialism, and so may be called on to cease enjoying benefits that are not rightly theirs. This is a common way of understanding how the burdens of correcting an injustice can be distributed. Indeed, this is the position adopted in paragraph 116, which (to recall) says that 'States, companies and individuals *who benefited materially*' from colonialism (and other injustices) are responsible for contributing to the reparations demanded. Straightforward as this position might seem, it however faces Waldron's 'indeterminacy' objection as noted above. The more distant the past injustice, the more difficult it is to determine how and which successive individuals are continuing to benefit from the injustice of their predecessors.

However, framing the issue in terms of corporate rather than individual responsibility will avoid the problem of unfair burdens. The idea of the nation as a corporate entity will help us to see why a country (and effectively its present citizens) can now be called on to make repairs for its past colonialist activities. It is the corporate entity that had done the wrong and it is the corporate entity that is now asked to make good the wrong. No responsibility is being passed on from a moral agent who committed the wrong to a moral agent who is innocent. The wrongful actor is the nation, and it is the nation that is now being asked to make repairs. We are not wrongly allowing responsibilities to travel across agents; the responsibility stays with the culpable agent, in this case the nation that is responsible for the harm. Nor is there any assumption here that present individuals who are being asked to make repairs are in fact benefiting from the unmitigated past injustice. The claim is that the corporate entity has done wrong, and the group (and this has to involve its current individual members) is now asked to make good this wrong.

As with the case for harm against groups, none of the above assumes any contentious group metaphysics. There is no attribution of an existence to a group that is independent of lives of the individuals that make it up. What it suggests is that we can talk of a group having responsibilities and rights that need not be necessarily reducible to the responsibilities and rights of distinct individuals of the group.[28] Our ordinary moral language allows for the concept of corporate responsibility without the need to presuppose that groups have independent moral lives. We, after all, do talk of a business corporation being responsible for a wrong even before we actually allocate the responsibility to particular individuals. We take corporations to be *structured* institutions that are capable of doing wrongs that are not simply the sum of the wrongs of any particular individuals within its ranks. Indeed, newly appointed executives of a corporation can be expected ordinarily to apologize for any past failings of the corporation even if these failings happened under the watch of their predecessors. Group responsibility, like group interests, need not be reducible to the personal responsibilities and interests of the individual members of the groups.

Of course, the actual discharge of the group's responsibilities will involve the division and allocation of responsibilities to *individual members* of the group. As Chandran Kukathas notes, although responsibility for a past injustice 'lies with the institutions', individuals, as members of these institutions, are responsible for performing their appropriate institutional duties.[29] This does not mean that these individuals are being unfairly blamed, in the sense of being morally culpable, for the wrong of their predecessors. As Kumar and Silver write, 'The wrongdoing of the state... reflects not on the character of the person but, rather, on the past quality of the ongoing state of which one is now a citizen'.[30] It is a civic duty, as Fullinwider calls it, for persons to share in the burdens of justice of their society even if they are not personally responsible for the injustice that needs correcting. As citizens or members of a nation, we have certain civic responsibilities that are independent of our choosing and past responsibility. The duty of justice is one of the civic responsibilities of citizenship—citizens have the duty to help sustain the justness of the institutions of their society by virtue of their being citizens, not by virtue of their past actions. If a nation owes reparations to another, this is a duty that has to be allocated in some appropriate way to its members, and it becomes part of their civic duties to their state or nation as citizens or nationals.[31] A member of a nation need not be personally culpable in order to have a share in the collective moral responsibility of her country, however this responsibility might arise. On this view, recent immigrants to a society can also acquire a share in the society's responsibility to make good its past injustices. The 'quality' of their state is of moral concern to them even though they had no role in contributing to that quality. This is in part what it means to become a citizen.

One reason why a member of a nation that has done wrong as a collective can be expected to bear responsibility for reparations even though the individual herself has done no wrong is that as a member of the nation, she belongs to a cooperative organization in which through her own ongoing contribution she benefits from her membership. David Miller calls this the 'cooperative practice model' of collective responsibility. And a nation, Miller argues, is a cooperative organization. 'Nations provide their members with a number of public goods, foremost among which is protection of the national culture itself... nations exhibit the features of a large-scale cooperative practice: each member makes certain sacrifices in order to support a national culture from whose continued existence each is presumed to benefit'.[32] Notice that the benefit to the member need not be the direct result of the past wrong done in the context of reparations; it is the benefit of belonging to a national community that imposes civic obligations of various sorts on her, and this can include, where relevant, taking on a share of her nation's responsibility for its past wrong, even if she is not directly benefiting from the wrong.[33]

As with the case of harm against a group, a collective can be responsible for its past action only if it is enjoys a continuous existence. But what is relevant is not that a particular state remains in existence, but that there is a continual national identity. Borrowing Kymlicka's terminology, perhaps we can say that the continuing existence of a distinctive 'societal culture' is evidence of a nation's continuing identity. A societal culture is not simply a statistical collection of persons with a shared ethnicity. It is, crucially, characterized by a set of public institutions and norms and practices; that is, there is a deliberative mechanism of some form that allows us to hold the corporate group as a morally responsible entity. A group of persons, even of the same ethnicity, randomly brought together do not constitute a nation, let alone a corporate moral agent that can be held accountable as a whole. What makes a nation different from a mere collection of individuals is that its members see themselves as part of a shared project and that there are in place various institutions that allow the collective to make decisions on behalf of the group.

It is important here to acknowledge the limits of reparative arguments with respect to global redistribution claims. One reason why proponents of colonial reparations often press their claims in terms of the benefits of colonialism (as in paragraph 116) is that this allows them to target rich countries such as Canada and the United States, which though not colonizers themselves, are arguably also indirect beneficiaries of Europe's colonial adventures. But if Waldron is right, arguments about benefits from past wrongs are hard to establish, and the kind of repayment for these wrongs even harder to ascertain. Indeed, on my account of reparations, claims about benefiting from past wrongs are put to one side. This may seem to some, however, to limit the fruitfulness of reparative arguments. Canada and the United States, countries that can contribute enormously to global redistribution of wealth, for example would not be called on, yet a poorer country like Portugal that has historically engaged in colonialism would be expected to contribute to the reparations fund. And this might seem perverse in addition to being ineffective. To defuse this worry, one needs to accept the limited status of reparative arguments. They are not meant, for example, to replace arguments from global justice but are meant, as I argued earlier, only to supplement them. So understood, as only one argument among others in the arsenal of global egalitarians, even though reparative arguments can target only wrongdoers but not rich beneficiaries, this need not have unacceptable results because, within the larger framework of global justice, these rich beneficiaries can be required on grounds of egalitarian justice to contribute to the global redistribution of wealth. The limited quality of reparative arguments is not a drawback so long as it is recognized that it is not the only claim of justice that people can make.[34]

Treating nations as corporate entities that can be wronged in ways that are not reducible to the wrongs against individuals, and as entities that can be collectively responsible for wrongdoing in ways that are not reducible to the actions of individuals, can help us make sense of reparative demands for colonialism. The people making the demands for reparations need not themselves have personally suffered under colonial rule; nor is there any need to assume that they are being made worse off personally because of colonialism. What is morally relevant is that the nation to which they belonged was wronged, and it is for this wrong against their nation that they are demanding reparation. Similarly, nations can act unjustly in ways that are not reducible to the sum of the actions of individuals. Present members of a nation are responsible for mitigating the wrongdoing of their country not because they have contributed personally to this wrong, but because they belong to a corporate entity that has done wrong. And they need not have benefited from the wrong before they can be asked to make amends. An injustice that profits no one is still an injustice, and culpable parties can still be asked to pay compensation even if they did not benefit from the injustice they committed.

(4) Another difficulty with reparative demands is that they sometimes seem to impose unduly heavy burdens on the agents responsible for providing the reparations. This is not the problem of imposing burdens on the wrong agents but that of imposing the wrong kinds of burdens on agents. For example, the demand for territorial repatriation in some indigenous claims may seem to impose an unreasonably heavy demand on persons who are now called on to surrender the disputed territory. Or, as in some of the republics of the former Soviet Union, the correction of the past injustice of the Russian occupation is thought to require the effective revocation of citizenship from the descendants of Russian immigrants. Even if we accept the idea of corporate responsibility, the distribution of this burden of correcting the past injustice to individuals, even if the corporate entity to which they belong must take responsibility for the past wrong, seems unreasonably harsh. So it is not enough for an account of reparation to show that the bearers of responsibility have not been unfairly selected to bear the burden of a past wrong; it has to show also that the burden is also an unreasonable one. In other words, the reparation itself must not constitute an injustice. In many cases of past injustices, given the complexity of history, full reparations may not always be possible given their unjust implications on the persons expected to bear the costs. What this means, however, is not that reparations per se are unwarranted; what may have to be limited against other considerations is the content of the demands for reparations. To put the point in a different way, it is not that the reparative principle no longer is valid in this case, but that the complexity of the situation renders salient other competing principles that need to be taken account of. The crucial point remains that a past wrong be acknowledged and that some sincere and appropriate steps be taken to make up for this wrong within the limits that other moral considerations can impose.

At any rate, the demands for colonial reparations presented in paragraph 116 are less complicated. As mentioned in the opening, they are demands for development assistance and other forms of cooperation that are independently defensible, many commentators would say, on grounds of global equality. These demands do not entail obvious grave injustice such as the mass transfer of persons, the revocation of citizenship, and so on. Rather, they are quite modest and are demands that can be defended on other grounds of justice. The reparative demands for colonialism proposed by the Group of 21 in their Draft Resolution for the World Conference against Racism are therefore not unreasonable. They are not demands that will incur further injustices if accepted and enforced; on the contrary they are demands that would be required by other (independent) considerations of justice.

Some commentators might point to the 'passage of time' that has passed between the injustice committed and the present in which reparations are being demanded. Perhaps there can be a moral equivalent of a statute of limitations?[35] Is it, after all, not unfair to suddenly impose an unexpected burden of repair on a violator when she could reasonably believe that bygones will be bygones because a significant amount of time has passed since the violation? One purpose of a statute of limitations, I take it, is to allow people to go on with their lives; to protect people's legitimate expectations by avoiding unexpected but intrusive demands and claims on them. My issuing a person with a burdensome summons for a past harm after many intervening years of silence about the matter could constitute an unexpected intrusion on that person's life, if the inaction on my part could be reasonably read by my past violator that I was prepared to let bygones be bygones. Yet my past inaction could be reasonably read in this way, if, among other things, it was wholly within my means and power and authority to raise a claim against my perpetrator earlier but that I freely opted not to. My sudden demand for reparations could plausibly be condemned as a violation of my past transgressor's legitimate expectations. Indeed, my raising the issue now, moreover, can be viewed with some suspicion, as a case of my wanting to take advantage of the past for the purpose of satisfying some new inclination or need, rather than a case of genuinely seeking justice. So the real and key question that the passage of time objection raises is whether demands for reparations for colonial injustices are similarly out of the blue, so to speak, that is, whether they are demands that former colonial powers could not reasonably expect would be made. It does not seem so to me. Claims against colonialism have been ongoing, from calls for equal treatment during colonialism itself to calls for independence from colonial rule, and currently for reparations after independence. At no point in the history of colonialism could colonizing authorities pretend not to know that claims were being made against them during colonialism or that claims were going to be made against them even after colonialism by their subjects. Indeed the practice of special immigration policies for members of former colonial peoples, the creation and awarding of scholarships for former colonial subjects, and other practices are evidence of the recognition by former colonial rulers of the special obligations they owe to their former colonies and the ongoing tie between them. The issue of colonial injustice, I believe, slides by the passage of time objection because at no time could colonizing authorities in good faith assume that bygones will be bygones. That the injustice of colonialism still reverberates in the minds of many former colonized peoples, and that the perceived injury is openly spoken about, renders such an assumption suspect.

12.4. CONCLUSION

I have tried to argue that the demands for reparations proposed in paragraph 116 can be meaningfully and justly made. Indeed, that these demands are also demands that can be made on grounds of egalitarian justice does not show that reparative demands are redundant but in fact shows that they are supportable because they are consistent with what global justice requires. And I argued that taking nations to be corporate entities capable of being responsible and of being wronged in ways that are not just the sum of individuals' responsibility and well-being avoids the common difficulties associated with reparations—namely, the problems of passing responsibilities and harm across moral agents. Reparative demands can be meaningfully made in the colonial context when the nations which were the historical antagonists still exist qua nations. That the individuals making up these groups are not identical to those at the scene of the injustice does not render reparative demands meaningless. That there is a continuing societal culture is sufficient for holding a collective responsible because there is in continuing presence a structured organization with identifiable institutionalized roles and responsibilities (that can be filled by different individuals) to which moral responsibilities can be fixed. It is an institution that is held morally culpable for the past wrong, not the individual who is occupying the office presently, even though the incumbent is expected to discharge her institutional responsibility because she is now occupying that office.

One might object that it can never be precisely determined how much reparations are owed—how much, for instance, should the debt relief be? How much development assistance should be offered as compensation? But the precise amount of reparations is not the central issue—within the bounds of justice, reparations can take the form of a sincere apology to a full and complete return of whatever was taken (like territory).[36] What is important is that the culpable party be prepared to confront the past, to acknowledge the wrongdoing, and to take seriously the claims of the wronged. This does not mean that the specifics and exact amount of reparations are nonnegotiable, but it means that there must be the readiness to deliberate over these terms as equals.

NOTES

1. See http://www.racism.gov.za/substance/confdoc/decldraft89b.html for the declaration.
2. See paragraph 99 of the final Declaration in http://www.unhchr.ch/html/racism/02-documents-cnt.html
3. I thus take European colonialism in Asia and Africa as my model example of colonialism. But in so restricting my discussion, I do not mean to endorse the so-called 'salt water' doctrine that confines colonialism to European colonialism, thereby limiting the right to colonial independence and self-determination to just these cases.
4. Rushdie (1992: 64). See also Achebe (1975: 91–103).
5. Fanon (1967*a*: 166–8). See also Rajeev Bhargava's discussion of the 'cultural injustices' of colonialism in this volume.
6. I thank Rahul Kumar for helpful discussion on the points in this and the preceding paragraphs.
7. See, e.g. Pogge (2002) and Beitz (1979). See also Debra Satz's essay in this volume.
8. Kymlicka (1995).
9. The restitution of cultural objects can thus be defended in terms of a people's rightful inheritance to its cultural goods (both tangible and intangible) and the right to its cultural identity more generally, without making references to past wrongs. The right of a people to its cultural heritage is sufficient to ground the demand for restitution.
10. Some philosophers argue that global equal respect does not entail global egalitarianism in the strict sense. See e.g. R. Miller (1998). Miller would prefer that his position be called global beneficence rather than global egalitarianism. Still, for my present point, all we need to note is that Miller accepts that equal respect will require the meeting of basic needs and rights through wealth and resource transfers and reformation of existing global institutions, and so, even on this weaker (beneficence) conception of global justice, there will be a convergence between what reparative justice demands and what global justice demands.
11. Thompson (2001: 116).
12. Waldron (1992: 14). For a discussion of the ongoing direct harms of colonialism, see Rajeev Bhargava in this volume.
13. See his chapter in this volume.
14. I try to defend the egalitarian view in Tan (2004).

15. Thompson (2002: 34–5).
16. Kumar and Silver (2004: 152).
17. Not surprisingly, many individuals in former colonies continue to regard the foreign policies, even when well meaning, of former colonial powers with deep suspicion, often interpreting them from the paradigm of neocolonial domination. E.g. attempts (some of which are sincere) by Western countries to support the development of human rights institutions in some of their former colonies are sometimes dismissed as neocolonial interventions.
18. Aristotle says that corrective justice aims to 'redress the inequality between persons' (*Nicomachean Ethics*, Book 5: ch. 4).
19. For more discussion on reparations as means of restoring the preconditions of justice, see Brandon Hamber and Debra Satz in this volume.
20. This does not mean that global egalitarians have given up on egalitarian arguments as a philosophical commitment. The substitution, if we like, is strategic rather than philosophical. Those making reparative arguments do not need to abandon egalitarian arguments altogether even as these arguments are put aside for strategic reasons. Thanks to Colin Macleod whose comments motivated this clarification.
21. 'General Introduction', in Pogge (2002).
22. My point is not that reparative arguments will guarantee success when egalitarian arguments fail. My claim is only that it can serve as a substitute when egalitarian arguments are rejected; but there is no requirement that a substitute has to ensure success. I thank Alistair Macleod for urging clarification of this point.
23. I am grateful for Richard Miller's comments at the APA Eastern Division Meeting that raised this challenge. I thus depart from Glenn Loury's view (in this volume) that focusing on reparations for African American slavery will be counterproductive and a distraction from the real concerns of present injustices against African Americans. Making arguments for reparations for African American slavery need not undercut the case for greater (present) social justice if reparations are not seen to constitute the whole of justice and that they are not the only kinds of justice-arguments that are made. To the contrary, as I suggested above, reparative arguments can help bolster the cause of social justice in different ways.
24. Aristotle would say that this idea is affirmed even in criminal law. As he writes, in punishing a criminal, what 'the judge aims at doing is to make the parts equal by the penalty he imposes, whereby he takes from the aggressor any gain that he may have secured' (*Nicomachean Ethics*, Book 5: ch. 4). For a contemporary account of criminal law as a form of reparation, see Barnett (1977).
25. Margalit and Raz (1994: 119).
26. Waldron (1992: 7ff.). Also see Waldron's contribution in this volume. For a direct response to Waldron, see Thompson (2001).
27. See Walzer (1980).
28. Dworkin (1986: 167–75). See also Christine Korsgaard's point that moral agency is not necessarily limited to human beings but can potentially be

attributed to any entity capable of deliberative decision making (like states) (Korsgaard 1996: 372–3). I should point out that Korsgaard does not treat nations as the sort of entities that have a deliberative structure. But this is because she is using a definition of nation distinct from that of say Kymlicka's and David Miller's—more like a collection of persons who share a common ethnic culture. On Kymlicka's and Miller's definition, nations are not merely ethnic communities but communities that have common public institutions and decision making structures. The difference between them here is more definitional than substantive.

29. Kukathas (2003: 181).
30. Kumar and Silver (2004: 155).
31. Fullinwider, (2000: 4).
32. Miller (2004: 263). See also Kukathas (2003: 183–5). As an aside, Miller would hold that the notion of national responsibility tells against any global distributive principle that cosmopolitans argue for because an ongoing global distributive principle would run against the idea of holding nations responsible for their choices and policies. See also Miller (2005: 55–79). Rawls has a similar argument in *The Law of Peoples*, Part III. But as we accept that it is possible to hold individuals responsible while accepting global distributive justice between them, so there is nothing per se difficult with the idea of national responsibility and global justice. Cosmopolitans will want to hold nations accountable for their actions within a just global order; the issue for them is what that just global order consists in. On their view, the principles for the global order must be determined independently of nations' past decisions and choices even though what nations are entitled to within the order can be affected by such decisions and choices. As Rawls points out, principles of justice do not derive from notions of desserts. Cosmopolitan egalitarian principles have to do with the global background rules and norms within which nations interact, and cosmopolitans can accept that nations are collectively responsible for their choices made *within* the rules of this global structure or for choices that offend against the requirements of a just structure. If we treat egalitarian distributive justice fundamentally as an institutional ideal and reparative justice as fundamentally an interactional one, I think my argument in favor of holding nations collectively responsible for past injustices need not run against the demands of cosmopolitan egalitarianism.
33. Understanding the demands for reparations for the wrong of colonialism as demands made by corporate entities against other corporate entities for harm against them also shows that the duty of reparations is not to the dead, but to existing persons by virtue of their membership in a group that was violated. Compare Ridge (2003).
34. I thank Will Kymlicka and Jay Drydyk for urging this clarification.
35. I am grateful to Dick Miller for bringing up and detailing this objection, and I can here only try to gesture at a response. For more discussion on the general 'let bygones be bygones' objection, see Rajeev Bhargava in this volume.

36. I do not mean here that an apology instead of monetary compensation may suffice *regardless of what the wronged community wants*. My point is that sometimes this is what victims of past injustice want. For instance, some Korean comfort women refused monetary compensation from the Japanese government for atrocities committed against them during World War II in the absence of any formal official apology. As Brandon Hamber points out in this volume, the symbolic value of reparations (in particular the inherent acknowledgment of wrongdoing) should not be underestimated. I thank Dick Miller for urging clarification here.

In addition to the 'Conference on Reparations' at Queen's University, this paper was also presented at a conference at Bryn Mawr, at a PHILAMORE meeting in Philadelphia, and at the 2004 APA Eastern Division Meeting (Boston). I am grateful for comments and questions from participants and members of the audience at these events, with special thanks to Colin Macleod for his comments at the Queen's conference, Dick Miller for his comments at the APA Meeting, and Christine Koggel for her comments at the Bryn Mawr conference. Thanks also to David Reidy (for his written comments), and to David Silver, Karen Detlefsen, Rahul Kumar, Will Kymlicka, Alistair Macleod, David Sussman, Henry Richardson, Nien-he Shieh, Milton Meyer, Jay Drydyk, Daniel Weinstock, Debra Satz and Leif Wenar for helpful discussions on various occasions. Finally, I thank Jon Miller for sharing his thoughts on the topic and encouraging the paper, and to him and Rahul Kumar again for very helpful substantive and editorial suggestions.

Conclusion: Essential Elements of Healing after Massive Trauma: Some Theory, Victims' Voices, and International Developments

Yael Danieli

This chapter will convey how victims and the professionals (primarily traumatologists) who have worked with them view some of the essential elements of healing after massive trauma. After describing and conceptualizing the aftermath of the victims' experiences, the chapter will examine some of the meanings of reparation compensation and will also draw attention to the often-neglected reparative aspect of commemoration. It then summarizes related developments in victimology and international law, and concludes with a discussion of the hard-won milestone provisions for victims in the Rome Statute of the International Criminal Court.

I.1. THE EXPERIENCE OF THE VICTIM

I.1.1. The Aftermath of the Experience

After liberation, as during the war, survivors were victims of a pervasive societal reaction comprised of obtuseness, indifference, avoidance, repression, and denial of their Holocaust experiences. Like other victims, survivors' war accounts were too horrifying for most people to listen to or believe. Similar to other victims who are blamed for their victimization ['You are stupid to live near the Bhopal plant'], survivors were faced with the pervasively held myth that they had actively or passively participated in their own destiny by 'going like sheep to the slaughter'. Additionally, bystander's guilt led many to regard the survivors as pointing an accusing finger at them and projecting onto the survivors the suspicion that they had performed immoral acts in order to survive. Like other victims, they were also told to 'let bygones be bygones' and get on with their lives.

Such reactions have ensured the survivors' silence about their Holocaust experiences. They were forced to conclude that nobody cared to listen and that 'nobody could really understand' unless they had gone through the same experiences. The resulting *conspiracy of silence* (Danieli 1982, 1988*a*) between Holocaust survivors and society in general, and survivors and mental health and other professionals in particular, has proven detrimental to the survivors' familial and sociocultural reintegration by intensifying their already profound sense of isolation, loneliness, and mistrust of society. This has further impeded the possibility of their intrapsychic integration and healing, and made their task of mourning their massive losses impossible (Eitinger and Krell 1985; Danieli 1989).

Children of survivors seem to have consciously and unconsciously absorbed their parents' Holocaust experiences into their lives.[1] As Bettelheim (1984) observed, 'What cannot be talked about can also not be put to rest; and if it is not, the wounds continue to fester from generation to generation' (166). Families of survivors are extremely small. The Holocaust deprived them of the normal cycle of the generations and ages, and of natural death (Eitinger 1980). Survivors of the Holocaust age early and have higher than average rates of early death from all causes. Old age, in itself, is a trauma for them (Danieli 1981). Each survivor's family tree is steeped in murder, death and losses; yet its offspring are expected to reroot that tree and reestablish the extended family and to start anew a healthy generational cycle. Edelman, Kordon, and Lagos (1992) similarly report that in Argentina 'a remarkably high number of fathers of missing people had major physical disorders and substantial increase of deaths, whereas mothers did not present the same symptoms' (1–2), and provide related speculations.

I.1.2. The Healing Process

Cognitive recovery involves the ability to develop a realistic perspective of what happened, by whom, to whom, and accepting the reality that it happened the way it did. For example, what was and was not under the victim's control, what could not be, and why. Accepting the impersonality of the events also removes the need to attribute personal causality and consequently guilt and false responsibility. An educated and contained image of the events of victimization is potentially freeing from constructing one's view of oneself and of humanity solely on the basis of those events. For example, having been helpless does not mean that one is a helpless person; having witnessed or experienced evil does not mean that the world as a whole is evil; having been betrayed does not mean that betrayal is an overriding human behavior; having been victimized does not necessarily mean that one has to live one's life in constant readiness for its reenactment; having been treated as dispensable vermin does not mean that one is worthless; and, taking the painful risk of bearing witness does not mean that the world will listen, learn, change, and become a better place (Danieli 1988*b*).

The Latin American Institute of Mental Health and Human Rights in Santiago, Chile stated that:

> The victims know that individual therapeutic intervention is not enough. They need to know that their society as a whole acknowledges what has happened to them ... Truth means the end of denial and silence ... Truth will be achieved only when literally everyone knows and acknowledges what happened during the military regime ... [They concluded:] Social reparation is thus ... simultaneously a sociopolitical and a psychological process. It aims to establish the truth of political repression and demands justice for the victims ... both through the judicial process and through the availability of health and mental health services ... The new democracy that now offers the possibility of reparation will deteriorate into a frail bureaucratic system if the process of social mourning is not realized fully.[2]

Thus, you need to heal the sociopolitical context for the full healing of the individuals and their families, as you need to heal the individuals to heal the sociopolitical context. This is a mutually reinforcing context of shared mourning, shared memory, a sense that the memory is preserved, that the nation transformed it into a part of its global consciousness. The nation shares the horrible pain. The survivors are not lonely in their pain.

I.1.3. The Conceptualization of the Experience

I.1.3.1. Trauma and the Continuity of Self: A Multidimensional, Multidisciplinary Integrative (TCMI) Framework

To conceptualize the consequences of massive trauma, I proposed the multidimensional, multidisciplinary integrative framework (Danieli 1998). It posits that an individual's identity involves a complex interplay of multiple systems, including: biological and intrapsychic; interpersonal, including the familial, social, and communal; ethnic, cultural, ethical, religious, spiritual, and natural; educational/occupational; material/economic, legal, environmental, political, national, and international. These systems coexist along the time dimension, creating a sense of life continuous from past through present to the future. Ideally, one should have free psychological access to and movement within all these identity systems. Each system is the focus of one or more disciplines that may overlap and interact, such as biology, psychology, sociology, economics, law, anthropology, religious studies, and philosophy.[3] Each discipline has its own views of human nature and it is those that inform what the professional thinks and does.

I.1.3.2. Trauma Exposure and 'Fixity'

Trauma exposure can cause a rupture, a possible regression, and a state of being 'stuck' in this free flow, which I have called 'fixity' (Danieli 1998). The intent, place, time, frequency, duration, intensity, extent, and meaning of the trauma for the individual, and the survival strategies used to adapt to it, will determine the degree of rupture and the severity of the *fixity*.

Fixity can be intensified in particular by the aforementioned *conspiracy of silence*, the survivors' reaction to the societal (including health care and other professionals) indifference, avoidance, repression, and denial of the survivors' trauma experiences (see also Symonds 1980). Society's initial emotional outburst, yet its demand for rapid return to apparent normality, is an important example. This *conspiracy of silence* is detrimental to the survivors' familial and sociocultural (re)integration by intensifying their already profound sense of isolation and mistrust of society. It further impedes the possibility of their intrapsychic integration and healing, and makes the task of mourning their losses impossible. Fixity may increase vulnerability to further trauma. It also may render *chronic* the immediate reactions to trauma (e.g. acute stress disorder), and, in the extreme, become lifelong (Danieli 1997) *post-trauma/victimization adaptational styles* (Danieli 1985). This occurs when survival strategies generalize to a way of life and become an integral part of one's personality, repertoire of defense, or character armor.

Recognition of the possible long-term impact of trauma on one's personality and adaptation and the *intergenerational* transmission of victimization-related pathology still await explicit inclusion in future editions of the diagnostic nomenclature. Until they are included, the behavior of some survivors, and some children of survivors, may be misdiagnosed, its etiology misunderstood, and its treatment, at best, incomplete. This framework allows evaluation of each system's degree of rupture or resilience, and thus informs the choice and development of optimal multilevel intervention. Repairing the rupture and thereby freeing the flow rarely means, 'going back to normal'. Clinging to the possibility of 'returning to normal' may indicate denial of the survivors' experiences and thereby fixity.

Immediately after September 11, I suggested that, more than ever, issues related to the time dimension emerged as paramount (Danieli 2001). *First* was the imperative to resist the culturally prevalent (American) impulse to do something, to find a quick fix, to focus on outcome rather than process, to look all too swiftly for closure, and to flee 'back to normal'. *Second*, knowing that there will be long-term effects not only of the disaster itself but also of the immediate interventions, we must recognize the necessity for and importance of long-term commitment, and systematically examine every short-term decision from a long-term perspective. Since the urge to act and help others and oneself in the immediate aftermath is near universal, it should be harnessed and incorporated into long-term planning. I also noted the necessity of considering *at-risk times* (e.g. family holidays, anniversaries) as well as the *at-risk groups* (Danieli 2001).

Integration of the trauma must take place in *all* of life's relevant (ruptured) systems and cannot be accomplished by the individual alone. Systems can change and recover independently of other systems. Rupture repair may be needed in all systems of the survivor, in his or her community and nation, and in their place in the international community. To fulfill the reparative and preventive goals of trauma recovery, perspective and integration through awareness and containment must be established so that one's sense of continuity and belongingness is restored. To be healing and even self-actualizing, the integration of traumatic experiences must be examined from the perspective of the *totality* of the trauma survivors' and family and community members' lives.

I.2. WHAT VICTIMS TELL US ABOUT REPARATION

In order to understand more fully the experience of receiving reparation, compensation, and how it can be helpful to individuals and to their society, as well as to gain a long-term perspective, I interviewed victims/survivors of the Nazi Holocaust and then newer populations, such as Japanese Americans, Argentineans and Chileans, and professionals working with them, both in and outside their countries. Following a description of the process of claiming redress are some quotations of statements, discussions, and conclusions, from these interviews.

I.2.1. Claiming Redress

The process of applying for German '*Wiedergutmachung*'[2] [meaning literally 'to make something good again'] was experienced by survivors as yet an additional series of hardships. The Allied Powers after World War II issued laws restricted to restoring to the original owners property confiscated by the Nazis. The laws did not take into account personal damage to victims of Nazi persecution—those who had suffered in mind and body, or had been deprived unjustly of their freedom, or whose professional or economic prospects had been summarily cut short. Nor did these laws consider assistance to the widows and orphans of those who had died as a result of Hitler's policies. The Western Allies placed the responsibility for the reparation of such damages in the hands of the newly constituted German Federal States. Following a few stages, the Federal Republic of Germany enacted the 'Final Federal Compensation Law' on September 14, 1965. Thus, indemnification for persecution of persons was differentiated from restitution for lost property. The implementation of the compensation law was traumatic in itself.

Kestenberg (1980), a reparation lawyer, states:

> Even when most German officials showed concern and willingness to compensate Jews for the wrong done to them, their so-called 'Wiedergutmachung'... was only concerned with monetary matters. A moral 'Wiedergutmachung' was not planned and did not exist. No one bothered to restore the survivors' dignity. On the contrary, the procedures inherent in some of the paragraphs of the Restitution Laws, inflict indignities upon the claimants while at the same time German authorities are elevated to the status of superior beings who adjudge the claimants' veracity and honesty and classify them in accordance with the degree of their damage (2–3)... [Even if] the applicant had indeed been confined in a concentration camp... they behaved as if he were trying to extort money from the German government under false pretenses (4).
>
> The survivors had to prove that they had been damaged. Their attempts at self-cure were destroyed once they had to admit that their damage was permanent, sealed and signed by the authorities. To receive payments, often sorely needed, the applicants had to subject themselves to the most humiliating and degrading, seemingly very correct legal type of investigation (5).
>
> Bureaucratic deadlines are used for the unfair and prejudicial practice of rejecting claims... The German treasury enriches itself when a claimant dies before his case is concluded. At this time 50% of claims are denied, 25% are still pending and only 25% have been resolved in favor of the claimants. A case in the highest court alone takes eight years for determination, while many of the elderly claimants are not only humiliated, but suffer from lack of economic necessities and moneys for treatment of ailments which exacerbate in old age (9)... [T]he victimization of the once persecuted continues (12).[4]

Crucial to having a claim processed was undergoing a psychiatric examination. To be an examiner, the only requirement was that the psychiatrist be able to speak and write German, not Yiddish or Polish, which were the languages spoken by many survivors. The psychiatric examiner had to determine, and try to express in numbers, how much, or what fraction of the patient's emotional illness is, in his opinion, due to the persecution he suffered. The law required a minimum of 25 percent damage in order for the applicant to receive pension.

Examiners had intense emotional and moral reactions to this process. These reactions motivated much of their writings and were poignantly expressed in most of them (Danieli 1982). Eissler (1967) speculates that one major reason for the experts' (and the courts') 'open or concealed hostility against those who have had to bear great sufferings' has to do with the 'universal', archaic, pagan 'contempt that man still tends to feel for the [weak and] humiliated, for those who have had to submit to physical punishment, suffering, and torture' (1357). He concludes:

> The minimum one may demand, under such circumstances, is that the responsible authorities recognize those who cannot control this archaic feeling and exclude them from the position of experts in matters of compensation for suffering. When a physician refers to concentration camp experiences as 'disagreeable' he has given away his secret contempt.... He has thrown away the right to be called an 'expert'; if he continues to avail himself of that privilege, he must share the blame with those who continue to use his services (1358).

Krystal and Niederland (1968) add, 'Even the hearing of the tales of the concentration camp survivors is so disturbing and traumatic, so abusive to the examiner that some are compelled to avoid obtaining the details of the traumatization.[5] They then arrive at a meaninglessly brief summary of the experiences' (341). Hocking (1965) reports cases 'where patients have been told not to describe their experiences, only their symptoms' (481).

FT, a Czech Jew of Viennese origins and the sole survivor of a well-to-do family, whose total possessions in Prague were taken over by the Germans, and then by the Communists... left, via France to the United States... and began pursuing compensation in the 50s. He describes his ordeal as follows:

> The fact that I was three and a half years in concentration camps didn't count. At that time unless you were literally disabled—such as missing a hand—they recognized nothing. I always found it distasteful to spend days fighting a bureaucracy that tried to tell me that I am not entitled to that money, providing documents, writing letters, having to prove that I was indeed worthy of compensation. When I tried to get payment for some medical bills they wanted copies of the bills from 1946 to 1956. I had no way of finding them so they figured out an 'average' and offered me $200 if I waive claims against medical bills and I said that that is an insult and told them to keep the money and leave me alone. Fighting for these things absorbs so much emotional energy... It is bad enough that I have to live with memories, but to have to stir them up and to also face one's persecutors. I don't have to face Nazis any more, but I still have to deal with German bureaucracy. I got disgusted and wanted to quit.

But I knew that if I didn't claim it, the money will remain in Germany. They won't give more to someone else.

I.2.2. Restitution and Compensation

Of course everybody says that money is not enough. There is a disagreement whether we should take money or not. Some people do not need it at all financially yet insist on getting reparations; for others the check is practically necessary, especially the elderly. Compensation is a symbolic act because you can never be compensated. It is minor in amount but major in significance. Many people are desperate and need the support; they are living on a pension and US$200 a month is critical. For a family in Bhopal even US$15 a month may make a difference even though it is a pittance.

How does one compensate for three and a half years in concentration camps? For the loss of a child? It is impossible. How do you pay for a dead person? For a Korean woman sexually abused by the Japanese in World War II? It is not the money but what the money signifies—vindication. It signifies the governments' own admission of guilt, and an apology. The actual value, especially in cases of loss of life, is, of course, merely symbolic, and should be acknowledged as such.

The complexities here are illustrated by the Argentinian experience. On the one hand, the Madres de Plaza de Mayo organization officially refused economic reparations as the government's attempt to buy their silence and in the absence of social and historical recognition that their children had been political or social opponents and not criminals. On the other hand, the former political prisoners, especially if they had been in prison for a long time, consider economic compensation as their rightful reparation. Mostly young people, their imprisonment deprived them of finishing their studies, progressing in a job, or establishing their own home and families. In married cases, the long period in jail caused great economic difficulties to their families. Many of them feel that this is a partial moral recognition of the damage they had suffered and that, albeit in a small way, they can at least win something from the State. For people who are ambivalent, their ambivalence increases when compensation is experienced as an offence, yet is very necessary economically.

Most Japanese Americans felt finally vindicated after fifty years, having spent ten years fighting the system, not as a Japanese American issue, but as an American constitutional one. So many of our people could now talk about it and express deep-seated feelings for the first time in fifty years. That was the positive, therapeutic side. It was only a token compensation. Twenty thousand dollars would not cover what was lost: jobs, names, all properties, horrible living conditions, dignity or citizenship. It is not the money but what the money signifies. Psychologically it lifted a big burden off the Japanese Americans who always feel that the system could not trust us but viewed us as potential enemies, as second-class citizens. At least we now feel not accepted but vindicated for what happened fifty years ago. The apology was more important than the amount of money. After fifty years of maintaining that they were right, the government did acknowledge that they were constitutionally wrong (for intergenerational effects, see Nagata 1998).

The money *concretizes* for the victim the confirmation of responsibility, wrongfulness, he is not guilty, and somebody cares about it. It is at least a token. It does have a meaning. Just a letter of apology does not have the same meaning and even if it is a token it adds. In our system of justice, of government, when damage occurred money is paid. Should there be one payment? No. The monthly check in some ways weakens the trauma. When it becomes routine, it transforms into something permanent that somehow enables overcoming survivor guilt. The routine swallows the guilt.

Economic compensation given to torture victims should be very substantial. The torturers should compensate for their crime by having confiscated all of their property in order to pay back to those they have tortured. Whether members of governments, police officers, and doctors who have participated in torture—*all* property should be confiscated from them—this is the most important aspect of restitution—and used for compensation to the victim. Furthermore, there should be general awareness in the whole population about this aspect and the situation as such. It might be very effective preventively if this principle was generally known.

Before anything else the victim wants an acknowledgment of a debt that somehow, sometime a government writes laws and one of them is 'Mr._____deserves the praise of the country'. The first step of a government such as Argentina is 'the state of Argentina has woefully wronged those people who were persecuted by the military and we feel contrite and wish to apologize'. The full sense of it is that it *should* be a *law*, nothing else. And put it on the books. We have done wrong, we acknowledge it. It is *very* important. As a *political* matter I would absolutely have the books open ... open the files and let the facts speak for themselves.

Let us find a way and make a general statement. Clearly victims of governmental wrong should be compensated and this is the way we should go about it. As we had established norms of international minimal behaviors, crimes against humanity, we need parallel legislation for compensation for the victims. Legal procedures against the victimizers and financial arrangements compensating the victims are necessary steps in the aftermath of man-made calamities. However, they are not sufficient steps for societies to recover. In societies which moved out of totalitarian regimes, into quasi-democratic ones (Argentina, Chile, Eastern Europe), victims and victimizers of the former regime go on living in the same society. As they do not have any social and psychological mechanisms to repair these past relations, these may just penetrate deeper inside, and thereby be transmitted to the next generations. Therefore, along legal and financial steps, in each of these countries, a sociopsychological institute should be established to work on the after-effects of the traumata with both children of victims and victimizers. The end result of this process should be to try to bring them together, to think about the overall social responsibility: What can they do together so that detrimental tensions will not burst out again and again within those societies? Because of the long-term and/or intergenerational transmission of victimization there should be no statute of limitation. If the victim, for moral reasons, refuses the meaning of the reparation payment, the money should, nonetheless, not remain in the hands of the perpetrators or the silently acquiescing proceeding socio/political system, but it or its equivalent sum should be put in a special long-term fund whose purpose should be future-oriented, both in terms of education, prevention, and later care as provisions for the future—for themselves and/or their offspring's care, if needed and necessary.

I.2.3. Commemoration and Education

The need for commemoration is for the victims and for society. Rituals are very important; there is no organized society, religion, or culture that does not have rituals of memory. Commemorations can fill the vacuum with creative responses and may help heal the rupture not only internally but also the rupture the victimization created between the survivors and their society.

It is a shared context, shared mourning, shared memory. The memory is preserved; the nation has transformed it into part of its consciousness. The nation shares the horrible pain. What may be an obligatory one-day-a-year ritual to others the victims experience as a gesture of support, of sharing the pain. They are not lonely in their pain.

There should be general awareness on a high level, with information and education about the situation, how it arose, and its consequences widely circulated. There should be statues of heroes or martyrs, paintings. Streets should be named after them, as could be rooms in colleges and museums. There should be memorial services, scholarship funds, concerts and theatre performances, and educational books.

Commemoration should be done with great dignity, and with a feeling that while it honors those who suffered, those who have died, it is also done for preventive purposes, in the spirit of the knowledge that compensation for loss of lives, health, hopes can never be fulfilled. Yet maintain the commitment to NEVER AGAIN! and the possibility for intergenerational dialog, which may include dialogs between children of survivors and of perpetrators.

In Elie Wiesel's words (1985), 'they have no cemetery; we are their cemetery'. Building monuments serves some important functions in the reestablishment of a sense of continuity for the survivors, and for the world. Much of the chronic grief, the holding on to the guilt, shame, and pain of the past have to do with these internally carried graveyards. Survivors fear that successful mourning may lead to letting go, thereby to forgetting the dead and committing them to oblivion. The attempt to make these graveyards external creates the need for building monuments so that the survivors might have a place to go to remember and mourn in a somewhat traditional way. Visiting Yad Vashem seems to provide such an opportunity for some survivors.

Building monuments also has the significant functions of commemoration, documentation, and education—an extension of bearing witness—and of leaving a legacy so that the victims, the survivors, and the Holocaust will not be forgotten. The latter are comforting to some of the essential components of the aging survivor's preoccupation: 'Who cares if I live?' 'Who loves me?' 'Who will remember me?' 'Will the memory of my people and of the Holocaust perish?' and, 'Did/Will the world learn anything from it?'

I.2.4. Goals and Recommendations

In the following I summarize what victims/survivors themselves believe are the necessary components for healing in the wake of massive trauma. As stated above, these components emerged from interviews with survivors of the Nazi Holocaust, Japanese and Armenian Americans, victims from Argentina and Chile, and professionals working with them, both in- and outside their countries. Presented as goals and recommendations, they are organized from the (1) individual, (2) societal, (3) national, and (4) international perspectives:

1. Reestablishment of the victims' equality of value, power, esteem (dignity), the basis of reparation in the society or nation. This is accomplished by (*a*) compensation both real and symbolic, (*b*) restitution, (*c*) rehabilitation, and (*d*) commemoration.
2. Relieving the victim's stigmatization and separation from society. This is accomplished by (*a*) commemoration, (*b*) memorials to heroism, (*c*) empowerment, and (*d*) education.
3. Repairing the nations' ability to provide and maintain equal value under law and the provisions of justice. This is accomplished by

(*a*) prosecution, (*b*) apology, (*c*) securing public records, (*d*) education, and (*e*) creating national mechanisms for monitoring, conflict resolution and preventive interventions.

4. Asserting the commitment of the international community to combat impunity and provide and maintain equal value under law and the provisions of justice and redress. This is accomplished by (*a*) creating ad hoc and permanent mechanisms for prosecution (e.g. ad hoc Tribunals and ultimately an International Criminal Court), (*b*) securing public records, (*c*) education, and (*d*) creating international mechanisms for monitoring, conflict resolution, and preventive interventions.

It is important to emphasize that this comprehensive framework, rather than presenting *alternative* means of reparation, sets out necessary *complementary* elements to be applied in different degrees, in different situations and cultures, and at different points in time. It is also crucial that victims/survivors participate in the choice of the reparation measures adopted for them.[6]

I.3. INTERNATIONAL DEVELOPMENTS ON BEHALF OF VICTIMS

Some of these elements have already been recognized among the measures recommended in the United Nations Declaration of Basic Principles of Justice for Victims of Crime and Abuse of Power,[7] the *Magna Carta* for victims. These elements include improving access to justice and fair treatment, restitution, compensation and necessary material, medical, psychological, and social assistance and support for such victims. Adopted in 1985 by the UN General Assembly, although it was conceived and drafted in what was then the UN Crime Branch, the Declaration was listed as well by the UN Commission on Human Rights as a human rights instrument—one of very few such documents.

The above framework partly informed the Basic Principles and Guidelines on the Right to a Remedy and Reparation for Victims of Gross Violations of International Human Rights Law and Serious Violations of International Humanitarian Law[8] which were adopted on April 13, 2005. During this same session, in April 2005, the United Nations Human Rights Commission also took note, with appreciation, of the recently revised Set of Principles for the Protection and Promotion of Human Rights Through Action to Combat Impunity, updated by Diane Orentlicher.[9] This set of principles includes the right to know, the right to justice, and the right to reparation/guarantees of nonrecurrence.[10]

The United Nations General Assembly first recognized the need for a permanent mechanism to prosecute mass murderers and war criminals in 1948, following the Nuremberg and Tokyo trials after World War II. Headquartered at The Hague, the ICC is a permanent institution not constrained by the time and place limitations of the two ad hoc Tribunals for the Former Yugoslavia and Rwanda. It is able to act more quickly and, as a permanent entity, its very existence will be a deterrent, sending a strong warning message to would-be perpetrators. It will also encourage States to investigate and prosecute egregious crimes committed in their territories or by their nationals, for if they do not, the ICC will be there to exercise its jurisdiction.

Calling for justice for victims as well as for society, the tone for the ICC's operation is set in the preamble to the Statute that notes that 'during this century millions of children, women and men have been *victims* of unimaginable atrocities that deeply shock the conscience of humanity'. It calls for an end to the impunity of perpetrators of crimes of concern to the international community.

Based theoretically on the above Declaration and Basic Principles, and practically on both the positive as well as negative practical/operational experiences of the ad hoc Tribunals for the former Yugoslavia and Rwanda, the sections relevant to victims in the Statute and Rules of Procedure and Evidence of the ICC make for the most progressive provisions for victims in any international court, in fact, in international law. Moreover, it is the provisions for the role of victims in the ICC that makes it unique.

Most of the victims' issues and much of the material on victims in the Draft Statute going into Rome, and in instruments that were drafted later, appeared to be controversial. But an ongoing process has continued in which governments and NGOs have been intimately involved in developing further positions relating to victims.

Victims have been the silent partners in the legal process, with little role other than as witnesses, and at the mercy of litigants. The Victims Declaration and the van Boven/Bassiouni principles attempt to remedy this anomaly, and the two ad hoc Tribunals have taken steps to address most of the protection and assistance issues faced by victims as witnesses. In many respects the fact that there remains little disagreement on these particular issues demonstrates how far the debate has moved on. Thus, it is now generally accepted that victims as witnesses are entitled to protection, sometimes even if this means that their identity is withheld from the accused until shortly before the trial, and may be permanently withheld from the public. The ICC has a sound theoretical basis, as well as a reservoir of practical experience, on which to build appropriate mechanisms for the protection of victims/witnesses and to provide assistance to them during the sometimes difficult appearances they will make before the ICC and their aftermath.[11]

To help victims and witnesses face the judicial process—without being (re)traumatized by it—the ICC has a Victims and Witnesses Unit to provide protective measures and security arrangements, counselling, and other assistance for witnesses and victims, while fully respecting the rights of the accused. The Court must take appropriate measures to protect the privacy, the dignity, the physical and psychological well-being and the security of victims and witnesses, especially when the crimes involve sexual or gender violence.

Article 75 of the Rome Statute of the ICC provides that '[t]he Court shall establish principles relating to, or in respect of, victims, including restitution, compensation and rehabilitation'. The Assembly of States Parties of the Court has begun the process of dealing with these issues.[12] The Court is empowered to determine the scope and extent of any damage, loss, and injury to victims, and to order a convicted person to make specific reparation. A Trust Fund was established for the benefit of victims and their families, the sources of which will include money and other property collected through fines and forfeiture imposed by the Court. The Member States of the ICC demonstrated the importance with which they consider the Trust Fund by electing the following prestigious individuals, representing their respective regions, for its board: HM Queen Rania al-Abdullah of Jordan, HE Mr. Tadeusz Mazowiecki from Poland, HE Mr. Oscar Arias from Costa Rica, Madam Minister Simone Veil from France (Chair), and HE Archbishop Emeritus Desmond Tutu from South Africa.

It is clear that, as a result of the Victims Declaration, the van Boven/Bassiouni principles, and the energetic work of NGOs, the terms of the debate have been changed and the position of victims has moved from the margins to being a central part of any discussion or practice of justice.[13] An essential advancement for victims' rights in the Rome Statute of the ICC is the historic recognition that victims have the right to participate in the ICC proceedings to express their views and concerns at stages and according to methods to be decided by the Judges. As appropriate, victims or groups of victims will be represented by a legal representative. In this respect, it is important to stress the significance of the January 17, 2006 decision of the pretrial Chamber of the ICC dealing with the Democratic Republic of the Congo. The Chamber admitted six survivors of atrocities committed in various regions of the Congo to participate in the ICC proceedings through a common legal representative.[14]

While the ICC's commitment to realizing victims' rights and meeting their needs and concerns is undeniable, there remain serious uncertainties regarding full victim protection (including its psychosocial aspects), and serious questions regarding the temptation to bureaucratize the process of relating to victims in general and their participation in court proceedings in particular. Two more grave challenges confronting the Court are realizing its reparative mandate when the number of victims and the nature of the suffering are so overwhelming, and balancing the victims' right to justice with society's need for peace. Much has been achieved in principle, but much more needs to be learned and put into practice, both in the ICC's work and in implementing its principles and practices in nations around the world.

Thus, the Statute of the Court represents a strong merger of the lessons of Nuremberg, of the Universal Declaration of Human Rights, and of the ad hoc tribunals. The rights of victims find their expression in the context of individual criminal responsibility.[15]

NOTES

1. See Bergman and Jucovy (1982), Danieli (1985, 1992, 1998), Dasberg (1987), Sigal and Weinfeld (1989), and Rubenstein, Cutter and Templer (1990).
2. Becker et al. (1990: 147–8). For related programs, see Kordon et al. (1988) and Genefke (1992).
3. More recently, Stover and Weinstein (2004) also utilize an ecological model of social reconstruction.
4. Elsewhere, Kestenberg (1985) elaborated on the difficulties particular to child survivors, a population whose special needs deserve special attention.
5. See the section 'In search for justice' in Danieli (2002) describing the toll paid by human rights and justice defenders in their work, particularly with victims.
6. 'A constant under all these approaches is the need to involve the victims and their organizations in discussions about what reparations, like other post-conflict strategies, should look like' (Roht-Arriaza 2004*b*: 121, 136).
7. G. A. res. 40/34, U.N. GAOR, 40th Sess., Supp. No. 53, at 213, U.N. Doc. A/40/53 (1986).
8. Commission on Human Rights Res. E/CN.4/2005/L.48 (2005).
9. U.N. Doc. E/CN.4/2005/102/Add.1 (2005).
10. See *The Administration of Justice and The Human Rights of Detainees, Revised Final Report*, prepared by Mr Joinet pursuant to Sub-Commission decision 1996/119, U.N. Doc. E/CN.4/Sub.2/1997/20/Rev.1 (1997).
11. Isabelle Wesselingh, 'Trauma and isolation await many witnesses of UN court at home,' Agence France-Presse, Jan. 16, 2004.
12. Rules of Procedure and Evidence, Rules 94–8, Doc. ICC-ASP/1/3 (2002); Regulations of the Trust Fund for Victims, paragraphs 69–75, ASP Res. ICC-ASP/4/Res.3, ICC-ASP/4/32 (2005).
13. Yael Danieli, *Sectoral Caucus Report: Victims Rights Working Group*, in Coalition for the International Criminal Court, Report on the Rome Statute of the International Criminal Court: The Role of Nongovernmental Organizations in the

Making of the International Criminal Court Treaty (2006). It is hoped that the Trust Fund will benefit from the vast experience of the major Jewish organizations, starting in 1948, to obtain restitution, compensation and rehabilitation from the West German government for the victims of Nazi persecution. See generally Ferencz (1979).

14. Pre-Trial Chamber I, Situation in the Democratic Republic of the Congo, Decision on the Applications for Participation in the Proceedings of VPRS 1, VPRS 2, VPRS 3, VPRS 4, VPRS 5 and VPRS 6, No. ICC-01/04 (2006). The victims were mobilized by the NGO, Federation Internationale des Droits de l'Homme (FIDH).
15. See generally R. S. Clark & D. Tolbert, *Toward an International Criminal Court*, in The Universal Declaration of Human Rights: Fifty Years and Beyond (Yael Danieli et al. eds., 1998). On victims' participation, see D. Donat Cattin, *Article 68*, in Commentary on the Rome Statute of the ICC (Otto Triffterer ed., 1999).

Bibliography

ACHEBE, C. (1975). *Morning Yet on Creation Day*. New York: Doubleday.

ALLEN, J., ALS, H., LEWIS, J., and LITWACK, L. F. (2000). *Without Sanctuary: Lynching Photography in America*. Santa Fe, NM: Twin Palms.

ANAYA, J. (2004). *Indigenous Peoples in International Law*. Oxford: Oxford University Press.

ANDERSON, M. L., and COLLINS, P. H. (eds.) (1995). *Race, Class, and Gender: An Anthology*, 2nd edn. Belmot, CA: Wadsworth.

ARISTOTLE (1955). *The Ethics*, trans. J. A. K. Thomson. Harmondsworth: Penguin.

ARROW, K. J. (1963). *Social Choice and Individual Values*. New Haven, CT: Yale University Press.

ASPEN INSTITUTE REPORT (1989). *State Crimes: Punishment or Pardon*. Queenstown, MD: Justice and Society Program of the Aspen Institute.

BAIER, A. (1994). *Moral Prejudices*. Cambridge: Harvard University Press.

BALFOUR, L. (2003). 'Unreconstructed Democracy: W. E. B. Du Bois and the Case for Reparations', *American Political Science Review*, 97.

BARKAN, E. (2000). *The Guilt of Nations*. New York: Norton.

____ and KARN, A. (eds.) (2006). *Taking Wrongs Seriously: Apologies and Reconciliation*. Palo Alto, CA: Stanford University Press.

BARNETT, R. (1977). 'Restitution: A New Paradigm of Criminal Justice', *Ethics*, 87.

BASS, G. (2004). 'Jus Post Bellum', *Philosophy and Public Affairs*, 32.

BASS, G. J. (2002). *Stay the Hand of Vengeance: The Politics of War Crimes Tribunals*. Princeton, NJ: Princeton University Press.

BEAUVOIR, SIMONE DE (1953). *The Second Sex*, trans. and ed. H. M. Parshley. New York: Knopf.

BECKER, D. (2001). 'Dealing with the Consequences of Organized Violence', in BERGHOF RESEARCH CENTER (2001).

____ LIRA, E., CASTILLO, M. I., GOMEZ, E., and KOVALSKYS, J. (1997). 'Therapy with Victims of Political Repressions in Chile: The Challenge of Social Reparations', *Journal of Social Issues*, 40. Reprinted in KRITZ (1997).

BEITZ, C. (1979). *Political Theory and International Relations*. Princeton, NJ: Princeton University Press.

BELLUCK, P. (2004). 'Brown U. to Examine Debt to Slave Trade', *New York Times*, March 13.

BERGHOF RESEARCH CENTER (2001). *Berghof Handbook for Conflict Transformation*. Berlin: Berghof Research Center for Constructive Conflict Management.

BERGMAN, M. S., and JUCOVY, M. E. (eds.) (1982). *Generations of the Holocaust*. New York: Basic Books.

BETTLEHEIM, B. (1984). 'Afterword' to VEGH (1984).

Bhargava, R. (2000). 'Restoring Decency to Barbaric Societies', in Rothberg and Thompson (2000).

—— (2001). 'Are there Alternative Modernities?', in Vohra (2001).

—— (2002). 'Ordinary Feelings, Extraordinary Events: Moral Complexity in 9/11', in Calhoun et al. (2002).

Biggar, N. (ed.) (2001). *Burying the Past: Making Peace and Doing Justice after Civil Conflict.* Washington, DC: George Town University Press.

Biondi, M. (2003). 'The Rise of the Reparations Movement', *Radical History Review*, 87.

Bittker, B. ([1973] 2003). *The Case for Black Reparations.* Boston, MA: Beacon Press.

Blackstone, W. (2001). *Blackstone's Commentaries on the Laws of England*, ed. Wayne Morrison. London: Cavendish.

Blaut, J. M. (1993). *The Colonizer's Model of the World.* New York: The Guilford Press.

Borrows, J. (2002). *Recovering Canada: The Resurgence of Indigenous Law.* Toronto: University of Toronto Press.

Boven, Theo van. (1983). 'Study Concerning the Right to Restitution, Compensation and Rehabilitation for Victims of Gross Violations of Human Rights and Fundamental Freedoms', UN Commission on Human Rights, Sub-Commission on Prevention of Discrimination and Protection of Minorities (UN document E/CN.4.Sub.2/1983/8).

Boxill, B. (1972). 'The Morality of Reparation', *Social Theory and Practice*, 2.

—— (2003). 'A Lockean Argument for Black Reparations', *Journal of Ethics*, 7.

Brookfield, F. M. (1999). *Waitangi and Indigenous Rights: Revolution, Law and Legitimation.* Auckland, New Zealand: Auckland University Press.

—— (2002). 'Moriori, Maori and the Crown: Reflections on the Waitangi Tribunal's Chathams (Rekohu) Report', *New Zealand Law Review*, 128–9.

Brooks, R. (1999). *When Sorry Isn't Enough.* New York: NYU Press.

—— (2004). *Atonement and Forgiveness: A New Model for Black Reparations.* Berkeley, CA: University of California Press.

Brophy, A. L. (2004). 'Reparations Talk: Reparations for Slavery and the Tort Law Analogy', *Boston College Third World Law Journal*, 24.

Cairns, A. (2003). 'Coming to Terms with the Past', in Torpey (2003).

Calhoun, C., Price, P., and Timmer, A. (eds.) (2002). *Understanding September 11.* New York: The New Press.

Card, C. (ed.) (1999). *On Feminist Ethics and Politics.* Lawrence, KS: University Press of Kansas.

Carr, E. H. (1965). *International Relations between the Two World Wars (1919–1939).* London: Macmillan.

Cassidy, J. (1998). 'Sovereignty of Aboriginal Peoples', *Indiana International and Comparative Law Review*, 9.

Chakrabarty, D. (2000). *Provincializing Europe: Postcolonial Thought and Historical Difference.* Delhi: Oxford University Press.

Chang, I. (1997). *The Rape of Nanking: The Forgotten Holocaust of World War II.* New York: Penguin.

CHATTERJEE, P. (1998). *Nation and Its Fragments*. Delhi: Oxford University Press.

CHOCK, J. (1995). 'One Hundred Years of Illegitimacy: International Legal Analysis of the Illegal Overthrow of the Hawaiian Monarchy, Hawaii's Annexation, and Possible Reparations', *University of Hawaii Law Review*, 7.

CHODOROW, N. (1978). *The Reproduction of Mothering: Psychoanalysis and the Sociology of Gender*. Berkeley, CA: University of California Press.

CLIFFORD, J. (1988). *The Predicament of Culture: Twentieth-Century Ethnography, Literature, and Art*. Cambridge, MA: Harvard University Press.

COATES, K. (1998). 'International Perspectives on Relations with Indigenous Peoples', in COATES AND MCHUGH(1998).

____ and MCHUGH, P. G. (eds.) (1998). *Living Relationships: The Treaty of Waitangi in the New Millennium*. Victoria: Victoria University Press.

CODE, L. (1995). *Rhetorical Spaces: Essays on Gendered Locations*. London: Routledge.

COHEN, M., NAGEL, T., and SCANLON, T. (eds.) (1977). *Equality and Preferential Treatment*. Princeton, NJ: Princeton University Press.

COLLINS, P. H. (1998). *Fighting Words: Black Women and the Search for Justice*. Minneapolis, MN: University of Minnesota Press.

COWAN, T. (1997). 'Discounting and Restitution', *Philosophy and Public Affairs*, 26.

CRAWFORD-PINNERUP, A. (2000). 'An Assessment of the Impact of Urgent Interim Reparations', in HAMBER and MOFOKENG (2000).

CRENSHAW, K., GOTANDA, N., PELLER, G., and THOMAS, K. (eds.) (1995). *Critical Race Theory: The Key Writings that Formed the Movement*. New York: New Press.

CUNNEEN, C., and LIBESMAN, T. (1995). *Indigenous People and the Law in Australia*. Butterworths, Australia: North Ryde.

DANIELI, Y. (1981). 'On the Achievement of Integration in Aging Survivors of the Nazi Holocaust', *Journal of Geriatric Psychiatry*, 14.

____ (1982). *Therapists' Difficulties in Treating Survivors of the Nazi Holocaust and their Children*, Ph.D. dissertation, New York University. *University Microfilms International* #949-904.

____ (1985). 'The Treatment and Prevention of Long-term Effects and Intergenerational Transmission of Victimization: A Lesson from Holocaust Survivors and their Children', FIGLEY (1985).

____ (1988*a*). 'Confronting the Unimaginable: Psychotherapists' Reactions to Victims of the Nazi Holocaust', in WILSON ET AL. (1988).

____ (1988*b*). 'Treating Survivors and Children of Survivors of the Nazi Holocaust', in OCHBERG (1988).

____ (1989). 'Mourning in Survivors and Children of Survivors of the Nazi Holocaust: The Role of Group and Community Modalities', in DIETRICH and SHABAD (1989).

____ (1992). 'The Diagnostic and Therapeutic use of the Multi-generational Family Tree in Working with Survivors and Children of Survivors of the Nazi Holocaust', in WILSON ET AL. (1993).

____ (1997). 'As Survivors Age: An Overview', *Journal of Geriatric Psychiatry*, 30.

____ (1998) (ed.) *International Handbook of Multigenerational Legacies of Trauma*. New York: Kluwer Academic/Plenum Publishing.

DANIELI, Y. (2001). 'ISTSS Members Participate in Recovery Efforts in New York and Washington, D.C.', *Traumatic Stress Points*, 15.

——(2002) (ed.). *Sharing the Front Line and the Back Hills: International Protectors and Providers, Peacekeepers, Humanitarian Aid Workers and the Media in the Midst of Crisis*. Amityville, NY: Baywood Publishing.

DASBERG, H. (1987). 'Psychological Distress of Holocaust Survivors and Offspring in Israel, Forty Years Later: A Review', *Israel Journal of Psychiatry and Related Sciences*, 23.

DAVIS, A. Y. (1983). *Women, Race and Class*. New York: Vintage.

——(1998). *The Angela Y. Davis Reader*, ed. Joy James. Malden, MA: Blackwell.

DE GREIFF, P. (ed.) (2006*a*). *International Centre For Transitional Justice Study on Reparations*. Oxford: Oxford University Press.

——(2006*b*). 'Justice and Reparations', in P. DE GRIEFF (ed.), *The Handbook of Reparations*. Oxford: Oxford University Press, 451–77.

——(forthcoming). 'Reparations Efforts in International Perspective: What Compensation Contributes to the Achievement of Imperfect Justice', in VILLA-VICENCIO AND DOXTADER (forthcoming).

DE SOUZA, P. (2000). *Contemporary India: Transitions*. New Delhi: Sage.

DIETRICH, D. R., and SHABAD, P. C. (eds.) (1989). *The Problem of Loss and Mourning: Psychoanalytic Perspectives*. Madison, CT: International Universities Press.

DIMSDALE, J. E. (ed.) (1980). *Survivors, Victims, and Perpetrators: Essays on the Nazi Holocaust*. New York: Hemisphere.

DIRKS, N. B. (2002). *Castes of Mind: Colonialism and the Making of Modern India*. Delhi: Permanent Black.

DU TOIT, A. (2001). 'The Moral Foundation of the South African TRC', in ROTHBERG AND THOMPSON (2001).

DWORKIN, R. (1986). *Law's Empire* (Cambridge, MA: Harvard University Press).

DYSON, M. (1995). 'The Plight of Black Men', in ANDERSON ET AL. (1995).

DYZENHAUS, D., and MORAN, M. (eds.) (2005). *Calling Power to Account: Reparations, the Law, and the Chinese Canadian Head Tax Case*. Toronto: University of Toronto Press.

EDELMAN, L., KORDON, D., and LAGOS, D. (1992). 'Argentina: Physical Disease and Bereavement in a Social Context of Human Rights Violations and Impunity', in L. H. M. van Willigen (Chair), *The Limitations of Current Concepts of Post Traumatic Stress Disorders Regarding the Consequences of Organized Violence*, session presented at the World conference of the International Society for Traumatic Stress Studies, Amsterdam, The Netherlands.

EISSLER, K. R. (1967). 'Perverted Psychiatry?', *American Journal of Psychiatry*, 123.

EITINGER, L. (1980). 'The Concentration Camp Syndrome and its Late Sequelae', in DIMSDALE (1980).

——and KRELL, R. (eds.) (1985). *The Psychological and Medical Effects of Concentration Camps and Related Persecutions on Survivors of the Holocaust: A Research Bibliography*. Vancouver, WA: University of British Columbia Press.

ELSTER, J. (2004). *Closing the Books*. Cambridge: Cambridge University Press.
____ and HYLLAND, A. (1986). *Foundations of Social Choice Theory*. Cambridge: Cambridge University Press.
EPSTEIN, R. (1985). *Takings: Private Property and the Power of Eminent Domain*. Cambridge, MA: Harvard University Press.
FANON, F. (1967*a*). *The Wretched of the Earth*. New York: Penguin.
____ (1967*b*). *Black Skin, White Masks*. New York: Grove Press.
____ (1970). *A Dying Colonialism*. England: Penguin Books.
FARLEY, R. (1996). *The New American Reality: Who We Are, How We Got Here, Where We Are Going*. New York: Russell Sage Foundation.
FEAGIAN, J. R. (2000). *Racist America: Roots, Current Realities, and Future Reparations*. New York: Routledge.
FEINBERG, J. (1968). 'Collective Responsibility', *Journal of Philosophy*, 65.
FELCH, J., and FRAMMOLINO, R. (2005). 'Getty Had Signs It Was Acquiring Possibly Looted Art', *Los Angeles Times*, September 25.
FEYTER, KOEN DE, PARMENTIER, S., BOSSUYT, M., and LEMMENS, P. (eds.) (2005). *Reparation for Victims of Gross and Systematic Human Rights Violations*. Antwerp, Belgium: Intersentia.
FIGLEY, C. R. (ed.) (1985). *Trauma and its Wake*. New York: Brunner/Mazel.
FINCH, G. A. (1919). 'The Peace Negotiations with Germany', *American Journal of International Law*, 13.
FIRESTONE, S. (1970). *The Dialectic of Sex*. New York: Bantam.
FRENCH, P. (2003). 'You Must Remember This/We'll Always Have Paris'. Unpublished manuscript.
FREY, R. G., and MORRIS, C. W. (eds.) (1991). *Liability and Responsibility*. Cambridge: Cambridge University Press.
FRYE, M. (1983). *The Politics of Reality: Essays in Feminist Theory*. Freedom, CA: Crossing Press.
FULLINWIDER, R. K. (2000). 'The Case for Reparations', *Philosophy and Public Policy*, 20.
____ (2004). 'The Reparations Argument: A Reply [to Hughes (2004)]', *Journal of Social Philosophy*, 35.
GANDHI, L. (1998). *Post Colonial Theory: An Introduction*. Sydney: Allen and Unwin.
GANDHI, M. (1997). *Hind Swaraj and other Writings*, ed. by Anthony J. Parel. Cambridge: Cambridge University Press.
GATTINI, A. (2002). 'The UN Compensation Commission: Old Rules, New Procedures on War Reparations', *European Journal of International Law*, 13.
GAUTHIER, T. S. (2006). *Narrative Desire and Historical Reparations*. New York and London: Routledge.
GELLNER, E. (1994). *Encounters with Nationalism*. Oxford: Blackwell.
GENEFKE, I. (1992). 'The Most Effective Weapon against Democracy: Torture—It Concerns Us All', Testimony to the subcommittee on foreign operations, export financing and related expenses for the Rehabilitation Centre for Torture Victims, Copenhagen, Denmark, May 1, 1992.

GILLIGAN, C. (1993). *In a Different Voice: Psychological Theory and Women's Development*, 2nd edn. Cambridge, MA: Harvard University Press.

GIYOSE, M. P. (2003). 'Jubilee, Reparations and the Lawsuits against Economic and Financial Backers of Apartheid', presented at the Civil Society Conference on Reparations, Randburg, August 27, 2003.

GONZALEZ, M., and COOK-LYNN, E. (2001). 'The Politics of Hallowed Ground: Wounded Knee and the Struggle for Indian Sovereignty', *Annals of the Association of American Geographers*, 91.

GOVERNMENT and COMMUNICATION and INFORMATION SERVICES (2002). *South Africa Yearbook 2002/2003*. Yeoville, South Africa: STE.

GROTIUS, H. (1901). *The Rights of War and Peace*, trans. by A. M. Campbell. New York: Walter Dunne.

GUHA, R. (1998). *Dominance without Hegemony: History and Power in Colonial India*. Delhi: Oxford University Press.

HABERMAS, J. (1990), 'Justice and Solidarity', in WREN (1990).

HALL, D. (2004). 'The Spirit of Reparation', *Boston College Third World Law Journal*, 24.

HAMBER, B. (1998). 'The Burdens of Truth: An Evaluation of the Psychological Support Services and Initiatives undertaken by the South African Truth and Reconciliation Commission', *American Imago*, 55.

—— (2001). 'Does the Truth Heal: A Psychological Perspective on the Political Strategies for Dealing with the Legacy of Political Violence', in BIGGAR (2001).

—— (2002*a*). 'Ere Their Story Die: Truth, Justice and Reconciliation in South Africa', *Race and Class*, 44.

—— (2002*b*). 'Repairing the Irreparable: Dealing with the Double-binds of Making Reparations for Crimes of the Past', *Ethnicity and Health*, 5.

—— (2005). 'The Dilemmas of Reparations: In Search of a Process Driven Approach', in DE FEYTER ET AL. (2005).

—— (2006). 'Narrowing the Micro and Macro: A Psychological Perspective on Reparations in Societies in Transition', in DE GREIFF (2006*b*).

—— and MOFOKENG, T. (eds.) (2000). *From Rhetoric to Responsibility: Making Reparations to the Survivors of Past Political Violence in South Africa*. Johannesburg: Centre for the Study of Violence and Reconciliation.

HAMPTON, J. (1981). 'The Moral Education Theory of Punishment', *Philosophy and Public Affairs*, 13.

—— (1988). 'The Retributive Idea', in MURPHY and HAMPTON (1988).

—— (1991). 'A New Theory of Retribution', in FREY and MORRIS (1991).

HARRINGTON, J., MILDE, M., and VERNON, R. (eds.) (2005). *Bringing Power to Justice*. Montreal and Kingston: McGill-Queen's University Press.

HASAGER, U., and FRIEDMAN, J. (eds.) (1994). *Hawai'i: Return to Nationhood*. Copenhagen: International Working Group for Indigenous Affairs.

HAUNANI-KAY, T. (1994). 'Politics in the Pacific Islands: Imperialism and Native Self-Determination', in HASAGER and FRIEDMAN (1994).

HENRY, C. P. (2003). 'The Politics of Racial Reparations', *Journal of Black Studies*, 34.

HERMAN, J. L. (1992). *Trauma and Recovery: From Domestic Abuse to Political Terror*. London: Pandora.
HERRNSTEIN, R., and MURRAY, C. (1994). *The Bell Curve*. New York: Free Press.
HESS, C., and POST, R. (eds.) (1998). *Human Rights and Political Transitions*. New York: Zone Books.
HEYES, C. (2000). *Line Drawings: Defining Women through Feminist Practice*. Ithaca, NY: Cornell University Press.
HILL, JR, T. E. (1991*a*). *Autonomy and Self-respect*. Cambridge: Cambridge University Press.
____ (1991*b*). 'The Message of Affirmative Action', *Social Philosophy and Policy*, 8.
HOCKING, F. (1965) 'Human Reactions to Extreme Environmental Stress', *Medical Journal of Australia*, 2.
HONNETH, A. (1996). *The Struggle for Recognition: The Moral Grammar of Social Conflicts*. Cambridge, MA: MIT Press.
HOOKS, B. (2000). *Feminist Theory: From Margin to Centre*, 2nd edn. Cambridge, MA: South End Press.
HOROWITZ, D. (2002). *Uncivil Wars: The Controversy over Reparations for Slavery*. San Francisco, CA: Encounter Books.
HOWARD, M. (1962). *The Franco-Prussian War: The German Invasion of France, 1870–1871*. New York: Macmillan.
HUGHES, P. M. (2004). 'Rectification and Reparation: What Does Citizen Responsibility Require?', *Journal of Social Philosophy*, 35.
HULME, P. (1993). 'The Profit of Language: George Lamming and the Postcolonial Novel', in WHITE (1993).
HUMAN RIGHTS and EQUAL OPPORTUNITIES COMMISSION (1997). *Bringing Them Home: Report of the National Inquiry into the Separation of Aboriginal and Torres Strait Islander Children from Their Families*. Sydney: Human Rights and Equal Opportunities Commission.
HYLTON, K. (2004). 'A Framework for Reparations Claims', *Boston College Third World Law Journal*, 24.
IVISON, D., PATTON, P., and SANDERS, W. (eds.) (2000). *Political Theory and the Rights of Indigenous Peoples*. Cambridge: Cambridge University Press.
JACOBSON, J. (1983). 'Is There a New International History of the 1920s?', *The American Historical Review*, 88.
JANOFSKY, M. (2005). 'A New Hope for Dreams Suspended by Segregation', *New York Times*, July 31.
KENNAN, G. F. (1996). *At a Century's Ending: Reflections 1982–1995*. New York: W.W. Norton.
KESTENBERG, M. (1980) 'Discriminatory Aspects of the German Restitution Law and Practice', in Yael Danieli (Chair), *Nazi Holocaust Effects*, session presented at the meeting of the First World Congress of Victimology, Washington, DC, August, 1980.
____ (1985). 'Legal Aspects of Child Persecution during the Holocaust', *Journal of the American Academy of Child Psychiatry*, 24.

KEYNES, J. M. (1963). 'Proposals for the Reconstruction of Europe (1919)' in his *Essays in Persuasion*. New York: W.W. Norton.

KINGSBURY, B. (1998). '"Indigenous Peoples" in International Law: A Constructivist Approach to the Asian Controversy', *American Journal of International Law*, 92.

—— (2002). 'Competing Conceptual Approaches to Indigenous Group Issues in New Zealand Law', *University of Toronto Law Journal*, 52.

KLEIN, M., and RIVIERE, J. (1964). *Love, Hate and Reparation*. New York: W.W. Norton.

KORDON, D. R., EDELMAN, L. I., and LAGOS, D. M., ET AL. (1988). *Psychological Effects of Political Repression*. Buenos Aires: Sudamericana/Planeta.

KORSGAARD, C. M. (1996). *Creating the Kingdom of Ends*. Cambridge and New York: Cambridge University Press.

KRITZ, N. J. (ed.) (1997). *Transitional Justice: How Emerging Democracies Reckon with Former Regimes*. Washington, DC: United States Institute of Peace Press.

KRYSTAL, H. (ed.) (1968). *Massive Psychic Trauma*. New York: International Universities Press.

—— and NIEDERLAND, W. G. (1968). 'Clinical Observations on the Survivor Syndrome', in KRYSTAL (1968).

KUKATHAS, C. (2003). 'Responsibility for Past Injustice: How to Shift the Burden', *Politics, Philosophy, and Economics*, 2.

KUMAR, R., and SILVER, D. (2004). 'The Legacy of Injustice', in MEYER (2004).

KUTZ, C. (2000). *Complicity*. Cambridge: Cambridge University Press.

KYMLICKA, W. (1989). *Liberalism, Community, and Culture*. Oxford: Clarendon Press.

—— (1995). *Multicultural Citizenship*. Oxford: Clarendon Press.

LERNER, G. (ed.) (1973). *Black Women in White America*. New York: Vintage.

LOCKE, J. (1978). *Two Treatises of Government*. London: Dent & Sons.

—— (1988). *Two Treatises of Government* [1689], ed. Peter Laslett. Cambridge: Cambridge University Press.

LOOMBA, A. (1998). *Colonialism/Postcolonialism*. London: Routledge.

LOURY, G. C. (1977). 'A Dynamic Theory of Racial Income Differences', in WALLACE and LAMOND (1977).

—— (1995). *One by One from the Inside Out: Essays and Reviews on Race and Responsibility in America*. New York: Free Press.

—— (2000). 'Twenty-Five Years of Black America: Two Steps Forward and One Step Back', *Journal of Sociology and Social Welfare*, XXVII.

—— (2002). *The Anatomy of Racial Inequality*. Cambridge, MA: Harvard University Press.

LU, C. (2002). 'Justice and Moral Regeneration: Lessons from the Treaty of Versailles', *International Studies Review*, 4: 3.

—— (2005). 'Delivering the Goods and the Good: Repairing Moral Wrongs', in DYZENHAUS AND MORAN (2005).

—— (2006). 'The International Criminal Court as an Institution of Moral Regeneration: Problems and Prospects', in HARRINGTON ET AL. (2005).

LYONS, D. (1977). 'The New Indian Land Claims and the Original Right to land', *Social Theory and Practice*, 4.

MAAKA, R., and FLERAS, A. (2000). 'Engaging with Indigeneity: Tino Rangatiratanga in Aotearoa', in IVISON ET AL. (2000).

MCCARTHY, T. (2004). 'Coming to Terms with Our Past, Part II: On the Morality and Politics of Reparations for Slavery', *Political Theory*, 32.

MCGARY, H. (2002). 'Achieving Democratic Equality: Forgiveness, Reconciliation, and Reparations', *The Journal of Ethics*, 7.

MACINTYRE, A. (1981). *After Virtue: A Study in Moral Theory*, 2nd edn. London: Duckworth.

MACINTYRE, S., and CLARK, A. (2003). *The History Wars*. Melbourne: Melbourne University Press.

MACKENZIE, M. K. (1991). *Native Hawaiian Rights Handbook*. Honolulu: University of Hawaii Press.

MACKINNON, C. (1987). *Feminism Unmodified: Discourses in Life and Law*. Cambridge, MA: Harvard University Press.

MACMILLAN, M. (2001). *Paris 1919: Six Months that Changed the World*. New York: Random House.

MAMDANI, M. (1996). 'Reconciliation without Justice', *South African Review of Books*, 46.

MANI, R. (2002). *Beyond Retribution: Seeking Justice in the Shadows of War*. Malden, MA: Blackwell.

MARAIS, H. (2000). *South Africa Limits to Change: The Political Economy of Transformation*. London: Zed Books; and Cape Town: University of Cape Town Press.

MARGALIT, A. (2002). *The Ethics of Memory*. Cambridge, MA: Harvard University Press.

—— and RAZ, J. (1994). 'Self-Determination', in RAZ (1994*a*).

MARKS, S. (1978). 'The Myths of Reparations', *Central European History*, 11.

MARTIN, D. F. (1997). 'The "Wik" Peoples of Western Cape York', *Indigenous Law Bulletin*, 4.

MATSUDA, M. (1987). 'Looking to the Bottom: Critical Legal Studies and Reparations', *Harvard Civil Rights-Civil Liberties Law Review*, 323.

—— (1995). 'Looking to the Bottom: Critical Legal Studies and Reparations', in CRENSHAW ET AL. (1995).

MAY, L., and HOFFMAN, S. (eds.) (1991). *Collective Responsibility*. Savage, MD: Rowman & Littlefield.

MEHTA, U. S. (1999). *Liberalism and Empire: India in British Liberal Thought*. New Delhi: Oxford University Press.

MEISTER, R. (1998). 'Forgiving and Forgetting: Lincoln and the Politics of National Recovery', in HESS and POST (1998).

MEMMI, A. (1965). *The Colonizer and the Colonized*. Boston, MA: Beacon Press.

MEYER, L. H. (ed.) (2004). *Justice in Time: Responding to Historical Injustice*. Baden-Baden, Germany: Nomos.

MEYER, M. (1995), 'To Set Right—Ho'oponopono: A Native Hawaiian Way of Peacemaking', *The Compleat Lawyer*, 30.

MILLER, D. (2004). 'Holding Nations Responsible', *Ethics*, 114.

—— (2005). 'Against Global Egalitarianism', *The Journal of Ethics*, 9.

MILLER, E. (2004). 'Reconceiving Reparations: Multiple Strategies in the Reparations Debate', *Boston College Third World Law Journal*, 24.

MILLER, R. (1998). 'Cosmopolitan Respect and Patriotic Concern', *Philosophy and Public Affairs*, 27.

MILLETT, K. (1969). *Sexual Politics*. New York: Ballantine.

MILLOY, R. E. (2001). 'Panel Calls for Reparations in Tulsa Race Riot', *New York Times*, March 1.

MILLS, C. (1997). *The Racial Contract*. Ithaca, NY: Cornell University Press.

MINOW, M. (1998). *Between Vengeance and Forgiveness*. Boston, MA: Beacon Press.

—— (2002). 'Breaking Cycles of Hatred', in MINOW AND ROSENBLUM (2002).

—— and ROSENBLUM, N. L. (eds.) (2002). *Breaking the Cycles of Hatred: Memory, Law and Repair*. Princeton, NJ: Princeton University Press.

MURPHY, J., and HAMPTON, J. (eds.) (1988). *Forgiveness and Mercy*. Cambridge: Cambridge University Press.

MYRDAL, G. (1944). *An American Dilemma: The Negro Problem and Modern Democracy*. New York: Pantheon.

NAGATA, D. K. (1998). 'Intergenerational Effects of the Japanese American Internment', in DANIELI (1998).

NANDY, A. (1983). *The Intimate Enemy: Loss and Recovery of Self Under Colonialism*. New Delhi: Oxford University Press.

NDUNGANE, N. (2003). Opening Address, presented at the Civil Society Conference on Reparations, Randburg, August 27, 2003.

New York Times (2005). 'North Carolina: Spouses Don't Want Charges', August 23.

NOZICK, R. (1974). *Anarchy, State and Utopia*. New York: Basic Books.

OCHBERG, F. M. (ed.) (1988). *Post-traumatic Therapy and Victims of Violence*. New York: Brunner/Mazel.

O'DONOGHUE, L. (2003). '"Practical Reconciliation": a dismal failure', *The Age*, December 11.

OFFE, C. (1999). 'How can we Trust our Fellow Citizens?', in WARREN (1999).

OGLETREE, JR, C. J. (2002). 'Litigating the Legacy of Slavery', *New York Times*, March 31.

—— (2003). 'Repairing the Past: New Efforts in the Reparations Debate in America', *Harvard Civil Liberties Law Review*, 38.

OLIVER, M. L., and SHAPIRO, T. M. (1997). *Black Wealth/White Wealth: A New Perspective on Racial Inequality*. New York: Routledge.

OLIVER, W. H. (1998). 'The Fragility of Pakeha Support', in COATES and MCHUGH (1998).

O'NEILL, O. (1996). *Towards Justice and Virtue*. Cambridge: Cambridge University Press.

OTTO, D. (1995). 'A Question of Law or Politics? Indigenous Claims to Sovereignty in Australia', *Syracuse Journal of International Law and Commerce*, 21.

PAREKH, B. (2000). *Rethinking Multiculturalism: Cultural Diversity and Political Theory*. Cambridge, MA: Harvard University Press.

PATTERSON, O. (1982). *Slavery and Social Death*. Cambridge, MA: Harvard University Press.

____ (1998). *Rituals of Blood: Consequences of Slavery in Two American Centuries.* Washington, NJ: Civitas.

PAUL, E. F. (1991). 'Set-Asides, Reparations, and Compensatory Justice', *NOMOS*, XXXII.

PETTIT, P. (1996). 'Freedom as Antipower', *Ethics*, 106.

PIETERSE, J., and PAREKH, B. (eds.) (1997). *The Decolonisation of Imagination.* Delhi: Oxford University Press.

POGGE, T. (2002). *World Poverty and Human Rights.* Cambridge: Polity.

POOLE, R. (1999). *Nation and Identity.* New York and London: Routledge.

POSNER, E., and VERMEULE, A. (2003). 'Reparations for Slavery and other Historical Injustices', *Columbia Law Review*, 689.

POVERTY & RACE RESEARCH ACTION COUNCIL (2005). *Poverty and Race*, 14.

RANDELZHOFER, A., and TOMUSCHAT, C. (eds.) (1999). *State Responsibility and the Individual: Reparations in Instances of Grave Violations of Human Rights.* The Hague: Kluwer Law International.

RASPBERRY, W. (2004). 'Still Battling "Massive Resistance"', *Washington Post*, February 29.

RAWLS, J. (1971). *A Theory of Justice.* Cambridge, MA: Harvard University Press.

____ (1972). *A Theory of Justice.* Cambridge: Harvard University Press.

RAZ, J. (1994*a*). *Ethics in the Public Domain*, rev. edn. (Oxford: Oxford University Press).

____ (1994*b*). 'Multiculturalism : A Liberal Perspective', in RAZ (1994*a*). Oxford: Oxford University Press.

REHG, W. (1994). *Insight and Solidarity: The Discourse Ethics of Jürgen Habermas.* Berkeley, CA: University of California Press.

RESCIA V. R. (1999). 'Reparations in the Inter American System for the Protection of Human Rights', *ILSA Journal of International and Comparative Law*, 5.

REYNOLDS, H. (2003). *Law of the Land*, 3rd edn. Harmondsworth, UK: Penguin.

RIDGE, M. (2003). 'Giving the Dead Their Due', *Ethics*, 114.

ROBINSON, A. (2004). 'Troubling "Settled" Waters: The Opportunity and Peril of African-American Reparations', *Boston College Third World Law Journal*, 24.

ROBINSON, R. (2000). *The Debt: What America Owes to Blacks.* New York: Dutton.

ROHT-ARRIAZA, N. (2004*a*). 'Reparations Decisions and Dilemmas', *Hastings International and Comparative Law Review*, 27.

____ (2004*b*). 'Reparations in the Aftermath of Repression and Mass Violence', in STOVER AND WEINSTEIN (2004).

ROTHBERG, R., and THOMPSON, D. (eds.) (2000). *Truth vs. Justice.* Princeton, NJ: Princeton University Press.

ROYAL COMMISSION INTO ABORIGINAL DEATHS IN CUSTODY (1991). Available at: www.autlii.edu.au/au/special/rsjproject/rsjlibrary/index.html

RUBENSTEIN, I., CUTTER, R., and TEMPLER, D. I. (1990). 'Multigenerational Occurrence of Survivors Syndrome Symptoms in Families of Holocaust Survivors', *Omega Journal of Death and Dying*, 20.

RUBIO, M. (1999). *Crimen e Impunidad.* Bogotá: TM Editores.

RUSHDIE, S. (1992). '"Commonwealth Literature" Does not Exist', in his *Imaginary Homelands*. New York: Penguin.

SANDEL, M. J. (1982). *Liberalism and the Limits of Justice*. Cambridge: Cambridge University Press.

SANÉ, P. (2001). 'In Defence of Durban: Racism is Back on the Agenda', October 2001, http://www.unesco.org/courier/2001_10/uk/planet.htm

SCHEDLER, G. (1998). *Racist Symbols and Reparations*. Lanham, MD: Rowman & Littlefield.

SEN, A. (1970). *Collective Choice and Social Welfare*. San Francisco: Holden-Day.

SHELTON, D. (1999). *Remedies in International Human Rights Law*. Oxford: Oxford University Press.

—— (2002). 'Righting Wrongs: Reparations in the Articles on State Responsibility', *The American Journal of International Law*, 96.

SHER, G. (1981). 'Ancient Wrongs and Modern Rights', *Philosophy and Public Affairs*, 10.

SHKLAR, J. (1990). *The Faces of Injustice*. New Haven, CT: Yale University Press.

SIGAL, J. J., and WEINFELD, M. (1989). *Trauma and Rebirth: Intergenerational Effects of the Holocaust*. New York: Praeger.

SINDERBRAND, R. (2005). 'A Shameful Little Secret', *Newsweek*, March 28.

SINGH, Y. (1988). *Modernisation of Indian Tradition*. Delhi: Rawat Publications.

SMITH, W. C. (1991). *The Meaning and End of Religion*. Minneapolis, MN: Fortress Press.

SOOKA, Y. (2004). 'South Africa, its Past, Human Rights and Reparations', keynote address at the Public Seminar on Reparations—International, Social, Legal, Economic Dimensions, Wits Institute for Social and Economic Research, July 6, 2004. Available at: http://www.apartheid-reparations.ch/documents/reparationen/e_2004-08_RedeSooka.pdf

SOUTH AFRICAN TRUTH and RECONCILIATION COMMISSION (1998*a*). *Final Report of the South African Truth and Reconciliation Commission*, Vol. 1–5. Cape Town: Juta.

SOUTH AFRICAN TRUTH and RECONCILIATION COMMISSION (1998*b*). *A Summary of the Reparation and Rehabilitation Proposal*. Cape Town: Juta.

SOWELL, T. (1983). *The Economics and Politics of Race: An International Perspective*. New York: William Morrow.

SPARKS, A. (2003). *Beyond the Miracle: Inside the New South Africa*. Johannesburg and Cape Town: Jonathan Ball.

SPELMAN, E. (1988). *Inessential Woman: Problems of Exclusion in Feminist Thought*. Boston, MA: Beacon Press.

STERBA, J. P. (1996). 'Understanding Evil: American Slavery, the Holocaust, and the Conquest of the American Indians', *Ethics*, 106.

STOVER, E., and WEINSTEIN, H. M. (eds.) (2004). *My Neighbor, My Enemy: Justice and Community in the Aftermath of Mass Atrocity*. Cambridge: Cambridge University Press.

STRELEIN, L. M. (2003). *Members of the Yorta Yorta Aboriginal Community v. Victoria [2002] HCA 58*. Canberra: Native Title Research Unit, Australian Institute of Aboriginal and Torres Strait Islander Studies.
SWAIN, C. (2002). *The New White Nationalism in America: Its Challenge to Integration*. Cambridge: Cambridge University Press.
SWINBURNE, R. (1989). *Responsibility and Atonement*. Oxford: Clarendon Press.
SYMONDS, M. (1980). 'The "Second Injury" to victims', *Evaluation and Change* (special issue).
TAN, K. (2004). *Justice Without Borders: Cosmopolitan, Nationalism and Patriotism*. Cambridge: Cambridge University Press.
TATE, K. (2004). 'Will America Ever Pay? Racial Justice and Reparations', *The Forum*, 3.
TAYLOR, C. (1992). *Multiculturalism and the Politics of Recognition*. Princeton, NJ: Princeton University Press.
THOMAS, L. (1980). 'Sexism and Racism: Some Conceptual Differences', *Ethics*, 90.
THOMPSON, J. (2001). 'Historical Injustice and Reparation: Justifying the Claims of Descendants', *Ethics*, 112.
____(2002). *Taking Responsibility for the Past*. Cambridge: Polity.
THOMSON, J. J. (1977). 'Preferential Hiring', in COHEN ET AL. (1977).
THUCYDIDES (1989). *The Peloponnesian War*, trans. by Thomas Hobbes. Chicago: University of Chicago Press.
TOMUSCHAT, C. (1999). 'Individual Reparation Claims in Instances of Grave Human Rights Violations: The Position under General International Law', in RANDELZHOFER and TOMUSCHAT (1999).
TORPEY, J. (ed.) (2003). *Politics and the Past: On Repairing Historical Injustices*. Lanham, MD: Rowman & Littlefield.
____(2004). 'Paying for the Past? The Movement for Reparations for African-Americans', *Journal of Human Rights*, 3.
TRACHTENBERG, M. (1980). *Reparation in World Politics: France and European Economic Diplomacy, 1916–1923*. New York: Columbia University Press.
TSOSIE, R. (2000). 'Sacred Obligations: Intercultural Justice and The Discourse of Treaty Rights', *UCLA Law Review*, 1615.
____(2005). 'Engaging the Spirit of Racial Healing Within Critical Race Theory: An Exercise in Transformative Thought', *Michigan Journal of Race and Law*, 21.
TULLY, J. (2000). 'The Struggles of Indigenous Peoples', in IVISON ET AL. (2000).
SIR TRAVERS TWISS (1884). *The Law of Nations*. Oxford: Clarendon Press.
U.S. DEPARTMENT OF STATE (1947). *The Treaty of Versailles and After: Annotations of the Text of the Treaty*. Washington, DC: U.S. Department of State.
VALLS, A. (1999). 'The Libertarian Case for Affirmative Action', *Social Theory and Practice*, 25.
____(2003*a*). 'Racial Justice as Transitional Justice', *Polity*, 36.
____(2003*b*). 'A Truth Commission for the United States?', *Intertexts*, 7.
VANDEGINSTE, S. (2003). 'Reparation', in *Reconciliation after Violent Conflict: A Handbook*. Stockholm: International Institute for Democracy and Electoral Assistance.

VEGH, C. (1984). *I didn't say goodbye*, trans. by Ros Schwartz. New York: E. P. Dutton.

VERDUN, V. (1993). 'If the Shoe Fits, Wear It: An Analysis of Reparations to African Americans', *Tulane Law Review*, 67.

VILLA-VICENCIO, C., and DOXTADER, E. (eds.) (forthcoming). *Repairing the Unforgivable: Reparations and Reconstruction in South Africa.*

VISWANATHAN, G. (1998). *Masks of Conquest.* New Delhi: Oxford University Press.

VOHRA, N. N. (ed.) (2001). *Culture, Democracy and Development in South Asia.* New Delhi: Shipra.

WALDRON, J. (1988). *The Right to Private Property.* Oxford: Clarendon Press.

—— (1992). 'Superseding Historical Injustice', *Ethics*, 103.

—— (2003). 'Indigeneity? First Peoples and Last Occupancy', *New Zealand Journal of Public and International Law*, 1.

—— (2004). 'Settlement, Return and the Supersession Thesis', *Theoretical Inquiries in Law* (Tel Aviv), 5.

—— (2005). 'Nozick and Locke: Filling the Space of Rights', *Social Philosophy and Policy*, 22.

WALLACE, P. A., and LAMOND, A. (eds.) (1977). *Women, Minorities and Employment Discrimination.* Lexington, MA: Lexington Books.

WALSH, C. (2004). 'Slave Descendents Sue Lloyd's for Billions', *The Observer* (UK), March 28.

WALZER, M. (1980). 'The Moral Standing of States', *Philosophy and Public Affairs*, 9.

WARREN, M. E. (ed.) (1999). *Democracy and Trust.* New York: Cambridge University Press.

WELCH, D. A. (1993). *Justice and the Genesis of War.* Cambridge: Cambridge University Press.

WELLINGTON TRIBUNAL (2001). *Rekohu: A Report on Moriori and Ngati Mutunga Claims in the Chatham Islands.* Wellington, New Zealand: Waitangi Tribunal Report.

WESCHELER, L. (1989). 'Afterword', in ASPEN INSTITUTE REPORT (1989).

WHITE, E. N. (2001). 'Making the French Pay: The Costs and Consequences of the Napoleonic Reparations', *European Review of Economic History*, 5.

WHITE, J. (ed.) (1993). *Recasting the World: Writing after Colonialism.* Baltimore, MD and London: John Hopkins University Press.

WIESEL, E. (1985). 'Listen to the Wind', in *Against Silence: The Voice and Vision of Elie Wiesel*, ed. Irving Abrahamson. New York: Holocaust Library.

WILLIAMS, B. (1993). *Shame and Necessity.* Berkeley, CA: University of California Press.

WILLIAMS, D. R., and COLLINS, C. (2004). 'Reparations: A Viable Strategy to Address the Enigma of African American Health', *American Behavioral Scientist*, 47.

WILSON, J. P., HAREL, Z., and KAHANA, B. (eds.) (1988). *Human Adaptation to Extreme Stress.* New York: Plenum Press.

WILSON, J. P., and RAPHAEL, B. (eds.) (1993). *International Handbook of Traumatic Stress Syndromes.* New York: Plenum Publishing.

WILSON, W. J. (1999). *The Bridge over the Racial Divide: Rising Inequality and Coalition Politics.* Berkeley, CA: University of California Press.

WINBUSH, R. A. (2003). *Should America Pay? Slavery and the Raging Debate on Reparations*. New York: HarperCollins.
WINDSCHUTTLE, K. (2003). *Fabrication of Aboriginal History*. Sydney: Macleay Press.
WOLFF, J. (2002). 'Addressing Disadvantage and the Human Good', *Journal of Applied Philosophy*, 19.
WREN, T. (ed.) (1990). *The Moral Domain*. Cambridge, MA: MIT Press.
YAMAMOTO, E. K. (2000). *Interracial Justice: Conflict & Reconciliation in Post-Civil Rights America*. New York: New York University Press.
YOUNG, I. M. (1990). *Justice and the Politics of Difference*. Princeton, NJ: Princeton University Press.
____ (1999). 'Public Address as a Sign of Political Inclusion', in Card (1999).
YOUNG, R. (2001). *Postcolonialism: An Historical Introduction*. Oxford and Malden, MA: Blackwell.
ZACK, N. (2003). 'Reparations and the Rectification of Race', *The Journal of Ethics*, 7.

Index*

Aboriginal culture: see native culture
Aborigines, 69–71, 73, 75, 77, 174n; Tasmanian, 82, 84
Activists, 6, 16, 82n; black women, 138, 141; white feminist, 142
Affirmative action, 121–122, 189, 262
African Americans, 87–90, 97, 108, 110, 112n, 116–118, 120–121, 126, 129, 132, 135, 173n, 181, 189, 192n, 275n, 285, 304n
African National Congress, 253, 261–262, 268
Amnesty, 5, 15, 254, 273n
America, 11, 87, 105, 110, 138
Americans, 51, 89, 128, 139; black, 105, 136–137; non-black, 88, 93
American society, 115, 118, 120–121, 123, 129. See also America, United States, and US society
Anarchy, State, and Utopia, 30, 36
Ancestors, 82, 87, 93, 110, 295
Apartheid, 12, 120, 257–261, 263, 267, 268, 271, 276n, 277n, 279n; legacy of, 253, 268
Apology, 18, 51, 56, 59–63, 66, 74, 81, 83n, 104, 118–119, 155, 176–177, 181, 183, 242, 278n, 306n , 315, 318
Aristotle, 69, 82n, 201, 304n

Baier, A., 175n
Barkan, E., 115, 127–128, 172n, 195, 211n
Bass, G., 198, 201–202, 211n, 212n
Bhargava, R., 278n, 279n, 303n,
Biondi, M., 130, 146n, 149n
Black Americans, 141–142, 144. See also Americans, black
Black community, 11, 139–143
Black liberation movement, 140, 145
Black masculinity, 138
Black men, 116, 136–138, 140–142, 219–220. See also blacks, black people
Blackness, 91, 95–96, 98, 110, 137
Blacks, black people, 91, 97–98, 100, 108, 110, 112n, 132, 142, 147n; poor, 105–106
Black women, 130, 132, 134–138, 140, 146n, 147n, 148n, 150n. See also blacks, black people

Boxill, B., 119, 192n
Brookfield, F. M., 34, 39n, 40n, 41n
Brooks, R., 119–121, 124, 127, 129
Brown v. Board of Education (1954), 117, 128
Bureau of Indian Affairs (BIA), 60–64

Capital, political, 110; social, 95
Capitalism, 106
Citizens, 161–164, 169, 206, 296, 298
Citizenship, 161, 271
Civic trust, 154, 157, 163, 166, 190, 279n. See also trust
Civil society, black, 141; white, 141
Claimants, 9, 172n, 184, 190, 204, 212n, 251n, 291
Class inequality. See inequality, class
Colonialism, 4, 8–10, 59, 215–216, 219, 221–228, 230–231, 233–235, 238, 241–242, 244–247, 248n, 251n, 279n, 280–283, 285–286, 288–297, 299–302, 303n, 305n; cultural, 229, 232
Colonial settlement, 32. See also European settlement
Colonization, 28–29, 76, 215, 217, 219, 244, 282, 293; cultural, 222; victims of, 281. See also victims
Colonized (people), the colonized, 215, 219, 220–223, 225–229, 231–233, 235, 239, 241–242, 244, 246, 249n, 278n, 281–282, 288, 290, 293, 302
Colonizer, 215–217, 220–223, 225–226, 228–229, 233, 240–242, 244, 278n
Commitment, 72–73, 290, 311
Compensation, 5, 13, 51, 74–75, 78–81, 87, 118–119, 124, 127, 145, 154–155, 157–160, 165–166, 176–191, 192n, 202–204, 206, 216, 258–259, 263, 267, 271, 280, 289, 293, 296, 300, 302, 306n, 314–315, 317–318, 322n; as restitution, 179, 188; token, 256
Congress, 14, 53, 60. See also US government
Critical Race Theory, 52, 138

Davis, A., 135, 140, 148n, 149n, 150n
de Beauvoir, S., 133, 147n

* The editors wish to thank Patrick Moran for his invaluable assistance in compiling this index.

Debt, 178, 190, 315; cancellation of, 279n; foreign, 288–289; relief, 280, 283, 302
de Greiff, P., 119, 192n, 276n, 277n, 278n, 279n
Democracy, 153, 160–161, 178, 215, 246, 253, 262, 268, 309
Descendants, 8, 26, 59, 80, 104, 119, 183, 185–189, 199, 218, 244, 280, 293
Development, 170–171, 263–264, 269–271, 272n, 276n, 289; cultural, 284; economic, 282, 285; social, 278n
Discrimination, 70, 272n; market, 90; racial, 89, 94, 102, 104, 108, 112n, 114, 117, 121; system of, 116
Dworkin, R., 304n

Entitlement, entitlements, 29–30, 36–37, 47, 51, 75, 77, 79–80, 82, 103, 186, 199, 203, 286, 293
Epistemological problems, 88, 125–126, 143
Equality, 164, 287; cultural, 242; global, 286, 288–290
European settlement, 69–70

Fanon, F., 219–220, 229, 240, 248n, 251n, 282, 289, 303n
Feminism, 134, 144
Feminists, 134, 138
Feminist philosophy, feminist theory, 133, 136
Feminist theorists, 133–134, 149n

Gandhi, M. K., 247, 251n
Gender, 11, 130, 132–140, 142, 146, 147n
Gender inequality: see inequality, gender
Gender reparations: see reparations, gender
Gilligan, C., 148n
Grotius, H., 31, 38, 40n
Guilt, 3, 239–240, 315

Habermas, J., 175n
Hamber, B., 273n, 278n, 303n, 304n, 306n
Holocaust, 16, 57, 117, 308, 317
Holocaust survivors, 308, 311
Human remains, 52, 54, 55, 60, 155
Human rights: see rights, human

Identity, 79, 220; collective, 59, 62, 92, 218; complexities of, 134; cultural, 281; family, 187; gender, 133, 137–138; individual, 218; moral, 296; national, 294, 299; racial, 112n, 133–134; self, 72
Immigrants, 105, 123, 298
Indigenous culture, 223, 226, 228, 230–231, 241, 246
Indigenous people, 13, 24–25, 27, 30–31, 34, 70, 174n, 233, 248n, 280–281
Inequality, 171, 253; class, 121; economic, 284; gender, 131, 139, 141; global, 289; internal, 141, 143; racial, 95–96, 98–102, 104, 108, 112n, 115, 118, 120–121, 123, 125–126, 129; socioeconomic, 252; structures of, 145; systemic, 145
Inheritance, 79–80, 110, 186–188
Injustice, 45, 81, 133, 142, 161, 177, 180, 183–184, 186–188, 192n, 194, 210, 211n, 215, 243, 248n, 272, 280, 282–285, 288, 291–293, 300; apartheid, 265; colonial, 295, 301–302; cultural, 216–219, 221–225, 227, 231–235, 238, 240–241, 244–246, 248n; economic, 216, 221, 270; gender, 139; global, 286, 291; historical, 32, 74–77, 124, 131, 177, 179, 182–186, 189–190, 215, 233–234, 287, 289, 292, 295; passive, 206, 212n; past: see injustice, historical; political, 216, 221; racial, 87, 115, 123, 125, 132, 144; social, 270; systemic, 134, 145
International Criminal Court (ICC), 205, 307, 318–321, 322n

Jim Crow, 87, 106, 112n, 115–120, 128–132, 135–139, 141–145, 146n
Justice, 125, 144, 146, 155, 157, 163, 165, 170, 172, 190, 196–197, 199, 201, 206, 209, 224, 276n, 298, 301, 317, 321, 321n; as accountability, 197–199, 202–203, 206, 210; corrective, 184; criminal, 153, 155, 161–162, 167; criterion of, 154; distributive, 80, 194–195, 206–209, 265, 283, 286, 290, 305n; duties of, 286; egalitarian, 281, 284–285, 287, 289, 290, 299; global, 275n, 284, 288, 290–291, 299, 303n, 305n; historical, 131; intercultural, 56, 58, 66; international, 287; measures of, 156; racial, 105, 110, 112n, 114, 121, 127, 130–131, 138; reparative, vi, 2, 6, 15, 19, 25, 34, 44, 50, 55, 69, 72–73, 75–77, 138, 141, 144, 153, 177, 182, 194–195, 199, 209, 290, 292, 296; retributive, 194–195, 197–199, 209, 268; social, 100, 103, 110, 232, 304n; transitional, 120, 160, 162; victims of, 187–188; victor's, 195

Keynes, J. M., 195, 210n
Khulumani Victim Support Group, 257–259, 272n, 274n, 275n

Korsgaard, C., 304n, 305n
Ku Klux Klan, 116, 128
Kymlicka, W., 84n, 249n, 283, 299, 303n, 305n

Land claims, 38, 53, 65
Law, American tort, 177; criminal, 304n; human rights, 154; international, 30, 154–155, 157, 174n, 201–202, 205, 319; natural, 30
Legal mechanisms, vi
Legal system, 31, 46, 48, 156–157, 163–165, 223; American, 137
Liberal, liberals, 10, 38, 110, 125–126, 249n, 250n
Liberalism, 10, 110, 111n, 112n; colonial, 225; color-blind, 89, 99, 100–101, 107, 109, 111n
Locke, J., 30, 35, 38, 39n, 40n, 41n, 83n; Lockean proviso, 36–37
Loury, G. C., 91–92, 103, 111n, 123–124, 126, 146n, 149n, 149n, 150n, 192n, 265, 276n, 285, 304n

MacIntyre, A., 83n
MacKinnon, C., 147n
Mandela, N., 254, 259, 274n, 275n
Massacre at Wounded Knee: see Wounded Knee
Matsuda, M., 52, 55, 63, 66n, 67n, 118
Mbeki, T., 253, 257–258, 260, 272n, 274n, 275n
Memmi, A., 56, 219, 231
Memory, 9, 220; collective, 168, 218; public, 62, 65
Minow, M., 50, 66n, 119, 191n, 192n, 194, 242, 251n, 278n
Money, 178, 181–182, 243, 256, 271, 314–316, 320
Moral regeneration, 193, 197, 208, 210, 210n
Moral responsibility: see responsibility, moral

Nagel, T., 161, 175n
Nandy, A., 223–224, 229–230, 234, 249n, 250n, 251n
Native Americans, 15, 52, 55, 60, 119. See also native people
Native culture, 14, 58
Native communities, 64
Native people, 14, 24, 43–44, 49, 51, 52, 55, 57–58, 60, 62, 65–66, 67n
New York Times, 128, 211n, 274n
Nicomachean Ethics, 211n, 304n. See also Aristotle
Non-native people, 43–45, 47, 55, 70, 73, 75
Nozick, R., 30, 36, 39n, 40n, 41n, 83n, 113n, 125, 191n

Oppression, 181, 146n, 147n, 148n; gender-based, 134–136, 138, 144, 147n, 148n; internal, 252; race-based, 134, 136, 138, 144, 146, 147n; of women, 241

Perpetrators, 7, 16–18, 59, 65, 69, 77, 106, 137, 153, 155, 158, 162, 172n, 177, 182–184, 194–195, 197–199, 201–203, 205–206, 209–210, 216–217, 233, 238–239, 244, 255, 263, 288, 292, 296, 301, 316, 319; states, 205
Political violence, 193–194, 202, 264, 270, 276n, 278n
Prison, 71, 110, 137
Property, 185, 187, 192n, 315
Punishment, 177, 197–198, 201, 216, 220, 229

Race, 131, 133, 134–135, 137–138, 144, 146n, 147n
Race-based or racial oppression: see oppression, race-based
Racial disparity: see inequality, racial
Racial inequality: see inequality, racial
Racial progress, 131
Racial stigma, 89–90, 92, 94, 97, 100–101, 108–109, 110, 112n
Racism, 137, 139, 142, 147n, 272n, 279n
Rawls, J., 2, 25, 125–126, 164, 175n, 191n, 305n
Raz, J., 248n, 295, 304n
Recognition, 13, 14, 154, 157, 161–162, 166, 264, 278n, 279n
Reconciliation 58, 65, 77, 115, 120, 127, 177, 194–195, 197, 208–210, 244, 253, 259, 265–267, 269
Redistribution, 13, 25, 139–140, 142, 145, 208; global or of global resources, 286, 288–290, 299; land or of land, 177
Redress, 8, 16, 18, 32, 53, 154, 157, 162, 190, 257, 263–264; for historical injustice, 59, 64; symbolic, 51
Rehabilitation, 155, 157, 194, 266, 282, 290, 317, 322n
Reparations, 76, 87, 90, 122, 124, 141–142, 144–145, 146n, 150n, 153, 156, 158, 161, 165–167, 169, 170, 172, 174n, 175n, 182, 190, 192n, 197–204, 206, 208–210, 211n, 217, 237, 248n, 252–261, 263–267, 269, 272, 275n, 276n, 278n, 280–283, 288,

290–296, 298–300, 304n, 306n, 314, 317–318, 321n; apartheid, 252, 257, 259, 261, 264, 270; atonement model of, 120; black or to blacks, 114–115, 118–119, 123–130, 136–137, 146; colonial, 286, 299; community, 252, 260, 262, 269; and criminal justice, 162; and civic trust, 164; definition of, 50, 154; financial, 7, 15, 45, 110, 279n, See also compensation; gender, 131, 143; individual, 252, 269–271; issues with, v–vii; material, 168, 155, 170, 193–195; opponents of black reparations, 119; philosophical literature on, 149n; programs, 155, 160, 171, 172n; and or as reconciliation, 65, 74, 251n; as restoration, 251n; social, 309; for slavery, 88, 99, 106, 115; symbolic, 155, 170, 255; tort model of (black), 120, 124–125, 129; for victims of human rights abuses, 157; war, 196
Responsibility, civic 298; of citizenship, 298; collective, 62, 72–74, 237, 298; corporate, 297, 300; criminal, 321; diffusion of, 277; false, 308; group, 297; moral, 61, 64, 206, 210, 290; personal, 297; social, 316; of the state, 160
Restitution, 17, 18, 74, 154, 158, 178, 202, 315, 317, 322n
Retribution, 178, 197–199, 205, 216
Rights, 154; cultural, 281, 284, 289; economic, 289; equality of, 161; human rights, 2, 7, 154, 262, 289, 321n; individual rights vs. community rights, 36; property, 25, 28, 37, 47, 61, 76, 187; right of a nation to self-determination: see rights, sovereignty; social, 289; sovereignty, 25, 28, 281; violations of human rights, 254–255, 263, 266, 276n, 279n

Sacred objects, 49, 51, 54
Sacred sites, 45, 60, 63, 75
Self-determination, 60, 63–64, 67n, 282, 293, 303n
Sexism, 134, 137, 147n, 148n; theories of, 133
Slavery, 8, 11, 87, 89, 92–93, 106, 112n, 117–119, 129–132, 135–146, 147n, 275n, 276n, 280, 285, 304n; sexual, 137
Slaves, 133, 137; black, 88; black female, 133; freed, 118
Social solidarity, 154, 157, 166, 168, 178; definition, 165
South Africa, 12, 15, 17, 113n, 120, 159, 175n, 252
Sufferer, 233, 238, 240, 244
Sufferer-response, 241, 244
Survivors, 59, 310–311, 316–318

Tan, K.-C., 265, 248n, 250n, 275n
Traducer, 233, 238, 240–241, 244
Traducer-response, 240–242, 244
Thompson, J., 24–25, 34, 41n, 43, 47–48, 57, 66n, 67n, 83n, 84n, 186–188, 191n, 192n, 210n, 211n, 248n, 250n, 284, 303n, 304n
Thomson, J., 178, 191n
Tsosie, R., 24–25, 28, 39n, 40n, 41n, 66n, 83n, 119
Trauma, 310–311, 315, 317
Trust, citizen, 164; definition, 163; restoration of, 162; social, 164, See also civic trust
Truth and Reconciliation Commission (TRC), 12, 15, 113n, 159, 254, 256–261, 264, 266–269, 273n, 274n, 276n, 277n
Truth-telling, 153, 161, 167, 242

Universal Declaration of Human Rights, 157, 173n, 321
United States, 70, 104, 111n, 112n. See also America
US courts, 15, 45, 259. See also legal system
US government, 13, 14, 46–49, 54, 61, 65–66
US Senate, 104. See also US government
US society, 89, 91, 93, 98–99. See also America
US Supreme Court, 45, 47, 116

Valls, A., 115, 117, 119–120, 124, 127, 149n
Victims, 7, 10, 14–18, 63, 69, 78, 104, 106, 113n, 120, 127, 153–158, 161–162, 164 166, 168–169, 172n, 173n, 174n, 177–178, 182–184, 186, 189–190, 194, 197–198, 201–203, 205–206, 209–210, 217, 233, 237–238, 244, 254, 256–257, 263, 267, 270–271, 274n, 276n, 278n, 280, 287, 291–292, 306n, 307–308, 311, 315–321, 321n, 322n

Waldron, J., 13, 19n, 41n, 42n, 44, 47–48, 75, 81, 83n, 84n, 124, 142, 150n, 184, 187, 192n, 233–234, 250n, 284, 296–297, 299, 303n, 304n
War, 193–196, 202; responsibility for, 197
White Americans, 88, 141
White civil society: see civil society, white

White, E., 195, 197, 210n
White men, 141, 147n, 148n, 244, 250n
Whites, white people, 55, 117, 122
White supremacy, 130, 136, 141, 149n
White women, 134, 142, 148n, 244; middle-class, upper-class, 133–134
Williams, B., 236, 240, 250n, 251n
Women, 132, 140, 147n; free, 133; slaves, 140. See also slaves
Wounded Knee, massacre at, 45, 57

Yamamoto, E., 55–56, 58, 66n, 67n